ARMSTRONGISM

THE "WORLDWIDE CHURCH OF GOD"
EXAMINED IN THE SEARCHING LIGHT OF SCRIPTURE

(An In-depth Study of a False Religion)

by DR. ROBERT L. SUMNER

BIBLICAL EVANGELISM PRESS
Brownsburg, Indiana 46112

ISBN: 0-914012-15-0

Cover Design by Ron Sumner

Printed in the United States of America

DEDICATION

To my pastor,

Rev. Donald Tyler,

Along with the staff, officers and members of the Bethesda Baptist Church. While strongly opposing everything that is evil, their primary emphasis is on winning souls to Christ and building them up in the Faith.

In grateful appreciation for their loyal and active support for all the ministries of Biblical Evangelism.

Table of Contents

Author's Preface

In Houston, Texas, a 46-year-old trained and experienced laboratory technician prepared a dextrose solution, she thought, for a hospital patient. Entering the room and pouring two ounces of the mixture into a glass, she told the woman it was what the doctor had ordered. Starting to take a sip from the glass, the patient shuddered and exclaimed, "Oh, that tastes terrible!"

Being assured it would do her good, the lady quickly gulped down the remainder of the contents of the glass. . .*then pitched over on her face dead!* Subsequent investigation by authorities proved what she had been given was deadly sodium cyanide.

The laboratory technician had been *sincere* in thinking she was administering a dextrose solution. The patient had certainly been *sincere* in believing the terrible-tasting potion would do her good. But the sincerity of neither was beneficial and the victim was just as dead as if she had deliberately committed suicide or the technician had willfully committed murder.

In this volume, I am not questioning the sincerity of Herbert W. Armstrong, Garner Ted Armstrong or any of their followers in the Worldwide Church of God. No doubt some are insincere, just as in any other religion, but that is not my accusation. My position in this book is that the entire movement is heretical, completely at variance with the Word of God and the historic Christian faith. I think this will be very easy to prove.

In noting that *sincerity* does not help apart from *rightness,* our attention is drawn to Solomon's inspired conclusion: "There is a way which seemeth right unto a man, but the end thereof are the ways of death" (Proverbs 14:12; 16:25). The Armstrong way has proven to be thus with thousands of sincere, but nonetheless misguided, souls.

The author of this present work was the very first one to publicly oppose the heresy of Mr. Armstrong and his Worldwide Church of God (then called the "Radio Church of God"). While pastoring in Texas in the late 1940s and early 1950s, I occasionally heard some of his radio broadcasts over one of the powerful border stations. One time I listened in amazement as Mr. Armstrong spent his entire broadcast belittling and ridiculing John 3:16 in a style I then—and still do today—considered blasphemy. While I felt at that time the man was a vicious heretic, I frankly did not think his unorthodox approach to the Scripture would gain a following of merit.

In the late 1950s, after several had inquired about the man and his ministry—and I had been able to offer only unsubstantiated and undocumented opinions—I decided to launch a more thorough investigation. I wrote to Pasadena and requested representative literature, asking also to be placed on the mailing list of *The Plain Truth* magazine. After spending considerable time examining these materials, I eventually wrote a brief expose.

Even then I was not sure it should be published. It was my thinking that if the movement were not a threat to any great number of people, printing the critique might be merely publicizing Armstrong and his work. This, of course, I did not want.

About this time I went to the Euclid Avenue Baptist Church in Lorain, Ohio, for an evangelistic crusade which would close out 1960 and launch 1961. During the meeting some of the members asked me to visit a young family man who had been serving in the church as both deacon and Sunday school teacher. It seemed he had just resigned his duties with the startling announcement he had come to the conclusion all organized religion was wrong and consequently he would be dropping out of the church. Since he had been an earnest, active worker, fellow Christians were concerned and felt I might be able to help.

Arriving at his home, it did not take long to discover he had been listening to Armstrong and reading that cult's literature, hence his current conclusions about God, the Bible and churches. I stated a few of Armstrong's claims about eventually becoming God and Creator, his radical legalism, his wild theory that Britain is Ephraim and America, Manasseh, plus some other extremisms of the cult.

He did not believe me for a moment!

My unpublished manuscript, which was then at my motel, came to mind. Saying, "I have a brief critique of Armstrong in my room, proving from his own writings what I have said to you, giving book and page numbers where the quotes are found. Will you wash your hands of Armstrong completely if I can prove my charges?" With tear-filled eyes he affirmed that he most certainly would.

My companion and I drove immediately to the motel, got the paper, then returned to the brother's home. I simply handed it to him and left. That night he was in the service with his family and, at the conclusion of the message, stepped out to confess his backsliding and publicly repudiate Armstrong and his entire movement.

That convinced me!

The next day the manuscript was sent to Dr. John R. Rice and *The Sword of the Lord,* a magazine with which I have served in one editorial capacity or another for almost 20 years. Dr. Rice published the expose in the February 24, 1961, issue under the title, HERBERT W. ARMSTRONG—A FALSE PROPHET. The response was immediate and the Sword Foundation republished it in an inexpensive 10¢ booklet for wider distribution, a form wherein it has enjoyed many printings and done considerable good. We have heard from many in various parts of the world who have been saved or/and delivered from this false cult through this small expose. Some are serving Christ full-time today. I can only pray that this larger, in-depth study will do far more good and deliver many times the souls.

In my original work I observed: "In analyzing Armstrong's printed utterances, one gets the impression that he is a strange mixture of many false sects and isms. His sensational and fantastic teaching adheres in many respects to prominent doctrines of Seventh-Day Adventism, British Israelism, Jehovah's Witnesses, and even a touch of Mormonism in his insistence that it is possible to eventually become God."[1]

At that time, because I did not have all the facts in hand about his background, I merely offered this as an observation. Now, a dozen years later and with an abundance of documention before me, I can only echo the previous sentiments. My original observation was an excellent appraisal.

In fact, Mr. Armstrong evidenced a very serious character blemish in trying to deny what I had written. Just a few months after my article appeared in *The Sword of the Lord,* Mr. Armstrong came out with what appeared to be a rebuttal in *The Plain Truth,* "If *YOU* Had Lived in the Time of *CHRIST.*" The subtitle asked: "*Would you have believed Him—turned against Him—or checked up on Him—Which? Don't be too sure!*" The gist of the article seemed to be that not only were the ministries of Christ and Armstrong alike, but they were receiving the same treatment by the people of their respective days. I quote just two paragraphs here:

"A very small printed bulletin was sent to us some little time ago, warning people against Christ's own Gospel, which we preach, calling it 'religious rubbish.' Of course such expressions are designed to discredit and set up prejudice. Then followed the false accu-

1. Page 4

sation that we preach 'a religion of works for salvation.' All who listen regularly, or read *The* PLAIN TRUTH, know we preach nothing of the kind!

"Reports have come that some here or there have claimed, falsely, that I have been a 'Seventh Day Adventist,' a 'Jehovah Witness' and many other such things. I *have* been—before conversion—a 'Quaker' and a Methodist. But I have never, directly or indirectly, in any form, shape, or manner, had any affiliation, association, or connection with ANY other denominations. Incidentally, the TRUE Church of Christ established is *not* denominational!"[2]

Although I did not use the expression "religious rubbish" in my booklet, and I will reserve comment on his denial about teaching "works for salvation" for a later chapter (wherein an abundance of proof will be given), I offer two observations now. First, if Mr. Armstrong will make a brief trip to his college library and look up the meaning of "denomination," "denominational," etc., in any standard dictionary, he will never make such a foolish statement again. Second, for a man who spends so much time teaching the law—especially exalting the Fourth Commandment, "Remember the sabbath day, to keep it holy"—he certainly tramples under foot the Ninth Commandment, "Thou shalt not bear false witness. . ."

In fact, *I would call his claim a blatant falsehood!*

It is easily proven. He acknowledges Quaker and Methodist affiliation "before conversion" (not *salvation* because he admits he is not saved, even yet). Elsewhere he says he "was born of solid old Quaker stock"[3] and when he registered for the draft at the time of World War I, he listed his religious affiliation as "Quaker,"[4] receiving a "conscientious objector"

---

2. June, 1961; p. 17
3. *The Plain Truth,* July, 1958; p. 18
4. *The Plain Truth,* August, 1958; p. 12

status. Shortly after marrying, he united with the River Forest Methodist Church of Maywood, Illinois, later acknowledging it was "more from social preferences than theological."[5]

Yet when he claims to have "never, directly or indirectly, in any form, shape, or manner, had any affiliation, association, or connection with ANY other denominations," he wanders far from the pathway of integrity. In one of his "Personal" columns, Armstrong says: "When I was first ordained, I accepted a very small salary from what I then believed to be God's true Church."[6] While he later quit this church and branded it apostate, if being on the payroll of a church was not being "directly or indirectly, in any form, shape, or manner, [having] any affiliation, association, or connection with ANY" denomination, I fail to understand what it was.

Again, in another "Personal" column, Armstrong wrote: "For a few months I had been receiving a salary of $20 per week as a minister, holding evangelistic campaigns. We had been able to live, very modestly, on that. But at the end of November that year, the salary was cut off. The Church Conference treasury was empty!"[7] Note that he was a salaried servant of a church (which he later admits was not a true church), and that this connection in turn was related to a "Conference treasury."

There is other evidence. In an official brochure of the movement, readers are told: "In 1930 the Oregon members, in order to revitalize the Work of God, incorporated under the name, 'Oregon Conference of The Church of God.'

". . .In June, 1931, Mr. Armstrong was ordained by this Oregon Conference, and entered the Work of

---

5. *The Plain Truth,* December, 1958; p. 7
6. *Tomorrow's World,* August, 1971; p. 2
7. *Tomorrow's World,* February, 1971; p. 2

God full time."[8] Here is proof positive that Mr. Armstrong did, indeed, have "affiliation, association, or connection" "directly or indirectly, in any form, shape, or manner" with others than pre-conversion Quakers and Methodists. He was an ordained, salaried servant of such a group. One of a false prophet's characteristics is his recklessness with truth in times of attempting to defend himself from outside opposition.

Perhaps a word would be in order about the background of this "Oregon Conference of The Church of God." I did a little research and discovered it had its roots in the movement known today as Seventh-Day Adventism. The members of this group, coming out of William Miller's misguided attempt at "date setting" for the Lord's return (a matter which he himself later repudiated, acknowledging to have been mistaken), got into a squabble over a name for the new denominational press they were setting up at Battle Creek, Michigan. Objection to the exalted "prophetess" status of Ellen G. White also contributed to the split. The dissenters moved from Michigan to Missouri and established headquarters at Stanberry. Their main offices are now in Denver and they number less than 100 churches, averaging about 45 members each. Much of today's Worldwide Church of God's theology stems from this early association of Armstrong. It seems absolutely incredible that Mr. Armstrong would deny this affiliation in a 1961 issue of his magazine.

"*Absolutely incredible*" is an excellent way of picturing Armstrong, however. A good example is how he described himself and his ministry at the time of the cult's 25th anniversary celebration. Talking about the launching of the work with a radio broadcast, he wrote: "What really occurred that Sunday morning precisely at 10 o'clock was a momentous event. It

8. *This Is The Worldwide Church Of God,* Written Anonymously; © 1970, 1971, 1972; p. 14

was the fulfilling of a definite corner-stone prophecy of Jesus. More than that, it was *the initial, start-off event of the fulfilling of some 90% of all the prophecies in the Bible!* And approximately *a third of the whole Bible* is prophecy!"[9] Now, any man who thinks his ministry fulfills almost a third of the entire Bible has some serious problems of an order that could keep a full staff of psychiatrists working day and night for years to come.

He says again, "The world did not know it, then. *I myself did not know it then!* But GOD'S TIME HAD COME—at precisely 10:00 A.M., the first Sunday in the year 1934! Between 10:00 and 10:30 that historic morning, a few hundred—perhaps a *very* few thousand—people heard a shocking half-hour broadcast. These people all lived in one county in Oregon. The program was then called the 'Radio Church of God'."[10]

In my rough notes I described those words: *"the ravings of a mad man."* I seriously doubt that any Hitler ever arose on the scene more obsessed with his own importance than Mr. Armstrong.

This brings up an issue which needs a comment. I honestly wanted to be objective in my writing and charitable in my language. Yet again and again I found my righteous indignation boiling over to where it was not always easy, and I confess that sometimes I have not been as tender as others think I should.[11] In my defense, I would like to point out that, although our Lord was kindly and gracious in His dealings with sinners of the worst repute, He was harsh and sometimes cruel in the language He directed at false

---

9. *The Plain Truth,* January, 1959; p. 3
10. Ibid.
11. To illustrate the problem, in Salem Kirban's expose of Armstrong he passionately declared: "Before we get to the heart of this treatise on the Radio Church of God. . . let me say one thing. Several articles have been written on Herbert W. Armstrong in derision. I do not intend to do this. I intend to show where Mr. Armstrong differs with Scripture. . .but with Christian courtesy." © 1970, Published by the author; p. 5 Yet he himself titled his work **Doctrines of Devils: Armstrong's Church of God!**

religious leaders. I assure all readers of this volume that my language will not approach the biting bluntness of His in Matthew 23:13-36.

In a somewhat related matter, many of Armstrong's followers have written me and accused me of "judging" in my original booklet; *then they invariably proceeded to judge me!* The characteristic complaint is, "God's Word tells us not to judge." But that is only a half truth. There are many things which the Bible *commands* us to judge.

A Christian *can* and *should* judge false doctrine. In the very passage where Jesus said, "Judge not, that ye be not judged," He went on to say: "Beware of false prophets, which come to you in sheep's clothing, but inwardly they are ravening wolves. Ye shall know them by their fruits. Do men gather grapes of thorns, or figs of thistles? Even so every good tree bringeth forth good fruit; but a corrupt tree bringeth forth evil fruit. A good tree cannot bring forth evil fruit, neither can a corrupt tree bring forth good fruit. Every tree that bringeth not forth good fruit is hewn down, and cast into the fire. Wherefore by their fruits ye shall know them" (Matthew 7:15-20). So the servants of God have both *right* and *duty* to judge doctrine and determine whether it is true or false, just as the Berean Christians did (Acts 17:11).

Not only so, it is right for Christians to judge the lives of other Christians, even to the extent of withdrawing fellowship from them and excluding them from the church congregation. I suggest that any reader who doubts this fact study such passages as Matthew 18:15-17; Romans 16:17,18; I Corinthians 5; II Peter 2:1-3; I John 4:1; and II John 9-11.

Another problem I have experienced in my dealings with Armstrong's followers is their absolute refusal to accept evidence when it is presented, manifesting a blind loyalty to the man which borders on the worship which should be reserved for deity. By way of example, one lady in South Carolina wrote calling me "a liar" (her words) for saying Armstrong taught he would eventually become God and Creator. When I sent her a photostat page of the book from which we had originally documented the statement, adding a comment that she owed me an apology for the false accusation, she amazed me by replying: "Yes, I very definitely *do* owe you an apology, and I humbly beg of you to accept my apology. Don't misunderstand me. I am *not* apologizing for believing in Mr. Armstrong's teaching, I am apologizing for labeling a part of your tract an out and out lie, for in doing this I committed the same sin that I accused you of, that of judging another."[12] She filled the remainder of the letter with defense of Armstrong and his teachings, even supporting the very things in my booklet she formerly found so shocking she branded them "an out and out lie." I have found this form of mesmerization common among supporters of the Worldwide Church of God.

Purchasers of this volume will probably expect an explanation of the division which arose between the father/son top echelon team of Herbert W. and Garner Ted Armstrong. They will be disappointed, unless something additional breaks before the type is completely set, as I can only speculate, along with others, on the basis of the scanty evidence before me.

Summed up: (1) There was some form of rift in the last half of 1971. (2) On October 14, 1971, Herbert W. Armstrong reported his son had been granted an indefinite "leave of absence" and that the boards "of both the Church and the College. . .made official the relieving of all responsibilities from my son Garner Ted. . ." (3) The younger Armstrong "repented" and was received back into the fold by his father late in 1971 or early 1972. (4) Alas and alack, the Senior Arm-

12. Personal letter to the author, dated October 10, 1968

strong wrote that "subsequent events, attitude and conduct, to our great dismay, demonstrated to the Board members, ministers, and myself that the process of repentance was not yet complete." (5) A "read and destroy" communication was sent to all the cult's congregations, written by the elder Armstrong and quoting Garner Ted's confession that he was "in the bonds of Satan." It was read on Saturday, the cult's "Sabbath," February 12. (6) Later that same year the son repented again, this time to the father's complete satisfaction, and was restored to fellowship and service in the movement. In fact, under date of May 31, 1972, the Senior Armstrong sent a letter to his "Inner Family of Co-Workers," announcing: "This letter is being written high in the air, with mingled emotions of thanksgiving and gratitude, hope and JOY! My most fervent heart-rending and prevailing prayers of the last ten months, combined with yours *have been answered!*

"Messrs. Portune, Antion and Dart — all Vice Presidents, Mr. Stanley Rader and I, are returning to Pasadena from a momentous meeting with my son Garner Ted Armstrong. I had spent the better part of two days with him last week, and I knew then that with God's help, and countless hours of submissive, prevailing prayer on his part, coupled with the prayers of thousands for him, his problems have now been overcome. There is no question in our minds that God is calling him back now, with plans for the greatest lunge forward this Work of God has ever taken. He is like a *NEW* Garner Ted Armstrong, and we believe God will now use him with far greater power in getting out Christ's Gospel to the world than ever before. We know God has forgiven, and filled him—and us—with a completely new dedication for the finishing of the Work for this age."

Most of the speculation regarding the problem has centered in two areas: *moral* and *doctrinal.* Perhaps the majority lean to the latter since Garner Ted, in an interview with religion columnist Lester Kinsolving, spoke lightly of one of the cult's major doctrines—the one his father seems most fond of and without which the movement would not have been nearly as successful—the Anglo-Israel theory.

Personally, I lean in the other direction for several reasons: (1) The father/son rift began in 1971, but the Kinsolving interview was not until 1972, being released in March of that year. (2) In a six-page clarification statement (which in reality was an attempt to clarify what the trouble was *not,* rather than what it *was*), released in the Spring of 1972 by the Senior Armstrong, he emphasized that the matter definitely did not involve "doctrinal dispute" or "personal conflict" between the two men. This would rule out anything regarding Anglo-Israelism, it would seem to me. (3) While doing research for this book and going through one of the cult's magazines late in 1971, the emphasis was so heavy on forgiveness for major sins like adultery that I commented to my wife, "This issue sounds like a whitewash for someone high in the movement who got caught." My comment was made before any public report of the conflict broke. (4) In the son's confession, quoted by the father, he acknowledged, "I have no excuses. I sinned mightily against God, against His Church and His Apostle; against the wife God gave me in my youth; against all my closest friends." He also described himself as one "afflicted of the devil," the one through whom "Satan sought to destroy God's work," and confessed, "I have acted like a mindless criminal; like an enraged beast; like someone bent on destruction, and on hurting, and tearing down." (5) Some former members of the cult expressed the opinion to me that the problem was the outgrowth of the immense power struggle which has been raging for several years among those high in the leadership structure at the Pasadena offices.

I offer no conclusions, simply stating the above for the reader to draw his own. If it were not for the "Watergate" kind of cover-up on the part of the Pasadena office, such speculation would not be necessary, of course. *If* and *when* the Armstrongs make a clean breast of the matter, we will be happy to pass the information on to others.

I would also like to point out that this study is an original work, based almost exclusively on the author's personal examination and evaluation of the cult. The first draft was written completely before checking other exposes, then a few items were added where I thought so doing might strengthen a point or further enlighten. Credit for these sources is given in full at the places in the text where they are used.

Another item for clarification relates to my sources for the Armstrong quotes. The reader will note that complete dates for magazine articles and all copyright dates from books, booklets and reprint articles are given, with the last in the series of copyright dates for a publication being the proper one for that particular quote, of course. I point this out because, as with all cults, changes in texts are made so frequently due to errors discovered about untenable positions, if one does not know the date of a particular quote, he might think it inaccurate when he checked the same title having a different copyright date. I was compelled to send out photostat copies of quotes used in my original article because later editions had changed or corrected the text.

This is especially important to remember with regard to the quotations in this work from a key text of the cult, *The United States and the British Commonwealth in Prophecy.* The reader will note that my quotes are from the 1954 edition, the only one I have been able to obtain. It is merely twenty-five pages in length. Later this was expanded to a 227-page tome. However, after an ex-member of the cult wrote an exposition in reply, it was allowed to go "out of print." I tried through several sources over the past two years to obtain a copy and each time the request came back: "Temporarily out of print." I understand it is now being reworked and revised again.

When quoting Armstrong or his leaders, I have given the quotes just as they originally appeared. These writers regularly use such heavy emphasis, usually no further stress is needed. In the rare cases of exception to this rule, I have plainly labeled the emphasis as mine.

I close this Preface by commenting that, after months and months of careful study into this cult's teachings, I feel akin to the brother who had been studying three modern religions, then sat down in despair to write:

"Across the moorlands of the Not
We chase the gruesome When;
We hunt the Itness of the What
Through forests of the Then.
Into the Inner Consciousness
We track the crafty Where,
We spear the Ego tough, and beard
The Self within its lair.

"With Nothingness of mind we catch
The Isness of the What
And in the copses of the Whence
We hear the Think-Bees buzz.
We climb the slippery Which to see
The pallid Thusness roll;
And lift the So beside the Why
Above the Over Soul!"[13]

---

13. Quoted anonymously in *Prophecy Monthly,* June, 1948

CHAPTER I

The Amazing, Astounding Armstrongs!

It was a Sunday morning in Southern Oregon back in 1933. A men's Bible class had assembled in a local church and the teacher was preparing to expound that day's lesson on the Ten Commandments. A stranger, in his early forties, entered the classroom and was handed a copy of the current quarterly. Being seated, he glanced hurriedly over the notes for that day's lesson.

Then something strange took place! The teacher began to stutter and stammer, fumble and bumble, completely unable to launch the lesson. Suddenly, without warning, he turned to the stranger—a man upon whom he had never laid eyes until a few moments before—and blurted out: "Mister, I don't know who you are, but for some reason I just can't teach this class this morning—and I know you can. Would you take my place and teach it?"

In recounting the incident decades later, that stranger wrote: "It was like a sudden bolt out of the blue. WHY was he suddenly unable to teach a class he had been teaching regularly? WHAT made him turn to *me*? WHY did he seem sure I could teach them, when he had never seen me before, and we had not even been introduced?"[1]

Was it a case of the mysterious, mighty moving of the Spirit of God? Or was it a case of demonism and the power of Satan working to accomplish his end? We think readers of this volume will arrive at very definite conclusions long before the last page has been reached.

The man of mystery was Herbert W. Armstrong.

---

1. *Which Day Is The Christian Sabbath?* Herbert W. Armstrong; © 1962,1964,1968, 1970,1971; p. 36

Now an octogenarian, he launched a ministry in January of the year following which, by any standard of measurement, has been highly successful. Pinpointing the origin of his work as January 7, 1934, by the early 1970's its growth, in four primary fields, has been described as phenomenal. The first year of this decade "brought a deluge of nearly 3 million letters" just to his United States address, requiring a staff in excess of 150 people to read and answer.[2] The Religious News Service reports the cult "has an annual budget of $40 million."[3] In an article in the magazine we edit, R. G. Glasgow of New Zealand reported an agent of the cult in Auckland "told me their work is doubling every 2 years and 7 months. I asked whether he meant magazines mailed or church members. He said everything in the work doubled every 2 years and 7 months."[4] Mr. Armstrong himself gives the growth figures "at the rate of approximately 30% a year. That rate of growth has continued for 36 years."[5]

The "Worldwide Church of God"

This hub of Armstrong's ministry is admittedly the smallest and by far the most difficult about which to obtain accurate information. Called the "*Radio* Church of God" when it was launched in 1934, the organization's name has recently been changed to "*Worldwide* Church of God." The reason information pertaining to the church is so hard to come by is that the local congregations meet at *secret* locations, huddled behind *locked* doors, its ministers are not identified to the general public, and members are told not even to allow their mates to read "*Good News*," the magazine exclusively for members. How this system of secrecy is squared with such Scriptures as John 18:20, "Jesus

2. *Tomorrow's World*, April, 1971; p. 35
3. Quoted in *Baptist Bible Tribune*, May 26, 1972
4. *The Biblical Evangelist*, April, 1970; "'The Plain Truth': A False Magazine"; p. 6
5. *The Plain Truth*, October-November, 1970; p. 38

answered him, I spake openly to the world; I ever taught in the synagogue, and in the temple, whither the Jews always resort; and in secret have I said nothing," is not clear.

However, a newspaperman with the *Akron Beacon Journal,* who was able to get into a service in that Ohio city without identifying himself, reported "the church claims 125,000 'co-workers' around the world—most of them in the U. S."[6] *Los Angeles Times* Religion Writer John Dart, reporting how Garner Ted Armstrong, the "No. 2 Man" in the movement, had confessed to falling into "the bonds of Satan," listed the number of congregations at 250.[7] The Associated Press, when reporting the younger Armstrong's restoration after "several months of exile in Colorado," described the cult as a "75,000-member religious group."[8] This latter figure is one acknowledged in a descriptive booklet published by Ambassador College Press.[9] According to one ex-member, however, the growth rate began declining in the late 1960's.[10]

The Printed Page

From the very launching of his movement, the dynamic, fast-talking founder, an advertising man by profession, recognized the value of mass literature circulation. His first magazine, *The Plain Truth*, was launched on February 1, 1934. Run off on a second-hand Neostyle, forerunner of the mimeograph, its circulation was less than 200 copies. Until late 1940, it continued to be mimeographed and issues appeared only spasmodically. For example, 1938 saw only 7 issues and the June, 1939, issue was only the third

6. Peter S. Geiger; quoted in *Baptist Bible Tribune,* October 16, 1970
7. April 1, 1972
8. *Indianapolis Star,* July 8, 1972
9. *This Is The Worldwide Church of God*, Written Anonymously; © 1970,1971,1972; p. 6
10. *The Marson Report Concerning Herbert W. Armstrong*, Richard A. Marson; © 1970; The Ashley-Calvin Press, Seattle, Washington; pp. 6,7

published that year. In fact, it was "out of business" for 2½ years, no issues being published from July, 1935, until January, 1938. Starting with the August-September, 1940, issue, the magazine enjoyed commercial printing and this means was used until 1964, when the movement began publishing the paper on its own presses.

In 1949 the magazine had grown to 16 pages; in 1956 it went to 24 pages; later that decade it went to 32 pages; in 1961 it jumped to 40 pages; and in 1962 it expanded to 48 pages. The following year, a heavy, glossy paper cover was added, making four additional pages—although they are not counted in the numbering. This is the current size. *The Plain Truth* has reached a circulation in the millions and is published, usually monthly, in California, England and Australia in English; a Spanish edition is published in Texas; and French, Dutch and German editions are published in England.

In 1969 a second magazine, *Tomorrow's World*, was launched, fluctuating between a monthly and a bi-monthly. It is described as an "International magazine of Biblical understanding published by the School of Theology, Ambassador College." The December, 1971, issue listed the circulation at 803,000. The difference between the two magazines is editorially explained: "*The* PLAIN TRUTH is now a vehicle for performing our *first* and *principal* commission of proclaiming the good news of coming world peace to the whole world as a witness. . . .TOMORROW'S WORLD is now a vehicle to help perform the *second* commission of FEEDING CHRIST'S SHEEP the deeper spiritual truths."[11] Since *Tomorrow's World* made its appearance, *The Plain Truth* has been very much like a *Newsweek* or a *U.S. News & World Report*, containing far more secular themes than religious.

---

11. *Tomorrow's World*, July, 1971; p. 24

A third magazine, *Good News*, has been published since the early 1950's. It is distributed among baptized members of the cult only and copies are extremely difficult to obtain.

In addition to the magazines, Ambassador College Press turns out tons of books and booklets. To expedite this, the group operates three major printing plants in Pasadena, California; Radlett, England; and North Sidney, Australia. It also has a smaller plant in Big Sandy, Texas.

To handle this voluminous load, Ambassador College Press has the latest and best equipment. For example, the Pasadena plant operates a giant, 180-ton 73-foot Goss P-50 press. It "can transform a reel of blank white paper 50 inches wide into printed pages with full-color pictures at the rate of 1200 to 1500 feet per minute. That's *one mile* of paper every three and one-half minutes!"[12] Since the magazine's pages are approximately 90 square inches, this means the Goss P-50 can turn out *three million* square inches of its pages "every three and one-half minutes!"

The August, 1971, issue of *Tomorrow's World* boasted: "The Ambassador College Press complex in Pasadena occupies more than 100,000 square feet of floor space. Last year this plant used 2,500 tons of paper and 70,000 pounds of ink to print 33 million pieces of literature—including 10 million PLAIN TRUTH's and 3 million TOMORROW'S WORLD magazines. Further facilities include 62,000 square feet in England; 24,700 in Australia; and 5,400 in Big Sandy.

"It's a big operation. It requires hard-working, dedicated people—125 in Pasadena, 80 in Radlett, 35 in North Sidney, and 11 in Big Sandy."[13]

To handle the voluminous load of mail—and to keep files up to date—the California office has a data

---

12. *Tomorrow's World*, July-August, 1970; p. 29
13. Page 34

processing center, using the big IBM System 360 computer, handling about 100,000 names and addresses for the multiple mailing list every month. About 80,000 of these are new contacts and the remaining 20,000 consist of address changes.

As for the content of the literature, most of the articles appearing in *The Plain Truth* and *Tomorrow's World*—as well as the "talks" on the radio and television programs—*advertise* much more than they *produce.* Most of them have sensational, eye-catching, appealing titles, headings and openings, but offer very little in the way of answers. Often a reader must digest an entire article as a buildup for some sensational answer not found until the last paragraph. Or, as often as not, he ends up finding the whole thing was just a "pitch" to get him to write for further literature.

In an expose we published in *The Biblical Evangelist,* R. E. Glasgow reported: "Editor Gentet writes a five-page article, '*The Desert Shall Blossom as the Rose,*' with magnificent photography and maps, using Armstrong's 'staggering' adjectives. The article news is a single paragraph that artesian water has been found beneath the Sahara, but insufficient to make all the Sahara blossom as the rose. You have to read carefully to discover even this detail. Advertising method draws interest but so seldom can you find the plain truth!"[14]

Glasgow presented an analysis of 43 main articles which had appeared "in a random 7 editions of 'The Plain Truth' in 1969." He reported finding "the following percentages of subject matter: Staggering, incredible news items: 39.53 per cent. Violence, sex and disasters: 27.91 per cent. Science: 13.95 per cent. False teachings: 11.63 per cent. Health and personality:

14. Op. cit.

6.98 per cent. Total: 100 per cent."[15]

He also gave an interesting evaluation of Garner Ted Armstrong's booklet, "*What Is a Real Christian?*" He said: "It starts with '*It's shocking, but it's true. Most professing "Christians" today are not really Christians!*' You then expect a gospel sermon, but the booklet, after insisting on law-keeping and proving that no one keeps the Sermon on the Mount, ends flatly with the sentence, 'May God help you to really see and change before it's too late!' Of the 143 paragraphs in the booklet, 136 paragraphs have italics or words in capitals or both, and 101 paragraphs end with an exclamation or question mark. The booklet's excited confusion has no real salvation to offer."[16]

"World Tomorrow" Radio & TV

On January 7, 1934, over KORE, a mere 100-watt station in Eugene, Oregon, the unknown Herbert W. Armstrong launched his radio ministry. Now expanded to television as well as radio—and with son Garner Ted Armstrong "restored" from the "bonds of Satan" as speaker—it is claimed that the radio audience alone numbers "*fifty million* regular listeners who tune in weekly around the world."[17] The network currently includes approximately 300 radio and 50 television stations.

Admittedly, the programs are top quality in production and high in human interest. Differing from the ordinary religious broadcast, such things as prayer and gospel music are never heard. Nor does the cult use this avenue for the "strong meat" of its distinctive doctrines. Quite the contrary, much of what is given would appeal to most Americans, even those fundamental and evangelical in religious beliefs. Broadcast

15. Ibid.
16. Ibid.
17. *Tomorrow's World,* February, 1971; p. 25

themes center around current events, patriotism, morality, attacks on evolution and other subjects calculated to win general approval. Garner Ted Armstrong appears to have patterned his program style from news commentator Paul Harvey. He even *sounds* like him and we have, on occasion, started listening to Armstrong thinking we were listening to Harvey. In fact, the radio programs and telecasts of the Worldwide Church of God are high-powered public relations for the movement as much as anything else. Most of the "discussions" on the airways are calculated to get the listener to write headquarters for additional information.

In describing how Garner Ted's programs are prepared, *Tomorrow's World* revealed: "As for his enormous supply of up-to-date factual information, Mr. Armstrong is assisted by a very well-organized News Bureau staffed with a crew of experienced analysts. The very latest happenings from the international scene are gathered continually from the news centers of the world. Scrutinized, analyzed, and collated, this material is passed on fresh to Mr. Armstrong. It is this extra effort which provides the up-to-the-minute news picture necessary to keep broadcasts timely and meaningful in the light of the very latest world events. AP, UPI, and Reuters teletypes bring reports in a steady stream, 24 hours a day. Important newspapers are scanned and clipped daily—the *New York Times, Washington Post, Wall Street Journal, Christian Science Monitor, Chicago Tribune, London Times,* and others. The nine-member News Bureau staff also receives and reads about 150 weekly and monthly magazines.

"Besides the Pasadena News Bureau, staffs are maintained in each of our regional overseas offices in London, Bonn, Geneva, Johannesburg, Manila, Sidney, and Mexico City for on-the-spot news reports from those areas of the world. . . .

"This vital material is all carefully organized and classified—and the high spot news of whatever subject

Garner Ted Armstrong is planning to speak on is brought to him daily, about an hour before broadcast time.

"Besides the generalized news picture provided through the News Bureaus, Editorial Research teams do in-depth studies into specific aspects of pollution, crime, urban renewal, the population explosion, economics, political situations, and many other pertinent subjects. These researchers interview experts, study technical reports and literature, do on-the-scene surveys—literally becoming experts themselves in these specific fields."[18]

There is little doubt as to *why* or *how* this format builds a large audience for the cult.

Ambassador College

Armstrong's school, Ambassador College, is described as "ONE COLLEGE with THREE uniquely different campuses." The original one, in a Pasadena, California, residential area, is a 45-acre campus with "contoured lawns, sparkling fountains and colorful gardens." The second campus, located in the "Green Belt" area of St. Albans, is just a few miles from London, England. The newest campus is in East Texas at Big Sandy. It has a 4,500-acre campus utilized largely by its agricultural research department.

Leslie L. McCullough calls the Big Sandy campus a "capsule society" and said: "We operate our own water treatment plant, dispose of our own waste, maintain our own grounds, produce the majority of our own dairy products, raise all our own beef (for both United States campuses) and grow a portion of our own vegetables."[19]

With the college motto, *"Recapture True Values,"* the three locations are currently matriculating in the

---

18. Ibid.
19. *Tomorrow's World*, September, 1971; p. 36

neighborhood of 2,000 students—a far cry from the original four students who enrolled for that initial semester in October of 1947. While we have seen several conflicting figures, the *Los Angeles Times* reported, in 1972, 700 students on the California campus, 550 students on the Big Sandy campus and 350 students on the English campus.[20]

In addition to its campuses, Ambassador College makes much of its Correspondence Course. In mid-1970 it reported "more than 165,000 enthusiastic students around the world" as being enrolled.[21]

Background of the Founder

Who is the man in whose fertile mind this strange cult was conceived? Herbert W. Armstrong was born in Des Moines, Iowa, on July 31, 1892. On July 31, 1917, he was united in marriage to Miss Loma Dillon of Motor, Iowa, a local schoolteacher, at the Hyde Park Baptist Church parsonage in Chicago by a Dr. Brown, pastor of the Oak Park Baptist Church and father-in-law of the Hyde Park minister, Dr. Gilkey. The latter had been scheduled to perform the ceremony but was unexpectedly called out of the city. Mrs. Gilkey was a witness.

From that union came four immediate descendants. Two daughters were born first: Beverly Lucille, on May 9, 1918; and Dorothy Jane, who arrived on July 7, 1920. Two sons followed: Richard David, born in October, 1928; and Garner Ted, born on February 9, 1930. At this writing, Mrs. Armstrong and the eldest son, Richard David, are deceased. Regarding the latter, a brief notice in the October, 1958, issue of *The Plain Truth* spoke of the "untimely accidental death of Richard D. Armstrong," and stated further: "An article concerning this tragedy, why God allowed it, and its

---

20. Op. cit.
21. *Tomorrow's World*, July-August, 1970; p. 8

tremendous significance to God's people and His Church at this time, will appear in the November number."[22] However, the November issue contained not a word on the subject, nor did any subsequent issue which we have in our possession.

The origin of the Armstrong cult can probably be traced to the early Fall of 1926, when the Armstrongs visited his mother in Salem, Oregon. Mrs. Loma Armstrong went next door to call on her mother-in-law's neighbor, a Mrs. O. J. Runcorn. This lady was a member of a small cult calling itself the Church of God, with headquarters at Stanberry, Missouri, and holding many of the beliefs the Worldwide Church of God has adopted. This cult was, in turn, a split from the Seventh-day Adventist movement in the mid-1800's brought about from debate over a distinctive name for the advent movement's publication ministry, plus objection to the status of Mrs. Ellen G. White in the group as a "prophetess."

Mrs. Runcorn had Loma read a series of biblical passages and they convinced her, right on the spot, that Saturday was the true Sabbath, still binding upon people today. Mrs. Armstrong ran back to her in-laws' home immediately to share the "great discovery" with her husband. Describing his reaction years later in his autobiography, Mr. Armstrong wrote: "'*Are you CRAZY?*' I had asked, shocked, incredulous!

"My wife gone into religious *fanaticism*! I was horrified, outraged! What would my friends—my business associates say?

"I demanded that she drop this ridiculous heresy at once! But she wouldn't. I argued. Week after week I argued. But all to no avail. I threatened divorce. I told her I would not have our children brought up in any such fanatical religion—and I was sure any sane

22. Page 17

court would grant me custody of our daughters."[23]

Eventually, to prevent the break-up of his home, Armstrong extracted a promise from his wife that, if he could convince her from the Bible that Sunday was the Sabbath, she would abandon her fanaticism. Since his business was about to collapse at the time, requiring only about 30 minutes of his time a week, he "spent a solid SIX MONTHS of virtual night-and-day, seven-day-a-week STUDY and research, in a determined effort" to prove his wife wrong.[24] At the end of that time, however, he had been convinced that his wife was right and that he, along with most of the rest of the world, had been wrong. The present "Worldwide Church of God" resulted from this discovery.

Incidentally, one expose of the movement says: "The message of Armstrongism began with Mrs. Herbert W. Armstrong. An angel revealed God's way to her and she shared the revelation with her husband."[25] But the writer offers no documentation for the claim and we have been able to discover absolutely no foundation whatsoever for it. None, that is, unless he is referring to a dream Mrs. Armstrong had shortly after their marriage. However, that was 5 or 10 years before Armstrong "got religion" and the only angel's message in it pertained to her husband's "movie habit." The angel said, "I have other things for you to do." Years later Armstrong identified this as his first "bona-fide call from God" to the ministry.[26]

For some time after their discovery of "the truth," the Armstrongs called Mr. and Mrs. Runcorn their "spiritual parents."[27] Mr. Armstrong insists he did not

---

23. *The Plain Truth*, March, 1959; p. 7
24. Ibid., p. 10
25. *The Plain Truth About Armstrongism*, Roger R. Chambers; Copyright, 1972; Baker Book House, Grand Rapids, Michigan; p. 9. We do not recommend this book. It deals almost exclusively with Armstrong's Anglo-Israelism and the author is almost as confused as Armstrong.
26. *The Plain Truth*, August, 1958; "The Autobiography of Herbert W. Armstrong"; p. 18
27. *The Plain Truth*, April, 1959; p. 7

join this Missouri-based cult, but acknowledges he was ordained to the ministry by them, preached for them, and received a salary from them. His first public preaching was to conduct an "evangelistic campaign" at Harrisburg, Oregon, the last eleven days of 1930. He saw four "conversions" during the crusade.

It is important to remember that Herbert W. Armstrong made the "discoveries" upon which his present work is based as an unconverted man. Acknowledging even today that he still is not "saved" [the movement teaches none has yet been saved but Jesus of Nazareth], it was not until *after* he made these "discoveries" that he even "wanted to accept Jesus Christ as personal Savior" and "surrendered, unconditionally," he said, to Him.[28] We remind our readers that the Bible itself claims to be a closed book to the unconverted. Paul wrote in I Corinthians 2:14, "But the natural man receiveth not the things of the Spirit of God: for they are foolishness unto him: neither can he know them, because they are spiritually discerned." So the foundation stones for the movement were conceived in the admittedly *un*converted mind of a *non*-spiritual man. *This is tremendously important!*

Much of the success of the movement, especially in the early days, was undoubtedly due to Mr. Armstrong's background as a successful advertising man. The first twenty years of his adult life were spent in the advertising game and all of the cult's work in radio, television and literature bears this imprint. Often an entire radio or television program will be geared to simply whetting the recipient's mind to desire further information, writing to the cult's head-

28. In light of this, we do not understand Salem Kirban's statement, "In his early days he was what may be termed a fundamentalist." [*Doctrines of Devils: Armstrong's Church of God*; © 1970; Published by the author; p. 6] According to Mr. Armstrong's repeated published testimony, he had no interest in spiritual things, rarely even attending church. He was controlled by a consuming passion to make money and be a success in the eyes of the world. (See *The Plain Truth*; August, 1958, p. 18; November, 1958, p. 28; December, 1958, p. 7; *Tomorrow's World*, February, 1972; p. 2)

quarters in order to obtain it, and getting on the mailing list thereby. Quite frankly, a usual headline for an article, a broadcast or a book promises far more than is ever actually revealed.

Perhaps this also explains the Armstrong penchant for emphatic writing. Capital letters, italics, capital letters in italics, and exclamation points are the norm. A complete paragraph in normal type is almost unheard of in a Worldwide Church of God publication.

As a sample, taken at random, note this paragraph from the booklet by Herbert W. Armstrong, "*Which* DAY Is the CHRISTIAN SABBATH?" While talking about what sin is, he says: "But that could be very *costly ignorance*! The first thing you need to get settled in your mind is this: THE LIVING GOD OF ALL POWER DOES NOT ALLOW US TO DECIDE *WHAT* IS SIN. HE DETERMINES *WHAT* IS SIN, AND COMPELS YOU TO DECIDE *WHETHER* TO SIN! And the PENALTY of sin is DEATH for *ETERNITY*! That penalty is *real*! It is a terrifying, *frightful* fate!"[29]

In fact, all the writers in *Tomorrow's World, The Plain Truth, et al*, sound exactly the same and have exactly the same writing style. All are imitators of the Senior Armstrong.

Speaking of the men in the movement, in addition to Herbert W. Armstrong—still living and heading the cult at this writing, in his early eighties—and Garner Ted Armstrong, the heir apparent [he is called *"second in authority"* in the cult's literature] despite having fallen into the "bonds of Satan" and being "restored," there are such men as Herman L. Hoeh, Roderick Meredith, Kenneth Herrmann, Raymond Cole, C. Paul Meredith, Raymond McNair, David Jon Hill,

---

29. Op. cit., p. 19; In this book we are not using type style to show it, but in Armstrong's writings where capital letters are in italics, they are in extra large letters—at least one-third greater in size.

Charles V. Dorothy, Jack R. Elliott, Gerald D. Waterhouse, David L. Antion, Clint C. Zimmerman, Benjamin L. Rea, James W. Robinson, Gene H. Hogberg, Dennis Prather, Charles F. Hunting, Vern R. Mattson, Paul W. Kroll, Leon Walker, Robert L. Kuhn, Brian Knowles, William F. Dankenbring, Albert J. Portune, Eugene M. Walter, Leslie L. McCullough, Vern L. Farrow, Arthur A. Ferdig, Harry Eisenberg, Ernest L. Martin and Basil Wolverton.

A False Prophet

We titled our original expose of the movement, HERBERT W. ARMSTRONG: A FALSE PROPHET! It was published first in *The Sword of the Lord*, an evangelistic weekly with which we have been associated for approximately two decades, then reprinted in booklet form. The description apparently rankles Mr. Armstrong and he refers to it repeatedly in his writings.

For example, on one occasion, talking about Satan, he said: "He palms himself off as GOD. He is called, in your Bible, the *god of this world* (II Cor. 4:4). He palms off his ministers as the ministers of CHRIST—accusing the *true* ministers of Christ of being 'false apostles' to divert suspicion from themselves!"[30]

Again he wrote: "The *modern* 'Pharisees' of this world's organized but deceived 'Christianity'—resisting *the same true Gospel* of the Kingdom of God, now being heard by the MILLIONS worldwide today through *this* work of God, use the same tactics against us! They falsely accuse us of being what they are—false prophets. They deliberately misrepresent what we teach. They falsely say we teach what we do not—and that we do not teach what we do!"[31] Mr. Armstrong frequently quotes II Corinthians 11:13-15, regarding

30. *Which Day Is The Christian Sabbath?* p. 54
31. *What Do You Mean..."The Unpardonable Sin"?* © 1967,1971,1972; p. 36

the ministers of Satan transforming themselves into the apostles of Christ, but apparently never sees himself or his co-workers in this passage.

It is both amazing and tragic that so many good people have been deceived as to the true character of the movement. Earnest Bible believers send money to the Armstrongs, faithfully listen to their broadcasts and avidly read their publications. By way of example, we noted recently that a 27-year-old Nazarene minister in White Springs, Florida, had written the editor of *Tomorrow's World* to enthusiastically say, "I deeply enjoy and appreciate the penetrating articles and programs you offer. An unteachable spirit is deadly to true wisdom so I intend with God's help to keep an open mind. Your article on 'The Real Jesus' is one of the best you have ever written—wish all Christians in the world would read it."[32]

Some of Armstrong's Extravagant Claims

While modesty is a virtue, Herbert W. Armstrong apparently does not even know the meaning of the word. [Even though a descriptive brochure of the cult calls his work ". . . the WAY of humility. . ."!][33] Let me list, for the benefit of the reader, some of his grandiose pronouncements and claims.

(1) His work is identified as *the* work of God on earth. He said of his readers: ". . . you are coming to *know*, and *know that you know* that you are in contact with the actual *Work of Almighty God* on this earth!"[34] One of his chief writers tells them: "*Thousands* of you have come to realize that you are getting the *truth* and *message* of God through this work—The *World Tomorrow* broadcast and the PLAIN TRUTH

32. June, 1971; p. 49
33. *This Is The Worldwide Church of God*, p. 6
34. *Tomorrow's World*, December, 1971; "Which Is The Religion BEST FOR YOU?" p. 8

Magazine. You are beginning to realize that this is the true Church of God."[35]

(2) He claims his work is the first true work of God on earth since the Apostle John's ministry. Brian Knowles wrote: "The true Church *recognized* the *true Gospel.* And undoubtedly the Gospel *was preached on a small personal scale.* But following the death of John, the *organized* preaching of the Gospel on a powerful basis ceased. The Church was persecuted and its numbers decimated in great martyrdoms. The concentrated power of the 'holy people' was scattered so that a worldwide Work was virtually impossible.

"It was not until *this modern twentieth century* that God again raised up a Work of sufficient size and influence to preach the Gospel on a *powerful world-wide basis!*. . .

"We state dogmatically and positively, THIS IS THE VERY WORK OF THE LIVING GOD! *We do not apologize for that!*"[36]

Or, as another expressed it: "For 18½ centuries — from 70 A.D. until 1934 A.D. — this Gospel was not proclaimed to the nations of the world."[37]

(3) He teaches that his work is absolutely the only work of God on earth today. In a pitch for money for the work, A. E. Carrozzo wrote: "There has never been a greater need to reach this dying world with God's lifesaving warning. And there is only one Work on the earth today performing that task. There is only one Work proclaiming the Good News of *Tomorrow's World!*

"That work is *this* Work."[38]

(4) He teaches that his work fulfills the prophecy regarding the coming of Elijah. In an article by John

---

35. *The Plain Truth,* July, 1959; Roderick C. Meredith, "*False* Conversion — A MORTAL DANGER!"; p. 15
36. *Tomorrow's World,* September, 1971; "What 'on Earth' Is God Doing?"; p. 13
37. *The Plain Truth,* July, 1962; Quoted in *Herbert W. Armstrong — The Plain Truth About His Shocking Heresies,* Bob L. Ross; Published by the author, n.d.; p. 2
38. *Tomorrow's World,* July-August, 1970; "About Tithing"; p. 33

Robinson and Alan Heath, "THE SALT of the EARTH," they wrote: "Also read Malachi 4:5-6. Look it up in your own Bible. Read it right now—for yourself. 'I will send you Elijah the prophet before the coming of the great and dreadful day of the Lord.' This is what God's Work is all about. This is the commission that we as the followers of Jesus Christ are being called to do. Elijah is a type of this Work—a work of which *you* are a part."[39]

In another article, "The Bible Defines—'THAT DAY!'" Dennis G. Luker declared: "Malachi 4:5 is a prophecy being fulfilled in your lifetime—right now! 'Behold, I will send you Elijah the prophet before the coming of the great and dreadful day of the Lord.' Luke 1:17 says that John the Baptist came 'in the spirit and power of Elias [Elijah]' to prepare the way before the first coming of Christ. Another Elijah is prophesied to warn the world 'before the coming of the great and dreadful day of the Lord'—the return of Jesus Christ *in power* and glory to punish the unrepentant nations of the earth! *This Work* is performing that commission."[40]

We presume the inference is that Herbert W. Armstrong is the promised Elijah.

(5) He compares his own ministry with that of our Lord's, pointing out they both started small. Writing of his visit to the synagogue in Nazareth, he said: "I have visited the synagogue. It brought vividly to mind the close resemblance, *in size*, to some of the little churches in which I preached in the early years of my ministry. It was very small—probably seating not more than 50 people. It was built entirely of stone. I thought, as I stood and walked around in that little room, of how even Jesus, by whom God *created the earth*, started out His earthly ministry in a very small, humble place. I can't describe my feelings at that

39. *Tomorrow's World*, September, 1971; p. 26
40. *Tomorrow's World*, August, 1971; p. 10

moment—but I assure you it was a tremendous experience!"[41]

(6) He equates himself with God. In writing about the early years of Ambassador College, in one paragraph he calls attention to his absolute control of the institution, saying, "I could not fill ALL the jobs of administration and instruction—I am not *many,* but only *one* man. But two things I could, and did, do. I kept myself as Chairman of the Board of Trustees, appointing as Board members *only* those who believed God's TRUTH, keeping the setting of all POLICIES in the hand of the Board. And second, I made myself the sole instructor in Bible and Theology for the first several years." But then, three paragraphs later, he says, "At all times, GOD has been kept at the HEAD of these campuses, and of His WORK!"[42]

(7) Garner Ted Armstrong is classed along with Old Testament prophets. Describing his public speaking engagements in Nashville and Cincinnati, *Tomorrow's World* reported: "Five power-packed meetings in each city presented the problems of America *as they are*—and, more important, offered *solid solutions.* Reminiscent of Amos, Jeremiah, Isaiah—God's men of the Old Testament who shed tears warning a nation *they loved* to return to God—Garner Ted Armstrong moved many in his audiences to tears in sharing his concern about this nation's going the way of Rome, away from God . . ."[43]

David Jon Hill, the managing editor of the magazine, who reported the crusade, closed his account by taking a Scripture completely out of context and applying it to Garner Ted, saying, "Just as these two cities now know, so the whole world will soon know, '. . . that a prophet hath been among them' (Ezekiel 33:33)."[44]

---

41. *Which Day Is The Christian Sabbath?* p. 24
42. *Tomorrow's World,* August, 1971; p. 48
43. July-August, 1970; p. 26
44. Ibid., p. 28

No wonder we laughed aloud when we read what this cult said of Pentecostal people: ". . . most 'tongues' people are not meek, but loud-mouthed and bragging. . ."![45]

(8) Garner Ted Armstrong is equated with writers of the Bible. In another article about Garner Ted Armstrong and his ministry on the airways, after describing how subject material for a current broadcast is organized, classified and put into his hands, the writer says: "When you add all this to what Mr. Armstrong already has in his mind, plus the inspiration of God's Spirit, then perhaps you will realize how the facts come flowing so fluently out of the loud speaker of your radio."[46]

(9) Armstrong puts himself and his work on a par with the Bible as "God talking to Israel." Referring to Ezekiel's commission to go to the house of Israel (Ezekiel 3:1,4), Mr. Armstrong informed his readers: "But Ezekiel never took that message to the lost house of Israel. He couldn't. He was a slave among the Jews.

"Yet he *is taking it to them*, today, by means of having written it in his book in the Bible—and by the fact that it is being taken to those very people today by *The* PLAIN TRUTH and *The* WORLD TOMORROW broadcast!

"IT IS A PROPHECY! It is a message for OUR PEOPLES TODAY! You are reading it NOW! *God help you to heed!*"[47]

Incidentally, to say that Ezekiel failed in the commission given him by Almighty God is an absurdity of absurdities! It hinges, of course, on Armstrong's false Anglo-Saxon/Israelite theory that no Jew is an Israelite!

(10) Armstrong claims that to join his group is to join the Body of Christ. Garner Ted Armstrong, writing

---

45. *The "Tongues" Question*, Written Anonymously; © 1957,1970; p. 33
46. *Tomorrow's World*, February, 1971; p. 25
47. *Which Day Is The Christian Sabbath?* pp. 79,80

on this subject, "Which Is The Religion BEST FOR YOU?" says: "But even *after* some have called on US, without any solicitation on our part, and have *asked us* if they can 'join' with us in this great Work of God—they want to be baptized, and become a very *member* of the Body of Jesus Christ—yes *even then* we do *not* baptize all of them, by any means." And he goes on to say: "We ARE the very servants of the LIVING Jesus Christ of Nazareth preaching HIS Word, fulfilling HIS great commission to HIS own Body! And we do baptize those we find truly repentant according to the Word of God."[48]

(11) Armstrong claims God's "true ministers" are associated only with his movement. In an article, "Here's How to RECOGNIZE GOD'S TRUE MINISTERS," written by Roderick C. Meredith, he says: "Frankly, there *are* such true ministers on earth today. They are affiliated with this magazine through the Ambassador College Graduate School of Theology. They are warm, friendly and *balanced*—NOT trying to 'pressure' or urge people into anything. But they will call to answer *your questions* upon *your personal request.*"[49]

(12) He warns that "Christians" who do not help in his work will "shrivel up and fall by the wayside." In a reprint release, "What'll You Be DOING In the NEXT LIFE?" by Herbert W. Armstrong, making an obvious pitch for funds for his work, he writes: "Those who are self-centered, caring nothing for the WORK OF GOD, having not enough *outgoing concern* to want to help GET CHRIST'S MESSAGE out to this blinded, deceived, dying world, fall away. Those who center their whole 'Christian' life and activity on developing *their own selves* spiritually, whose hearts are not in or concerned about this great OUTGOING worldwide WORK OF GOD, actually directed by the *living*

---

48. *Tomorrow's World*, December, 1971; pp. 8,45
49. *Tomorrow's World*, July-August, 1970; p. 32

CHRIST, develop only INWARDLY, until they shrivel up spiritually and fall by the wayside! Those whose hearts, their active, constant, earnest, fervent PRAYERS, and their tithes and offerings are in GOD'S WORK continue to EXPAND spiritually—they become HAPPIER—they become greatly BLESSED—their lives become richer and fuller—and their faces beam in smiles. They RADIATE! They PROSPER!"[50]

Armstrong in Prophecy

That the Worldwide Church of God, founded by Herbert W. Armstrong, is experiencing tremendous growth is not denied. It is like a joke he once told in his "Personal" column in *The Plain Truth* about a new pilot on a commercial airline flight. Approximately an hour after take-off, the captain announced over the plane's intercom: "Ladies and gentlemen, I have an announcement to make. I have both good news and bad news. I'll give you the bad news first: WE ARE LOST! Now the Good News: WE ARE MAKING EXCEPTIONALLY FAST TIME!"[51]

For a movement whose founder and followers frankly acknowledge they are not "saved," and whose basic doctrines were formulated by its founder before he made any kind of a professed surrender to Christ, and whose theological pronouncements today are a maze of confusion and contradiction, *they are making exceptionally fast time*!

However, never lose sight of the fact summed up in the old proverb regarding error going around the world while truth is getting its boots on. Mormonism, founded by the "glass looker" and adulterer, Joseph Smith, has experienced phenomenal growth. In fact, the Religious News Service reports it is right now enjoying the greatest membership advance in its history, in-

50. © 1967,1969; p. 8
51. Page 1

creasing 50% in the United States in the past dozen years. Its American constituency now totals 2,133,758 and the world figures have reached 3,090,953.[52] Christian Science, founded by a woman with myriad psycological problems, who had to be rocked to sleep in a specially constructed cradle as an adult, Mary Baker Patterson Glover Eddy, is now a worldwide religion. If growth and numbers indicated God's blessing, perhaps Armstrong should convert to Islam, or, if he wished to remain Christian in name, pledge allegiance to the Pope and unite with Roman Catholicism. But, as Mr. Armstrong was so fond of pointing out when his movement was very tiny and insignificant, size and growth have nothing to do with Truth.

Actually, Herbert W. Armstrong and his Worldwide Church of God were indeed prophesied in the Word of God centuries ago. He and his followers love to amaze their readers with such claims, but the passages to which they point in pride are not the proper ones. The Scripture prophesying this movement came from the pen of Paul in a letter to Timothy, when he warned: *"For the time will come when they will not endure sound doctrine; but after their own lusts shall they heap to themselves teachers, having itching ears; And they shall turn away their ears from the truth, and shall be turned unto fables"* (II Timothy 4:3,4).

This fact, that the Worldwide Church of God is founded upon fables, will become very apparent as you read on.

52. *Baptist Bible Tribune*, August 11, 1972

CHAPTER II

The Armstrongian "Key" to Success: Deception, Misrepresentation, Perversion of Scripture

The Armstrongs have a flair for *keys*. For example, in his original "The United States and the British Commonwealth in Prophecy," Herbert W. Armstrong wrote, ". . .the vital KEY, needed to unlock prophetic doors to understanding, had become lost. That KEY is a definite knowledge of the true identity of the American and British peoples in biblical prophecy."[1] And he titled one of his booklets, "The *Key* to the Book of REVELATION," then said about that Book, ". . .*this Book is the very KEY to understanding of all prophecies! CAN it, then, be understood? It can, if you have the key to this Book, itself. We give you, here, this KEY.*"[2]

Yet, contrary to what the Armstrongs claim *for* and *about* themselves, after wading through stacks of the cult's literature, we have experienced a growing conviction that their *real* "key" is indicated in deception, misrepresentation and perversion of the Word of God. We have sadly concluded that this is a basic Armstrongian principle: "*Scriptures are written to be twisted!*"

Strangely, in a fashion reminiscent of the proverbial pot and the kettle, this is the charge the Armstrongs make of others. On one occasion, Garner Ted Armstrong wrote: "People do not seem to really *fear* to misapply, to misinterpret, wrest, distort and twist the sacred word of God! People do not really RESPECT the divinely inspired words of Almighty God!

"That's why people don't understand the Bible! You

1. Copyright, 1954; p. 1
2. © 1952; p. 2

can come to understand the Bible, and Biblical prophecy, ONLY when you begin to really FEAR and RESPECT *what the Bible says!"*[3]

On another occasion, Herbert W. Armstrong, trying to prove his strange theory that Jesus Christ had to be born again, said: "To *interpret* the Bible is to put your meaning into it—to twist it to mean what YOU want to make it mean, instead of what GOD made it to mean and wants you to understand."[4]

In this chapter the reader is going to discover that more accurate appraisals of self-condemnation have never been written. This is exactly what the Armstrongs do: they "misapply, misinterpret, wrest, distort and twist the sacred word of God." They twist the Bible to mean what they want it to mean, not what God made it mean and wants you to understand. And that is why *they* fail to "understand the Bible!"

In this chapter, we are not so concerned with the practice of the Armstrongs to switch from translation to translation, paraphrase to paraphrase, *sometimes* in the *same passage*, because the wording better suits their purpose, although we think such a practice is deplorable and dishonest. Nor are we so much concerned with the looseness with which they treat fact, especially when talking about their own work, sometimes contradicting themselves in the same passage. [For example, in the "News of the Work" feature of one issue of *Tomorrow's World*, the opening paragraph referred to "a deluge of nearly three million letters" in 1970, "just in the United States alone." But by the last paragraph of the same article, that flow had swelled to "over three million letters."[5] The same uncertainty about numbers prevails with the first edition of *The Plain Truth* magazine. In one place the reader is told, "It started with some 175 or 200

---

3. *Why Prophecy?* © 1960, 1970; p. 4
4. *The Plain Truth,* February, 1963; p. 7
5. April, 1971; pp. 35-38

copies."[6] Less than 2½ years later, he is told, "it started as a little hand mimeographed 'magazine' of 150 copies. . ."[7] But ten pages later in the very same issue the figure had shrunk even more, describing it as "starting with 108 the first issue, February 1934."[8]

Ignorance of Biblical Truth

Nor are we especially concerned in this chapter with the errors they often make in biblical facts, although we think it shows a basic untrustworthiness. As samples of the looseness with which the historicity of the Word of God is treated, note the following:

(1) One of the cult's key men—a member of the board of trustees, a vice-president of Ambassador College, and deputy chancellor at the Pasadena campus—Roderick C. Meredith, writing about "Seven 'Keys' to Mental Mastery," declared: "It may surprise some to learn that most, if not all, of the great leaders of the Bible were *highly educated men.*"[9] He then listed three examples—Daniel, Moses and Paul—but, out of the scores of biblical leaders, this is a small percentage. And his claim that *perhaps* "all" were highly educated is amazing in the light of Acts 4:13, which says, "Now when they saw the boldness of Peter and John, and perceived that they were unlearned and ignorant men, they marvelled; and they took knowledge of them, that they had been with Jesus." In fact, what Meredith is claiming would have been against stated scriptural principle. Paul wrote: "For ye see your calling, brethren, how that not many wise men after the flesh, not many mighty, not many noble, are called: But God hath chosen the foolish

6. *The Plain Truth,* January, 1959; p. 6
7. *The Plain Truth,* June, 1961; p. 2
8. Ibid.; p. 12
9. *Tomorrow's World,* December, 1971; p. 11

things of the world to confound the wise; and God hath chosen the weak things of the world to confound the things which are mighty; And base things of the world, and things which are despised, hath God chosen, yea, and things which are not, to bring to nought things that are: That no flesh should glory in his presence" (I Corinthians 1:26-29).

(2) In one of Herbert W. Armstrong's "Personal" columns, advising his followers never to "preach" to the unconverted, he used Paul as an illustration of one who did not use the negative approach, but always the positive, never arguing with those he sought to win. Among other things, Armstrong said: "When he talked to an unconverted Jew, do you suppose he spoke as a Christian, thinking he is 'witnessing for Christ'? Do you suppose Paul said to the unconverted Jew: 'Have you received Christ as your personal Saviour? Oh, *won't* you just kneel with me right here, dear brother, and give your heart to the Lord right now?' Or, do you suppose he said: 'Look here, my Jewish sinner-friend, you're on the way to hell. Your religion is all wrong. Every day you reject Christ as your Saviour you are crucifying Him afresh. You are worse than a thief or a murderer. I'm going to keep after you, and pester you with my arguments, and drum them into your stubborn ears, and beat them into that stiff rebellious mind of yours until I *force* you to become a Christian.'

"No, that is not the way Paul spoke to unconverted Jews. Paul said: 'Unto the Jews I became *as a Jew*' (I Cor. 9:20,22). Paul spoke to others *from their point of view*! He talked to a Jew just like *another Jew*—from the *Jewish viewpoint*—showing sympathy and understanding of the *Jews'* way of looking at Christianity. They were—and mostly are today—hostile to the idea of Jesus being the promised Messiah. Paul did not rouse hostility—he put it down. He got on the inside, so to speak, just as *one of them*, so that they were *sympathetic* toward him, not hostile. He became *as* a Jew, 'that I might gain the Jews.' Even so he gained only a small minority, yet it was a large number."[10]

Aside from the dishonest portrait of how today's evangelical soul winners witness, note the complete misrepresentation of Paul's methods when Armstrong says he "did not rouse hostility." Then why was Paul run out of town nearly everywhere he went? Why was he beaten, stoned, imprisoned and finally martyred? To show how completely Armstrong has misunderstood the Pauline method, let me quote from the pen of an associate: "Following through the Acts we find that Paul also demonstrated a similar manner in his dealing with people. In Acts 13:43 he and Barnabas, having witnessed to Jews and proselytes, 'persuaded them' to continue in the grace of God. Goodspeed renders this, '*urged them to rely on*'; Phillips has '*urged them to put their trust in the grace of God*'; and we find that the 1901 American revision, Weymouth, Twentieth Century, Montgomery, and Amplified also have '*urged,*' while the New American Standard, Wuest and Williams vary the tense slightly, making it '*urging them.*' Berkeley gives, '*influenced them to entrust themselves to the grace of God.*'

"Since the leading original word here for 'persuaded' can well be cited in other places, it would be to the point to see how that word has been defined. Thayer's *Lexicon* suggests for this ('*pietho*'): 'to persuade, i.e. to induce one by words to believe;. . .to persuade unto i.e. move or induce one by persuasion to do something.' Vine's *Expository Dictionary of New Testament Words* gives: 'to apply persuasion, to prevail upon or win over. . . .' And it was such a real effort which the apostles exerted.

"This word is employed again in Acts 18:4 and 13.

10. *Tomorrow's World,* July-August, 1970; p. 41

In the first instance Paul 'persuaded' the Jews and Greeks, or as Weymouth has it, he '*tried to win over*' both of those groups. In the thirteenth verse it was said by his accusers that Paul 'persuadeth men to worship God contrary to law,' or as Weymouth again has it, '*inducing people to. . . .*'

"In the next chapter of Acts we read that Paul 'spake boldly. . .disputing and persuading the things concerning the kingdom of God' (Acts 19:8). The 'persuading' here is the same word. The Amplified version renders this '*spoke boldly, persuading and arguing and pleading about the kingdom of God.*' As a result of the zeal and urgency Paul displayed, an accusation against him in this place was that he 'hath persuaded and turned away much people' (vs. 26), or as it is in Weymouth, '*has led away a vast number of people by inducing them to believe. . . .*' "[11]

(3) In his book, "*Which Day is the* CHRISTIAN SABBATH?" Armstrong shows his confusion of Bible history when he writes: "So the tribe of Judah *seceded from the nation* ISRAEL. They formed a separate kingdom, called the Kingdom of JUDAH. The tribe of Benjamin went with them."[12]

But it was not Judah that seceded from Israel, it was the reverse: *Israel seceded from Judah*! The story is recorded in I Kings 12:16-24 and II Chronicles 10:12-11:4, but we will merely quote verses 16 and 19 of the latter passage here: "And when all Israel saw that the king would not hearken unto them, the people answered the king, saying, What portion have we in David? and we have none inheritance in the son of Jesse: every man to your tents, O Israel: and now, David, see to thine own house. So all Israel went to their tents. . . .And Israel rebelled against

---

11. *The Public Invitation: Is It Scriptural? Is It Wise? Is It Necessary?* Samuel Fisk; Copyright, 1970; Biblical Evangelism Press, Brownsburg, Indiana; pp. 7,8
12. Page 62

the house of David unto this day." In fact, God stopped Judah from going after the rebellious ones who had declared their independence, saying, "This thing is done of me" (II Chronicles 11:4).

(4) In a reprint article first published in 1957, "Who—What—was Jesus *before His Human Birth*?" Garner Ted Armstrong, dealing with the transfiguration, denies that the voice from Heaven was the voice of God. He said: "As the disciples stood, gazing with awe and wonder at the brilliance of the vision, there came a '. . .voice out of the cloud, which said, This is my beloved Son, in whom I am well pleased; hear ye Him' (Matt. 17:5). But notice, did the scripture say it was God the Father who spoke? NO! *Read it in your own Bible!*"[13] But who else would have called Christ "my beloved Son"?

This same error is repeated in the "*ANSWERS* to your Questions" column of a 1971 issue of *Tomorrow's World*, explaining: "It was not THE voice of God, but merely *a voice.* It did not come from the heights of heaven but from the cloud which overshadowed them. This was the voice of an angel acting as a spokesman for God."[14] But, if so, the angel would have had to say: "This is the Father's Son, in whom He is well pleased!"

In both instances, the "proof" is given as John 5:37, where Jesus said, "And the Father himself, which hath sent me, hath borne witness of me. Ye have neither heard his voice at any time, nor seen his shape." But these words about not having heard the Father's voice were addressed to the wicked, unbelieving religious leaders of that particular day who were seeking to kill Jesus, those who had "not his word abiding in" them (vs. 38). They were not intended as a blanket statement covering all mankind. Quite the

13. Page 3
14. June, 1971; p. 45

contrary, since the Bible uses phrases like "the Lord spake," "God said," etc., "nearly seven hundred times in the Pentateuch alone, and they are scattered throughout the Scriptures no less than three thousand times altogether."[15]

In fact, Armstrong himself acknowledges this in his booklet on the Sabbath, saying, "It was *not* Moses' voice which delivered God's LAW. It was THE VOICE OF *GOD*! The whole nation of people heard the VOICE OF GOD!

". . .the voice of GOD spoke to that mass of people. . ."[16]

(5) Another major blunder, showing the unfamiliarity of the cult leaders with the Sacred Scriptures, pertained to Garner Ted Armstrong's identification of "Nazareth" as the birthplace of our Lord. He wrote: "Nevertheless, Jesus did, continually, enter into a home, which very likely was His own home, in Capernaum, as well as the home of which He spoke in the city of Nazareth, the city of His birth." This is a "goof" on a par with Joe Smith's listing of "Jerusalem" as the birthplace of Jesus in his *Book of Mormon.*

These are just a few examples of the kind of statements men make who are not familiar with what the Bible actually teaches.

Deception, Misrepresentation, Perversion

Without making any attempt to classify them, let us list some of the cases of the Armstrongian "Key" in action, noted at random while going through the cult's literature.

(1) Repeated efforts are made, especially in appeals to the general public both over the airwaves and in

---

15. *And God Spake These Words,* W. H. Griffith Thomas; Copyright, 1926; The Sunday School Times Company, Philadelphia; p. 87
16. Page 43
17. *Tomorrow's World,* June, 1971; "The 'Jesus Trip' One-Way Ticket to Nowhere?"; p. 31

print, to leave the impression that giants of the Christian faith would agree with them. For example, while trying to prove his Anglo-Saxon Israelism of America and the British Commonwealth, Armstrong says: "One of Britain's most famous clergymen of the 1800's, C. H. Spurgeon, said: 'I judge that *God* has blessed the *two great nations* of the Anglo-Saxon race — England and the United States — and given them pre-eminence in commerce and in liberty on purpose that in such a time as this they may spread abroad the *knowledge of the glory of God. . . .*'"[18] But Charles Haddon Spurgeon would have been among the first and the most vehement to condemn Armstrong and his Anglo-Saxon Israelism — along with all his other heresies — had the latter gentleman launched his work a century sooner. In fact, Spurgeon commended a brother who was opposing this theory back then, writing in a letter: "Dear Sir: I wish you every success in your warfare against this silly craze. I was at one time rather amused with the delusion as a freak of human folly; but it evidently has its moral and spiritual bearings, and must therefore be met and exposed. I have not time for this contest, and therefore I am the more pleased to see others in the field. Yours truly, C. H. Spurgeon."[19]

In his booklet, "*The* RESURRECTION *was* NOT *on Sunday*!" Herbert W. Armstrong says: "The PLAIN TRUTH concerning the crucifixion and the resurrection of Christ is fast sweeping the world. Thousands are coming to see it. This truth has been published in the Sunday School Times. The Oxford University Press, in their 'Companion' Bible, publish a table proving this newly-revealed truth of the Bible."[20] The inference is that this noted evangelical magazine, which is no longer being published, would agree with Armstrong's

18. *The Plain Truth,* October-November, 1970; p. 8
19. Quoted by Charles U. Wagner in *Temple Tidings,* June 11, 1970; p. 3
20. Copyright, 1952; pp. 11, 12

teaching. While the *Times* did teach that the crucifixion was not on Friday, it just as vehemently denied the Armstrong position that the resurrection was on Saturday.

In two of his books, Armstrong gives lengthy passages of praise to George Mueller. In one he describes him as "a great man of FAITH,"[21] and, in the other, he says, "he probably was the greatest modern apostle of FAITH."[22] In fact, he quotes a definition of faith by Mueller and calls it "a true Bible definition."[23] But George Mueller and Herbert Armstrong were poles apart in their understanding of the Word of God—*and in their understanding of scriptural faith.* George Mueller would have described Armstrong as a heretic of the worst order and Armstrong, if he were to go by his own teaching as revealed elsewhere, would have to say that Mueller was not a true Christian, but rather an unconverted man and a false prophet. Yet in these books he writes of Mueller in a way that would cause the uninformed reader to think the two men believed alike.

(2) Misrepresentation and vilification of today's Christian leaders by the cult are not unknown, despite pious claims to the contrary. For example, the noted Irish evangelical and Member of Parliament, Ian Paisley, is described in *The Plain Truth* by Raymond F. McNair as "very vociferous in his anti-Catholic, pro-Protestant speeches, both in and out of Parliament."[24] Yet in a sister magazine, Garner Ted Armstrong wrote: "We do *not* attack organizations, churches, or individuals."[25]

(3) A favorite Armstrong trick, in endeavoring to prove a point in his teaching, is to add words in

---

21. *Does God Exist?* © 1957, 1960, 1970, 1971; p. 27
22. *What Is Faith?* Copyright, 1952; p. 8
23. Ibid.
24. August-September, 1970; p. 11
25. *Tomorrow's World,* December, 1971; p. 8

brackets while quoting Scripture, completely changing the scriptural meaning and thus making it conform to his theories. By way of illustration, in an article, "*Just What Do You Mean. . .BORN AGAIN?*" Herbert W. Armstrong quotes from Romans 8:11 like this: "But if the Spirit of him that raised up Jesus from the dead dwell in you, he that raised up Christ from the dead shall also quicken [change to immortal spirit] your mortal bodies by his Spirit that dwelleth in you."[26] But the word "quicken" here is *zoopoieo*, which simply means to "make alive." Armstrong's bracket/insertion changes the meaning entirely: from the raising and making alive of a dead body, to the transformation of a dead body into an immortal spirit.

Later in the article he quotes Romans 8:21 as follows: ". . .because the creation [RSV] itself also *shall be delivered* [a *birth*] from the bondage of corruption into the glorious liberty of the children of God."[27] Since he is trying to prove that one is not born again until the resurrection, the insertion of his interpretation of the word "delivered" as "birth," completely out of context, is thus transformed *ipse dixit*—or, more correctly, *hocus pocus*.

Still later in the article Armstrong quotes Hebrews 11:39,40, as follows: "And these all, having obtained a good report through faith, received not the promise [were not born into the KINGDOM]: God having provided some better thing for us, that they without us should not be made perfect."[28] Here, again *ipse dixit/hocus pocus*, he turns "received not the promise" into being born into the kingdom of God. This, in spite of the fact the context shows "the promise" to be the covenants God made with Old Testament Israel regarding the Promised Land.

---

26. *Tomorrow's World,* October, 1971; p. 8
27. Ibid.; p. 41
28. Ibid.; p. 44

If the Armstrongs had to use typewriters without brackets, they would be compelled to abandon three-fourths of their creed!

(4) Garner Ted Armstrong, in an article, "What Is Satan's Faith?" palms off as "false doctrine" an isolated case of "figure of speech." He writes: "Most of you are well aware of the false doctrines circulated in modern 'churchianity' about Satan the devil. The familiar tunes of the 'preachy-toned' tent-camp evangelist shouting, 'We're sure gonna twist ole Satan's tail tonight!' is just one of many examples."[29] To use such a facetious figure of speech as "proof" of false doctrine among today's evangelicals is either inexcusable ignorance or deliberate deception.

(5) Three times in Mark 9 (verses 44,46,48), in warning of Hell, our Lord declared: "Where their worm dieth not, and the fire is not quenched." Interpreting this as maggots which feed on dead carcasses, a writer in one of the cult's releases said: "It was to *these worms* that Christ was referring when He said 'their worm dieth not.' But Christ didn't mean that each *individual* worm continued to live forever!

"Actually, these worms, or maggots are the larvae which develop from eggs deposited by flies. They continue for only a *few days* in this larval stage, and then they pupate and finally emerge as flies, later dying. These are scientific facts, known by any real student of science. And yet some people think that Christ *ignorantly* stated that these larvae continued to live forever in that stage of development! This just goes to show that we should always be careful to use wisdom and common sense in studying God's Word. The Holy Spirit is the spirit of a *sound mind* (II Tim. 1:7). Let's rightly use the minds God gave us!"[30]

But there never has been a single evangelical

29. *Tomorrow's World,* June, 1971; p. 6
30. *There Is A Real Hell Fire,* David Jon Hill; © 1962,1963,1971; p. 5

preacher in the history of mankind, to our knowledge, who has ever given such an absurd interpretation to that passage. What a terrible perversion this is of what Bible preachers have always taught; yet the writer sets it forth as a straw man to attack, implying that he is refuting what people who have believed in eternal Hell have always taught.

(6) On one occasion, trying to prove his legalism, Armstrong asks: "Why have you been taught that MOSES 'gave the law'? WHY has this law been called the 'Law of Moses'?"[31] To answer the first question, we have been taught that Moses "gave the law" because that is what the Word of God says. John 1:17 declares, "For the law was given by Moses, but grace and truth came by Jesus Christ." And to answer the second question, the law has been called "the Law of Moses" because that is what it is called in the Bible. Joshua 8:32 says, "And he wrote there upon the stones a copy of the law of Moses, which he wrote in the presence of the children of Israel." And Nehemiah 8:1 says, "And all the people gathered themselves together as one man into the street that was before the water gate; and they spake unto Ezra the scribe to bring the book of the law of Moses, which the Lord had commanded to Israel." In the first verse the reference is to the Ten Commandments; in the second verse the reference is to the first five books of the Bible. Both are called "the law of Moses." In fact, Herbert W. Armstrong, himself, speaks of "the Law of Moses."[32]

(7) In an effort to distinguish between the Ten Commandments and the other laws given by Moses, Armstrong quotes Deuteronomy 5:22, which, after listing the Ten Commandments, says, ". . .and he added no more." Armstrong comments: "That was a COM-

---

31. *Which Day Is The Christian Sabbath?* © 1962,1964,1968,1970,1971; p. 43
32. *What'll You Be Doing In The Next Life?* © 1967,1969; p. 2

PLETE LAW! It is a SPIRITUAL LAW. It is COMPLETE. He added no more—to THAT LAW! Any other laws are different, separate laws—NO PART OF THAT SPIRITUAL LAW! It is complete in itself!"[33] But the *adding no more* has to do with what God wrote on the two tables of stone, not the instructions he gave Moses at that time. In fact, just nine verses on in Deuteronomy 5, we read: "But, as for thee, stand thou here by me, and I will speak unto thee all the commandments, **and the statutes, and the judgments,** which thou shalt teach them, that they may do them in the land which I give them to possess it" (vs. 31). Mr. Armstrong makes a distinction that God does not make.

(8) In his effort to make his legalism binding today, Mr. Armstrong declares: "And if you think this law was for 'Jews only,' you couldn't be more wrong! Have you not read, in Acts 7:38, that those Israelites 'received the lively oracles *to give unto* US'—for US who, under the New Testament, are Christians?"[34] My, what a perversion of Scripture is this! The "us" here does not refer to New Testament Christians, but to the unconverted Israelites at Jerusalem to whom Stephen was speaking. The "us" of that verse were the very ones who moments later picked up stones and stoned Stephen to death because of his preaching. If that is the best Mr. Armstrong can do while advocating his legalism, he is in mighty sorry shape. The more one reads what Armstrong writes, the more it seems he is totally ignorant of the overall teaching of the Scriptures. His acquaintance with the Word of God is limited to his few pet passages.

(9) Another example of his misrepresentation, then drawing a conclusion from what he has misrepresented, is seen in his argument: "Consequently, many have

33. *Which Day Is The Christian Sabbath?* p. 45
34. Ibid.

used the argument, without any Scriptural authority of course, that the Ten Commandments were abolished at the cross. Of course they never stop to realize that, *if* there is no law, there is no transgression—as Paul plainly states in Romans 4:15—and no one has sinned since the cross—and therefore we should not *need* a Saviour!"[35] This is a complete misrepresentation of what evangelical Christianity has always maintained. We know of no one who teaches that the Ten Commandments were abolished at the cross. What evangelicals believe, and what the Scripture states, is that the ceremonial law—which includes the Sabbath—was abolished at the cross. The moral law is just as much in effect as it was when the Ten Commandments were given; yea, just as much as it was *before* the Ten Commandments were written on tables of stone. God's *moral* law has been in effect from the creation of man!

(10) Another example of Armstrong's twisting of Scripture to support his brand of legalism is seen in the opening paragraph of a *Tomorrow's World* article: "Much of the professing Christian world today suffers from the mistaken notion that Christ came to do away with His Father's religion—the religion of the Old Testament. Nothing could be further from the truth! Jesus Himself said, 'Think *not* that I am come to destroy the law, or the prophets: I am not come to destroy, but to fulfill [fill to the brim]' (Matt. 5:17)."[36] But the word translated "fulfill" is the Greek word *pleroo*, meaning to finish, complete, execute—*and this is the meaning consistent with the context.* Jesus went on to say in the next verse, "For verily I say unto you, Till heaven and earth pass, one jot or one tittle shall in no wise pass from the law, till all be fulfilled."

35. Ibid.; p. 51
36. September, 1971; Ernest Martin and Harry Eisenberg; "Between the Testaments" p. 20

Both the British and American revisers used the word "accomplished" instead of "fulfill." Jesus Christ *did* perfectly complete [or, *accomplish*] the law in our behalf, and now, just as Paul said in Romans 10:4, "Christ is the end of the law for righteousness to every one that believeth."

(11) A sample of how the Armstrongites twist Bible prophecy is seen in the statement: "Now as for Russia burying the United States and Britain, God says that America and Britain—after a downfall—will rise and bury Russia! It's in your Bible, hidden to the world only because the world has failed to look.

"Notice what God says about *our burying Russia* in the prophecies of Ezekiel: 'Son of man, set thy face against Gog, the land of Magog, the chief prince of Meshech and Tubal [Russia] and prophesy against him. . .And it shall come to pass in that day, that I will give unto Gog a place there of graves in Israel, the valley of the passengers on the east of the sea: and it shall stop the noses of the passengers: and there shall they bury Gog and all his multitude: and they shall call it the valley of Hamongog. And *seven months* shall the house of Israel [which includes Britain and America] be *burying of them*, that they may cleanse the land. Yea, all the people of the land shall bury them; and it shall be to them a renown the day that I shall be glorified, saith the Lord God' (Ezek. 38:2; 39:11-13)."[37]

Here, absolutely without any justification whatsoever except the writer's own insertion in brackets of the totally false assumption that Britain and America are included in "the house of Israel," a prophecy dealing exclusively with Israel is attributed to the United States and Britain.

(12) On one occasion, Herbert W. Armstrong wrote: "WHY do most of those who claim to be the very

---

37. *Tomorrow's World,* July-August, 1970; P. S. Royer, "Who Will Bury Whom?"; p. 34

CLERGY of Jesus Christ say there are 'NO WORKS WHATEVER' in the Christian life?

"Because of their false pagan and unscriptural doctrine about what 'salvation' is. Their conception of salvation seems to be an eternity of idleness and ease—with nothing to do. The development of the very CHARACTER of the living GOD—preparing for RULERSHIP—qualifying for SERVICE—have no place in their false pagan theology."[38]

This is complete misrepresentation on both counts. In the first place, Bible believers do not say there are "no works whatever" in the Christian life. Quite the contrary, they teach that the Christian life is one of continuous works. The difference between evangelical Christianity and Armstrongism, however, is that evangelical Christianity says there are "no works whatever" *as a basis* for salvation.

Neither does Bible-believing Christendom have a concept of "an eternity of idleness and ease—with nothing to do." This is another figment of the fertile Armstrong imagination. Again, to the contrary, evangelicals believe and preach an eternity of worship, adoration and service to Almighty God.

(13) In the same article, Armstrong makes the statement: "We are to become a CREATION (Gal. 6:15, margin)."[39] But that passage is not talking about the future, it is talking about the present. We are not going "to become" new creatures, the individual in Christ Jesus is *right now* a new creation! Second Corinthians 5:17 declares: "Therefore if any man be in Christ, he is a new creature: old things are passed away; behold, all things are become new." It says "he is," not "he will be."

(14) If a little fabrication will help Armstrong's cause, then he is ready and willing to weave it. Con-

38. *What'll You Be Doing In The Next Life?* p. 8
39. Ibid.

sider the following example of biblical history being re-written to suit his own purposes: "So immediately Jeroboam set up two great idols for his people to worship. He ordered the fall Festivals to be observed in the EIGHTH month, at a place in the north of Palestine of HIS choosing—instead of in the seventh month, and at Jerusalem as GOD ordered (I Kings 12:28-32). Also Jeroboam changed the Sabbath day from the seventh to the eighth—that is, to the day *following* the seventh day, which, actually of course, was the *first* day of the WEEK. Thus he set the day for worship to coincide with the pagan DAY OF THE SUN, now called Sunday!

"Through the rule of 19 kings and seven successive dynasties, the ten-tribed house of ISRAEL continued in the basic twin sins of Jeroboam—idolatry and Sabbath-breaking. Several of the kings added other evil and sinful practices."[40]

This is pure fiction. There is no indication whatsoever that Jeroboam changed the Sabbath from the seventh day of the week to the first. And any who will read his "proof passage" in I Kings 12:28-32 will discover that this is definitely *not* what this portion of Scripture is saying. However, Armstrong, a few pages after stating this fabricated history as fact, argues another matter from his assumption: "This was because they had rejected GOD'S SABBATH, and followed King Jeroboam's custom of observing the first day of the week (today called SUNDAY) as their 'sabbath.'"[41] This is typical Worldwide Church of God procedure: *fabricate a proof, then argue from the fabrication.*

(15) The amazing extreme to which Armstrong will take Scripture out of context to prove his point is seen in his reference to Hosea 2:6, where God said, "Therefore, behold, I will hedge up thy way with

---

40. *Which Day Is The Christian Sabbath?* p. 63
41. Ibid.; pp. 66,67

thorns, and make a wall, that she shall not find her paths." Armstrong wrote: "That is, the house of Israel shall *lose her way*—as she migrates from Assyrian captivity, to the northwest into Europe, to the Atlantic coastlands, Scandinavia, and Britain—she *shall lose her identity*—BECOME LOST—the Lost Ten Tribes!

"Read those first two chapters of Hosea—a prophecy for the Ten-Tribed HOUSE OF ISRAEL. It portrays them as having lost all knowledge of WHO their True God is!"[42] This, of course, takes the passage completely out of context.

Next he quotes Hosea 2:8, "For she did not know that I gave her corn, and wine, and oil, and multiplied her silver and gold, which they prepared for Baal," saying: "That pictures Britain and America TODAY! God has given us the unprecedented national WEALTH He unconditionally promised Abraham—not because of our SINS, but because of Abraham's OBEDIENCE!"[43] But the passage is not talking about Britain and America **TODAY!** It is talking about Israel **THEN!**

Such a technicality does not bother Armstrong; he moves right on, calling attention to the next verse and saying: "'Therefore will I return, and take away my corn in the time thereof, and my wine in the season thereof. . .'—that is, the FAMINE already *now* beginning in its early years—prophesied by Joel, Ezekiel, by Christ, and in Revelation! Yes, this is a prophecy for NOW! FOR OUR PEOPLE! It is even NOW, as *you* read, beginning!"[44] No doubt our readers will be amazed to know that we are in famine and have been since Armstrong wrote those words in 1962! Although America is having her annual surpluses of crops and able thereby to feed many other nations of the world with those surpluses, Mr. Armstrong tells

42. Ibid.; p. 67
43. Ibid.
44. Ibid.

us we are experiencing famine. This shows to what extremes fanatical heresy will lead men.

The amazing thing is that Mr. Armstrong has the audacity to tell his readers, right in the midst of his blasphemous twistings of biblical teaching, "Probably you never *understood* the prophecy of Hosea before!"

(16) In the July-August, 1970, issue of *Tomorrow's World* was an article by G. Freibergs, "DOOR-TO-DOOR PREACHING. . .A CHRISTIAN PRACTICE?" The writer's conclusion was that such a custom of soul-winning visitation is paganism, not true Christianity at all. This, in spite of the fact that the Scripture says of the apostles, "And daily in the temple, AND IN EVERY HOUSE, they ceased not to teach and preach Jesus Christ" (Acts 5:42).

After quoting "authorities" who prove that such a system of spreading God's Good News is obnoxious, the writer concludes: "Such a way of 'winning souls,' needless to say, is diametrically opposed to the practices and teachings of Jesus. Christ *never* preached from door to door. He did not hand out one religious tract. He specifically instructed His disciples, 'Go not from house to house' (Luke 10:7). John, the last survivor of the original twelve apostles, admonished the followers of Christ: 'If there come any unto you, and bring not this doctrine [which John preached and which only the one true Church of God preaches], receive him not into your house' (II John 10). No truth could be learned from the preachings or the writings of these disseminators of error. Paul warned about the type of fellow Plutarch wrote about. 'For of this sort are they which creep into houses, and lead captive silly women laden with sins, led away with divers lusts' (II Tim. 3:6)."[45]

Note at least four major twistings of Scripture in this one paragraph: (1) To say that Christ never preached

45. Pages 32,33

from door to door is to go beyond what is written. Nowhere are we told He did *not* engage in this type ministry; on the other hand, the Scripture repeatedly refers to homes where He *did* visit. Whether He gave out any religious tracts is not revealed in the Bible; but, if He did not, that is begging the point. He did not preach sermons on the radio, as the Armstrongs do today, either! (2) The statement regarding His instruction to His disciples not to go from house to house is wicked perversion and misrepresentation. He simply told His disciples not to go from house to house *for their hospitality*, remaining instead in the same home throughout their ministry in a particular city. The entire verse, which the writer did not quote, says: "And in the same house remain, EATING AND DRINKING SUCH THINGS AS THEY GIVE: for the labourer is worthy of his hire. Go not from house to house." (3) To quote II John 10 as proof that door-to-door evangelism is wrong "takes the cake" in perversion. This has absolutely nothing to do with "going," but rather "receiving." And it does not have anything to do with truth; it has to do strictly with error. (4) Perhaps the worst perversion in the paragraph pertains to the "warning" by Paul in II Timothy 3:6. To compare twentieth century soul winners, going from house to house with the dynamic gospel of Christ and its life-changing results, with those who sneak into houses and lead silly women into sin is the perversion of one in the last throes of frantic desperation!

(17) As an example of how Armstrongites twist Scripture to fit their confusing ideas (in this case, the theory that no one is yet a child of God, simply "conceived," not yet "born"), Herman L. Hoeh writes: "We are called the 'begotten *children* of God' (I John 3:1). God, then, has the power to beget us as His children. He begets us 'by his Spirit.' Each portion of the Spirit by which we are begotten is termed in the Bible a germ or 'seed.' Peter tells us we are

'begotten again, not of corruptible SEED, but of incorruptible, through God's word, which liveth and abideth' (I Peter 1:23). Jesus completes this by saying we must finally be *born* again at the resurrection—when we shall *be* spirit. Now we are only flesh with the spiritual *germ of eternal life* impregnating us."[46]

Notice the twisting of what the Bible really says: (1) Christians are called in I John 3:1 "sons of God," not "begotten children," a term which suits the Armstrong theory better. (2) Note that the "seed" in I Peter 1:23 is the Word of God, not the "portion of the Spirit," as Hoeh would have it. (3) Finally, the reference to what Jesus said contains two lies: He did not say we must "finally" be born again, nor did He say that the new birth would be "at the resurrection." This is Armstrongian misrepresentation, plain and simple.

(18) Leaders in the Worldwide Church of God often quote only a portion of Scripture, taking it out of context, to try to prove a point. Consider, for example, this gem: "It is by the fruits of the Spirit that you *know* you have received the Holy Spirit of God. 'By their fruits shall ye know,' said Jesus (Matt. 7:20)."[47] But Jesus, in this passage, was warning of "false prophets, which come to you in sheep's clothing, but inwardly they are ravening wolves" (vs. 15), and His conclusion in Matthew 7:20 is, "Wherefore by their fruits ye shall know them." Far from this verse teaching that one with the fruits of the Holy Spirit will know he has received the Holy Spirit, this passage is merely showing how false prophets are identified. (And they are very definitely identified by such fruits of misrepresentation as Hoeh manifests here!)

(19) Another example of the Armstrongian twisting of Scripture is seen in the following statement from the

---

46. *How You Can Be Imbued With The Power Of God!* © 1958,1967,1970,1971; p. 3
47. Ibid.; p. 2

pen of Herbert W. Armstrong: "No Gentile can become a Christian *until* he becomes an ISRAELITE—read Ephesians 2:11-22."[48] In case the reader misses that, four paragraphs further he is told again: "Read Ephesians 2:11-22. YOU HAVE TO BECOME AN ISRAELITE TO BE SAVED! You have heard a lot of *false* and *anti-Scriptural* teaching leading you to suppose salvation is for Gentiles. IT IS NOT!"[49] We challenge anyone to read the passage in Ephesians indicated by Armstrong, apart from wearing the spectacles of an Anglo-Saxon/Israelite, and come up with any conclusion that it is necessary to become an Israelite *before* he can be saved!

(20) Believe it or not, Mr. Armstrong, who has a vendetta against any kind of a celebration—even one's own birthday or Valentine's Day—claims that the Bible condemns Christmas trees! Here are his own words: "But if the Bible is silent about telling us to observe Christmas, or recording any such observance by the apostles or early true Church it *does* have something to say about the Christmas tree!

"This will come as a real surprise to many. But here it is:

"Jeremiah 10:2-6: 'Thus saith the Lord, *learn not the way of the heathen. . . .For the customs of the people are vain*: for one cutteth a tree out of the forest, the work of the hands of the workman, with the ax. They deck it with silver and with gold; they fasten it with nails and with hammers, that it move not.'

"There is a perfect description of the Christmas tree, termed by the Eternal as 'the way of the heathen—the custom of the people.' We are commanded not to learn that way or follow it! It is also viewed in this passage as idolatry. The fifth verse

48. *Which Day Is The Christian Sabbath?* p. 88
49. Ibid.; p. 89

shows that these trees cannot speak—cannot walk—must be carried. 'Be not afraid of them; for *they* [the trees] cannot do evil, neither also is it in them to do good.' They are not gods to be feared. Some people *mis*-read this to make it say there is no harm in having a Christmas tree, but that is not what it says."[50]

If we had not read with our own eyes Armstrong's exegesis of this passage, we could not believe it! Since one of the Christmas songs speaks of "decking," we suppose Mr. Armstrong concluded that the "decking" (vs. 4) of these trees is the "trimming" of the twentieth century Christmas tree! But it ought to be obvious to anyone of intelligence that the entire passage is talking about making "gods" [idols] out of wood, then covering them with silver and gold. (Who, today, would gold-plate or silver-plate a Christmas tree?) These "gods" cannot talk or walk, but must be carried by their worshipers. (Who would carry around a Christmas tree, pray tell?) They are called "gods" (vs. 11), and the reader is told further: "Every man is brutish in his knowledge: every founder [*goldsmith,* R.V.] is confounded by the graven image: for his molten image is falsehood, and there is no breath in them. They are vanity, and the work of errors: in the time of their visitation they shall perish" (vss. 14, 15). This passage has no more to do with Christmas trees than it does Mount Vesuvius.

(21) The Armstrongs teach that God is going to raise unconverted people from the dead and give them an opportunity to be saved. Their perversion of Scriptures, while trying to justify this position, is enough to make the angels weep. Here is a sample: "Read what Revelation 20:11-12 says about this resurrection: 'And I saw a great white throne. . .and I saw the dead, small and great, stand before God [these

50. *The Plain Truth About Christmas* © 1952,1970; pp. 17,18

people are standing—a resurrection]. . .and another book was opened, which is the book of life [they are given life]; and the dead were judged out of those things which were written in the books.'

"It is the great white throne judgment!

"Even the worst of the sinners who never had a chance will be in this resurrection, for even the inhabitants of Sodom will be there! 'When thy sisters, Sodom and her daughters, shall return to their former estate, and Samaria and her daughters shall return to their former estate, then thou [Jerusalem—refer to Ezekiel 37]. . .shall return to your former estate' (Ezekiel 16:55).

"Isaiah 65:20 indicates these resurrected at that time will live for a hundred years.

"God is indeed a just God (Deut. 32:4) and all will have their chance to be saved!"[51]

Note how the writer jumps around, picking a Scripture here and a Scripture there, taking them all out of context and assembling them together again in a manner reminiscent of the one who put the following three Scriptures together: "[Judas] departed, and went and hanged himself. . .Go, and do thou likewise. . . That thou doest, do quickly" (Matthew 27:5; Luke 10:37; John 13:27).

For one thing, observe how the writer put in brackets after the opening of the Book of Life: "they are given life." But there is not the slightest indication that the opening of the Book of Life means the impartation of life. It would be every bit as logical to suppose that others are "given works" when those books are opened. Quite the contrary, the passage goes right on to say, "And whosoever was not found written in the book of life was cast into the lake of fire" (vs. 15). And to make Ezekiel 16:55 refer to a physical resur-

51. *If You Die. . .Will You Live Again?* C. Paul Meredith; © 1958,1971; p. 7

rection of Sodom and Samaria goes far beyond the bounds of sanity. That a *spiritual* Sodom and a *spiritual* Samaria is indicated in the passage is seen by the context (vss. 44-46). And how Isaiah 65:20 proves that those supposedly resurrected at that time will live a hundred years, only an Armstrongite would understand.

In another article, quoting the same passage in Revelation 20:12, the writer says: "'. . .which is the book of life [there is a chance of obtaining eternal life], and the dead were judged out of those things which were written in the books. . .'"[52] He does not say they have been given life, as in the other reference, but that the opening of that book means "there is a chance of obtaining eternal life." Again, this foolishness is refuted by the context (vs. 15).

(22) The Worldwide Church of God quotes Ezekiel 37:13,14 as proof that unconverted Israelites of ages past are going to be resurrected and given an opportunity for salvation. Their interpretation is: "This is speaking of ancient Israel—a people who had been scattered among the nations almost 150 years before this was written!"[53]

However, as William E. Biederwolf points out: ". . .what we are concerned about is whether [the passage] is to be taken as a direct and immediate prophecy of that great event which is still in the future [the resurrection from the dead], or merely as a type or figure of the waking up to new life of the Israel then dead in captivity. That it is the latter is seen not only from the fact that in the vision itself there are certain features to be found that do not apply to the literal resurrection of the dead, but as well from the fact that no other explanation can exhaust the

---

52. *Is This The Only Day Of Salvation?* C. Paul Meredith; © 1958,1971; p. 4
53. *If You Die. . .Will You Live Again?* p. 7

meaning of the words in the first clause of verse 11."[54]

The writer in *Ellicott's Commentary on the Whole Bible* agrees, saying: "In verses 1-10, Ezekiel, in a vision, sees a plain full of bones and is directed to prophecy to them; in consequence of which they come together, are clothed with flesh, and become alive. In verses 11-14, the vision is expressly explained to mean that the children of Israel, in their scattered and apparently hopeless condition, shall yet be brought together again and restored to national life. The vision is not at all concerned with the future resurrection. . ."[55]

Several things in the passage itself indicate this to be the case. For one thing, the bones are spoken of both as being scattered about in an "open valley" (vss. 1,2), and being "in graves" (vss. 12,13)—a liberty granted for similes, but not for literal events. Again, the coming to life is for a particular kind of dead men: those who have been "slain" (vs. 9)—a simile of Israel's destruction by her enemies. We might also point out that these dry bones are "the whole house of Israel" (vs. 11), not just the ones Armstrong calls "ancient Israel," by which he means the so-called "lost ten tribes."

The meaning of this simile for "the whole house of Israel" is further indicated in Ezekiel 39:25-29: *restoration to the land from "captivity among the nations."*

(23) Part of Armstrong's success with the uninformed pertains to the fashion in which he uses "circular reasoning" in his arguments—a system, incidentally, by which anyone can *conclusively prove* just about anything! This is undoubtedly one reason for his verbosity; one must read page after page before Armstrong even begins to answer the "sensational" question he has advertised he will explain. An illustration of

---

54. *The Second Coming Bible* [formerly, "The Millennium Bible"]; Baker Book House, Grand Rapids, Michigan; Reprint edition, 1972; p. 186
55. Dr. F. Gardiner; Zondervan Publishing House, Grand Rapids, Michigan; Vol. V, p. 306

this is seen in his effort to prove the Sabbath binding on both Jew and Gentile today. Here is what he says:

"Now read ISAIAH'S PROPHECY! Isaiah 56, begin verse 1.

"Notice, first, it comes from the Supreme AUTHORITY!

"'Thus saith the Lord. . .' *there is your AUTHORITY!*

"Continue: '. . .Keep ye judgment, and do justice: for my salvation is near to come, and my righteousness to be revealed' (Isa. 56:1)."

Now note how he jumps from this subject: "Here is the *TIME* to which the prophecy applies. *WHEN* is God's salvation near to come! *WHEN* is His righteousness to be revealed?

"That is explained in Hebrews 9:27-28!

"UNDERSTAND THIS: 'And as it is appointed unto men once to die, but after this the judgment: So Christ was once offered to bear the sins of many; and unto them that look for him shall he appear the second time without sin UNTO SALVATION!'"[56]

Note that Armstrong has jumped to the time of Christ's return to identify "the day of salvation." He completely ignores passages like II Corinthians 6:2, which list the day of salvation as being current 1,900 years ago; and Luke 4:17-21, where Jesus announced it at the very start of His earthly ministry. But, no, these plain statements would not suit Armstrong's purpose. Apparently he searched for a verse with the word "salvation" in it that would fit his theory. . .*and used it*!

Going on, Armstrong said: "Christ brings SALVATION, *when* He appears *the second time*! A better translation of the last part of the above sentence would be: 'And unto them without sin that look for Him, shall He appear the second time UNTO SALVATION.'"[57]

56. *Which Day Is The Christian Sabbath?* p. 73
57. Ibid.; p. 74

(This is *not* a better translation; it does violence to the original.) But back to Armstrong:

"The Revised Standard Version renders it: 'So Christ, having been offered once to bear the sins of many, will appear a second time, not to deal with sin, but to save those who are eagerly waiting for Him.'"[58]

Note how this paragraph from Armstrong's pen contradicts his previous paragraph. But it seems of no consequence to him, and he proceeds: "WHEN does Christ's SALVATION *appear*? This is explained also in Revelation 12:10: '*Now* is come salvation, and strength, and the kingdom of our God, and the power of his Christ.' That is speaking of the time of Christ's second coming!

"Again, Jesus said: 'And, behold, I come quickly; *and my reward is with me*, to give every man according as his work shall be' (Rev. 22:12). The TIME: Christ's second coming!"[59]

Although the latter passage does not speak of salvation, it speaks of *reward* (and salvation is no reward; *it is a gift*), we are now ready for Armstrong's conclusion: "So the TIME of Isaiah's prophecy is just shortly before the second coming of Christ. The TIME, then, IS NOW—*TODAY!*

"Now notice what Christ, the SUPREME AUTHORITY, says:

"'Blessed is the man that doeth this, and the son of man that layeth hold on it; *that keepeth the sabbath from polluting it*, and keepeth his hand from doing any evil. Neither let *the son of the stranger* [GENTILE], that hath joined himself to the LORD, speak, saying, the LORD hath utterly separated me from his people' (Isa. 56:2-3).

"NOTICE THAT! Let no GENTILE, in our 20th century, now, that has been converted, and joined

58. Ibid.
59. Ibid.

himself to the LORD JESUS CHRIST, say that Christ has separated him from GOD'S PEOPLE ISRAEL. No, the Sabbath was *NOT* assigned to separate Gentiles from Israelites! Gentiles were NOT excluded!"[60]

What an amazing twisting of unrelated Scriptures! Yet this is what Armstrong calls "PROOF POSITIVE" and "*irrefutable* 'thus saith the Lord.'"

(24) The Armstrong practice of jumbling Scriptures together whenever the same word can be found in separate passages is seen again: "The first resurrection of man to immortality that has ever occurred in this world (except Christ's), will occur when Christ comes at the last trump. I Thessalonians 4:16-17 describes this: 'For the Lord himself shall descend from heaven with a [great] shout, with the voice of the archangel, and with the trump [last trump] of God: and the dead in Christ shall rise first.

"'Then we which are alive and remain shall be caught up together with them in the clouds to meet the Lord in the air: and so shall we ever be with the Lord.' But they will go *immediately* to Jerusalem to start their 1000-year rule. Read Zechariah 14.

"This is the resurrection just ahead now! I Corinthians 15:51 through 56 describes this same resurrection and Revelation 11:15 describes the blowing (sounding) of the 'last trump' which ushers this period in. Read these verses!"[61]

These completely unrelated events are harmonized simply because the word "trump" is used in each place!

(25) In trying to prove that the British are Israelites, Armstrong refers to the Abrahamic promise in Genesis 22:16-18, saying: "Notice an additional detail of the promises—the nations who are Abraham's racial descendants are to 'possess the gate of his enemies.' A gate is a narrow passage of entrance or exit. When

60. Ibid.
61. *If You Die. . . Will You Live Again?* p. 6

speaking nationally, a 'gate' would be such a pass as the Panama Canal, the Suez Canal, the Strait of Gibralter. This promise is repeated in Gen. 24:60."[62]

He does not say it "could be," but that it definitely "would be." This is, of course, the wildest form of speculation, not in the least supported by the Word of God.

(26) Armstrong teaches that God does not want to save many now, preferring to wait until He has resurrected them. With this in mind, one of his writers wrote: "Astounding as it may seem, God has deliberately clouded the meaning of His message so the vast majority cannot understand. God explains in Isaiah 28:10-13: 'For precept must be upon precept, precept upon precept; line upon line, line upon line; here a little, and there a little. . .that they might go and fall backward, and be broken, and snared and taken.'

"God purposely wrote His Word so that it could be misunderstood. He intended that only those whom He is calling and choosing will understand."[63]

But is that what this passage is saying? Of course not!

Those words were written as a curse upon Ephraim, people who had ". . .erred through wine, and through strong drink are out of the way; the priest and the prophet have erred through strong drink, they are swallowed up of wine, they are out of the way through strong drink; they err in vision, they stumble in judgment" (vs. 7).

(27) A favorite Armstrong ploy is to put in years when no mention of years is made. For example, commenting on Leviticus 26, he writes: "But, said God, (verses 14-33), if they refused to obey those Commandments, they would suffer sickness and disease, lose all prosperity for 2520 years, be invaded, conquered,

---

62. *The United States And The British Commonwealth In Prophecy,* Copyright, 1954; p. 3
63. *Tomorrow's World,* May, 1971; Alfred E. Carrozzo, "Is God Calling You?"; p. 31

and driven from their land as slaves to their enemies' lands."[64]

We invite our readers to examine minutely the verses referred to and see if there is the slightest reference to 2,520 years. The "seven times" repeated four times in this chapter has to do with severity of chastening. To turn them into a prophetic multiplication table would result in all kinds of fantastic figures. This is merely a liberty Armstrong feels he has the right to take with Sacred Scripture in order to bolster an argument.

(28) Armstrong used his bracket/insertion method to pervert another passage, writing: "Notice I Corinthians 15:12-18: 'Now if Christ be preached that he ROSE from the dead, how say some among you that there is no resurrection of the dead?. . .For if the dead rise not, then is not Christ raised: and if Christ be not raised, your faith is vain; ye are yet in your sins. Then [unless there is to be a RESURRECTION from the DEAD] they also which are fallen asleep in Christ are perished.' Strong scripture, that!

"The dead IN CHRIST are PERISHED, not alive enjoying the promised inheritance already somewhere, but perished—utterly perished—UNLESS there is to be a RESURRECTION FROM THE DEAD! How different from the modern fables to which a deceived people have been turned today!"[65]

The whole argument hinges on what Armstrong has inserted in the brackets—*and it is a perversion of the context.* If you leave out what Armstrong has placed in brackets and reread the passage, you will see that the "then" refers back to Christ being not raised. The apostle is merely saying that unless Christ was raised from the dead, there is no hope for those who have "fallen asleep in Christ." But the dead in Christ

64. *Which Day Is The Christian Sabbath?* pp. 78,79
65. *Tomorrow's World,* November, 1971; p. 46

are not "perished," because He *did* rise from the dead!

(29) Armstrong, who does not think Christians are going to go to Heaven, said: "Jesus Christ did not say we should go up to heaven, to be with Him *there*. Instead, He said in John 3:13: 'No MAN hath ascended up to heaven, but he that came down FROM heaven, even the Son of man'—that is, Himself! He went again to heaven, from where He had come. But He said, 'Whither [where] I go, ye *cannot come*.' That's in your Bible in John 8:22 and John 13:33!"[66]

But when Jesus said, "Whither I go, ye cannot come," He was not talking to Christians. He was talking to those who refused to put their trust in Him (John 8: 21-24). When He repeated it later to His disciples, He pointed out that it was only a *temporary* problem for them, as Mr. Armstrong could have discovered by reading just a few more verses. John 13:36 tells us: "Simon Peter said unto him, Lord, whither goest thou? Jesus answered him, Whither I go, thou canst not follow me now; **but thou shalt follow me afterward.**" So Jesus told His disciples that the matter of going to Heaven was not something that would happen for them immediately, but He promised them that "afterward" they would! Armstrong denies any "afterward" for the disciple of Christ.

(30) Armstrong again ridicules the thought of going to Heaven, saying: "Also He said, 'I go' (to heaven) and 'I will come again' (John 14:2-3). Yes, come again BACK TO EARTH. And when He comes—when He is again here—He will come as He said, 'Receive you unto myself; that where I am [here on earth], there ye may be also.'"[67]

Once again Armstrong uses his bracket method to change the meaning of a passage. Actually, this kind of interpretation makes the disciples receiving Jesus

66. Ibid.; pp. 5,6
67. Ibid.; p. 6

instead of Jesus receiving the disciples! It has Him coming back so He can be where they are, rather than coming back to receive them so they can be where He is!

(31) A reader wrote the Armstrongs to inquire: "Why do you seem to judge people in your *Tomorrow's World* magazine, when Jesus told us not to judge one another?" The answer given was, in part: "The scripture you undoubtedly have in mind is found in Matthew 7:1-2. 'Judge not, that ye be not judged. . . .' The word 'judge' as used in this passage should be rendered 'condemn' or 'damn.' We are never to condemn or damn anyone. That is God's prerogative—and He only exercises it as a last resort in dealing with incorrigible, unrepentant humans after giving them every opportunity."[68]

This twisting of what the Scripture says makes it become meaningless. If only God can damn (and this is true, of course), then why should Christ tell man *not* to do what only *He* could do in the first place?

(32) An illustration of how Garner Ted Armstrong misquotes and misapplies Scripture is seen in this statement from his pen: "He says He is *not willing* that ANY should perish, but that ALL should finally come to repentance! (II Peter 3:9.)" But that passage does not say everyone is going to "finally" come to repentance. It merely states God desires for all to come to repentance *right now.* It says: "The Lord is not slack concerning his promise, as some men count slackness; but is long-suffering to us-ward, not willing that any should perish, but that all should come to repentance."[69]

(33) In his book on the Sabbath, Armstrong says: "Christ said, in the sermon on the mount: 'THINK NOT that I am come to destroy the law,' so professing

68. June, 1971; p. 44
69. *Tomorrow's World,* June, 1971; "What Is Satan's Fate?"; p. 7

Christians think He *did* come to destroy it!"[70] But he misrepresents both the Scripture and the position of evangelicals when he quotes only part of Matthew 5:17. The full verse says, "Think not that I am come to destroy the law, or the prophets: I am not come to destroy, but to fulfil." There is a difference between "destroying" and "fulfilling."

(34) Another case of misrepresentation is when a Worldwide Church of God leader writes: "I know that this is hard to believe. Some of you probably were taught that you cannot receive the Holy Spirit. . .until you REJECT God's law."[71] We know of no one who teaches such and we seriously doubt that the writer does, either.

(35) On one occasion, a Worldwide Church of God writer quotes Isaiah 28:11,13, commenting: "Observe also what God said He would do to Ephraim—Great Britain today—head of the ten tribes of Israel. . ."[72] Yet there is not the slightest indication in these verses that Great Britain is Ephraim.

(36) Armstrong and his followers have a habit of stating a blatant falsehood as fact, then arguing from that supposed fact. For example, Hermon Hoeh, writing about Easter in *Tomorrow's World*, says: "Remember that up to this point the Churches of God universally understood that Jesus rose after three days—on Saturday evening shortly before sunset."[73]

Such a statement impresses the uninformed, no doubt, but it stands completely apart from all reliable scholarship. For example, Ignatius, who was martyred around 110 A.D. in Rome, wrote: "If, then, those who lived in ancient ways attained a new hope, no longer keeping the sabbath but observing the Lord's Day, on which our life too rose through him and his death (which

---

70. Op. cit.; p. 46
71. *How You Can Be Imbued With The Power Of God!* p. 2
72. *Is This The Only Day Of Salvation?* p. 2
73. March, 1971; "Four Thousand Years of Easter"; p. 44

some deny). . . . —*Magnesians* 9:1 (shorter version)."[74]

In fact, Philip Schaff, recognized as an authority even by Hoeh in his article, declares: "The Lord's Day took the place of the Jewish Sabbath as a weekly day of public worship. . . .The day was transferred from the seventh to the first day of the week, not on the ground of a particular command, but by the free spirit of the Gospel and by the power of certain great facts which lie at the foundation of the Christian church. It was on that day that Christ rose from the dead; that He appeared to Mary, the disciples of Emmaus and the assembled Apostles; that He poured out His Spirit and founded His church; and that He revealed the Mysteries of the future. Hence, the first day was already in the Apostolic age honorably designated 'the Lord's Day.' On that day Paul met with the disciples at Troas and preached until midnight. On that day he ordered the Galatian and Corinthian Christians to make, no doubt in connection with divine service, their weekly contributions to charitable objects according to their ability. It appears, therefore, from the N.T., itself, that Sunday was observed as a day of worship and in special commemoration of the Resurrection, whereby the work of redemption was finished. The universal and uncontradicted observance in the second century can only be explained by the fact that it had its roots in Apostolic practice."[75]

He said again: "There is no dissenting voice."[76]

Again, under the heading "Sunday" in the *Schaff-Herzog Encyclopedia of Religious Knowledge*, it is declared: "Sunday. . .the first day of the week, was adopted by the early Christians as a day of worship. . . .

---

74. Quoted by Richard Bird in *Theology Of Seventh-Day Adventism,* © Copyright, 1961; Wm. B. Eerdmans Publishing Company, Grand Rapids, Michigan; p. 112
75. *History Of The Christian Church:* Vol. I, pp. 477-479; Quoted in *Another Look At Seventh-Day Adventism,* Norman F. Douty; Copyright, 1962; Baker Book House, Grand Rapids, Michigan; p. 88
76. Ibid.; Vol. II, p. 201; Quoted in *The Armstrong Error,* Charles F. DeLoach; © 1971; Logos International, Plainfield, New Jersey; p. 48

Sunday was emphatically the weekly feast of the resurrection of Christ, as the Jewish Sabbath was the feast of the Creation. It was called 'the Lord's Day' and upon it the primitive church assembled to break bread (Acts 20:7; I Cor. 16:2). No regulations for its observance are laid down in the N.T., nor, indeed, is its observance even enjoined; yet Christian feeling led to the universal adoption of the day, in imitation of Apostolic precedence. In the second century its observance was universal."[77]

Tertullian, in 200 A.D., wrote: "We solemnize the day after Saturday in contradistinction to those who call this day their Sabbath. . ."[78](*Apology,* Chapter XVI).

Justin Martyr, 140 A.D., wrote: "But Sunday is the day on which we all hold our common assembly, because it is the first day on which God, having wrought a change in the darkness and matter, made the world; and Jesus Christ, our Saviour, on the same day rose from the dead" (*Apology*, Chapter LXVII).[79]

Barnabas, 120 A.D., wrote: "Wherefore, also, we keep the eighth day with joyfulness, the day, also, on which Jesus rose again from the dead" (Chapter XV).[80]

So for Hoeh to claim that the churches of God "universally understood that Jesus arose. . .on Saturday evening shortly before sunset" is either flagrant deception or gross ignorance. We leave it to our readers to determine which.

(37) In his article, "Four Thousand Years of Easter," Herman L. Hoeh has the audacity to quote Ezekiel 8:15,16, referring to the followers of Tammuz who "worshipped the sun toward the east," and saying: "Notice this abomination which Ezekiel saw—the

77. Third Edition (1891); Quoted in *Another Look At Seventh-Day Adventism,* p. 89
78. Quoted in *Seventh-Day Adventism Renounced,* D. M. Canright; Reprint from 14th edition, 1914; Baker Book House, Grand Rapids, Michigan; p. 225
79. Ibid.; p. 221
80. Ibid.; p. 217

Easter sunrise service. This is what professing Christians are doing today—celebrating pagan custom on Easter Sunday supposedly in honor of Christ, who did not rise from the dead on Sunday at all!

"Surely the people today are sincere—but so were the pagans!—*they didn't know better.*"[81]

Now it just so happens that we have never been overly excited about sunrise services on Easter Sunday. We have always used Easter as a day to try to reach the unconverted and not many lost people show up at sunrise. Not only so, but Christians who rise before daybreak and go to a hilltop for services are usually not too "alert" during the regular Sunday morning services!

However, there are two obvious flaws in using this passage as something comparable to an Easter sunrise service, making it a gross misrepresentation. For one thing, it says nothing about worshiping *at sunrise* in the Ezekiel passage, simply that it was in the morning. In the second place, the Ezekiel passage talks about worshiping the sun. Surely not even an Armstrongite, in his wildest and grossest extremes of misrepresentation, would suggest that Christians were worshiping the sun during an Easter sunrise service.

This is falsification and perversion of the very lowest order.

(38) Another example of how Scripture is twisted to substantiate the Armstrong heresy is seen when one of the cult's writers, attempting to nullify the impact of Paul's exhortation regarding Sunday collections in I Corinthians 16:1,2, wrote: "The poor saints—Church members—at Jerusalem were suffering from famine during this time (Rom. 15:25). Paul was collecting contributions from the churches in his area to provide for their needs (Rom. 15:26-27). This collection included 'FRUIT'! (verse 28.)

---

81. Op. cit.; p. 43

"Therefore the Apostle Paul was actually telling the Corinthians that they should go out into the fields on Sunday, and collect the fruit and vegetables, and put them in storage, so they would have the food ready when Paul arrived—'that there be no gatherings when I come' (I Cor. 16:2). Obviously, he wasn't even going to be there on that Sunday."[82]

Surely the writer must know that if Paul were talking about literal fruit, it would have rotted by the time Paul got there, to say nothing of by the time it got to Jerusalem! The word Paul used in Romans 15:28 is *karpos* and although it can refer to either literal or figurative fruit, it is used in the Book of Romans only in the figurative sense. The word is used three other times in Romans as follows: Romans 1:13: "Now I would not have you ignorant, brethren, that oftentimes I purposed to come unto you, (but was let hitherto,) that I might have some **fruit** among you also, even as among other Gentiles." Romans 6:21: "What **fruit** had ye then in those things whereof ye are now ashamed? for the end of those things is death." Romans 6:22: "But now being made free from sin, and become servants to God, ye have your **fruit** unto holiness, and the end everlasting life." We suggest that Writer Dankenbring try to make these usages of *karpos* mean going out into the fields and gathering crops! For those who would like to pursue the subject further, the same word is used in Galatians 5:22,23; Ephesians 5:9; Philippians 1:22; Philippians 4:17; Hebrews 12:11; and Hebrews 13:15.

(39) In trying to nullify the impact of Acts 20:7, a writer in *Tomorrow's World*, declared: "Notice: 'And upon the first day of the week, when the disciples came together to *break bread*, Paul preached unto them, ready to depart on the morrow; and continued

---

82. *Tomorrow's World,* March, 1971; William F. Dankenbring, "Does It Matter Which Day You Keep?"; p. 35

his speech until *midnight.* And there were *many lights* in the upper chamber, where they were gathered together' (verses 7-8).

"Yes, this meeting occurred on the first day of the week, no doubt about that—but notice! This occurred when they came together to break bread—or in other words, to eat dinner (Acts 2:46). Paul preached till *midnight* of the first day of the week! Many lights were lit.

"Now when did this meeting actually occur? According to the Biblical reckoning, each day begins at sunset and ends the following sunset (see Lev. 23:32). The first day of the week, therefore, begins at sunset Saturday and lasts until sunset Sunday (not from midnight to midnight, which is the modern reckoning).

"Therefore, this meeting occurred during the night portion of the first day of the week—or on what we, today, call Saturday night! It was NOT a 'Sunday meeting' at all! But on Sunday, at daybreak (Acts 20:11,13), Paul walked from Troas to Assos, a distance of about 20 miles—a good long hike. Thus, rather than preaching on Sunday, Paul LABORED on Sunday."[83]

Notice, first of all, how this writer fluctuates from designating days (sunset to sunset, or midnight to midnight) as it suits his purpose. In the second place, remember that these people were Gentiles under Roman rule, not Jews, and the Roman reckoning of time was exactly the same as ours: from midnight to midnight.

In the third place, however—and this shows the deliberate misrepresentation which we are pointing out—ignoring all the fancy talk about how to reckon time, the Bible plainly states that the meeting was "upon the first day of the week" and Paul's journey from Troas to Assos was "on the morrow," or the

83. Ibid.; pp. 34,35

second day of the week. So, as plain as day, using our calendar days, the meeting took place on Sunday and the journey took place on Monday. This attempt to pervert plain biblical statements shows how desperate are the Armstrong seventh-day sabbaticants!

(40) Armstrong, in an article trying to justify his brand of the new birth and denying the possibility of being born into the kingdom of God in this life, declared: "therefore Jesus did not waste words. He struck straight through to the crux point—the Kingdom of God is *not* of *this* world—this time—this age—but of the WORLD TOMORROW—a different and a following AGE. Not composed of humans, but of immortals—the GOD FAMILY!"[84]

But does "this world" mean "this time," "this age"? Just what did Jesus actually say? The record is in John 18:36,37: "Jesus answered, My kingdom is not of *this world*: if my kingdom were of *this world*, then would my servants fight, that I should not be delivered to the Jews: but now is my kingdom not from hence. Pilate therefore said unto him, Art thou a king then? Jesus answered, Thou sayest that I am a king. To this end was I born, and for this cause came I into *the world*, that I should bear witness unto the truth. Every one that is of the truth heareth my voice."

The word translated "world" in this passage is *kosmos* and means world-system. The word for "age" is *aion*. Jesus was not saying He came into "this time—this age." That would not have even made sense. He was saying He had come into this world-system.

(41) The Armstrong followers have a problem with the biblical expression, "the Lord's Day," since down through the centuries it has been attributed to the first day of the week. One writer, in an attempt to discredit the force of this argument, argues thusly: "What day,

---

84. *Tomorrow's World*, October, 1971; p. 6

then, is 'the Lord's day'? Generally, when the Bible speaks of 'the Lord's day,' or the 'day of the Lord,' it is referring to a future time in prophecy—the time of God's intervention in world affairs (see Zeph. 1:14-17; Isa. 2:1-12,19-21). In Revelation 1:10, the Apostle John simply meant that he was carried 'in spirit,' in vision, into the period of prophecy known as the 'day of the Lord' (see Rev. 6:15-17).

"If Sunday, however, is 'the Lord's day,' or 'day of the Lord,' then I Thessalonians 5:2-3 is a very strange passage of scripture. We read: 'For yourselves know perfectly that the *day of the Lord* so cometh as a THIEF IN THE NIGHT. For when they shall say, Peace and safety; then sudden destruction cometh upon them. . .'!

"Does every Sunday sneak up on you like a thief? Does 'sudden destruction' come upon the world every Sunday? Obviously not. It should be clear that often when the Bible speaks of the 'day of the Lord,' it is not talking about a day of the week, but a particular period in prophecy!"[85]

This is deception and perversion on its lowest level! Note how the writer states, as if it were a simple fact understood by everyone, that "generally, when the Bible speaks of 'the Lord's day,' or the 'day of the Lord,' it is referring to future time in prophecy. . ." He mingles the two phrases together, trying to make out that these two completely different things are one and the same. Of course the term "day of the Lord" refers "to future time in prophecy," but "the Lord's Day" is something entirely different. Even the Seventh-Day Adventists, who are as strong in their Saturday/Sabbath worship as anyone, acknowledge that this expression "the Lord's Day" refers to a specific day of the week. But the Armstrongian writer confuses and clouds the issue in the fashion so typical with the cult,

85. William F. Dankenbring, op. cit.; p. 34

setting up a straw man and proceeding to attack it by quoting completely unrelated Scripture.

(42) In an effort to deny that man has an immortal soul, one writer of the cult says: "Eternal life with unending spiritual power is a *gift* of God. It is an attribute of the Holy Spirit. 'For the wages of sin is death; but the free *gift* of God is eternal life'—if we already had it, it would not be a gift; it would be inherited—(Romans 6:23)."[86]

In the first place, the fact of man possessing an immortal soul has nothing to do with eternal life, which is something spiritual received at the time of conversion. In the second place, note how the writer inserts the word "free" into Romans 6:23 preceding the word "gift." This without the slightest indication that he has added anything, although the usual practice of the cult is to place such words in brackets. In this case, the added word does not change the meaning, but it is entirely superfluous. What could a gift be but free? If it were not free, it would no longer be a gift.

(43) In one Worldwide Church of God booklet, an unnamed writer, seeking to prove the cult's "soul sleep" heresy, says: "Abraham died, and was still DEAD at the time of Christ's earthly ministry. We read in John 8:52, 'Abraham is dead.' At that time—centuries after he died—Abraham was *not living* on earth or in heaven or anywhere! He is still dead today. When, then, is he to inherit the promises?"[87]

What a strange, dishonest way to try to prove a point. You will note that the entire verse is not quoted, just the three words, "Abraham is dead." Why not quote the whole verse? *Because it would explode the writer's argument*! Here is the complete verse: "Then said the Jews unto him, Now we know that thou hast a devil. Abraham is dead, and the prophets; and thou

---

86. *How You Can Be Imbued With The Power Of God!* p. 3
87. *Lazarus And The Rich Man* © 1953,1971, p. 9

sayest, If a man keep my saying, he shall never taste of death."

Who said, "Abraham is dead"? It was the ungodly Jews who, in the same breath, were saying that Jesus was demon possessed! What an authority to use to prove a point!

(44) In one of his books, Herbert W. Armstrong wrote: "There are those who say: It is IMPOSSIBLE for us to live righteously, so Christ lived a righteous life IN OUR STEAD, and, if you just believe, God IMPUTES Christ's righteousness to you. These people mean that YOU do not need to live righteously. Actually, THEY CONDONE SIN—their false argument means you are free to go on deliberately SINNING, but God PRETENDS you are righteous, by a sort of hocus-pocus of transferring *Jesus*' righteousness to you. Those are the 'ungodly men' Jude warns against, 'turning grace into license.'

"Others say that, since it is IMPOSSIBLE for us to keep God's Law, Jesus *did away with* the Law. So—if that be true, you are FREE to go on sinning."[88]

What a perversion this is of what evangelicals have always believed about imputed righteousness and about the law! We do not know of a single evangelical preacher—and we challenge Armstrong to come up with a single one—who teaches that if you have Christ's righteousness "you are free to go on deliberately sinning." Such a statement on Armstrong's part is gross dishonesty. And this, indeed, from the pen of a man who claims others misrepresent what he teaches!

(45) In his booklet, *1975 in Prophecy*—which is not nearly as sensational or revealing as the title implies—Armstrong advocates his theory about Britain and America by quoting Christ's words of Matthew 24:9 in the following manner: "Jesus Christ said, 'Ye shall be HATED of ALL NATIONS. . .Then shall they

88. *What Do You Mean. . ."The Unpardonable Sin"?* © 1967,1971,1972; pp. 18,19

deliver you up to be afflicted, and shall KILL YOU."[89] He identifies Britain and the United States as the "ye" our Lord meant here, referring to his *The United States and the British Commonwealth in Prophecy* booklet as proof, adding, ". . .He meant US. We are *the* nations that are HATED by all other nations today—or hadn't you realized that alarming *fact?*"

However, once again we see the Armstrong deceit at work in a feeble, futile attempt to prove his false contentions, even at the price of perverting Scripture. Note that, in this quotation of our Lord's statement, he omits Christ's words, "*for my name's sake.*" Obviously, Britain and the United States are not being "hated" for Jesus' sake, so Armstrong must scrap that part in his effort to deceive the gullible.

Note, too, that Armstrong quotes the last half of the verse *first* and the first half *last*, yet gives no indication that he has done anything amiss.

Why does he change the order?

Because it changes the meaning to suit his purpose! The "Armstrong Version" has the affliction and killing the aftermath of the hatred. His reversal puts the "then" of the statement *after* the hatred, not before (or *with*) it!

(46) In misrepresentation of a different kind—but blatant falsehood nonetheless—the cult repeatedly advertises *Tomorrow's World* as "a sparkling nonsectarian magazine of Biblical understanding."[90] In truth and in fact, no magazine could possibly be *more* sectarian.

(47) Boasting about its "everything free" policy (in a soft-sell type pitch for funds), Herbert W. Armstrong claims: "This organization operates in *a way* none ever did before."[91] This is a falsehood. Many

89. Copyright, 1956; p. 14
90. One example: "Pull out" insert in *Does God Exist?*
91. *The Plain Truth*, October-November, 1970; p. 38

other religious organizations—past and present—have operated exactly the same way with regard to finances.

(48) In trying to establish that Jacob's pillow stone and the stone in the Throne of England, called the Throne of David by the Armstrongites, are one and the same, we are told: "This same rock—the coronation stone—accompanied the Israelites during their forty years wandering in the wilderness. Paul says in I Corinthians 10:4 that just as the Israelites had manna as a type of Christ, so they had, as a type of Christ, *a rock* which gave them water and which *followed* or *went with* them in their wanderings! Christ provides spiritual waters—the Holy Spirit, and Jacob's shepherd stone, a type of the Divine Shepherd, miraculously provided material water in the wilderness."[92]

Aside from the fact not one word is stated in Scripture about Jacob's stone after he used it as a pillow, and certainly not the slightest hint that it accompanied the Israelites in their wanderings, what does I Corinthians 10:4 really say? "And did all drink the same spiritual drink: for they drank of that spiritual Rock that followed them: and that Rock was Christ." As Hoeh is so fond of saying, "How plain!" The Rock was Christ, not Jacob's pillow. To interpret it as Hoeh has done is nothing short of blasphemy.

(49) Another ridiculous misrepresentation of truth, while endeavoring to establish the Anglo-Israel heresy, is this tidbit: "Open your Bible to II Kings 11:14. The event mentioned here occurred at the time when Josiah was proclaimed king in the temple when wicked Athaliah, who had usurped the throne, was about to meet her doom. Notice what it says: 'And when Athaliah heard the noise of the guard and of the people, she came to the people into the temple of the Lord. And when she looked, behold'—what? 'the king

92. *The Plain Truth*, July, 1959; "The Bible Answers Short Questions From Our Readers"; pp. 31,32

stood by a *pillar,* as the manner was, and the princes and the trumpeters by the king, and all the people of the land rejoiced, and blew with trumpets.'

"So it was the manner or custom even in that day to have the pillar of stone—Jacob's pillar stone—used in the coronation ceremonies!"[93]

If such perversion were not tragic, it would be hilarious! Imagine trying to make out that one of the huge columns in Solomon's temple (which were "thirty and five cubits high" with a capital five cubits high "on the top of each"; see II Chronicles 3:15; 4:11-13) was the same little stone pillow "twenty-two inches long, thirteen inches broad and eleven inches deep" now resting under the royal chair in Westminster Abbey in London and purported to be the same stone used by Jacob! The Armstrongs should be ashamed of themselves for resorting to this kind of silly nonsense!

(50) A gentleman in New York read my previous expose and was convinced of its truth, so he wrote to Armstrong cancelling his subscription to *The Plain Truth* and to the Ambassador College correspondence lessons, explaining his action and enclosing my booklet. He received a reply from David G. Hunsberger of the "Letter Answering Department," saying "...the author of that booklet has grossly MISREPRESENTED what we believe and preach. He has not told the truth."[94] Although the letter was a lengthy one of a page and a half, Mr. Hunsberger did not give one single example of misrepresentation, just his unsubstantiated charge. Since I had quoted verbatim from Armstrong's writings, always very careful to give the source of the quote with the exact page number where the statement could be found (just as we have in this book), we rather think Mr. Hunsberger *could not* and *dared not* be specific.

93. Ibid.; p. 32
94. Dated, May 31, 1967; Original in author's file

However, our purpose in mentioning the letter here is to quote this paragraph: "*A False Prophet* takes tiny excerpts from our free booklets out of context, presents them in a slanted context, greatly distorting what we teach. Then the result is sold for ten cents! The Bible plainly says that the *priceless* Gospel must go free of charge (I Cor. 9:18). When someone charges a nickel or a dime for their material, it isn't the Gospel of Christ!"[95]

The Word of God says no such thing! Truth would be truth no matter the manner of distribution and error is still error regardless of how freely it is dispensed. But does I Corinthians 9:18 teach that it is wrong to charge money for literature containing spiritual truth? *Most certainly not*! The entire context, verses seven through twenty-three, is teaching the exact opposite, proving that Paul certainly had the right to receive material reward for his spiritual labor, just as others did. He quotes Scripture to substantiate that such action is a basic Bible principle. The only thing I Corinthians 9:18 is saying is that Paul chose not to exercise his biblical right while ministering at Corinth. Nothing more! See Galatians 6:6 and I Timothy 5:18 for other examples of Paul's recognition of this biblical principle.

Mr. Hunsberger has done wicked violence to the Scripture in twisting this text to try to prove that charging money for literature is wrong. We will see the *real* truth about Armstrong and his "everything free" boast in Chapter XIII.

(51) Mr. Armstrong, of course, believes there is only one True Church —**his!** So he writes in the following vein: "Notice, too, the Church is here referred to as 'one body.' In several passages the Church is referred to as 'the body of Christ.' I Corinthians 12:12

---

95. Ibid.

says: 'For as the body is one, and hath many members. . . .' "[96]

Again he says: ". . .are there MANY CHURCHES? No, every where the New Testament speaks of the ONE Body—*ONE* CHURCH. . . .

"Christ is NOT divided (I Cor. 1:13). There is ONE true Church. All in it 'speak the same thing' (I Cor. 12:13)."[97]

While we certainly subscribe to the unity of the body of Christ, such an argument, intended to identify the Worldwide Church of God as the One True Church, is base hypocrisy. The truth of the matter is that the New Testament speaks of "churches" (plural, not singular) some thirty-seven different times. It is "the church*es* of Christ" (Romans 16:16); "the church*es* of Galatia" (Galatians 1:2); "the church*es* of Judaea" (Galatians 1:22); "church*es* which are in Asia" (Revelation 1:11); and "the church*es* of the Gentiles" (Romans 16:4).

The amazing thing is that Armstrong admits this, saying they are local congregations of the One True Church. At first thought this seems to be what many evangelicals have taught, pointing out that the true church is *an organism* while local congregations are *organizations*; the former is invisible, the latter visible. But this is not what Armstrong is saying. He is saying that the One True Church is both an organism and an organization. He says: "But did Christ, the HEAD of the Church, ORGANIZE that Church? Does it have a definite form of organization?

"Indeed He did—and indeed it has!"[98]

Armstrong leaves no doubt but that he thinks the Worldwide Church of God is the One True Church and the organizational headquarters are in Pasadena, Cali-

96. *Just What Is The Church?* © 1970; p. 1
97. *Where Is The True Church?* © 1965,1969; p. 6
98. *Just What Is The Church?* p. 2

fornia, with Herbert W. and Garner Ted the top men in authority, respectively. This we flatly deny as the most absurd thing since some one said Santa Claus came down chimneys and Easter bunnies laid eggs!

Perhaps it would prove interesting if we closed this section of Armstrong's perversions with an official explanation. When a reader wrote to complain of checking on his references and finding "the wording and even the context was entirely unrelated to your quote," admitting, however, that his was the Douay Version, the editors replied: "The answer lies in the fact that in our publications we generally quote from such Bible translations as the King James Version (KJV), Revised Standard Version, etc., most of which basically use the official Hebrew Masoretic Text for the Old Testament.

"The Douay Version has been *mainly* translated from the Latin Vulgate Text. This version not only includes the additional books of the Apocrypha, but also has certain books of the King James Version with *different titles*. For example, I and II Samuel (KJV) are titled 'I and II Kings' (Douay); I and II Kings are called 'III and IV Kings'; I and II Chronicles are 'I and II Paralipomenon'; the book of Nehemiah is 'II Ezdras'; the Song of Solomon is called 'Canticle of Canticles.'

"Anyone using the Douay Version of the Bible should note these variations."[99]

That was the entire explanation except for the usual "write and request" additional literature on the subject. We invite our readers to check the perversions listed in this chapter in any and every translation on the market. It will have absolutely nothing to do with the "out of context" conclusions which the Worldwide Church of God sets forth.

---

99. *Tomorrow's World,* February, 1972; p. 23

Armstrong's Straw Men

Before we close this chapter, it might be helpful to point out that one of Armstrong's favorite tactics is to manufacture a straw man, then tear the straw man apart. Some of this has already been indicated, but we want to list just a few more.

(1) Garner Ted Armstrong, talking about Heaven and endeavoring to bolster his "soul sleep" theory, wrote: "If Christians GO TO HEAVEN IMMEDIATELY WHEN THEY DIE—IF they are ALREADY in heaven, where they have been living in beautiful mansions for hundreds or even thousands of years—WHY BOTHER WITH THE RESURRECTION!

"If they have been *released* from this sin-sick world, from their old, worn-out, disease-ridden corruptible bodies, and if they have been WITH Jesus Christ IN heaven—*why* would Jesus *take them OUT* of heaven, bring them *back* to earth, plunge them BACK INTO their graves, and then go to the fantastic, laborious effort of RESURRECTING THEM?

"Isn't this a little difficult to believe?

"Does it really make sense?"[100]

Yes, it is difficult to believe. *No*, it really doesn't make sense. One reason *why* is that this is merely an Armstrong straw man. We know of no one who teaches that Jesus is going to bring saints back to earth and plunge them into their graves. Nor can Armstrong produce a single individual who has ever taught any such thing. It is simply a straw man he has manufactured to prop up an untenable theory.

(2) Christmas is a favorite straw man with the Armstrong movement. One writer in *Tomorrow's World* waxes eloquent when he enthused: "Prove it for yourself! Look in your Bible. Search for a mention of Santa Claus. Search for Jesus or His apostles ever decorating

---

100. *Tomorrow's World*, July-August, 1970; p. 10

a Christmas tree or Jesus ever *saying* we should do so in honor of Him. Examine the Bible carefully for any place Jesus said to celebrate His birthday—to exchange gifts among OURSELVES. Search for the *proof* December 25th WAS Jesus' birthday. Search for holly wreaths, mistletoe and Christmas cards.

"They are not there!"[101]

The ridiculousness of such arguing could be seen by asking the same questions about almost anything the Armstrongs are doing. One might say: "Prove it for yourself! Look in your Bible. Search for a mention of a radio broadcast or a telecast. Search for where Jesus or any of His apostles ever mailed out any monthly magazine. Examine the Bible carefully for any place Jesus said that we should establish a college."

This is merely a straw man established solely for the purpose of tearing it down and impressing the ignorant.

(3) A writer in *Tomorrow's World*, trying to prove the seventh-day Sabbath, wrote: "The word 'Sunday' does not once appear in the Bible, in the original Hebrew and Greek languages."[102]

How silly! Neither does the word "Saturday"! Nor does "Monday," "Tuesday," "Wednesday," "Thursday," or "Friday"!

This is just a foolish straw man set up for the purpose of shooting it down.

(4) Herbert W. Armstrong, himself, uses a kindred straw man in his booklet, "*Which Day is the* CHRISTIAN SABBATH?" saying: "*You cannot find* any such term as 'the *Jewish Sabbath*' anywhere in the Bible!"[103] Again, how silly! Neither can you find his term, "the *Christian* Sabbath" anywhere in the Bible!

(5) A writer in *Tomorrow's World* establishes a strange "Gospel" straw man to shoot down, declaring:

101. December, 1971; Albert J. Portune, "Is Christmas Christian?"; p. 16
102. William F. Dankenbring, op. cit.; p. 34
103. Op. cit.; p. 88

"The 'gospel' of churchianity is hollow, watery, meaningless.

"Their 'gospel' says certain goody-good individuals will one day find themselves wafted off to 'heaven.' Each will be issued a white toga, a sparkling halo and a fluffy cloud. Each of these A-1 harpists will sit benignly strumming while enjoying his 'beatific vision.' Look the Bible through and you won't find any such thing."[104]

Of course you won't find any such thing. You won't find it anywhere else, either. This is strictly the figment of the writer's imagination and we challenge anyone connected with the Armstrong movement to quote a single evangelical who has ever said any thing even remotely like this. It is baseless, gross deception and misrepresentation.

(6) The same writer, in the same article, went on to say: "World-renowned preachers are content to say, 'The Gospel is the good news that, on the first Good Friday, Christ died for our sins and that He rose from the dead on that first Easter morning—and that God is willing to forgive us our sins—and give us new life, peace and joy.'

"All too many preachers—and their followers—say this *is the Gospel.*

"The 'experts' are WRONG!"[105]

Again, this is a perversion of what "world-renowned preachers" and other Bible scholars teach—and have always taught—about "the Gospel." They define the gospel exactly as did the Apostle Paul, who wrote: "Moreover, brethren, I declare unto you the gospel which I preached unto you, which also ye have received, and wherein ye stand; By which also ye are saved, if ye keep in memory what I preached unto you, unless ye have believed in vain. For I delivered

104. July-August, 1970; Clint C. Zimmerman, "Gospel Pollution"; p. 47
105. Ibid.

unto you first of all that which I also received, how that Christ died for our sins according to the scriptures; And that he was buried, and that he rose again the third day according to the scriptures" (I Corinthians 15:1-4).

This is "the Gospel" and no Armstrong ridicule can change it.

(7) If Armstrong can convince his hearers that his opponents teach a license to sin, he has discredited them, of course. So a favorite straw man is stating such an idea, then shooting it down. For example, in one of his major booklets, he says: "It is the FALSE prophets of our day who try to deceive you into believing 'GRACE' means permission to BREAK GOD'S LAW!"[106]

To say that this is what evangelicals believe is a deliberate lie.

In the same article, he says again: "WHY do most of those who claim to be the very CLERGY of Jesus Christ say there are 'NO WORKS WHATEVER' in the Christian life?

"Because of their false pagan and unscriptural doctrine about what 'salvation' is. Their conception of salvation seems to be an eternity of idleness and ease—with nothing to do."[107]

This is a gross misrepresentation on both counts. Evangelicals most certainly do not say that there are "no works whatever in the Christian life." Quite the contrary, we believe, as Paul told Titus, "This is a faithful saying, and these things I will that thou affirm constantly, that they who have believed in God might be careful to maintain good works. These things are good and profitable unto men" (Titus 3:8). Because evangelicals do not join Armstrong in his heresy that works are a part of salvation, he falsely misrepresents

106. *What'll You Be Doing In The Next Life?* p. 4
107. Ibid.; p. 8

what they teach about life *following* conversion.

Also, what he says regarding our "concept of salvation" is completely false—a straw man—as we have already pointed out.

Many, many more illustrations could be given, but we have offered enough to conclusively prove our thesis in this chapter: *the Armstrong "key" to success is based upon deception, misrepresentation and perversion of Scripture!*

CHAPTER III

The Armstrong Teaching About God

A basic tenet in the Worldwide Church of God is the flat and bold denial of the Trinity. One of the cult's writers, in an article trying to prove the "family of Gods" theory, stated their position: "At the present time—*today*—there are only *two* beings in the God Family:

"1) God the Father—the *Possessor* of heaven and earth (Genesis 14:18,19; Psalm 110:1; Daniel 7:13; John 5:19)—the Father of Jesus Christ.

"2) The God of Abraham, Isaac and Jacob—the active *Creator* of heaven and earth—the One who became Jesus Christ."[1]

The following month, in the same magazine, the same writer stated again, still trying to prove the same thesis about a family of Gods, wrote: "How much clearer could one state that the God Family—comprising, at the present time, only two Persons, God the Father and God the Son. . ."[2]

Herman L. Hoeh, answering the question, "God a Trinity?" declared: "How plain that God is a Family—a Kingdom, not a limited trinity. The doctrine of the trinity was foisted upon the world beginning with the council of Nicaea. It is merely a continuation of the pagan Babylonish trinity of Nimrod, Semiramis and Tammuz—of father, mother and child—except that in this instance the apostate churches substituted the Holy Spirit for the mother (Semiramis) and called it a 'person.'"[3]

Herbert W. Armstrong says almost exactly the same thing, word for word: "The doctrine of the Trinity is

---

1. *Tomorrow's World,* May, 1971; Robert L. Kuhn, "The God Family"; pp. 29,30
2. "Your Destiny—*The God Family";* p. 36
3. *The Plain Truth,* August, 1958: p. 17

false. It was foisted upon the world at the council of Nicaea. It is the pagan Babylonish trinity of Nimrod, Semiramis and Horus—of father, mother and child—substituting the Holy Spirit for the mother, Semiramis, and calling it a 'person.'"[4]

Obviously, the member of the Trinity denied is the Holy Spirit. The Armstrongs make repeated reference to the Holy Spirit (even capitalizing the first letters, just as with Father and Son), but they deny His personality. In an article in *Tomorrow's World*, collaborated on by two of the cult's leaders, we are told: "God is a FAMILY of spirit beings. At present, that family is composed of *two* separate beings: God the *Father* and God the *Son*. The Holy Spirit is the *power*, the life, and the mind of God. It is not a 'person.'"[5]

In another article in the same issue, another writer says: "God's Spirit is a part of His very CHARACTER placed within you to enable you to live as you should."[6]

And in still another article in the same issue, still another writer defines the terms as follows: "We start with the basic definition of God's Holy Spirit: It is His POWER—the *power* of the Almighty Creator. . . .

"Power can be simply defined as 'the ability to act'—or, more technically, as 'the capacity to do *work*.' This most certainly applies to the power of God's Holy Spirit."[7]

We will go into the cult's teaching about the Holy Spirit further before we finish this chapter, but these quotes are sufficient to show the denial of the Trinity.

God the Father

One amazing facet of the Armstrong theology about God the Father is a denial that He is the God of the

---

4. *The Missing Dimension In Sex*, © 1964, 1971; p. 37
5. February, 1971; David Jon Hill and Brian Knowles, "Does God *Really* Understand People?"; p. 9
6. Roderick C. Meredith, "Why You Need to Change!"; p. 12
7. Robert L. Kuhn, "Receive the Gift of the Holy Spirit"; p. 21

Old Testament. As Garner Ted Armstrong wrote: "Most people have assumed the God of the Old Testament was the Father of Jesus Christ. This is proven by God's own inspired Word to be a great error."[8]

The senior Armstrong is even more emphatic, saying: "It is commonly supposed that 'Yahveh,' or, as commonly called, 'Jehovah,' or, as in the Authorized version, 'The LORD,' of the Old Testament was God the FATHER of Jesus Christ. *This is a flagrant error*!

"'Yahveh' was the God of Israel, the only One of the Godhead known to Israel. When He came in human flesh they did not recognize Him. 'He was in the world, and the world was made by Him and the world knew Him not' (John 1:10-11). Neither did they know God the Father (Mat. 11:27 and Luke 10:22). 'No one knoweth. . . who the Father is, save the Son, and he to whomsoever the Son willeth to REVEAL him.'"[9] The idea is, of course, that the only God in the Old Testament was Jesus Christ.

In a reprint article, a writer declared: "In the Old Testament, men did not pray to the Father."[10] He does not mean men did not pray to God; he is merely assuming that the God of the Old Testament was not God the Father.

A writer in *Tomorrow's World* denies, in essence, the omniscience of God the Father. In trying to describe what it will be like in eternity when Armstrong's followers become gods and equal with Father and Son, he declares: "Furthermore, as strange as it sounds, we will counsel and advise our Creator Father—we will have suggestions and opinions which will actually help God the Father administer all reality, suggestions and opinions which will be original and unique."[11]

---

8. *Who—What—Was Jesus Before His Human Birth?* © 1957; p. 3
9. *The Plain Truth*, September, 1958; "Is Jesus God?"; p. 7
10. *How You Can Be Imbued With The Power Of God!* Herman L. Hoeh; © 1958,1967, 1970,1971; p. 4
11. April, 1971; Robert L. Kuhn, "What It Means to Be. . .*Equal* with *God*"; p. 45

This is utter blasphemy! To even suggest that Almighty God needs our counsel about anything is heresy of the rankest and lowest order!

Another divine attribute which is denied, at least in essence, is His omnipresence. In one of the cult's releases, the writer declares: "Even though the Father and the Son are in definite locations with respect to each other, spirit proceeds from them and fills the entire universe much like air fills everything on earth. Note David's words that God's Spirit permeates *everything* (Psalm 139:7-11). *Spirit* is *God's* life. *Air* contains the physical *life-giving oxygen of man.* Notice how similar the comparison is."[12]

What the writer is saying is that the "two Gods" are in two locations and that the Spirit of God (which, remember, according to them is merely an impersonal force) is pervading everything much like air does. But this means that God is not omnipresent, only His impersonal force is!

It ought to be obvious that the "God Father" of the Armstrongs is not the "God the Father" of the Bible.

God the Son

The Armstrong teaching about Jesus Christ is equally strange.

Herbert W. Armstrong questions: "But *when* did Christ actually found, or *start* God's Church—while still a mortal human, or after His resurrection and ascension to heaven?"[13]

An evangelical would think, in reading the expression "a mortal human," that the phrase was intended merely to describe the human nature of Jesus, not denying His divine nature. But that is not what Armstrong means, as we shall see.

---

12. *How You Can Be Imbued With The Power Of God!* p. 5
13. *Which Day Is The Christian Sabbath?* ©1962, 1964, 1968, 1970, 1971; p. 14

Talking about the new birth, and trying to weave in his theory that Jesus had to be born again, Armstrong says: "Before Jesus was conceived by Mary, He was not the SON of God."[14] Yet centuries before He was conceived by Mary, the psalmist wrote: "Thy throne, O God, is for ever and ever: the sceptre of thy kingdom is a right sceptre. Thou lovest righteousness, and hatest wickedness: therefore God, thy God, hath anointed thee with the oil of gladness above thy fellows" (Psalm 45:6,7). Then the writer of Hebrews takes these exact verses and credits them to THE SON: "But unto the Son he saith, Thy throne, O God, is for ever and ever: a sceptre of righteousness is the sceptre of thy kingdom. Thou hast loved righteousness, and hated iniquity; therefore God, even thy God, hath anointed thee with the oil of gladness above thy fellows" (Hebrews 1:8,9).

In a *Tomorrow's World* article, a leader of the cult declares: "But *quantitatively*, man will *never* equal God the Creator, just as surely as *God the Creator* (Jesus Christ) will Himself never quantitatively equal God the Father (John 14:28).[15] In other words, Jesus is inferior, as God, to the Father.

In an article about mental mastery, one leader of the cult said that Jesus gave up being God when He came into this world. His words were: "Although Jesus was equal with God, and had been *very God*, He 'emptied Himself' as the original Greek should be translated, 'and took upon him the form of a SERVANT, and was made in the likeness of men.' Even though Jesus had shared the GLORY of God, even though it was *His* voice that had said: 'Let there be light,' when God reformed the earth at the time of Adam, Jesus was more than willing to *give that up* in order to SERVE

14. *Tomorrow's World,* October, 1971; "Just What Do You Mean. . .*Born Again?"*; p. 43
15. April, 1971; Robert L. Kuhn, op. cit.; p. 44

the lowly human beings He Himself had helped to create (Eph. 3:9)."[16]

Note the past tense: "*had been* very God"! Armstrong's teaching, unlike that of historic Christianity, does not claim that Christ merely emptied Himself of the outward manifestation of deity, but that He emptied Himself of that very deity!

Answering the question, "Does God REALLY Understand People?" two writers in *Tomorrow's World* teach Christ experienced physical sickness while on earth. They said: "Christ even knows what it is like to be *sick*. . ."[17]

This creates a problem for them, since the founder of their cult himself, in one of his "Personal" columns, wrote: "The Almighty God made the human body so that—even though composed of material substance from the ground—its *normal condition* is one of robust, invigorating, radiant GOOD HEALTH!

"Sickness and disease are ABNORMAL—they are the PENALTY of VIOLATION OF NATURAL LAWS. They are PHYSICAL *SIN*!"[18]

He then went on to quote "philosopher-author-lecturer-publisher Elbert Hubbard," saying: "He said: 'Of two things, being thrown in jail, or becoming sick, becoming sick is the *greater disgrace*!' One is thrown in jail for violation of a *man-made* law—it could be a nonsensical law—he could have been falsely accused. But when one is sick, a NATURAL law has been broken—and there was no false arrest."[19]

So, since the founder of their cult teaches so strongly that sickness is always a result of human sinfulness, the writers in the above-mentioned article find it necessary to qualify their statement. The full sentence was:

---

16. *Tomorrow's World,* December, 1971; Roderick C. Meredith, "Seven 'Keys' To Mental Mastery"; p. 40
17. David Jon Hill and Brian Knowles, op. cit.; p. 10
18. *Tomorrow's World,* April, 1971; p. 1
19. Ibid.

"Christ even knows what it is like to be *sick*, although He *never* broke the physical laws that normally cause human sickness."[20]

Just how these two conflicting statements can be harmonized is not clear. But, nonetheless, no matter how they are explained, the Christ of the Armstrongs is a *sickly* Christ!

Incidentally, one might ask whether Christ, when He got sick, remained ill or experienced healing. If He were healed, Armstrong has another problem to unravel because he teaches: "*Consequently, healing is nothing more or less than the* FORGIVENESS OF SIN—the consequent removal from us of the PENALTY we have incurred. . ."[21]

Garner Ted Armstrong said that Christ was completely without confidence in Himself. He declared: "CHRIST had absolutely NO *self-confidence*! *How much less, then, can you and I accomplish by trusting in ourselves?* (John 5:19, 30). . . .*Christ did not have one iota of self-confidence—but He had* ALL *confidence in God!*"[22]

While the Word of God certainly teaches the fact that Christ performed His earthly ministry in complete dependence upon the Father, as the Holy Spirit worked in and through Him, we deny emphatically that this was because He had a lack of confidence in Himself. Nothing could be farther from the case! Christ purposefully limited Himself during His earthly ministry, not because of any deficiencies, but because He was putting Himself in our place, "leaving us an example" that we "should follow his steps" (I Peter 2:21).

The Armstrongs also teach that it was "entirely possible" for Jesus to have fallen into sin. Herbert W. Armstrong writes: "Look at Jesus Christ Himself!

---

20. Op. cit.
21. *Does God Heal Today?* Copyright, 1952; p. 8
22. *Tomorrow's World,* February, 1971; "Don't Let Doubt, Despondency and Discouragement Ruin Your Life!"; p. 47

The Scriptures say He *did not sin*—yet they teach plainly that at all times *it was entirely possible* for Him to sin. Jesus, in the human flesh, '*was in all points tempted* like as we are, yet without sin' (Heb. 4:15). No scripture says that He *could not* sin. . . .it was NOT IMPOSSIBLE even for Jesus!"[23]

The junior Armstrong agrees, saying that it was a lifelong struggle for Christ to keep from falling. Garner Ted wrote: "Jesus constantly had to CRY OUT to God *day and night* to keep Himself from falling! MILLIONS of people, not understanding the tremendous *battle*, the lifelong *struggle* Christ had with *Himself*, in overcoming His own human nature—the natural pulls of the flesh—*do not fully realize the extent of the sacrifice their Saviour made*, and in many cases are trusting in a FALSE SAVIOUR!"[24]

Note that this teaching, apart from the point we are here emphasizing, means that Jesus had a *fallen* human nature. If this be the case, He might just as well have been the son of Joseph, receiving His humanity from him. Quite the contrary, our Lord said, ". . .the prince of this world cometh, and hath nothing in me" (John 14:30).

In our original expose of Armstrong, we called attention to the cult's strange teaching about Jesus' getting saved. In that booklet, we said: "One of this antichrist's (I John 2:18) most amazing declarations is that Jesus got saved. He writes: 'Jesus, *alone*, of all humans, has so far been SAVED! By the resurrection power of GOD! When Jesus comes, at the time of the resurrection of those IN CHRIST, He then brings His reward with Him!' (Page 11, *Why Were You Born?*)

"Again he says, 'Jesus, the captain or LEADER of our salvation—the one who *led off*, setting us an example—the *only* one so far completed—even HE was

23. "Just What Do You Mean. . .*Born Again?*," op. cit.; p. 47
24. *Who—What—Was Jesus Before His Human Birth?* p. 2

made perfect, and THROUGH SUFFERINGS!' (Page 13, *Why Were You Born?*)

"Then still again he insists: 'Jesus is the *author* of our salvation—He WROTE that salvation BY HIS EXPERIENCE, and that was the *first writing* of it—He was the *first* human ever to achieve it—to be perfected, finished as a PERFECT CHARACTER!' (Page 14, *Why Were You Born?*)

"But to say that Jesus needed salvation is to say that He was a sinner. This the Bible repeatedly and emphatically denies, describing Him as One who 'was in all points tempted like as we are, *yet without sin*' (Heb. 4:15) and 'who did no sin, neither was guile found in his mouth' (I Pet. 2:22).

"It is a strange doctrine of a strange religion which requires Jesus to 'get saved'!"[25]

Armstrong denies, however, that he is teaching our Lord was a sinner. Yet one of his most prominent writers made this strange observation: "Only when one is born of God by a resurrection does a person become perfect (I John 3:9-10). Christ is the only human being thus far *born* of God. He *is* perfect."[26] But if perfection comes *only* through the new birth—and Christ was not born again until His resurrection—He must have been imperfect (a sinner) until that time. This is just another example in the long line of confusing, contradictory teachings of this cult.

In thinking about Armstrong's insistence that Jesus Christ needed to be born again, it might prove profitable to read the most thorough discussion of what being born again involves in the entire Word of God. In John 3:1-15, we read: "*There was a man of the Pharisees, named Nicodemus, a ruler of the Jews; The same came to Jesus by night, and said unto him, Rabbi, we know that thou art a teacher come from*

25. *Herbert W. Armstrong—A False Prophet;* Copyright, 1961; Sword of the Lord Foundation, Murfreesboro, Tennessee; pp. 19,20
26. *The Plain Truth,* August, 1958; Herman L. Hoeh; p. 15

God: for no man can do these miracles that thou doest, except God be with him. Jesus answered and said unto him, Verily, verily, I say unto thee, Except a man be born again, he cannot see the kingdom of God. Nicodemus saith unto him, How can a man be born when he is old? can he enter the second time into his mother's womb, and be born? Jesus answered, Verily, verily, I say unto thee, Except a man be born of water and of the Spirit, he cannot enter into the kingdom of God. That which is born of the flesh is flesh; and that which is born of the Spirit is spirit. Marvel not that I said unto thee, Ye must be born again. The wind bloweth where it listeth, and thou hearest the sound thereof, but canst not tell whence it cometh, and whither it goeth: so is every one that is born of the Spirit. Nicodemus answered and said unto him, How can these things be? Jesus answered and said unto him, Art thou a master of Israel, and knowest not these things? Verily, verily, I say unto thee, We speak that we do know, and testify that we have seen; and ye receive not our witness. If I have told you earthly things, and ye believe not, how shall ye believe, if I tell you of heavenly things? And no man hath ascended up to heaven, but he that came down from heaven, even the Son of man which is in heaven. And as Moses lifted up the serpent in the wilderness, even so must the Son of man be lifted up: That whosoever believeth in him should not perish, but have eternal life."

Note that the "how" of the new birth is not even brought up until verse ten. This is followed by a rebuke because Nicodemus, "a master of Israel," did not know. Then the heart of the issue is declared: "As Moses lifted up the serpent in the wilderness, even so must the Son of man be lifted up: That whosoever believeth in him should not perish, but have eternal life" (vss. 14, 15). This being "lifted up" is explained in John 12:32, 33 as referring to the cross.

Dr. Noel Smith comments in this regard: "It was a serpent: a symbol of sin. It was a brass serpent: a symbol of judgment of sin. The brass serpent upon the pole made a cross. And how were they healed? By grace through faith. Not one work of the law, or all the works of the law, would have healed them.

"Our Lord was talking to Nicodemus about being saved from sin. He told him that he 'must be born again.' And when Nicodemus asked him how a man could be born again, our Lord told him that he could be born again by the same faith in the same grace that brought healing to the Jews in the wilderness. Our Lord pointed Nicodemus to His Cross, not to His Resurrection.

"If Armstrong is right, and Jesus Christ had to be born again in the **same manner** that He told Nicodemus he must be born again—and through Nicodemus told all men they must be born again—then Jesus Christ had not only been tempted by the serpent, He had been bitten by it, and the poison of sin was coursing through His veins.

"And that's blasphemy!

"And if Armstrong is right, and Jesus Christ wasn't born again until His resurrection, then He never saw the 'kingdom of God' until He was resurrected.

"And that's blasphemy!"[27]

In another article, Armstrong says that the Father gave Jesus "eternal life." He said: "Jesus Christ *only*, of all who have been human, has immortality (I Tim. 6:16). GOD is IMMORTAL (I Tim. 1:17). He has given eternal life, inherent, to Jesus, who has eternal life inherent *in Himself* (John 5:26)."[28]

This is justified by Armstrong in light of his teaching that "immortality" and "eternal life" are one and the same. According to this, then, it could be said with

---

27. *Herbert W. Armstrong And His World Tomorrow;* Copyright, 1964; Baptist Bible Tribune, Springfield, Missouri; pp. 49,50
28. *What'll You Be Doing In The Next Life?* © 1967,1969; p. 2

equal authority that Satan has "eternal life" because he is the possessor of Armstrong's understanding of immortality, that is, endless existence.

Regarding the death of Christ on the cross, the Armstrongs teach that He bled to death. Garner Ted Armstrong declared: "How did Christ die? Any extremely *casual* student of the Bible knows it was His shed BLOOD that caused His death, not the sentimental 'idea' of humans that Jesus died of a broken heart! . . .Jesus died because of the loss of His life BLOOD!. . .Jesus Christ died because He BLED to death. . ."[29]

How at odds this is with what the Bible actually teaches. For example, John 19:30 says, "When Jesus therefore had received the vinegar, he said, It is finished: and he bowed his head, and gave up the ghost"; that is, literally, He "delivered up His spirit." Matthew describes it, "Jesus, when he had cried again with a loud voice, yielded up the ghost" (Matthew 27:50).

Dr. C. I. Scofield comments here: "Literally, 'dismissed His spirit.' The Gr. implies an act of the will. This expression, taken with Mk. 15.37; Lk. 23.46; John 19.30, differentiates the death of Christ from all other physical deaths. He died by His own volition when He could say of His redemptive work, 'It is finished.' 'No man taketh it from me, but I lay it down of myself' (John 10.18)."[30]

The cult is as confused about the resurrection of Christ as about His death. In fact, its leadership has borrowed a page from the Jehovah Witnesses' theology in teaching that the resurrection of Christ was not physical. His body, they say, simply "disappeared." *It vanished*! One of their writers states it: "Christ's

---

29. *Do You Have An Immortal Soul?* © 1957,1969,1970,1971; p. 3
30. From *The Scofield Reference Bible,* edited by C. I. Scofield. Copyright, 1917,1944 by Oxford University Press, Inc., and reprinted by permission; p. 1042

body did disappear though! Christ was resurrected as a divine spirit being!"[31]

How different this is from what the Bible actually teaches. When Jesus appeared to His disciples following the resurrection, and they "were terrified" supposing "they had seen a spirit," the Savior said: "Why are ye troubled? and why do thoughts arise in your hearts? Behold my hands and my feet, that it is I myself: handle me, and see; for a spirit hath not flesh and bones, as ye see me have. And when he had thus spoken, he showed them his hands and his feet" (Luke 24:38-40). The reference to his hands and feet, of course, was a reference to the nail holes in His physical body. He then proceeded to eat a meal of broiled fish and honeycomb, something rather strange for a spirit!

Regarding the resurrection, the Armstrongs, being sabbatarians, are also confused about the day of the resurrection. Herbert W. Armstrong says, "The resurrection of Christ actually occurred on *the Sabbath*, not on Sunday!"[32]

He said again: ". . .we now may know THE RESURRECTION OF CHRIST OCCURRED LATE SATURDAY AFTERNOON.

"The Sabbath day ended at sunset. It was late on that day, before the beginning of the first day of the week. It was not, then, a Sunday resurrection at all—it was a Sabbath resurrection!"[33]

We answered this in our original expose, saying: "However, what *are* the facts?

"In revealing how Christ prophetically told His followers of His coming crucifixion and resurrection, the Word of God tells us: 'From that time forth began Jesus to show unto his disciples, how that he must

---

31. *If You Die. . .Will You Live Again?* C. Paul Meredith; c 1958,1971; p. 6
32. *Which Day Is The Christian Sabbath?* p. 56
33. *The Resurrection Was Not On Sunday!* c 1952; p. 8

go unto Jerusalem, and suffer many things of the elders and chief priests and scribes, and be killed, *and be raised again the third day*' (Matt. 16:21).

"Then, in Luke 24:17-21, the two on the road to Emmaus, talking with Jesus without knowing who He was, pin-pointed that resurrection day. The Scripture says: 'And he [Jesus] said unto them, What manner of communications are these that ye have one to another, as ye walk, and are sad? And the one of them, whose name was Cleopas, answering said unto him, Art thou only a stranger in Jerusalem, and hast not known the things which are come to pass there in these days? And he said unto them, What things? And they said unto him, Concerning Jesus of Nazareth, which was a prophet mighty in deed and word before God and all the people: And how the chief priests and our rulers delivered him to be condemned to death, and have crucified him. But we trusted that it had been he which should have redeemed Israel: and beside all this, *to day is the third day since these things were done.*'

"What day was that 'third day'?

"The opening verse of Luke 24 tells us, 'Now upon *the first day of the week*, very early in the morning. . . .' And, in the thirteenth verse, we are told 'that same day'! Hence, it was on the first day of the week that the disciples said '. . .to day is the third day since these things were done.'

"*Christ arose on the first day of the week*! It says the same thing in Mark 16:9, '*Now when Jesus was risen early the first day of the week*, he appeared first to Mary Magdalene, out of whom he had cast seven devils.'

"To use an Armstrongian expression, the PLAIN TRUTH is that Christ arose from the grave on the first day of the week, not on Saturday afternoon."[34]

---

34. *Herbert W. Armstrong—A False Prophet!* pp. 13,14

Since writing the above, we received scores of irate letters from followers of Armstrong, all screaming that the crucifixion could not have possibly been on Friday. Note carefully we did not say it was! For one thing, we do not believe it. Dating back to the time we were first converted and investigated the subject of the resurrection, we came to the conclusion that Christ was crucified on Wednesday—a position we still hold. Others have some strong arguments for a Thursday crucifixion. But, as we have patiently replied to all the critics, there might be a difference of opinion as to the day of His crucifixion, since the Bible does not name the day, but there can be no difference of opinion about the day of the resurrection since it is plainly identified in the Word of God as being "the first day of the week."

We might also point out that the three days and the three nights refer to the time of Christ's *burial* and should not be pin-pointed from mid-afternoon, which was the time of His *death*. The Scripture does not say He would be dead for three days and three nights, but that He would be "in the heart of the earth" for that length of time (Matthew 12:40).

Before we leave the Armstrong's teaching about Christ, perhaps we should mention a strange idea the group teaches about Jesus owning His own home! In the introduction of an article on the "Jesus People" movement by Garner Ted Armstrong, readers were promised: "Read, then, in this article, of the TRUE Jesus Christ: how He *paid taxes*, *slept in homes*, at least one of which was His *own*, DID NOT come 'head to head' with the 'establishment,' and DID NOT have long hair."[35]

In the article, Armstrong said: "Time and time again, when Jesus' remarkable teachings resulted in the gradual *gathering* of a crowd, even about a house

---

35. *Tomorrow's World,* June, 1971; p. 19

which very definitely appears to have been *His own*. . . ."[36]

He said again: "However, notice the account in Mark the 6th chapter. As Jesus was teaching in the synagogue, some of His persecutors began to say, 'Is not this the carpenter, the son of Mary, the brother of James, and Joses, and of Juda, and Simon? And are not his sisters here with us? And they were offended at him. But Jesus said unto them, A prophet is not without honor, but in his own country, and among his *own kin*, and in his own house.'

"Notice! Jesus plainly said, 'Among his OWN KIN'!

"He plainly admitted, then, that He, the prophet who was being dishonored, was, at that time, in His own country, and AMONG HIS OWN KIN!

"He also plainly stated that He was IN HIS OWN HOUSE!"[37]

Still later he said: "Again, Jesus sent the crowds away and entered into a house. Very likely, this was *His OWN* since it was in Capernaum, and Jesus continually went in and out of Capernaum, remaining in the area of Capernaum for much of His Galilean ministry. . . . Then follows the account of their questioning, and their statements concerning Christ's family. Jesus said, 'A prophet is not without honour, save in his own country, and in his OWN HOUSE'! (Matt. 13:57.)"[38]

How contrary is this wild speculation when compared with our Lord's own statement in Matthew 8:20, where we read: "And Jesus saith unto him, The foxes have holes, and the birds of the air have nests; but the Son of man hath not where to lay his head."

Mr. Armstrong offers his readers convincing "proof" that he is right. He refers to those words of Christ, "a prophet is not without honour, but in his own country, and among his own kin, and in his own

36. Ibid.; p. 26
37. Ibid.; p. 29
38. Ibid.

house," saying this "Proves that 'house' is not synonymous with 'kin.' "[39]

It proves no such thing! Quite the contrary, "kin" would be *all* His relatives, while "house" would be His *immediate family.* He was simply narrowing the field down from the wide "country," to the narrower "kin," to the narrowest, "house."

God the Holy Spirit

We have already seen that the Worldwide Church of God's definition of the Holy Spirit identifies Him merely as an impersonal force, not as a Person or a member of the Godhead. The Holy Spirit is never referred to by anyone in this cult in a personal sense. It is always "what" instead of "who," "it" instead of "Him." By way of example, Herbert W. Armstrong says: "Next, UNDERSTAND, it is important you realize that God's Spirit *will not* remain dormant within you. You can't put a cork over it and bottle it up."[40]

He says again: "The Holy Spirit imparts power to UNDERSTAND *what is* God's Way, revealed in the Bible. It thus *leads*—but never *pulls*, pushes, shoves, or forces!. . .It gives you spiritual POWER!. . .But it is still UP TO YOU what you *do* with it!"[41]

One of the movement's key writers said: "How many professing Christians really know what the Holy Spirit is—why they need it—and how they can receive it?. . .Why do almost none of the churches and ministers agree about what the Holy Spirit *is*—or about *why we need* the Holy Spirit?"[42]

Armstrong teaches that God's Spirit is God's love. In his book on the unpardonable sin, he says: "In John 7:37-39 Jesus spoke of the Holy Spirit as 'rivers

---

39. Ibid.
40. *What Do You Mean. . ."The Unpardonable Sin"?* © 1967,1971,1972; p. 9
41. Ibid.; pp. 22,23
42. *How You Can Be Imbued With The Power Of God!* p. 1

of living water,' *flowing into* us from Him, and then *flowing out of us*, in fulfilling God's Law. God's Spirit is God's LOVE—'the LOVE of God shed abroad in our hearts BY the Holy Spirit' (Rom. 5:5)."[43] Contrary to what he is saying, the Scripture quoted separates and differentiates between love and the Holy Spirit, saying that the love is shed abroad BY the Holy Spirit!

Armstrong repeats the same idea later in the book, saying, "God's Spirit dwelling in you is God's own divine LOVE, which *can* fulfill God's Law. . . .It MAY put His righteousness within you!"[44]

In one of the Worldwide Church of God publications, the Holy Spirit is called "a seed." The writer says: "Whenever we become members of God's begotten Family, we receive a *portion*—a seed or germ—of the Father's Holy Spirit.' On the nations also was *poured out* the gift of the Holy Spirit' (Acts 10:45). This gift is called a *seed*."[45]

To which we merely inquire, **"WHERE?"**

How does one receive the Holy Spirit, according to Armstrong? Well, for one thing, it is necessary to be baptized. But, lest anyone misunderstand, Armstrong wants it perfectly clear that you must be baptized by one of his representatives or the baptism will do no good. As a writer in *Tomorrow's World* expressed it: "When you have repented and have been baptized in the name of Jesus Christ for the remission of sins, then you *shall* receive the gift of the Holy Spirit when God's ministers lay their hands on you after the actual baptism (Acts 8:17). And there are no *'perhaps's'* or *'probably's'*. You *SHALL* receive the gift of the Holy Spirit. It is an absolute promise of God. It is sure. . . .

"There is a concrete act that you must do. You

43. *What Do You Mean. . ."The Unpardonable Sin"?* p. 9
44. Ibid.; pp. 21,22
45. *How You Can Be Imbued With The Power Of God!* p. 4

cannot baptize yourself. You *must* have a true representative of Jesus Christ baptize you.

"How can you arrange this? As many of our readers already know, God has His ministers within easy reach of all areas of the United States, British Commonwealth and Western Europe. . . .This is all *you* have to do. Then it becomes *our responsibility* to arrange the most convenient time and place."[46] Mailing addresses are then given for the United States, Canada, the United Kingdom and Europe, South Africa, Australia and Southeast Asia and New Zealand.

Before we leave the teaching of the Holy Spirit, however, it might be wise to show from the Word of God that He *is* a Person! To do this, we will quote from Henry C. Thiessen's *Lectures in Systematic Theology*, principally because he says so much in such a short space. Dr. Thiessen wrote:

"But the *Holy Spirit* is also called God. Before we present the proof of this fact, we wish to show that the Holy Spirit is a Person. And first, we note that personal pronouns are used of Him (John 14:17; 16:13, etc.). In the last reference the neuter substantive *pneuma* is referred to by the masculine pronoun *ekeinos,* recognizing the Spirit's personality. The neuter 'itself' in Rom. 8:16,26, has in the A.S.V. been properly changed to 'himself.' Again we prove His personality by the name Comforter. The term occurs only in John 14:16,26; 15:26; 16:7 of the Spirit. It is applied to Christ in John 14:16; 1 John 2:1 (Greek); and since it expresses personality when applied to Christ, it must do so also when applied to the Spirit. Thirdly, we prove it by the personal characteristics ascribed to Him. He has the three essential elements of personality; Intellect (1 Cor. 2:11), sensibilities (Rom. 8:27; 15:30), and will (1 Cor. 12:11). Fourthly, we prove the same

46. "Receive the Gift of the Holy Spirit," op. cit.; p. 23

thing by the personal acts which are said to be performed by Him. He works (1 Cor. 12:11), searches (1 Cor. 2:10), speaks (Acts 13:2; Rev. 2:7), testifies (John 15:26), teaches (John 14:26), reproves (John 16:8-11), regenerates (John 3:5), prays (Rom. 8:26), guides into truth (John 16:13), glorifies Christ (John 16:14), calls man into service (Acts 13:2), and directs him in service (Acts 16:6,7). Fifthly, His personality is established by the fact of His association with the Father and Son. This is the case in the baptismal formula (Matt. 28:19), in the Apostolic benediction (2 Cor. 13:14), and in His office as Administrator of the Church (1 Cor. 12:4-6). And finally, we prove His personality by the fact that He is susceptible of personal treatment. He can be tempted (Acts 5:9), lied to (Acts 5:3), grieved (Eph. 4:30; Isa. 63:10, A.S.V.), resisted (Acts 7:51), insulted (Heb. 10:29), and blasphemed (Matt. 12:31,32). An influence, manifestly, is not susceptible of such treatment. All these things prove that the Holy Spirit is a Person.

"But He is a divine Person. This is evident from a number of things. First, attributes of Deity are affirmed of Him, as eternity (Heb. 9:14), omniscience (1 Cor. 2:10,11; John 14:26; 16:12,13), omnipotence (Luke 1:35), and omnipresence (Ps. 139:7-10). Secondly, works of Deity are ascribed to Him, such as creation (Ps. 104:30; Gen. 1:2; Job 33:4), regeneration (John 3:5), the inspiration of the Scriptures (2 Pet 1:12), and the raising of the dead (Rom. 8:11). Thirdly, the way in which He is associated with the Father and the Son proves not only His personality, but also His Deity, as in the baptismal formula (Matt. 28:19), the Apostolic benediction (2 Cor. 13:14), and in the administration of the Church (1 Cor. 12:4-6). Fourthly, the words and works of the Holy Spirit are considered as the words and works of God. See Isa. 6:8-10 and Acts 28:25-27; Ex. 16:7; Ps. 95:8-11 and Heb. 3:7-9;

Gen. 1:27 and Job 33:4. And finally, He is expressly called God (Acts 5:3,4 cf. 2 Cor. 3:17,18, where we read in the A.S.V., 'the Lord the Spirit'). All these references prove that the Holy Spirit, equally with the Father and the Son, is God.

"There has been little opposition to the doctrine of the Deity of the Holy Spirit. Arius and his followers held that the Holy Spirit was 'the first being created by the Son,' and Macedonius, Bishop of Constantinople from A.D. 341-360, and his followers, held that the Holy Spirit was a creature subordinate to the Son. This doctrine was condemned by the Council of Constantinople in 381."[47]

Surely the god of the Worldwide Church of God could, under no circumstance or by any stretch of the imagination, be called the God of the Bible.

---

47. Copyright, 1949; Wm. B. Eerdmans Publishing Company, Grand Rapids, Michigan; pp. 144,145; Used by permission

CHAPTER IV

The Armstrong "Family of Gods"

Over a quarter of a century ago, Dr. Roy L. Aldrich made an intensive search and came up with the conclusion that in all the heresies of the ages, not one taught that man is God until modern times. The Worldwide Church of God comes mighty close. A unique feature in the Armstrongian salvation is that he, like Joseph Smith to his followers in Mormonism, holds out to them the hope of eventually becoming deity. He tells the faithful they are on the road to becoming creators. He promises them that others will worship them and adore them, just as Heaven's deity is worshiped and adored today.

Garner Ted Armstrong assures his readers:

"*You* are a POTENTIAL DYNAMO!

"*You* are a potential power!

"YOU can come to be sheer FORCE—compacted together into huge, limitless, driving, surging, energizing, irresistible, immovable, omnipotent power!

"*You can become God!*"[1]

Armstrong senior wrote: "The PURPOSE of life is that in us God is really re-creating *His own kind—reproducing Himself* after *His* own kind—for we are, upon real conversion, actually *begotten* as sons (yet unborn) of GOD; then, through study of God's revelation in His Word, living by His every Word, constant prayer, daily experience with trials and testings, we grow spiritually more and more like God, until, at the time of the resurrection we shall be instantaneously CHANGED from mortal into *immortal*—we shall then be BORN of God—WE SHALL THEN BE GOD!. . .

"Do you really grasp it? The PURPOSE of your

---

1. *Tomorrow's World,* November, 1971; "God's Power"; p. 12

being alive is that finally you be BORN into the Kingdom of God, when you will actually BE GOD, even as Jesus was and is God, and His Father, a different Person, also is God!

". . .you now begin to develop CREATIVE instead of destructive powers. You are setting out on a training to become CREATOR—to *become* GOD!"[2]

Robert L. Kuhn, one of the cult's chief writers, wrote in a *Tomorrow's World* article: "THE BIBLE states that the purpose of human life—the ultimate goal for all human beings—is to eventually be born into the God Family, to eventually become equal with the Creator of the universe!

"*Equal with God*!"[3]

Later in the article, he says: "It cannot be repeated too often:

"*We were born for the express purpose of literally becoming equal with the Creator of the universe—members in the same eternally ruling God Family-Kingdom.*

"But what will we be like?

"Like God!

"Exactly!

"Exactly like God!

"We will *do* what God does. We will *feel, act, enjoy* and *experience* at precisely the same presently incomprehensible level of awareness at which God feels, acts, enjoys and experiences."[4]

Another one of the cult's principal writers, Roderick C. Meredith, in another *Tomorrow's World* feature, put it like this: "God is RULER. If we become His children through *repentance, baptism,* and receiving the *Holy Spirit* (Acts 2:38), we may be 'born again' (John 3:1-8)—changed into, actually *born of spirit* as *literal* sons of God!

---

2. *Why Were You Born?* Copyright, 1957; pp. 21,22
3. April, 1971; "What It Means To Be *Equal* with *God*"; p. 43
4. Ibid.; p. 44

"God is reproducing Himself! He—the Creator and Ruler of the universe—is begetting human beings through His Spirit to be *born* as His Sons—to be in His own family—to inherit eternal life. But we must *first* learn *how to live* before God will grant us eternal life and make us His own sons."[5]

By this latter statement, Meredith means what the cult teaches, that no one except Jesus has ever yet been born again. Everyone who has ever received Christ as personal Savior is merely a "pregnancy" thus far, not yet having been delivered to actual birth.

According to Kuhn, God's purpose with humanity is to make more gods. Referring to Genesis 1:26, he says: "Here God succinctly gives the purpose of human life: Whereas animals reproduce after the animal kind, man reproduces after the God kind! Or, more properly phrased, human beings are the instruments through which *God is reproducing Himself.*"[6]

However, even a casual reading of Genesis 1:26 should show anyone that it cannot possibly be teaching what the Worldwide Church of God is saying. If God's creation of man in His image and likeness was "God reproducing Himself," then Adam was created as God and all the descendants of Adam were Gods. But not even Armstrong believes this!

Leaders in the cult make much of the fact that this teaching is unique with them and that they, alone, of the world's religions have this "truth." For example, Kuhn writes: "You can scrutinously investigate all of the myriad denominations, synods, sects, cults, orders and offshoots that this world has to offer—and never find even a remote allusion to the fact that God is a Family, that God is reproducing Himself, and that man was created to literally become God. . . .

"We repeat: No religion of this world even comes

5. July-August, 1970; "Here's How to *Recognize God's True Ministers*"; p. 31
6. "What It Means To Be *Equal* with *God*" op. cit.; p. 43

close to hinting that man's purpose in life is to be born *as a Son* into the Family of Almighty God.

"Now that all by itself should seem rather odd. In all the wide spectrum of religious beliefs it would seem that at least *one* would have stumbled upon the obvious, literal word-by-word meaning of the Bible. But none has."[7]

While this is not quite true—to mention the Mormons as just one example—the writer gets around this by saying that others who have offered the bait of "becoming God" as enticement for their followers did not really have the Bible thought. But the "god" of Joseph Smith and his Mormons is every bit as much "God" as the "god" of Herbert W. Armstrong and his followers.

In all fairness, we should point out that Armstrong does not believe that being "equal with God" *really means* being "equal with God" or that "exactly like God" *really means* becoming "exactly like God." It is another example of the confusing double-talk for which he and his followers are noted.

Go back and read some of the statements quoted earlier in this chapter and note how strong is the insistence that their followers will become "exactly like God." Yet Kuhn backs off and says he really doesn't mean what he is saying. He wrote: "When mankind is promised to be made 'equal with God,' that of course means that individual human beings will eventually become *qualitatively* equal with God—and obviously does *not* mean that individual human beings will eventually become quantitatively equal with either God the Father or Jesus Christ. Being 'equal with God' only means that we will be in the same God Family as the Father and Christ are in—and has nothing to do with an equality of power, authority, intelligence, etc., *within* the Family."[8]

So this is a horse of a different color and the equal-

7. Ibid.
8. Ibid.; p. 44

ity offered is divided between what he calls *qualitative* and *quantitative.* He says again: "But *quantitatively*, man will *never* equal God the Creator, just as surely as *God the Creator* (Jesus Christ) will Himself never quantitatively equal God the Father (John 14:28).

"These two original Beings in the God Family will always remain in over-all command. Their absolute authority will never be questioned—although they will delight in sharing progressively more of their responsibilities with their offspring as the God Family continues to expand throughout space and time."[9]

He goes on to say: "Every individual person has been created to grow toward *Sonship* (Romans 8:14-15)—to become a literal Son of God—a Son who is in every way *qualitatively equal* to his Father, yet a Son who is always in thankful and gracious submission to his Creator Father."[10] Note how Kuhn places a capital "S" on Son throughout this paragraph, just as when Son is used of our Lord, indicating deity.

What is this "deity" like? For one thing, Kuhn says those who become gods will be able to "generate" eternal life. He writes: "For example, one of God's *qualities* is that He has inherent life—He generates *eternal life intrinsically within Himself.* Because *God is life.* 'For as the Father hath life in himself; so hath he given to the Son to have life in himself' (John 5:26). Consequently, since the two original Beings in the God Family created all mankind to grow to become *qualitatively* like themselves, when we individual human beings are changed into new, individual *God*-Beings, we, too, will generate eternal life *intrinsically* within ourselves (John 7:38; 4:14; 3:16,36; 6:47; 10:28; 17:2, etc.)"[11]

Again, we are told that these Gods will counsel and

---

9. Ibid.
10. Ibid.
11. Ibid.

advise God the Father. He says: "Furthermore, as strange as it sounds, we will counsel and advise our Creator Father—we will have suggestions and opinions which will actually help God the Father administer all reality, suggestions and opinions which will be original and unique."[12]

Again, Kuhn says this means those who reach the God status will look just like Jesus Christ looks today. He quotes Revelation 1:13-17, then says: "As unheard of as it may sound, what you have just read is a prophetic description of what *you* can look like in a very few years."[13]

Again, we are told that reaching this level will mean having "exactly the same glory now possessed by God."[14]

Not only so, but Kuhn tells his readers that those who earn the God-Family status will be worshiped just as the Father and Christ are worshiped now. Without quoting the verse, he says: "Revelation 3:9 states that physical human beings in Tomorrow's World—living under the soon-coming Government of God—will *worship* before the feet of God's present-day human servants."[15]

True, Revelation 3:9 does say that those "of the synagogue of Satan" will be forced to "worship before thy feet," but it most certainly does not say they will be forced to worship *them.* Actually, the Greek word is *proskuneo* and means "to *fawn* or *crouch to,* i.e. (lit. or fig.) *prostrate* oneself in homage *(do reverence to, adore)*: —worship," according to Strong. We hardly think that members of the synagogue of Satan will be among the throngs of worshipers in God's future kingdom.

---

12. Ibid.; p. 45
13. *Tomorrow's World,* May, 1971; "The God Family"; p. 30
14. *Tomorrow's World,* June, 1971; "Your Destiny—*The God Family";* p. 37
15. Ibid.; p. 39

Kuhn acknowledges that he has a problem, since Revelation 19:10 and Revelation 22:8,9, warn against worshiping anyone but God. His conclusion is: "Now there is *only one logical way* for these two statements not to be in diametric contradiction of one another—there is only one way to make sense out of these scriptures—that is *if God's human servants of today will literally be changed into individual members of the God Family in the World Tomorrow.*"[16]

The "Proof"

How does the Worldwide Church of God prove its "family of gods" philosophy? That is a good question! In one of Kuhn's articles on the subject, about two-thirds of the way through, he says: "We have seen that God is reproducing Himself."[17] We wrote in the margin of our copy: "Haven't 'seen' any such thing!" Actually, Kuhn had merely made the claim earlier in the article; now he was arguing from his hypothesis as though it were fact. But the cult does offer "proof" to its followers.

To quote Kuhn again: "The Proof centers around *Elohim*—the Hebrew word translated 'God' in so many Biblical verses (for example, Genesis 1:1). *Elohim* is a *plural* word—it ends in '*im*,' which is the regular sign of the plural in the Hebrew language. Now read 1:26 and observe that *the God Family refers to itself in the plural:* 'Let *us* make man in *our* image, after *our* likeness.'"[18]

We readily acknowledge that *Elohim* is a plural word—it is one of the major arguments for the Trinity and God does say "us" and "our" in speaking of man's creation. However, we are astounded with what nonchalance Kuhn puts his "God Family" into Genesis

16. Ibid.
17. *Tomorrow's World,* April, 1971; p. 44
18. *Tomorrow's World,* May, 1971; op. cit.; p. 29

1:26 without an iota of proof. In fact, in another article, he quotes this verse (with the typical "brackets" of the cult) as follows: "*Let us* [*the God Family*] *make man in our* [*the God Family's*] *image and after our* [*the God Family's*] *likeness.*"[19]

In other words, all an Armstrongite needs is a plentiful supply of brackets and he can prove just about anything; *then he will argue from his brackets*!

Incidentally, the dishonesty of the cult is indicated when Kuhn makes the statement which will amaze Hebrew scholars everywhere: "'*Elohim*'—the Hebrew word that should be translated 'the God Family'. . ."[20]

Another "proof" is summed up: ". . .*God is singular*, God is ONE—*GOD IS ONE FAMILY*—yet the God Family can and will comprise an almost infinite number of individual distinct Sons. Ephesians 3:14-15 proclaims that the whole FAMILY in heaven and earth is named after God the Father. Or, in other words, the whole family is named the *God Family*."[21]

This proof is entirely the figment of the writer's imagination. Certainly, when someone receives Christ as Savior, he is born into the family of God. But this is an entirely different matter from ending up with a family of gods to be worshiped, create worlds and advise God the Father with His problems!

In a major article in *Tomorrow's World*, Kuhn sets forth, with a flourish, "the PROOF!" of his thesis, "*Your* Destiny—THE GOD FAMILY."[22] Most of his proof verses he does not quote; he merely gives the reference. Right here, in the same order as he has given them, we will give the references and let our readers check them and see if there is any such thing as a family of gods; Genesis 1:1; Genesis 1:26; Genesis 17:8 with Leviticus 25:23 with Romans 4:13,

---

19. *Tomorrow's World,* June, 1971; op. cit.; p. 36
20. Ibid.
21. *Tomorrow's World,* May, 1971; op. cit.; p. 29
22. June, 1971; pp. 35-40,48

17 with Hebrews 11:13; Leviticus 11:44, 45; Job 14:14; Psalm 17:15; Psalm 82:6 with John 10:34; Isaiah 58:8; Malachi 3:17; Matthew 5:48 with Genesis 17:1; Matthew 6:9 with John 6:27; Matthew 13:43 with Revelation 1:16; John 6:46 with Revelation 22:4; John 17:5,22; Romans 6:5 with John 17:5; Romans 8:14-16 with Genesis 32:32; Romans 8:17 with John 5:18 with Philippians 2:6; I Corinthians 15:49; II Corinthians 3:18 with Philippians 3:21; Ephesians 4:13 with Revelation 1:13-17; Philippians 2:5,6; I Peter 1:23; II Peter 1:4; I John 2:24,25; I John 3:1,2; Revelation 3:9 with Revelation 19:10 and Revelation 22:8,9; Revelation 3:12 with Revelation 21:22; Revelation 21:7; and Genesis 3:5.

Some of these proof texts would be humorous if the situation were not so serious. For example, he quotes Job 14:14, "If a man die, shall he live again? all the days of my appointed time will I wait, till my change come." His entire comment on this text consisted of less than a dozen words: "Change? To what? To a GOD-LEVEL of existence."[23] The proof? Absolutely none! Just a wild hypothesis on the part of the writer.

His reference to Psalm 17:15, where David says, ". . .I shall be satisfied, when I awake, with thy likeness," is summed up: "How then can David bear the *likeness (timoonah)* of God without being in God's Family? The answer is, he can't."[24] But David did not say anything about bearing God's likeness; he was talking about *beholding*, not *becoming*. The obviousness of this is seen when the entire verse is quoted (perhaps this is why Kuhn did not quote the verse), "As for me, I will behold thy face in righteousness: I shall be satisfied, when I awake, with thy likeness." In fact, the American Revised Version translates the

23. Ibid.; p. 36
24. Ibid.; p. 37

latter phrase, "I shall be satisfied, when I awake, with *beholding thy form.*"

Leaders in the Worldwide Church of God, incidentally, are obsessed with this "likeness" phase of creation. They argue that since man was to be made in the "likeness" of God, this must mean that he is going to be God. Kuhn even argues, "Why is the phrase 'after its kind' *never* applied to man. . .?"[25] Well, it is never applied to God, either, for that matter. There is a difference between *likeness* and *kind.* Do you have a "likeness" of a loved one in your billfold? Because that picture is a "likeness" of your loved one, does it make the picture the loved one? Does it even make the picture of the same "kind"—flesh, blood, hair, bones? Of course not.

Probably the strongest argument the Worldwide Church of God has for this family of gods is in Psalm 82:6 and John 10:34, the latter being a quote of that verse by Christ. Kuhn, in referring to these verses says: "'*Ye are Gods* [*Elohim*]; and all of you are children of the most High.' Can anything be clearer? Or easier to understand? Or more obvious? *You are Gods*! Plain and simple.

"Of course, *people* have *interpreted* this basic three-word statement (just *two* words in the Hebrew) as they have wished. . . .

"*Anything* but what the text actually *says*!

"*It says, 'You are Gods.'*"[26]

Without going into an examination of these verses here, suffice it to say that they *disprove* rather than *prove* the Armstrong thesis. Whatever these verses mean, as Kuhn pointed out, it couldn't be plainer that they say, "You **are** gods." Notice the tense. It is not "will be" gods, but "are" gods. This is completely opposite to what the Armstrong cult teaches.

25. Ibid.; p. 36
26. Ibid.; p. 37

For example, in the same article, we find: "How much clearer could one state that the God Family—comprising, at the present time, only two Persons, God the Father and God the Son. . . ."[27] So, according to this cult leader, Psalm 82:6 and John 10:34 would disprove, not prove their contention. Armstrong says people are *not* gods now, but that they are *going to be*. These verses, whatever they mean, are saying that people are gods **now**!

The reader will note, from the texts listed earlier and offered as proof in Kuhn's article, the Scriptures are listed chronologically until the last one, which reverts back to Genesis 3:5. Since this was one of his major arguments, he saved it until last—**but it is a quotation from the lips of Satan himself!** Without quoting him in great detail, let us simply say that the gist of his argument is that some of his critics have used this text in this fashion: "In Genesis 3:5 Satan is quoted as saying 'ye shall be as gods'—and since Satan is a liar, this statement *cannot* be correct. Therefore, because Satan asserted it, God could *not* possibly have created human beings to be 'as Gods.'"[28]

He answers this by referring to various statements uttered by Satan which were true, then argues: ". . .the very fact that Satan mentioned to Eve 'ye shall be as gods' in *his* first 'sermon' suggests that God had *already* told Adam and Eve precisely that same truth sometime before."[29]

Such an argument is, of course, pure hypothesis developed through an overworked and eager imagination. However, Genesis 3:5—which quoted in its entirety says, "For God doth know that in the day ye eat thereof, then your eyes shall be opened, and

27. Ibid.; p. 36
28. Ibid.; p. 40
29. Ibid.

ye shall be as gods, knowing good and evil"—offers not the slightest suggestion that anyone will ever become God. Whether what Satan said here was true or false is immaterial to the discussion. He did not say "ye shall become gods"; he said "ye shall be AS gods."

He was saying they would be as gods *only* in the sense that they would know good and evil. When Adam and Eve sinned their eyes *were* opened and they *did* know the difference between good and evil. In like manner, all the descendants of Adam have possessed "opened eyes" in this respect—they know the difference between good and evil. Would anyone suggest that a Hitler or an Al Capone, knowing the difference between good and evil, was god because he knew that difference? The very suggestion is absurd.

Armstrong's philosophy of a family of gods is without a single shred of foundation in the Word of God. In fact, we will close this chapter about such a possible status with a denial from the lips of the Son of God. Discussing the resurrection life with the Sadducees, He said: "The children of this world marry, and are given in marriage: But they which shall be accounted worthy to obtain that world, and the resurrection from the dead, neither marry, nor are given in marriage: Neither can they die any more: FOR THEY ARE EQUAL UNTO THE ANGELS; and are the children of God, being the children of the resurrection" (Luke 20:34-36).

Not *superior* to the angels, like God (Hebrews 1:1-14) . . .*only equal*!

CHAPTER V

The Armstrong Teaching About Salvation

The salvation featured by the Worldwide Church of God is "an *amazing*, ASTOUNDING" thing. *Uncertainty* is a keynote. The founder, Herbert W. Armstrong, and the number two man in the organization, Garner Ted Armstrong, have no assurance of "making it"—nor do the other leaders. In his booklet, "What'll You Be DOING In the NEXT LIFE?" the elder Armstrong confessed, "Today God is using me, my son Garner Ted Armstrong, our active staff of several hundred, and our growing family of Co-Workers who contribute financially—all FELLOW WORKMEN for God. Our WORK. . .will EARN a better position—a higher glory—IF we make it into God's Kingdom."[1] It is merely "IF we make it" with them.

The salvation offered by the Worldwide Church of God to its followers is a process and cannot actually be received in this life. In the "*ANSWERS* to your Questions" of *Tomorrow's World*, we read: ". . .a loving God has provided a method by which we might be granted eternal life. This is salvation. Like most English words ending with '*tion*,' salvation is a *process*. And as a process salvation is analagous to birth (John 3:1-8). Before a baby is born, it must be begotten or conceived. I Peter 1:3 shows we are *begotten* to a hope, the hope of being resurrected, just as a baby is begotten in hope it will be born.

"At the resurrection, those whom God will grant salvation will be given incorruptible spirit bodies that can never be destroyed (I Cor. 15:42-54). *At that time*, it will be impossible for those saved to become 'lost.' "[2]

---

1. ©1967,1969; p. 7
2. May, 1971; p. 47

According to the Armstrongs, it was not possible for people in the Old Testament to even have an opportunity for salvation ". . .because Christ had not yet come to make it available" and ". . .the Holy Spirit from the Father was not available to people on the earth until after Christ ascended!"[3]

Strange indeed is the salvation plan which denies that Abraham was saved (Romans 4:1-5), or that David was saved (Romans 4:6-8 with Psalm 32:1,2), or that other Old Testament giants such as Moses, Elijah, Joshua, Elisha, Daniel and Isaiah had experienced God's "so great salvation."

According to this cult, Jesus Christ is the only one in all the world's history who has been "saved." In Herbert W. Armstrong's booklet, "*Why* Were You BORN?" he declares: "Jesus, *alone*, of all humans, has so far been SAVED!"[4] Another leader, C. Paul Meredith, expressed it: "Only one person has been born into this Kingdom so far—this is Jesus Christ."[5]

One reason for this is that the salvation teaching of the cult hinges on the resurrection from the dead. No one experiences salvation until he has been resurrected. Referring to Romans 8:11, Herbert W. Armstrong writes: "This passage shows that the final SALVATION means being GIVEN ETERNAL LIFE *at the time of*, and *through* the resurrection. It says, of that final GIFT of being made IMMORTAL, 'he. . . *shall also*' (AS He raised Christ by resurrection)—and note that it is *future tense*—'quicken your mortal bodies BY HIS SPIRIT which dwelleth in you.'

"Notice carefully! It is the Holy Spirit of God 'dwelling in you' *at the time* of the resurrection. Or, more specifically, *at the end of this mortal life*. IF the Holy Spirit of God is 'dwelling in you' at *that time*, which

3. *If You Die. . .Will You Live Again?* C. Paul Meredith; © 1958,1971; p. 7
4. Copyright, 1957; p. 11
5. Op. cit.; p. 8

is the *time* of the second coming of Christ, (or at the time of your death, whichever comes first), THEN your mortal body will be resurrected, or CHANGED, to an IMmortal body—given ETERNAL life."[6]

He explains further in the booklet: "When you receive God's Holy Spirit, you have received the very *life* of God. But that does not make you, as yet, an *inheritor* of eternal life. You are *not yet* IMmortal.

"You are then an HEIR of God—and a joint-heir with Christ. You are a BEGOTTEN child of God, not yet Spirit-BORN; that is, an *heir, not yet* a *possessor* or *inheritor.* Still mortal flesh and blood—not yet composed of spirit."[7]

The Worldwide Church of God teaches that *none* was converted before Pentecost. A writer in *Tomorrow's World* expressed it: "As astounding as it may be, *not one single individual was ever converted during the ministry of Christ!*"[8] The reason for this teaching, obviously, centers in the cult's theory revolving around salvation and the Holy Spirit, outlined above—and the Holy Spirit had not yet been given.

But this statement is very strange in the light of numerous declarations within the Gospels. For example, Jesus assured Zacchaeus that he was saved. Luke 19:9,10, tells us: "And Jesus said unto him, This day is salvation come to this house, forsomuch as he also is a son of Abraham. For the Son of man is come to seek and to save that which was lost." We think of the woman "which was a sinner" in Luke 7, who washed our Lord's feet with her tears, wiped them with hairs of her head and then anointed them with expensive ointment. There we read: "And he said unto her, Thy sins are forgiven. And they that sat at meat with him began to say within themselves, Who is this that for-

6. *What Do You Mean. . ."The Unpardonable Sin"?* ©1967,1971,1972; p. 8
7. Ibid.; p. 12
8. July, 1971; Richard A. Wiedenheft, "Why Christ Spoke in Parables"; p. 15

giveth sins also? And he said to the woman, Thy faith hath saved thee; go in peace" (Luke 7:48-50).

Another amazing facet of the Armstrong brand of salvation is the teaching about who can get in on it in this life. Actually, according to this cult, God has not the slightest interest in converting *everyone* in this age. C. Paul Meredith makes light of the idea that there is *"a 'great controversy' between God and Satan—God doing His best to get everybody saved—Satan trying to keep them lost—with time now fast running out on God."*[9] His entire booklet was written to answer "the common teachings that salvation is open to everyone today."[10] He denies that everyone is "free to accept salvation and be saved any time one wishes to be."[11] His thesis is that God has "purposely *blinded* some to salvation in this day."[12]

Another writer of the cult, David Jon Hill, agrees, commenting: "Down through the ages God has selected some few whom He called *out of* this world to realize His plan of salvation. . ."[13] Going on to teach the cult's philosophy of an offer of salvation in the next world to those who didn't realize it in this one, Hill says: "When Jesus Christ returns to this earth in the very next few years, He will *for the first time* in mankind's history set His hand to save the whole world—that is, all people who are alive on the earth at that time. He will offer them the same salvation that He has in the past only offered to a few whom He has called *out of* the world. Then, at the close of a thousand years of this reign, all of those who have ever died, but never had a chance to know the true Jesus and His true Gospel message, will be resurrected and given their ONE opportunity to obey and

---

9. *Is This The Only Day Of Salvation?* © 1958, 1971; p. 1
10. Ibid.
11. Ibid.
12. Ibid.
13. *There Is A Real Hell Fire!* © 1962, 1963, 1971; p. 6

by the strength of God's Holy Spirit to enter into His Kingdom."[14]

In light of such a strange teaching about salvation, it would naturally follow that members of the cult do do not believe in trying to "convert" others. As the founder, Herbert W. Armstrong, declares: "Have YOU tried to get others converted—'saved,' as many express it? Have YOU started to 'preach'?

"If you have, you have probably stirred controversy, antagonism—lost a friend, or even a wife or husband.

"But if you haven't —*DON'T!!!*"[15]

He says again, "Of all the things evil and harmful a newly converted Christian can do, the very WORST is to try to talk your husband or wife into your religion. WHATEVER else you do, let me *plead* with every such reader, *NEVER* commit this tragic sin. If you love your husband or wife, *don't do it*!! If you love your Saviour who died for you, and now lives for you, *DON'T DO IT!!*"[16]

Mr. Armstrong practices what he preaches in this area. He testifies: "I am glad I learned that lesson early. I have had to maintain certain business connections with many people, since being plunged into God's Work. I must maintain contacts with radio men, publishers, professional men. I get along splendidly with them. A big reason is that I never talk religion to them.

"I never try to talk *anyone* into accepting Bible truth or being converted. I go *to* the world over the air and in print, and everyone is free to listen or read—or to dial out or not to read. No one gets our literature unless he personally requests it. We try never to force God's precious truth on anyone. That's GOD'S WAY!!"[17]

---

14. Ibid.
15. *Should You Try To "Convert" Others?* ©1966,1970,1972; p. 1
16. Ibid.; p. 2
17. Ibid.; pp. 2,3

While Armstrong teaches that one cannot be saved without receiving the Holy Spirit (hence none could have been saved before Pentecost), he equally denies that one is saved who *has* received the Holy Spirit. He writes: "Well is, then, the receiving of the Holy Spirit SALVATION? Is one already 'saved' when he receives this Spirit?

"GOD'S WORD SAYS *NO!* Not *FINALLY!*"[18]

The Word of God disagrees! Titus 3:5 says, "according to his mercy he SAVED us." Second Timothy 1:9 declares, "Who HATH SAVED us." Paul assured the Ephesians, "by grace ye ARE SAVED" (Ephesians 2:5). He reminded the Corinthians, "unto us which ARE SAVED" (I Corinthians 1:18, and spoke of their being a sweet savour to others "that ARE SAVED" (II Corinthians 2:15).

In the same manner, Armstrong denies it is possible for one to receive "eternal life" *now.* He says: "So, then, ETERNAL LIFE is something YOU DO NOT NOW HAVE."[19]

This is certainly strange teaching in light of the host of scriptural portions which insist that one *does have* eternal life the very moment he places his faith and trust in Jesus Christ. For example, John 3:36 says, "He that believeth on the Son HATH EVERLASTING LIFE. . ." Not "will some time receive," but "hath"—present tense, **right now!** Jesus said in John 5:24, "Verily, verily, I say unto you, He that heareth my word, and believeth on him that sent me, HATH EVERLASTING LIFE, and shall not come into condemnation; but is passed from death unto life." In John 6:47, He declared, "Verily, verily, I say unto you, He that believeth on me HATH EVERLASTING LIFE." And I John 5:11-13 guarantees: "This is the record, that God HATH given to us eternal life, and this life is in his Son. He that hath the Son HATH LIFE; and he that hath not the Son of God hath not

---

18. *What'll You Be Doing In The Next Life?* p. 3
19. Ibid.; p. 2

life. These things have I written unto you that believe on the name of the Son of God; that ye may KNOW that ye HAVE ETERNAL LIFE, and that ye may believe on the name of the Son of God." These are just samples among scores of Scriptures which might be given. Undoubtedly, the principle problem here is the inability—or refusal—of the cult to distinguish *spiritual* life as something entirely different from *physical* life.

History shows one of the earmarks of a false prophet's teaching regarding salvation to be that it is extremely difficult—if not impossible—to obtain apart from yoking up with his movement. Armstrong is no exception. He grudgingly acknowledges that a limited few "might" make God's Kingdom apart from him, but the way he says it you can tell he does not think it happens very often!

He asks: "Can one who does not know of the true organized Body doing God's Work, and therefore is outside of it, be a member of the true Church which Christ built? The answer is yes—for it is possible for one to have truly repented, believed, and received God's Spirit—and be following that Spirit as far as he sees and understands—who does not know of the organized Work Christ is using today. But surely God's Spirit in him would lead one, in due time, into his part in the organized Body the living Christ is directing.

"Is it possible that one who has joined a sect, church, or denomination NOT doing God's Work, might be truly converted, and led by God's Spirit in him? The answer is YES—I have known of a few. But in every case, either they came INTO the organized spiritual organism Christ is using in the real Work of God—or, when their eyes were opened to further light and truth, they rejected it and LOST the Spirit of God. And this was amply demonstrated by the fruits."[20]

---

20. *Tomorrow's World,* July-August, 1970; "Just what is *The Church?";* pp. 6,20

In short, Armstrong says there are some who might be a part of Christ though they do not know about his work; but if they really belong to God, then God will reveal Armstrong's work to them and they will hurry and join. If they don't join up with him after being thus "enlightened," they will become a spiritual miscarriage and the Holy Spirit will depart from them.

Ridicule of Bible Salvation

In typical Armstrong fashion, he both perverts the teaching of evangelicals regarding salvation and scoffs at the idea of redemption coming merely by grace through faith. According to Armstrong: "When God's Word says, 'BELIEVE on the Lord Jesus Christ, and thou shalt be saved,' it does not mean the DEAD faith now popularly taught! The common teachings of this day distort this to mean a mere belief in the FACTS of Christ's existence, His sacrifice, and His saving work. Just accept these FACTS, and accept Him—without any obedience to God's Laws! But the demons believe these things—and they TREMBLE—but they are *not* thereby *saved*!"[21]

However, evangelicals have never taught that salvation was merely a matter of head knowledge. Accepting "facts" saves no one. And evangelicals have always pointed out, just as Armstrong did in his comment, that believing *facts* does not make one a Christian any more than the devils believing those facts would make them Christians. This is a dishonest perversion and misrepresentation of what Christianity has always taught.

In one of his "Personal" columns, Armstrong wrote: "Today most professing Christians—and most of the cheap 'tracts' passed out indiscriminately, purporting to show 'sinners' how to 'get saved'—how to become

---

21. *Tomorrow's World,* August, 1971; "What Kind of *Faith* Is Required for *Salvation?"*; p. 5

a Christian—quote one verse, Acts 16:31, 'Believe on the Lord Jesus Christ, and thou shalt be saved.'"[22]

Then, referring to those in John 8 who merely had intellectual faith, he continued: "They 'believed on the Lord Jesus Christ,' just as these cheap tracts tell 'sinners' to do to 'be saved.' Yet they tried to KILL the very Saviour they 'BELIEVED ON.' And they DID NOT BELIEVE *HIM*—did not believe what He said.

"There is a DIFFERENCE between 'believing ON Christ,' and BELIEVING CHRIST!"[23]

This is exactly what evangelicals themselves have always taught.

Armstrong derides the biblical brand of "instantaneous" salvation and sneers at the thought of a salvation merely by grace through faith. As one of his writers in *Tomorrow's World* says: "So many people, today, seem to think that all Christians have to do is 'believe on Christ' and they are automatically SAVED. The common concept is that life is a one-way 'train ride' destined for hell. But at the moment you 'accept Christ,' a switch is changed, and your 'train' is then rerouted to heaven when you die!

"According to this concept, all a Christian has to do, then, is 'accept Christ,' and wait. There are NO WORKS to salvation! There is NOTHING he must then do—except wait at the station with his bags packed, so to speak.

"What's wrong with this prevalent conception—this common belief?

"Just this—it is a surefire method to LOSE OUT on the very salvation a person might think he has!"[24]

The funny thing is, six paragraphs on in the article he says: "All our good works, of course, will never in a million years EARN us our salvation."[25]

---

22. *Tomorrow's World,* July, 1971; p. 1
23. Ibid.; p. 2
24. December, 1971; William F. Dankenbring, "What Should You Do Until *Christ Returns?";* pp. 34,35
25. Ibid.; p. 35

Another writer, in another issue of *Tomorrow's World*, sneered at what he called "merely 'nicey-nice' talk about 'givin' your heart to the loarrd.' "[26]

Another writer says, ". . .God doesn't want the worldly kind of repentance which is manifested by a trip down the sawdust trail."[27]

Mr. Armstrong scoffs: "The favorite 'invitation' or 'altar-call' hymn sung by the popular denominations in revival or evangelistic services is 'JUST AS I AM!'

"But *be not deceived*—God WON'T RECEIVE YOU JUST AS YOU ARE!"[28]

In an article intended to show any conversion but theirs to be false, Roderick C. Meredith warns his readers: "Your *misplaced confidence* in a *FALSE* CONVERSION is a *great* and MORTAL *deception* which could very easily cause you to forfeit *eternal life!* It is such a *dangerous* deception because your own personal VANITY will in many cases prevent you from admitting that *you have never been converted*!"[29]

Armstrong shows his lack of understanding regarding the biblical subject of imputed righteousness and, at the same time, ridicules what evangelicals have always taught. He calls it God "kidding Himself," declaring: "God does not 'kid Himself.' Some religious teachers tell you Christ lived a righteous life FOR you 1930 years ago, and since you '*can't* keep the Law,' as they claim, God 'IMPUTES' Christ's righteousness of 19 centuries ago to you—by sort of 'kidding Himself' that you are righteous, while you are given license to still be a spiritual CRIMINAL breaking His Law! GOD does not impute to you something you do not have."[30]

---

26. August, 1971; Gary Alexander, "The Greening Of The World"; p. 18
27. *Tomorrow's World,* December, 1971; Leslie L. McCullough, "Just What do you mean—*Repentance?"*; p. 31
28. *The Plain Truth,* August, 1963; Quoted in *Herbert W. Armstrong—The Plain Truth About His Shocking Heresies,* Bob L. Ross; p. 9
29. *The Plain Truth,* July, 1959; "*False* Conversion—*A MORTAL DANGER"*; p. 14
30. *The Plain Truth,* July, 1961; "Just What do You *Mean—Salvation?"*; p. 39

He says again: "There are those who say. . .Christ lived a righteous life IN OUR STEAD, and, if you just believe, God IMPUTES Christ's righteousness to you. These people mean that YOU do not need to live righteously. Actually, THEY CONDONE SIN—their false argument means you are free to go on deliberately SINNING, but God PRETENDS you are righteous, by a sort of hocus-pocus of transferring *Jesus*' righteousness to you. Those are the 'ungodly men' Jude warns against, 'turning grace into license.'"[31]

This, of course, is not true. Evangelicals have always taught that the very best of man's righteousness is "filthy rags" before God and completely unacceptable to Him (Isaiah 64:6). So Christ lived a perfectly sinless and righteous life in our behalf (Matthew 5:17; Romans 10:3,4), and when one trusts Christ and His finished work at Calvary, that righteousness is imputed to him (II Corinthians 5:21; Romans 4:1-8). As for this doctrine condoning sin, Paul said, after teaching it (Romans 5:15-21), "What shall we say then? Shall we continue in sin, that grace may abound? God forbid. How shall we that are dead to sin, live any longer therein?" (Romans 6:1,2).

This brings us to the heart of a burning issue:

Does Armstrong Teach "Salvation by Works"?

He vigorously denies it!

The thing that disturbed Armstrong the most, apparently, when my booklet, HERBERT W. ARMSTRONG—A FALSE PROPHET, was published, although it listed ten major points, revolved around my seventh charge, "Teaches Salvation by Works!"

In one of his "Personal" columns, he wrote: "Understand, first, being 'saved'—that is, being born into the Kingdom of God—given God's GIFT of eternal

31. *What Do You Mean. . ."The Unpardonable Sin"?* p. 18

life—is altogether by GRACE, as God's free GIFT. *You can't earn it*! I have ALWAYS taught that! In spite of the false accusations of persecutors, who try to make you believe I teach 'salvation by WORKS' (and they know better!!!), I have NEVER taught that. I do not believe that! I have always taught that salvation—what religious people call 'being saved'—inheriting eternal life—being born into the Kingdom of God—just *getting there*—comes ONLY by *GRACE* (which means undeserved pardon) and as God's FREE GIFT. You CAN'T *earn it*! All your OBEDIENCE—all your good WORKS—won't buy it!"[32]

In another "Personal" column, he said: "So UNDERSTAND! Salvation is *from sinning*! It comes as God's GIFT—by grace.

"'Works' do not earn or produce it. 'Works' determine the degree of 'reward' or office, or glory, in God's Kingdom, *IF* you are born into that Kingdom, by grace!"[33]

But we insist just as vigorously today as we did originally—yea, even *more* so—that Armstrong teaches a salvation of works. He talks out of both sides of his mouth. On the one hand he maintains, as just quoted, that salvation is by grace, purely the gift of God. Then he turns right around and presents a grace that is anything but grace and faith that is anything but faith. In fact, in the very next sentence after the paragraph quoted above, Armstrong said: "To be 'saved'—to inherit eternal life in God's Kingdom—you must still be traveling THAT WAY at the end of your life!"[34] In other words, the ultimate receiving of salvation depends upon the individual's WORKS following the moment God "started him" along the road by grace.

---

32. *Tomorrow's World,* September, 1971; p. 2
33. *Tomorrow's World,* July, 1971; p. 46
34. Ibid.

His definition of grace is, in reality, legalism. He says, "And those who, thru repentance, obedience and FAITH have turned from disobedience and are, thru faith, KEEPING the Law, are the only ones who are UNDER GRACE!"[35]

That "keeping the law" is hardly grace is seen from the fact Galatians 3:10 tells us, "For as many as are of the works of the law are under the curse: for it is written, Cursed is every one that continueth not in all things which are written in the book of the law to do them," and by James 2:10, which warns, "For whosoever shall keep the whole law, and yet offend in one point, he is guilty of all." Yet this is the "grace" Armstrong offers his followers.

Trying to prove that salvation is not by simple faith in Christ, Armstrong says: "Is it possible to BELIEVE in Christ—to worship Him—in the customary manner of the day, *and yet be lost*? Christ Himself says, 'YES!'

"'Not every one that sayeth unto me, "Lord! Lord!" shall enter into the kingdom of heaven; but he that DOETH the will of my Father which is in heaven,' He said (Matt. 7:21).

"Hear Him again!

"'Howbeit IN VAIN do they worship me, teaching for doctrines the commandments of men. For laying aside the commandments of God, ye hold the traditions of men!' (Mark 7:7-8).

"There it is! From Jesus' own lips! Such a dead faith—such worship—is IN VAIN! Those who trust in it, and in the men and denominations which teach it, *ARE LOST*! And the quicker we come to realize it, the better!"[36]

This is typical Armstrong "proof"! His first proof text, in Matthew 7, says absolutely nothing about "believing" or "worshiping." The second proof text,

---

35. *What Kind Of Faith Is Required For Salvation?* Copyright, 1952; p. 5
36. Ibid.; pp. 9,10

which speaks of worshiping Christ in vain, is talking about hypocrites who were *doing*, not believing—the exact opposite of what Armstrong is trying to prove. Yet, after quoting these unrelated texts out of context, he tells his gullible followers: "There it is! From Jesus' own lips!"

The constant Armstrong teaching on this subject can be summed up: Salvation is a *gift,* but you have to *earn* the gift! One of his writers in *Tomorrow's World*, discussing the subject of "Gospel Pollution," expresses it: "Their works could not buy salvation or entrance into the Kingdom. The GRACE of God provides for sin's *pardon.* But men must prove their willingness to come under the good, holy, just laws which God commands."[37] You cannot "buy" salvation by your works, but you receive it through living according to the "good, holy, just laws" of God. This is double talk, plain and simple, of course.

Another illustration of this two-faced reasoning is when Herbert W. Armstrong writes: "So UNDERSTAND! Salvation is *from sinning*! It comes as God's GIFT—by grace.

"'Works' do not earn or produce it. 'Works' determine the degree of 'reward,' or office, or glory, in God's Kingdom, IF you are born into that Kingdom, by grace!"[38]

Do you fathom what he is saying? He is saying that salvation is strictly by God's grace—it is God's gift, absolutely not of works. Then he qualifies it by saying works have to do with "rewards." To all of this no evangelical today would disagree. But then Armstrong turns right around and says if you don't have proper "works" you will never get into that Kingdom—and he makes the "works" the deciding factor of whether or not you "arrive." As he says in the next sentence:

---

37. July-August, 1970; Clint C. Zimmerman; p. 48
38. *What Do You Mean. . ."The Unpardonable Sin"?* p. 34

"To be 'saved'—to inherit eternal life in God's Kingdom—you must still be traveling THAT WAY at the end of your life!"[39]

Armstrong continues his theme that works have to do with "rewards," when he says, defending himself from my charges: "But THAT explains, I think, WHY some ministers falsely accuse me of 'proclaiming a salvation by WORKS.' Since we are to be SAVED, as your Bible states repeatedly, by GRACE, therefore these people simply cannot conceive of any WORKS whatsoever. They don't understand that the Christian life is one of TRAINING for WHAT WE SHALL BE DOING through eternity IN THE NEXT LIFE. They miss the WHOLE PURPOSE of salvation!. . .

"Nowhere does the Bible teach earning your salvation by your own 'WORKS.' But what most do NOT understand is that the Bible DOES teach, over and over again, that we shall be REWARDED according to our WORKS!"[40]

He says again: "'WORKS' means the wages you earn—or the REWARD to be given—*either* good or bad. Evil works (sin) can EARN eternal punishment, but GOOD WORKS can EARN a better position or office in God's Kingdom *IF* you get there—but it *cannot* earn salvation!"[41]

Note the contradiction, the confusion. Good works will not earn you salvation, he says, but if you do not have good works then, obviously, you have evil works and evil works earn for you eternal punishment. It is six of one and a half-dozen of the other.

Do not misunderstand. We are not objecting to his "rewards" for "works" in the Christian life. We are objecting to his teaching of "works" to *stay on the road to "eventual" salvation*—which is salvation by

39. Ibid.
40. *What'll You Be Doing In The Next Life?* p. 1
41. Ibid.; p. 4

works. As Armstrong says: "So, SALVATION. . . depends not only on once *receiving* the Holy Spirit, but BEING LED BY God's Spirit *through life* (Rom. 8:14), and God's Spirit DWELLING IN US, *at the end of life's race!*"[42]

He says again: "Your 'WORKS' won't get you converted—won't earn you God's Spirit—won't earn salvation—as I have made PLAIN in this article. BUT THE LACK OF GOOD WORKS CAN GET YOU *LOST*, if persisted in!"[43]

There you have it! The salvation depends upon your works! If you do not have the proper works, then you become "lost." He is saying that grace will "introduce" you to Christ, but from there on, *it is up to you*!

Armstrong's problem is that he tries to do something the Bible says cannot be done; that is, *mingle* grace and works for salvation. As Armstrong himself says: "So what we WANT is not GRACE *or* WORKS, but GRACE *and* WORKS."[44]

That may be what Armstrong wants, but it is what the Word of God says is totally impossible. Romans 11:6 plainly declares: "And if by grace, then is it no more of works: otherwise grace is no more grace. But if it be of works, then is it no more grace: otherwise work is no more work."

Armstrong continues his confusion of grace and works when he says: "You shall be saved by GRACE, but God does lay down conditions. You can comply, and receive glorious GRACE—or you can rebel, and pay the DEATH PENALTY for eternity!"[45] Armstrong's salvation is by grace, plus "conditions"—and those conditions are *the works* of the individual.

In the light of all the times Armstrong declares works to be a matter of "reward," it is important to

---

42. Ibid.; p. 5
43. Ibid.; p. 6
44. Ibid.; p. 4
45. *Which Day Is The Christian Sabbath?* ©1962, 1964, 1968, 1970, 1971; p. 94

note that he also teaches *salvation* is the "reward" Christ is going to give. For example, he writes: "Christ brings SALVATION, *when* He appears the *second time*!. . .WHEN does Christ's SALVATION *appear*? That is explained also in Revelation 12:10: '*Now* is come salvation, and strength, and the kingdom of our God, and the power of his Christ.' That is speaking of the time of Christ's second coming!

"Again, Jesus said: 'And, behold, I come quickly; *and my reward is with me*, to give every man according as his work shall be' (Rev. 22:12). The TIME: Christ's second coming!"[46]

As Armstrong would say, "Don't take my word for it! Read it for yourself!"

As plain as day, he is saying that salvation is received when Christ comes again. To prove it, he quotes Jesus as saying that when He comes "*my reward is with me*" (note that Armstrong has this phrase in italics for added emphasis) "to give every man according as his work shall be." He insists that *works* have to do with *reward*, then he says the Lord's reward is *salvation*! How, in light of such statements as this, he has the audacity to say people are misrepresenting him when they accuse him of teaching salvation by works, is beyond this writer's comprehension. After all of Armstrong's double-talk is sifted through, one fact of his teaching is undeniable: **If you don't have the works you don't get the salvation!** Perhaps that is not "salvation by works" to Armstrong, but it is to intelligent people everywhere.

How does Armstrong get around the clear-cut Bible teaching that salvation is not by works? Here is a sample: "But *this* kind of 'works' is *not our* 'works'—for that (God's Spirit—God's LOVE) which PRODUCES this fruit of righteousness comes from GOD by HIS GRACE, freely given. THIS IS NOT OUR OWN

---

46. Ibid.; p. 74

RIGHTEOUSNESS—it is *not* OUR 'works' at all—it is GOD'S righteousness *given* by His grace, through His Spirit!"[47]

While evangelicals have always held that acceptable righteousness is produced by God's Spirit working in and through the Christian, they have always maintained this to be a *result* of salvation. Armstrong makes it a *prerequisite* of salvation and this is where the contradiction lies.

Armstrong's philosophy is that the salvation hinges upon the individual. God, he tells his followers, merely gives them the "tools" to work with; after that, it is up to the individual. He writes: "So UNDERSTAND! God gives you the *spiritual equipment* to go HIS WAY. The Holy Spirit imparts power to UNDERSTAND *what is* God's Way, revealed in the Bible. It thus *leads*—but never *pulls*, pushes, shoves, or forces! God's Spirit gives you the spiritual LOVE—God's own LOVE—which *only* may fulfill His law. His Spirit imparts to you CHRIST'S OWN FAITH, to make possible obeying His law. It gives you spiritual POWER!

"That's a lot of spiritual EQUIPMENT! A lot of HELP!

"But it is still UP TO YOU what you *do* with it! Jesus said that road *is not easy*. . . .YOU must exert your WILL and DETERMINATION to *follow* God's Spirit leading you to see and understand GOD'S way. You have the spiritual equipment to go that way."[48]

A few paragraphs on, under the subhead, "**It Takes STRIVING,**" Armstrong writes: "Notice what God says about the Christian life.

"It is not EASY to overcome sin. You simply DON'T succeed in every encounter—in every incident!

"Jesus said, 'STRIVE to enter in at the strait gate. . .' (Luke 13:24). The Greek word which Jesus

---

47. *What Do You Mean. . ."The Unpardonable Sin"?* pp. 9,10
48. *Tomorrow's World,* July, 1971; pp. 42,43

spoke for *'strive'* means 'to strain, to agonize.' It means a hard STRUGGLE. A 'strait' gate is a very narrow one—difficult to squeeze through. 'For,' continued Jesus (Matthew 7:13-14), 'WIDE is the gate, and broad is the way, that leadeth to destruction, and MANY there be which go in thereat: because *strait* is the gate, and *narrow* is the way, which leadeth unto life, and few there be that find it.'

"Paul, to the Colossians, spoke of his struggle to overcome, saying: '. . .I also labour, STRIVING according to his working, which worketh in me mightily' (Col. 1:29).

"Paul knew that the Christian has a fierce BATTLE with his own nature, the world, and the powers of Satan, when he said, 'Ye have not yet *resisted unto blood,* STRIVING against sin' (Heb. 12:4)."[49]

Now, admittedly, these statements taken at face value do not seem so bad—other than the fact he runs together salvation passages with those about victorious Christian living. But it is important to remember that, to Armstrong, the "Christian living" is the determining factor on which the salvation eventually is based! Without it, there would be no hope of attaining God's Kingdom. So when Armstrong talks about straining, struggling and agonizing to "enter in," he is actually talking about what individuals must do in order to be "saved" in "the end." As previously noted, Armstrong says: "To be 'saved'—to inherit eternal life in God's Kingdom—you must still be traveling THAT WAY at the end of your life!"[50]

William F. Dankenbring, one of his associate editors, says: "All our good works, of course, will never in a million years EARN us our salvation. Rather, salvation is a gift which God will bestow upon us because we have accepted Christ's sacrifice for payment of the

49. Ibid.; p. 43
50. Op. cit.

penalty of our sins. **BUT GOD DOES REQUIRE THAT WE LIVE ACCORDING TO HIS WAY OF LIFE, THE WAY SET FORTH BY HIS COMMANDMENTS**—the way of love for God and love for our neighbor!"[51] (Emphasis ours). Again we remind our readers of Romans 11:6: "And if by grace, then is it no more of works: otherwise grace is no more grace. But if it be of works, then is it no more grace: otherwise work is no more work." Romans 3:28 answers his insistence that living according to the law is a requirement for receiving salvation, declaring, "Therefore we conclude that a man is justified by faith **WITHOUT THE DEEDS OF THE LAW.**"

Incidentally, one of Armstrong's favorite texts in this area is Matthew 24:13. He quotes it repeatedly and always his emphasis is the same: *salvation in "the end" depends upon "holding out" until then!* He says: "Remember, Jesus tells us it is 'he that shall endure unto the END, the same shall be saved' (Matt. 24:13). He means the END of this Spirit-LED road, which every Christian must travel—if LED BY the Holy Spirit. That is LIFE'S road. So it means the remainder of your life."[52]

For Armstrong to make this passage refer to the salvation of a soul from the consequence of sin is to completely ignore the entire context of the passage. Our Lord was not talking here about personal salvation, He was discussing the terrible great tribulation and those who would survive its judgments of wrath.

In fact, we will let one of Armstrong's own writers answer him in this matter. Robert L. Kuhn, trying to prove that Jesus Christ is coming back again in the next couple of years, wrote about Matthew 24:22 as follows: "'And except those days should be shortened, there should no flesh be *saved*: but for the elect's

---

51. "What Should You Do Until *Christ Returns?"*; op. cit.; p. 35
52. *Tomorrow's World,* July, 1971; p. 46

sake those days shall be shortened.'

"In this popular King James translation, the meaning of 'saved' is ambiguous.

"What is meant by 'saved'? Spiritual salvation? Or simply, as we have explained here, the preservation and continuance of physical human life? If this verse refers to the *spiritual* condition of individual human beings during a certain period of history, then the whole prophetic significance would be lost. The original Greek can go either way. The answer must be determined from the context.

"And the context is very physical. The entire twenty-fourth chapter of Matthew deals with the basic problem of *staying alive* during wars (verse 6), famines, pestilences, and earthquakes (verse 7), religious persecution (verse 9), great tribulation (verse 21), etc. Consequently, more modern translations emphasize that Matthew 24:22 refers to the fact that human *life* would literally be on the verge of total annihilation—and this was to be a sure sign that the last days of the end-time generation had arrived.

"'If that time of trouble were not cut short,' begins *The New English Bible,* 'not a soul would be saved alive,' continues Moffatt; 'not a mortal would survive,' states the Berkeley Version of the New Testament; 'no living thing would have escaped,' paraphrases E. V. Rieu; 'no human being would survive' concludes Phillips."[53]

We would have to agree with Kuhn, who in this matter has ably answered his master, that salvation—or being "saved"—in Matthew 24 has to do with the physical, not the spiritual. And Armstrong's repeated use of the verse in Matthew 24:13 is either *ignorance* or *dishonesty.* We leave our reader to make his own choice.

---

53. *Tomorrow's World,* August, 1971; "Is This The Time of *The End?*"; p. 16

Some "Proof" Quotes

While we have already given numerous passages from Worldwide Church of God literature—and from Armstrong himself—pointing out the salvation the cult teaches is, in reality, a salvation by works, let us quote just a few more as added proof.

(1) Armstrong, in defining *conversion* and *a real Christian*, writes: "What, then, IS a true 'conversion'? WHAT constitutes a real Christian *in the sight of* GOD?

"The WAY to become a Christian was given, in few words, on the very day that the New Testament Church of God began, by the apostle Peter. There were three steps. The first two, we humans must do. These do not 'save' us, or make us Christians—they are merely required conditions. The third, GOD does.

"They are: 1) REPENT, 2) be baptized (which is the outward action testifying to inward FAITH in Christ as Saviour—Acts 8:36-37), and 3) you shall receive THE GIFT of the HOLY SPIRIT (Acts 2:38)."[54]

It should be noted, however, that even these "required conditions" do not produce salvation in the eyes of Armstrong. To these must be added the "works" and "holding out to the end" of the individual throughout the remainder of his earthly life.

(2) C. Paul Meredith writes: "The JUST DEAD will be raised by the power of God exerted through Jesus Christ (John 6:44). These are they who have repented (i. e., turned from their former ways), been baptized, received the gift of the Holy Spirit and were overcomers to the end (Acts 2:38 and Romans 8:11)."[55]

Again, here is a salvation depending upon "overcoming," the works of the "candidate" for salvation.

(3) Armstrong, in writing about "How to Be an

---

54. *What Do You Mean. . ."The Unpardonable Sin"?* p. 7
55. *If You Die. . .Will You Live Again?* p. 6

OVERCOMER," says: "But God is now calling SOME to a life of separation—to a new and different and Spirit-filled and Spirit-led life—in order that they may by wholly CLEANSED of sin, and that they may GROW in grace and knowledge, thus being prepared, trained, fitted for a position of solemn responsibility—that of king or priest—in God's KINGDOM! And it is *only* those who qualify by the training, the overcoming, the spiritual development and growth, DURING THIS PRESENT LIFE, who shall thus reign with Christ. Study the parable of the pounds in Luke 19:11-27."[56]

Notice how he bases "a life of separation" as being "in order that they may be wholly CLEANSED of sin." And notice that it is only those who live that separated life—who overcome—who will reign with Christ. As we have elsewhere seen, Armstrong equates eventual salvation with being a ruler in God's Kingdom.

(4) Roderick C. Meredith, in a *Tomorrow's World* article, talking about how to become sons of God, says that before one can be granted eternal life and become a son of God: "We must develop God's *wisdom*, God's *character*. We must '*live* by every word of God.' Realizing that our Creator knows best, we should OBEY Him."[57] So, according to Meredith, eventually receiving eternal life and becoming a child of God will come only through personal development and obedience. If this is not "works," words no longer have sensible meanings.

(5) In one of the "Answers" columns of *Tomorrow's World*, a reader wanted to know, "Should we really strive to be kings in God's Kingdom?" While the reply may be slightly confusing in light of evidence already given, namely, that David and other Old Testament saints "never had the chance of salvation," perhaps it is clear to a member of the cult. But, in his re-

56. *Tomorrow's World,* April, 1971; p. 3
57. July-August, 1970; "Here's How to Recognize God's *True Ministers";* p. 31

sponse, the editorial writer said: "Did David only exercise minimum effort in his quest to obtain Sonship in the Kingdom of God? Did David approach things in a half-hearted way? Notice a few scriptures: 'Now I have prepared *with all my might* for the house of my God. . .' (I Chron. 29:2). 'And David danced before the LORD *with all his might. . .*' (II Samuel 6:14). 'My soul followeth hard after thee. . .' (Psalm 63:8). David strove hard—exerted maximum effort to achieve God's Kingdom."[58]

Aside from the humor we see in David's dancing "with all his might" as an evidence of how sincerely he strove "to achieve God's Kingdom," note the clear teaching that he received it **because of his effort.** In fact, the writer's next sentence was: "Because of his wholehearted attitude and approach, God promised him a position of HIGH AUTHORITY in God's Kingdom (Ezekiel 34:24)."[59]

David himself had an entirely different idea about it. He wrote, in Psalm 32:1,2, "Blessed is he whose transgression is forgiven, whose sin is covered. Blessed is the man unto whom the Lord imputeth not iniquity, and in whose spirit there is no guile." Paul quoted this testimony of David in Romans 4 as evidence that salvation is entirely by faith, completely apart from any human effort.

(6) Armstrong's whole teaching about salvation hinges upon "keeping the commandments," and, we need to emphasize, upon *his understanding* of those commandments. In his book on the unpardonable sin, Armstrong says: "If WE profess to be Christians—if we SAY we have fellowship 'with the Father and with His Son Jesus Christ' (verse 3)—yet if we *are living* in darkness—if our lives are going the way of SIN—we are liars. He is not talking here of one who, under temptation, commits *an act* of sin, and then repents.

58. December, 1971; pp. 36,37
59. Ibid.; p. 37

He is talking directly of those followers of the FALSE PROPHETS who teach that GOD'S LAW is DONE AWAY. If you say you are a Christian because you BELIEVE IN CHRIST, or worship Christ—yet DO NOT KEEP HIS COMMANDMENTS, you WALK in 'darkness.' You then do NOT have any fellowship with Christ, and if you claim to be a Christian, you are a LIAR! (I John 2:4.)"[60]

Anyone who has read Armstrong very much understands him to be saying, for example, that if you do not observe the Sabbath on the seventh day, as he does, and keep all of the Old Testament feasts, as he *says* he does, then you are not a Christian—you cannot receive eternal life, you cannot be saved in the end! We do not know how it could be plainer that he insists *commandment keeping* is the criterion for salvation.

(7) In one of Armstrong's definitions of salvation, he writes: "SALVATION means being BORN into GOD'S KINGDOM, changed from a flesh-and-blood mortal HUMAN, *to* a Spirit-*composed*, life-*inherent*, IMmortal son of God the Father—the Father of the divine Family. *That* change will come at *the time* of Christ's return. This salvation depends upon God's Holy Spirit *dwelling in* one at the END of the ROAD—end of your life—or, as Paul characterized it, the end of the race."[61] In other words, if you have not held out faithfully, if your works have not been sufficient and the Holy Spirit has departed from you before "the end of the race," then salvation will not be yours. If Armstrong can convince his followers that this is salvation by grace through faith, he should be able to persuade a Harvard professor he is a 26-toed anthropoid who came to this planet from Mars in a sailboat!

In examining the kind of salvation taught by Armstrong and his Worldwide Church of God, we can well

60. *What Do You Mean. . ."The Unpardonable Sin"?* p. 27
61. Ibid.; p. 29

understand why, if someone lost it, he might not want it back. Armstrong himself confesses this to be the case when he says, talking about someone getting off the road: "You may never WANT to get back on the *right road*, traveling with the living CHRIST!"[62] The salvation Armstrong offers is a funny salvation, indeed, if one who had it—and lost it—might not want it back again!

That certainly does not describe the biblical salvation available in Jesus Christ!

Armstrong's "New Birth" Teaching

Before we leave the Worldwide Church of God teaching about salvation, perhaps we need a closer examination of the cult's doctrine of the new birth. It is a unique among all professing Christian groups—past and present—and the interpretation given is wild and weird when examined by the Word of God. *In a nutshell*: no one but Jesus has yet been born again. Any new birth experience in the present life is merely a "conception," not a birth. Christians in this age are simply in a state of pregnancy. Miscarriages, preventing actual birth, are not only possible, they are plentiful.

As representative of what the cult teaches, consider these words by Herman L. Hoeh: "First, notice that the Holy Spirit—the germ by which we are begotten—comes from the Father. God has masculine characteristics. That is why we call Him *'Father.'* We are called the 'begotten *children* of God' (I John 3:1). God, then, has the power to beget us as His children. He begets us 'by his Spirit.' Each portion of the Spirit by which we are begotten is termed in the Bible a germ or 'seed.' Peter tells us we are '*begotten again*, not of corruptible SEED, but of incorruptible, through

62. Ibid.; p. 34

God's word, which liveth and abideth' (I Peter 1:23). Jesus completes this by saying we must finally be *born* again—at the resurrection—when we shall *be* spirit. Now we are only flesh with a spiritual *germ of eternal life* impregnating us."[63]

Mr. Armstrong himself continues this theme: "No HUMAN can *inherit* the Kingdom. The Kingdom of God is not a human kingdom. There are NO HUMANS IN IT! It is a DIVINE Kingdom—the God Kingdom!

". . .'that which is born of the Spirit,' said Jesus, 'is spirit.' When we are born of the Spirit, then we shall BE spirit—so said Jesus—did Jesus know what He was talking about—or do some of us think we know better, today?"[64]

However, if being "born again" is the resurrection, how can Armstrong say Jesus is the only one thus born? What about the saints who were resurrected at the time of Christ's crucifixion? Matthew 27:51-53 tells us: "And, behold, the veil of the temple was rent in twain from the top to the bottom; and the earth did quake, and the rocks rent; And the graves were opened; and many bodies of the saints which slept arose, And came out of the graves after his resurrection, and went into the holy city, and appeared unto many." This is just one more incidence in Armstrong's network of contradictions.

Another writer of the cult, David Albert, emphasizing that the new birth does not take place until the resurrection, said: "After baptism and the receiving of the Holy Spirit, we become part of the *begotten* Family of God and as such have the right and privilege of calling God our *Father.* We have been immersed *into* the very family name of God (Eph. 3:15). We are literally His newly begotten sons looking forward

63. *How You Can Be Imbued With The Power Of God!* ©1967,1970,1971; p. 3
64. *Tomorrow's World,* November, 1971; "What Is The *Reward* of the Saved. . .*Heaven?*"; pp. 6,46

to the resurrection when we will be finally *born into* the divine Family of God!"[65]

This new birth will make it possible for the individual to join God the Father and God the Son in creative works. As Hoeh expressed it: "Man is put here on earth to learn to develop tools for limited creative work—to train himself for the ETERNAL GOAL—becoming part of the *God family*, which means *sharing* control of the creative Spirit of God."[66] (Incidentally, the Armstrongites have no difficulty in speaking of "sharing control" of the Holy Spirit, since they teach that the Holy Spirit is only a force, denying His personality.)

The major portion of Armstrong's argument concerning the new birth seems to be wrapped up in his claim that being born again means becoming spirit—and that no one is a spirit now. For example, he writes: "But, said Jesus plainly, when one is born of the Spirit HE WILL *BE* SPIRIT! Look at it! Read it in your own Bible.

"The Kingdom of God will be composed of SPIRIT BEINGS—not of humans!. . .

"When BORN AGAIN he will *BE* spirit—a spirit being, no longer human. . . .

"But we cannot BE spirit in this present age.

"THERE IS A TIME ELEMENT CONCERNED WITH BEING BORN AGAIN!. . .

"*Until* the resurrection, at Christ's coming, we shall not be changed from corruptible flesh into incorruptible SPIRIT (Paul—I Cor. 15:50-53 and verses 22-23).

"*Until* the resurrection, therefore, we cannot *see*, *enter* into, or *inherit* the Kingdom of God. WE CANNOT BE BORN AGAIN UNTIL THE RESURRECTION!

". . .When *born* of the Spirit, said Jesus, they shall BE spirit. . .

---

65. *Tomorrow's World*, February, 1971; "In the *Name* of Jesus"; p. 18
66. Op. cit.; p. 5

"Of the *first birth* we are, and remain, FLESH! HUMAN BEINGS!

"Of the *second birth,* which is spiritual, we shall BE spirit, no longer flesh—but SPIRIT beings—Divine Beings!"[67]

Notice that all of this is based upon a presumption that we are not now spirit beings—we are entirely flesh—but at that time we will be entirely spirit beings, not with physical bodies. That this presumptuous foundation is faulty is easily proven.

For one thing, Paul said in I Thessalonians 5:23: "And the very God of peace sanctify you wholly; and I pray God YOUR WHOLE SPIRIT and SOUL and BODY be preserved blameless unto the coming of our Lord Jesus Christ." Man is already spirit as well as body. He is not merely "flesh" today, with the possibility of being merely "spirit" in the future.

Neither will one be without a physical body in the resurrection. Our resurrection will be the same as our Lord's and He was raised with a physical body. After His resurrection, He said to His followers: "Behold my hands and my feet, that it is I myself: handle me, and see; for a spirit hath not flesh and bones, as ye see me have" (Luke 24:39). While we do not deny that the resurrection body will be a changed body, a spiritual body, nonetheless it will still be a physical body in the sense of "flesh and bones," a body capable of being "handled" by mortals.

The writers of the Worldwide Church of God do not at all mind twisting Scripture while attempting to prove a point. For example, I Peter 1:23 says: "Being born again, not of corruptible seed, but of incorruptible, by the word of God, which liveth and abideth for ever." Mr. Armstrong writes of this: "'Being born again. . .' (I Pet. 1:23). *Being*—in process of—not having *been*—

67. *Tomorrow's World,* October, 1971; "Just What Do You Mean. . .*Born Again?";* pp. 6,7, 44

not yet an immortal person—but *being* 'born again, not of corruptible seed, but of incorruptible. . . .' (Other translations use the term 'begotten.') *Greek: annagennao*—to begin anew—(Young). Peter is here referring to the process having *started* within us by the incorruptible Spirit of God—*not* as our human life was begotten by human physical sperm."[68]

But the simple truth of the matter is, Peter is not talking about something in the future—or even something in process now. He was discussing an experience that had already taken place.

Another writer in *Tomorrow's World* inadvertently acknowledges this fact through the use of another translation, saying: "'For you are sons of God now [in the process of being born again]: the live, permament Word of *the living God has given you his own indestructible HEREDITY*' (Phillips translation)."[69] Note with what suave nonchalance the writer makes a positive statement regarding something that has already happened ("*are* sons of God *now*"), then adds his own interpretation in brackets to entirely change the meaning, namely, "in process of being born again."

Armstrong has his own way of neutralizing the force of Peter's argument. Peter goes on to say, just a few verses further, "As newborn babes, desire the sincere milk of the word, that ye may grow thereby" (I Peter 2:2). Peter definitely describes these babies as already born, not merely unborn fetuses. What does Armstrong say of this? He passes it off as merely "an analogy."[70] But how is this the "likeness" of a fetus? Does a fetus desire milk? Whatever this "analogy" is the likeness of, it is the "analogy," the likeness of something ALREADY BORN!

In fact, Armstrong's claim that the new birth doesn't

---

68. Ibid.; p. 43
69. June, 1971; Robert L. Kuhn, "*Your* Destiny—*The God Family*"; p. 39
70. "Just What Do You Mean. . .*Born Again?*" op cit.; p. 43

happen until the resurrection—that the "convert" is just a "conception" up until then—gets him into serious trouble. For example, writing about the Christian life, he says: "But, as he WALKS this WAY of life, HE IS A 'BABE IN CHRIST,' actually *learning* to walk spiritually, just as a human baby must *learn to walk* physically. He must TRY not to fall, yet he is bound to fall down a few times along the road, learning to walk spiritually."[71]

Are we really to believe that a baby learns to walk before he is born? Mr. Armstrong wants the baby to be fully grown, able to walk, talk, and even "overcome" before he is born! What a strange kind of "birth" is this! In fact, it is the only case of "birth" we know of where the birth depends upon the unborn, rather than upon the parents.

Armstrong is not too clear about what happens when this "fetus" apostatizes. Since he teaches a "second chance" for his apostates in this life, if such took place and these individuals were "re-converted," would they be re-begotten, re-conceived, or what? They would not be re-born, since he doesn't believe in "birth" in this life. Would the same fetus be put back into the womb and given another start, would it be a "new" fetus, or what? Yes, we would be very much interested in knowing what happens to a Worldwide Church of God miscarriage.

Actually, to try making the new birth something which happens at the resurrection violates the entire Word of God. Just by way of example, note the language of the First Epistle of John. In I John 2:1 his remarks are addressed to "my little children. . ."; this is hardly an expression of the embryo or fetus. John does not even call them "babes," but "children"—small children, perhaps, but still children.

In I John 3:2, he says, "Beloved, now are we the

---

71. *What Do You Mean. . ."The Unpardonable Sin"?* p. 30

sons of God. . ." He does not say we *are going to be* sons some day at a resurrection (maybe!), but that we *are sons* right now.

In I John 3:10, he says: "In this the children of God are manifest, and the children of the devil. . ." Note that some are *right now* "the children of God" and some are *right now* "the children of the devil." He is not talking about the embryo or fetus, he is talking about "already born" children!

Some Christians are called "babes" (I Peter 2:2). Some are called "little children" (I John 2:1). Some are called "sons" (I John 3:2). But none is called a "fetus" or an "embryo"; this is merely a figment of Armstrong's overworked and highly active imagination. As a matter of fact, the writer of the Book of Hebrews speaks of those who "are of full age," no longer needing milk, but "strong meat" (Hebrews 5:14). It would be a little difficult to imagine "a fetus" being of full age and needing strong meat!

How much better to simply take the Bible at face value. John 1:11-13 says: "He came unto his own, and his own received him not. But as many as received him, to them gave he power to become the sons of God, even to them that believe on his name: Which were born, not of blood, nor of the will of the flesh, nor of the will of man, but of God." Note that those who received Christ during His ministry "WERE BORN." They were not *conceived,* they were *born.* They are not *going to be* born, they *have been* born.

Evangelicals everywhere have been shocked and angered by Armstrong's repeated insistence that Jesus "got saved," and that He needed to be "born again." To offset this criticism, Armstrong counters: "Emphatically this does NOT imply that Jesus was a sinner needing salvation. He was a pioneer, setting us the example, that we, too, may be BORN of God."[72]

---

72. "Just What Do You Mean. . .*Born Again?*" op cit.; p. 41

To this we reply, **Example of WHAT?**

If He did not need salvation as a sinner, why did He need salvation at all? He was not setting us an example of becoming a "Spirit Being," as Armstrong seems to indicate. He writes: "Jesus was, in the human flesh—His first birth—a descendant of David, and, by the resurrection from the dead—(born AGAIN)—the Son of God, now no longer human, but composed of SPIRIT—a Spirit Being. He thus became the FIRST SO BORN of many brethren who *shall be* BORN AGAIN at the time of the resurrection of those who are Christ's."[73]

But the truth of the matter is that Jesus *was* Spirit *before* coming into the world! He did not need to come into the world and be "born again" in order to *become* a Spirit Being.

Regarding the "firstborn" aspect, Armstrong likes to make that "first*born*," putting the emphasis on the birth. But he puts the emphasis on the wrong half: it should be *first*born. The Greek word is *prototokos* and it refers to POSITION, not chronology, as Armstrong repeatedly tries to make it. For example, in Colossians 1:15-19 (one of the five passages where *prototokos* is used of Christ), the reference relates back to eternity past—before creation—not something that chronologically took place through a resurrection.

To show that the new birth is a *present* experience—not something delayed until the resurrection—it might be well to point out what the believer *already has* in Christ. Homer Duncan lists "at least 72 stupendous transactions [which] take place the very moment a person exercises saving faith in Christ," adding he is "confident that a more thorough study of the Scriptures would enable the student to add" to it: **1.** We were lost (Luke 19:10); now we are saved (Matthew 1:21; Acts 16:31; Romans 1:16; Ephesians 2:8). **2.** We

73. Ibid.

were in Adam; now we are in Christ (I Corinthians 15:22; Ephesians 1:3,4,6,7,10,12). 3. We were spiritually dead (Ephesians 2:1); we now have everlasting life (John 5:24; I John 5:12). 4. We were condemned (John 3:18); now we are justified (Romans 3:28; 5:1). 5. We were enemies; now we are reconciled (Romans 5:10). 6. We were afar off; now we are made nigh (Ephesians 2:13). 7. We walked according to the course of this world (Ephesians 2:2); now we walk in Christ (Colossians 2:6) and in the Spirit (Galatians 5:16). 8. We were energized by Satanic power (Ephesians 2:2); we are now empowered by the Holy Spirit (Acts 1:8). 9. We were in the flesh; now we are in the Spirit (Romans 8:9). 10. We had our conversation (manner of life) in the lust of the flesh (Ephesians 2:3); we now have our conversation (manner of life) in Heaven (Philippians 3:20). 11. We walked according to the flesh (Ephesians 2:2,3); we now live in and walk in the Spirit (Galatians 5:16,25). 12. We were interested in the things of the flesh; now we are interested in the things of the Spirit (Romans 8:5). 13. We were carnally minded; now we are spiritually minded (Romans 8:6). 14. We could not please God (Romans 8:8); now we desire to please God and to please Christ (II Timothy 2:4). 15. We were under the law of sin and death; now we are made free from the law of sin and death (Romans 8:2). 16. We lived in the spirit of bondage and fear; now we have the spirit of adoption (Romans 8:15). 17. We were by nature the children of wrath (Ephesians 2:3); now we are the children of God (I John 3:2). 18. We were without Christ; now we are in Christ (Ephesians 2:13). 19. We were aliens from the commonwealth of Israel (Ephesians 2:12); now we are children in the family of God (Romans 8:17). 20. We were strangers from the covenants of promise (Ephesians 2:12); we now have exceeding great and precious promises (II Peter 1:4). 21. We were without peace (Isaiah 57:20,21); now Christ is our peace

(Ephesians 2:14), we have peace with God (Romans 5:1), and the peace of God that passeth all understanding keeps our hearts and minds in Christ (Philippians 4:6,7). 22. We were without hope (Ephesians 2:12); now we are saved by hope (Romans 8:24). 23. We were part of the old creation; now we are new creatures in Christ (II Corinthians 5:17). 24. We were as slaves in the market place of sin (Romans 7:14); now we are redeemed from the market place of sin (Galatians 4:5). 25. We were under the curse of the law; now we are redeemed from the curse of the law (Galatians 3:13). 26. We were born of the flesh; now we are born of the Spirit (John 3:5). 27. We were building on shifting sands; now we are building on Christ (Ephesians 2:20; I Corinthians 3:11,12). 28. We were scattered individuals or were held together by human organization; now we are builded together for a habitation of God through the Spirit (Ephesians 2:22). 29. We sought for happiness; now we have joy (John 16:22). 30. We lived in fear of death; now we are delivered from the fear of death (Hebrews 2:15). 31. We were under the wrath of God; now we are delivered from the wrath of God (I Thessalonians 1:10). 32. We were prisoners of Satan (Isaiah 14:17; 61:1); now we are free in Christ (John 8:36). 33. We were slaves to sin (John 8:34); now we are made partakers of the divine nature (II Peter 1:4). 34. We were a part of the Satanic world system (Galatians 1:4); now we are in the kingdom of His dear Son (Colossians 1:13). 35. We were in the power of darkness (Colossians 1:13); now we are light in the Lord (Ephesians 5:8). 36. We are in God the Father (I John 4:15,16). 37. We are in the Lord Jesus Christ (Ephesians 1:3). 38. We are in the Holy Spirit (Galatians 5:25). 39. God the Father is in us (Ephesians 4:6; I John 4:12,16). 40. The Lord Jesus Christ is in us (Colossians 1:27). 41. The Holy Spirit is in us (I Corinthians 6:19). 42. We were adopted as adult sons into the family of God (Ephesians 1:4,5). **43.** We became heirs of God and joint-heirs with Jesus Christ (Romans 8:17). **44.** We have access to God (Romans 5:2; Ephesians 2:18; Hebrews 4:16). **45.** We are accepted in Christ (Ephesians 1:6). **46.** We were crucified with Christ (Romans 6:6; Galatians 2:20). **47.** We were raised with Christ (Ephesians 2:6). **48.** We ascended with Him (Ephesians 2:6). **49.** We are seated with Him (Ephesians 2:6). **50.** We are now reigning with Him (Romans 5:17). **51.** We are blessed with every spiritual blessing in Him (Ephesians 1:3). **52.** We are complete in Him (Colossians 2:10). **53.** We are married to Christ (Romans 7:4). **54.** We are delivered from so great a death (II Corinthians 1:10). **55.** Christ is made unto us wisdom (I Corinthians 1:30). **56.** Christ is made unto righteousness (I Corinthians 1:30; II Corinthians 5:21; Philippians 3:9). **57.** Christ is made unto us sanctification (I Corinthians 1:30). **58.** Christ is made unto us redemption (I Corinthians 1:30). **59.** We were made a royal priesthood (I Peter 2:9). **60.** We were made a chosen generation (I Peter 2:9). **61.** We were made a holy nation (I Peter 2:9). **62.** We were made a peculiar people (I Peter 2:9). **63.** We were made heavenly citizens (Philippians 3:20). **64.** We have a High Priest (Hebrews 4:14; 8:1). **65.** We have a minister of the New Covenant (Hebrews 8:6). **66.** We have a new hope (Hebrews 6:19). **67.** We have an anchor for our soul (Hebrews 6:19). **68.** We have rest (Hebrews 4:9,11). **69.** We have an inheritance (Ephesians 1:11; I Peter 1:4). **70.** We are born of the Spirit (John 3:3,5). **71.** We are baptized by the Spirit into the body of Christ (I Corinthians 12:13). **72.** We are sealed by the Spirit (Ephesians 4:30).[74]

Does all this sound like the one trusting Christ is "not yet born"? Does this impressive list of *present*

---

74. *So Great Salvation,* Homer Duncan; n.d.; Missionary Crusader, Lubbock, Texas; pp. 10-15

tense inheritance sound like the believer can only *hope* that someday, sometime, somehow, in the next life, maybe, if he "overcomes," salvation may eventually be his? To ask these questions in the light of the above Scriptures is to answer them.

Armstrong's "Election"

The Worldwide Church of God's theory regarding election would make a hyper-Calvinist green with envy. It is so extreme John Calvin looks like an Arminian by comparison! According to Armstrong, God doesn't really want to save people in this age and He is only "electing" a very limited few. It is a strange philosophy indeed. As one writer says: "Unless God *elects* or *selects* an individual to be CALLED AT THIS TIME, unless God expands his mind to discern real spiritual truth, he remains blinded."[75]

While we have already dealt with this odd belief elsewhere, an additional word might be helpful. A writer in *Tomorrow's World*, claiming God doesn't want many people saved in this age, says: "True Christians know and understand that God is the One who calls and converts people (John 6:44). They recognize, therefore, that it would be completely futile—and actually contrary to God's will—to go out and attempt to win converts by force."[76]

Another one of the cult's writers says God did not want to save many from among the multitudes to whom Paul ministered. He insists: "Most who heard Paul preach were not being called by God—yet he talked their language so they would listen long enough to hear his witness. And for the few whom God was calling, Paul used terms they understood so they would not be offended or held back in any way."[77]

---

75. *Tomorrow's World,* July, 1971; Richard A. Wiedenheft, "Why Christ Spoke in Parables"; p. 15
76. July-August, 1970; G. Fribergs; p. 33
77. *Be Seen And Not Heard,* Richard A. Wiedenheft; © 1971, 1972; p. 5

This, of course, puts the blame for people not being converted squarely upon God. One of the cult's writers acknowledges this, bluntly declaring: "God himself has blinded the eyes of many to the truth at this time (Rom. 11:7,8). It is His *responsibility* that they don't know the truth yet."[78]

The Armstrongites, however, unlike the extreme Calvinists of our day, get God "off the hook" regarding His indifference to the plight of the non-elect by saying He is going to give them a full opportunity to get saved in the next world. We will deal with that claim before the chapter is concluded.

The "Security" of the Believer

According to the Worldwide Church of God's doctrine of salvation, no believer has any security whatsoever. We opened this chapter showing that even the leaders have no assurance of eventual salvation. In fact, members are warned, "To cause another human being to LOSE SALVATION is the most dastardly act a person can commit."[79] Since the cult teaches no one but Christ has yet reached salvation status, just how someone can commit this dastardly deed of causing another to *lose* something he *doesn't have* isn't quite clear.

Mr. Armstrong explains this insecurity as follows: "During our converted human Christian life, we are already children of God, as yet unborn. We have within us through the gift of the Holy Spirit, the presence of ETERNAL LIFE—Spirit life—divine life—BUT, only from and through GOD. We do not, yet, have any eternal life *inherent*—of *ourselves*, independent of God. And, WE COULD LOSE IT—be aborted!

"This compares to the unborn physical fetus, in the gestation period. It has human life—but only through

78. *The Answer to Unanswered Prayer,* Roderick C. Meredith; ©1956,1970; p. 3
79. *The Plain Truth,* October, 1958; Garner Ted Armstrong, "*Who* Should *God's* Ministers Be?"; p. 15

the umbilical cord and FROM the mother—NOT independently of itself. And it can be aborted!"[80]

In his booklet on the unpardonable sin, Armstrong says: "A Christian, then, in GOD'S terms, is one who has, at the moment, God's HOLY SPIRIT dwelling in him.

"BEFORE this change has taken place, he is NONE OF HIS—*not* a Christian. *IF* the Holy Spirit *no longer dwells* in him, then he is no longer a Christian. He is a Christian *while*, and *only while*, the Holy Spirit is dwelling in him.

". . .There is, however, a limit somewhere along life's way where, unless you are definitely GROWING spiritually, that God's Spirit will no longer 'dwell in you,' and if you let that time come, you shall, like a dead grape branch, be ultimately cast into the final 'Gehenna fire'."[81]

Later in the booklet, Armstrong describes how someone can lose salvation. He writes: "I want to be even more specific. I want every reader to UNDERSTAND. And I feel very few DO fully understand this question.

"There are at least TWO ways in which a Spirit-begotten Christian may LOSE the gift of God's Holy Spirit.

"1) By deliberate choice. This may come from wrong reasoning; from wrong desire thought out to a final fixed, permanent decision as to his WAY OF LIFE; or, from allowing *resentment* in his heart toward either God or some person who may have wronged him. To allow resentment to embitter him, until he comes to change his whole life course, turning from God. . . .

"2) The converted Christian can *lose* the presence of God's Spirit by CONTINUED NEGLECT. Neglect of prayer, neglect of Bible study, neglect of spiritual fellowship with God's people. Or, by continuing too

---

80. "Just What Do You Mean. . .*Born Again?*" op. cit.; p. 43
81. *What Do You Mean. . ."The Unpardonable Sin"?* pp. 8,10

close a friendship with unconverted people—letting participation with them and material interest, pleasures, sports, entertainments, cause NEGLECT of spiritual interests. . . ."[82]

We wonder from this if Armstrong doesn't believe God's "pledge" to be any good. Note his acknowledgement in the following passage: "The receiving of the Holy Spirit, NOW, is the TOKEN PAYMENT—or the EARNEST payment from God on the gift of eternal life. Notice: '. . .Christ. . .in whom also after that ye believed, ye were sealed with that Holy Spirit of promise, which is the *earnest of* our INHERITANCE, *until* the redemption of the purchased possession. . .' (Eph. 1:12-14). The Moffatt translation renders it in more understandable English, '. . .the long-promised Holy Spirit, which is the pledge and installment of our common heritage, that we *may* [in the future] *obtain* our divine possession. . . .' "[83]

In other words, the very gift of the Holy Spirit is God's guarantee (His "pledge," His "earnest") that the believer will eventually receive the *entire* "purchased possession."

This, thank God, is exactly the case! In the words of Paul: "Being confident of this very thing, that he which hath begun a good work in you will perform it until the day of Jesus Christ" (Philippians 1:6).

Armstrong's "Second Chance" After Death

According to the Worldwide Church of God, the wicked, lustful Sodomites will be raised from the dead and given an opportunity to obtain eternal life. So will the wicked inhabitants of ancient Tyre and Sidon. All the hardened, ancient Israelites of ages past will be raised from the dead and granted the offer of everlasting redemption. In fact, some of the wickedest

82. Ibid.; pp. 32,33
83. *What'll You Be Doing In The Next Life?* p. 3

sinners of all ages will be resurrected from the dead and offered an opportunity to be saved, according to Armstrong.

In the cult's Bible story book, written by Basil Wolverton, words are put into the mouth of Jehovah, telling Noah that, although He must destroy man because of his sin, He will give him another opportunity centuries later. The little readers are told: "It was a loving and merciful thing God planned, because He would be bringing them back to life thousands of years later when Jesus Christ would be ruling Earth. Then they would be brought to see how much wiser, safer and happier they could be by obeying their Creator. . . .

"One day Noah was startled to hear the Eternal speaking to him. Said God, 'Because man has disobeyed me and become so evil, and because people's lives are so miserable and unhappy in all their violence and fighting, I am going to take away their lives for now. But I shall bring them all back to life again in the future when my Son Jesus will be ruling Earth, and when people will live by my rules and be happy.' "[84]

A *Tomorrow's World* article puts it bluntly: "The Bible makes very plain the fact that the vast majority of all humanity will receive its opportunity—its first and only opportunity for salvation—in the future."[85]

Garner Ted Armstrong, with his usual sarcastic sneer, says: "Does it make *sense to you* that millions of people could be sent to a supposedly 'ever-burning hellfire,' helplessly and uselessly beating at the flames that threaten to engulf them, shrieking in hideous and all-consuming agony forever and ever and ever—*for all eternity*, just because a missionary had a flat tire?"[86] (No! It will be because of their own deliberate

---

84. *The Plain Truth,* January, 1959; pp. 19,20
85. July, 1971; Richard A. Wiedenheft, "Why Christ Spoke in Parables"; p. 15
86. *What Is Death?* ©1966,1967,1969,1970,1971; p. 5

sin, willful rebellion against God and rejection of the light He gave them!)

Another *Tomorrow's World* author put it like this: "When Jesus Christ returns to this earth in the very next few years, He will *for the first time* in mankind's history set His hand to save the whole world—that is, all people who are alive on the earth at that time. He will offer them the same salvation that He has in the past only offered to a few whom He hath called out *out of* the world. Then, at the close of a thousand years of this reign, all of those who have ever died, but never had a chance to know the true Jesus and His true Gospel message, will be resurrected and given their ONE opportunity to obey and by the strength of God's Holy Spirit to enter into His Kingdom!"[87]

In talking about how almost everyone will eventually be saved (the theory borders on, but never quite crosses the line of, universalism), the writer continues: "There have been, and there will be, however, some few who will utterly REBEL against doing God's will—who will set their wills against obedience to His laws so completely that *nothing can be done with them.*"[88]

Yet how contrary this is to what Jesus Himself said in Matthew 7:13,14: "Enter ye in at the strait gate: for wide is the gate, and broad is the way, that leadeth to destruction, and MANY there be which go in thereat: Because strait is the gate, and narrow is the way, which leadeth unto life, and FEW there be that find it."

A writer in *Tomorrow's World*, after quoting Revelation 20:12, says: "Notice. This is a resurrection to life. The book of LIFE was opened. Those coming up in this resurrection will be judged 'according to their works'! This is not a resurrection to condemnation.

87. *There Is A Real Hell Fire;* p. 6
88. Ibid.; pp. 6,7

Rather, these people will be the uncountable billions who lived and died in this life, who never even had a chance for salvation—those who lived and died in ignorance, those who never even heard the true Gospel of Christ during their lives! At that time they will be given a period of time in which God will open their eyes, show them His truth, and give them their *first* and *only* chance for salvation!"[89]

How in the world the writer gets both a resurrection and an opportunity for salvation from that verse is beyond the bounds of most people's imagination. In order to see what God is saying in the context, here is the entire passage: "And I saw a great white throne, and him that sat on it, from whose face the earth and the heaven fled away; and there was found no place for them. And I saw the dead, small and great, stand before God; and the books were opened: and another book was opened, which is the book of life: and the dead were judged out of those things which were written in the books, according to their works. And the sea gave up the dead which were in it; and death and hell delivered up the dead which were in them: and they were judged every man according to their works. And death and hell were cast into the lake of fire. This is the second death. And whosoever was not found written in the book of life was cast into the lake of fire" (Revelation 20:11-15). Can you see any opportunity for anyone getting saved in that passage? This is one more example of the extremes to which the imaginations of wicked men can take them.

Still another author of the Worldwide Church of God declares: "Many millions of people have lived and died without ever hearing the name of Jesus Christ. What about those people? What about little babies that live

89. July-August, 1970; William F. Dankenbring, "What Is This Place Called *Hell?*"; p. 17

only a few hours? Has God caused them to be doomed? What about the millions living under atheistic Communism? Are they lost forever?

"ABSOLUTELY NOT! EVERYONE will have a chance!

"The *shocking* fact is, *God is not trying to get everyone saved now!*

"It is a lack of understanding of God's plan that causes the evangelist to shout: 'Give your heart to the Lord before it's too late!' The inspired Word of God reveals that NO ONE can come to Jesus Christ UNLESS THE FATHER SPECIFICALLY CALLS HIM (John 6:44).

"In other words, this IS NOT THE ONLY DAY OF SALVATION!! This is an absolute fact of your Bible.

"All those who are *not* now called, or given a chance for salvation, will come up in the *second* resurrection. They will come up as physical human beings and be given their one and only chance for salvation. This resurrection takes place one thousand years later, after what Bible students call 'the millennium.'"[90]

This appears to us as if God were going to an awful lot of trouble when He could have given these people the opportunity of being saved in this age! But that is a minor matter to the Armstrongs, who accuse God of *deliberately* confusing people today, for Carrozzo went on to say: "God purposely wrote His Word so that it could be misunderstood. He intended that only those whom He is calling and choosing will understand."

Armstrong and his followers are very dogmatic and insistent that they are not talking about a "second chance." In what is probably one of the plainest statements of the doctrine we have seen, C. Paul Meredith declares: "This scene in Revelation 20 pictures the climax of God's plan—the great white throne judgment, when the vast number of unsaved dead will be resur-

---

90. *Tomorrow's World,* May, 1971; Alfred E. Carrozzo, "Is God Calling You?"; p. 31

rected and be given their first chance for salvation—all those millions and millions who have lived and died since the time of Adam up through our age, and have not known the true way to eternal life!

"Salvation will be open to all then resurrected, just as in the thousand-year reign of Christ on earth, only now there will be many more to accept it after the millennium.

"This will not be a SECOND CHANCE! Here is why: If they were blinded by God when they formerly lived, they never had a first chance! The ancient inhabitants of Tyre and Sidon will be resurrected and those evil people who were formerly blinded will be given their first chance (Matthew 11:22). Also, the people of Sodom and Gomorrah will be resurrected (Matthew 10:15), and their evil citizens will have their first chance. God is a just God. He is giving even the worst of the people who were blinded before Christ's second coming their first opportunity to receive salvation!"[91]

What a twisted, perverted picture of the actual truth he presents! The people referred to by Meredith were blinded because of their own deliberate sin and their willful rejection of what light God had already given them. We trust our readers will read the texts in the above paragraph (Matthew 11:22 and Matthew 10:15), and see if there is anything about an opportunity to be saved in either one of those passages. Quite the contrary is the case. Once again, we have a writer's wishful imagination working overtime.

Talking about Israel, Garner Ted Armstrong declares: "God has a TIME SCHEDULE He is working out. He WILL finally give all those ancient Israelites—whose hearts were hardened, who DID NOT KNOW the way to salvation—their FIRST chance!"[92]

His proof?

---

91. *Is This The Only Day Of Salvation?* p. 4
92. *What Is Death?* p. 6

He goes on: "Notice it. 'And SO ALL ISRAEL *SHALL BE SAVED*'! (Rom. 11:26.)"[93]

However, if the reader will trouble himself to check Romans 11, he will discover that this is not talking about the Israelites of ages *past*, but the Israelites *alive at the time Christ comes back to earth*, when the times of the Gentiles have been completed. There is not the slightest suggestion in Romans 11 that dead Israelites are going to be resurrected and given an opportunity to be saved. Again, it is merely the imagination of the writer.

In one of the "Answers" columns of *Tomorrow's World*, when a reader wrote to inquire about Armstrong's "third resurrection," the answer was, in part: "The second category of people is the millions and billions of individuals who never heard or understood the Gospel, never had a chance or opportunity for salvation during their lifetime. They are referred to as the *'rest of the DEAD'* in Rev. 20:5 who 'live not again UNTIL the thousand years were finished.' They will be resurrected to *physical* life and given their *first* opportunity for salvation (no 'second chance' doctrine here) in what is called the Great White Throne Judgment. See Ezek. 37:1-6; Rev. 20:11-12; Luke 10:12-14. Notice that in Ezek. 37:5-6 a resurrection to *physical* life is referred to because these people will have sinews, flesh, and breath. This is obviously NOT the *first* resurrection."[94]

Ignoring for the moment Ezekiel's meaning in that passage, we invite our readers to look up and read carefully each Scripture reference given in the paragraph above. While some of them do refer to a resurrection, in not a one will you find someone being given an opportunity to be saved after that resurrection. It is simply the imagination of the writer.

93. Ibid.
94. August, 1971; p. 43

Coming back for a moment to the passage in Revelation 20 and the claim of the cult that the opening of the book of life is an opportunity to get saved, Meredith quotes verses 11 and 12, putting in the familiar brackets, of course, as follows: "And I saw a great white throne. . .and I saw the dead, small and great, stand before God [these people are standing—a resurrection]. . .and another book was opened, which is the book of life [they are given life]; and the dead were judged out of those things which were written in the books."[95]

This is so completely out of context and so thoroughly out of harmony with what the passage is saying, it would be hilarious if not so tragic. In fact, just a couple of verses further, Meredith's theory is annihilated, since we read: "And whosoever was not found written in the book of life was cast into the lake of fire" (vs. 15). So, rather than being given an opportunity for salvation, these individuals are proved to be worthy of eternal judgment on the basis that their names are not written in the Book of Life. An interesting sidelight to Meredith's bracket insertion "they are given life"—a positive declaration—is that on another occasion, quoting the same verses, his bracket insertion at the same spot was merely "there is a chance of obtaining eternal life"—something entirely different.[96]

One of Armstrong's writers attempts to prove their thesis by referring to the parable of the wheat and the tares in Matthew 13. He says: "At the end of the thousand years, during which time Christ has been ruling the world and the earth has been full of the knowledge of the Eternal (a condition that certainly has not been present up to now), there will be another resurrection!

95. *If You Die. . .Will You Live Again?* p. 7
96. *Is This The Only Day Of Salvation?* p. 4

"Matthew 13:24 through 30 and verses 36 through 42 (the parable of the tares), describes this harvest! Note verse 30: 'Let both grow together until the harvest.'

"Also note verse 39: '. . .The harvest is the end of the world'—or consummation of the age—the one thousand-year age and the time of resurrection which will follow. Matthew 25:31 to 34 describes the salvation of the world during the millennium and this resurrection also!"[97]

What does this have to do with the subject? Is the writer trying to say that tares are going to have an opportunity to turn into wheat? Or does the passage say what evangelical Christianity has always understood it to say: that converted and unconverted will continue on the earth till Jesus comes, so the converted ought not to try to "pull up"—to kill, to execute God's vengeance and judgment on them now, in this life—the unconverted? We are confident that any honest reader of the passage will conclude the latter.

Before we leave the Armstrong doctrine of a second chance, perhaps we should point out that when Armstrong and his adherents speak of a "first chance," they are not talking about hearing "the gospel" as it has been universally understood. They are talking about their particular brand of the gospel and their particular message. This eliminates everyone from apostolic days down to the time Herbert W. Armstrong stepped to the microphone in Eugene, Oregon, and began his ministry in 1934. About the only ones they eliminate from this second chance are those who have heard the Armstrong message and rejected it. We rather doubt the cult holds much hope for this writer.

Armstrong himself, incidentally, would acknowledge that the whole thesis of an opportunity for salvation

---

97. *If You Die. . .Will You Live Again?* p. 7

after death hinges on the premise that it is not a "second chance." In other words, he must maintain that it is a "first chance." For one to disprove that thesis would be to disprove the whole argument.

Believe me, it is very simple to disprove. As Paul said in Romans 1:18-20: "For the wrath of God is revealed from heaven against all ungodliness and unrighteousness of men, who hold the truth in unrighteousness; Because that which may be known of God is manifest in them; for God hath shewed it unto them. For the invisible things of him from the creation of the world are clearly seen, being understood by the things that are made, even his eternal power and Godhead; **so that they are without excuse.**"

There it is! As Armstrong would say, "It is in your Bible! Read it and believe it!"

The entire world, through God's creation—apart from the Word of God—has enough light so that every lost man will be completely "without excuse" when he stands before God. This is what the Bible teaches and this is what true Christendom has always accepted as PLAIN TRUTH!

CHAPTER VI

The Armstrong Teaching About Legalism

Herbert W. Armstrong and his Worldwide Church of God teach and preach that the Old Testament law is every bit as binding upon God's people today as it was when first given to the young nation Israel, under Moses. His hearers — and all the world who will listen — are warned that evangelical Christendom disagrees only because her ministers preach for money and, therefore, tell the people what they want to hear. Armstrong says: "There is just one thing, it seems, that most of Satan's ministers can agree upon. 'God's LAW' they chorus in unison, 'is DONE AWAY!' Yes, they have to tell that in order to draw their salaries! Today the people of organized religion refuse to HEAR the Law of the Lord (Isa. 30:8-11). They demand that their ministers preach the soft and smooth things — the deceits! They have turned away from the TRUTH, and are accepting and believing FABLES (II Tim. 4:2-4). They are BITTER against God's Law, and against the few who have courage today to proclaim the PLAIN TRUTH of God's Word!"[1]

The Worldwide Church of God's position on legalism is so strong and so complete one of his ex-followers refers to it, for want of a better word, as "baptized Judaism!"[2] When Armstrong speaks about being under the law, he means all of the law! He is a strict legalist, insisting that followers of the Eternal in this age are to observe even the "holy days" of the Old Testament. Ignoring the fact that Paul calls this "bondage" to "weak and beggarly elements," Armstrong says: "Passover, the days of unleavened bread, Pente-

---

1. *Tomorrow's World,* February, 1971; "Is God Fair?"; p. 4
2. *The Armstrong Error,* Charles F. DeLoach; © 1971; Logos International, Plainfield, New Jersey; p. 19

cost, and the holy days God had ordained *forever* were all observed by Jesus, and the early apostles, and the converted Gentile Christians (Acts 2:1; 12:3; 20:6; 18:21; I Cor. 5:7-8; Acts 20:16; I Cor. 16:8)."[3]

However, in checking his "proof" references, one immediately observes that there is not the slightest intimation that Jesus, the early apostles, or the converted Gentile Christians observed these holy days. The only exception might be Acts 18:21 and, obviously, Paul was not referring there to keeping a legalistic feast. He was simply expressing his hope to reach Jerusalem in time to proclaim the liberating Gospel to those in Judaistic bondage from all over the known world who would be assembling for the observance of that feast at that particular time.

Mr. Armstrong ignores the fact that this same Apostle Paul wrote a letter to some others who were confused about legalism, specifically stating to them: "Howbeit then, when ye knew not God, ye did service unto them which by nature are no gods. But now, after that ye have known God, or rather are known of God, how turn ye again to the weak and beggarly elements, whereunto ye desire again to be in bondage? Ye observe days, and months, and times, and years. I am afraid of you, lest I have bestowed upon you labour in vain" (Galatians 4:8-11).

A sample of Armstrong's dishonest twisting of Scripture to serve his purpose is noted in the use of Acts 2:1 as a proof text for the statement that the apostles and early Christians observed Pentecost. It is a simple matter to turn to Leviticus 23:15-22 and discover what the observance of Pentecost involved. Obviously, the apostles and early Christians who were assembled "with one accord in one place" were *not* observing that holy day in the legalistic sense. In like manner, his

---

3. *Easter Is Pagan,* Written Anonymously; Copyright, 1952; p. 4

proof text in I Corinthians 5:7,8 actually teaches the exact opposite of a *literal* holy day observance. It is significant to note that he does not bother to explain how it would be possible to *literally* eat "the unleavened bread of sincerity and truth."

One of Armstrong's chief writers, arguing for twentieth century legalism, declared: "Any honest Bible student knows that throughout the Old Testament—even from the time of Abraham—God required men to OBEY *His commandments* in order to receive His blessings. All ten of the Ten Commandments were in *force* and *effect*. But somehow, men reason, this is *no longer* the Father's will. Many argue that Jesus came to *do away* with God's law—to nail it to His cross.

"However, when a young man came to ask Him how to inherit eternal life, Jesus Himself answered: 'Why callest thou me good? There is none good but one, that is, God: But *if thou wilt enter into life*, KEEP *the commandments*!' (Matt. 19:16-17). Then Jesus showed which commandments He meant by naming some of the Ten Commandments (verses 18-19).

"In literally *hundreds* of places in your New Testament, Jesus Christ and His inspired apostles teach absolute OBEDIENCE to *all ten* of the Ten Commandments!"[4]

Note the twisting and distortion of Scripture in the above. Meredith makes a true statement (that God's blessings in a life hinge on obedience to His commands), then ties the truth into a blatant misrepresentation (that when the Scripture speaks of God's commandments it always means the Ten Commandments), capping it off with a historical falsehood, completely unsubstantiated by the Word of God (that the Ten Commandments, as such, were known to

---

4. *The Plain Truth,* November, 1959; Roderick C. Meredith, "*Revival* in Our Time?"; p. 18

Abraham; they were not given by God until centuries later through Moses).

Note also his deceitful handling of the incident relating to our Lord and the rich young ruler. Meredith does not quote the passage; he merely infers that Jesus meant ALL of the Ten Commandments because He quoted SOME of them. Probably this is because Christ did not mention the Sabbath as one of the commands. While we are not interested here in the exegesis of the passage, we think it is of special import to note that Christ did not mention one single commandment pertaining to the young man's responsibility to God. In this instance, He mentioned only those relating to the ruler's responsibilities to his fellow man.

One thing further: Meredith's preposterous statement, "In literally *hundreds* of places in your New Testament, Jesus Christ and His inspired apostles teach absolute OBEDIENCE to *all ten* of the Ten Commandments," is probably one of the most blatant, unprovable falsehoods we have ever seen from the pen of a religious writer—*anywhere*! For example, although on occasion there are commands relating to the other nine commandments, *not one single time in the New Testament is there a command regarding seventh-day Sabbath observance*! Even if Meredith counted every time in the New Testament *any* commandment keeping was enjoined—whether pertaining to the ten, or a commandment about prayer, soul winning, etc.—he could not come up with "hundreds"—a fact regarding which he is probably well aware.

What about the clear teaching of the Bible that Christians of this dispensation are not under the law? As Paul wrote to the church at Rome: "For sin shall not have dominion over you: for ye are not under the law, but under grace. What then? shall we sin, because we are not under the law, but under grace? God forbid" (Romans 6:14,15). To Armstrong, being "under the law" merely means that "the law stood over you, claiming its penalty."[5]

This, of course, makes little sense in the light of what Paul had previously told the same church: "Now we know that what things soever the law saith, it saith to them who are under the law. . ." (Romans 3:19). In other words, if being "under the law" means only being under its penalty, then once the individual is freed from the penalty, the law has *nothing* more to say to him. This certainly is not what Armstrong would accept.

Isn't it strange, thinking of the legalism taught by the Worldwide Church of God, how people can look into a mirror and not recognize themselves? A writer in *Tomorrow's World*, discussing how the gospel message has been polluted by myriads of false teachers, declared: "Paul, too, *knew* there would be those who would PERVERT the Gospel of Christ and he *thundered* against them—saying they were 'ACCURSED' (Gal. 1:7-9)."[6] Yet the context of the Book of Galatians will show it was written to answer those who were teaching about the Law the very things Armstrong and his followers teach about it today.

In discussing their brand of legalism, Mr. Armstrong and his writers love to set up straw men and then attack them. One of their favorites is that people today have rejected the law on the basis "no one can keep it." After setting up that straw man on one occasion, Armstrong said: "Think! Could a just God command men to do what is IMPOSSIBLE to do? Or can we conceive of Jesus as a smart-aleck young man who knew more than His FATHER, and who did away with His Father's COMMANDMENTS? How absurd! Yet this is the popular conception today!"[7]

---

5. *The Plain Truth,* July, 1961; "Just What Do You *Mean—Salvation?"*; p. 38
6. July-August, 1970; Clint C. Zimmerman, "Gospel Pollution"; p. 46
7. *Tomorrow's World,* August, 1971; "What Kind of *Faith* Is Required for *Salvation?"*; pp. 4,5

This, however, is not the point. The law was given, not as a standard of perfection for us to measure up to and live by, but to point out how hopeless and helpless we were to live by such standards because of our sinful, depraved natures. Romans 3:19,20 declares: "Now we know that what things soever the law saith, it saith to them who are under the law; that every mouth may be stopped, and all the world may become guilty before God. Therefore by the deeds of the law there shall no flesh be justified in his sight: for by the law is the knowledge of sin." As sinners look into the mirror of God's law, they see how dirty they are and how desperately they need a cleansing. Then—and only then—are they ready for the blood of Christ to be applied.

Paul said again, having in mind men like Armstrong: "Desiring to be teachers of the law; understanding neither what they say, nor whereof they affirm. But we know that the law is good, if a man use it lawfully; Knowing this, that the law is not made for a righteous man, but for the lawless and disobedient, for the ungodly and for sinners, for unholy and profane, for murderers of fathers and murderers of mothers, for manslayers, For whoremongers, for them that defile themselves with mankind, for menstealers, for liars, for perjured persons, and if there be any other thing that is contrary to sound doctrine" (I Timothy 1:7-10).

Another favorite ploy of the Armstrongs is to say those who teach we are not under law but under grace are "destroying" the law—then triumphantly quote the Lord's words in Matthew 5:17,18 to disprove it: "Think not that I am come to destroy the law, or the prophets: I am not come to destroy, but to fulfil. For verily I say unto you, Till heaven and earth pass, one jot or one tittle shall in no wise pass from the law, till all be fulfilled."

Al Kersha, writing in *Tomorrow's World,* makes a typical statement: "So contrary to popular belief, He came not to destroy, but to fulfil or MAGNIFY the very Law that *He Himself wrote* on two tables of stone at Mount Sinai over fourteen centuries previously. As any honest scientist knows, to magnify does not mean to destroy, but to *show forth* and enlarge an object or thing to the fullest possible extent."[8]

This is begging the issue. The point is that Jesus "fulfilled" the law and fulfilling is not destroying. If this writer entered into a contract with Ambassador College to provide 5,000 copies of this book at a special price of $1 per copy, then delivered the 5,000 copies and picked up a check for $5,000, could the college charge him with destroying the contract? Hardly. The contract would have been fulfilled, not destroyed.

Jesus came to fulfill the law and this is exactly what He did. Paul says in Romans 10:4: "For Christ is the end of the law for righteousness to every one that believeth." He is the only One who ever lived the law perfectly. He fulfilled it. He kept it.

As a matter of fact, Mr. Kersha, in the above-mentioned article, acknowledges that the Greek word translated in Matthew 5:17 *fulfil* includes "*do* or *perform*" in its meaning.[9] The guarantee that one jot or one tittle would not pass from the law was only *until* the law had been fulfilled. It *has been* fulfilled. Jesus came to do this, *and do it He did*!

Armstrong's Understanding of the Law

While the Worldwide Church of God leaders make a strong distinction between the Ten Commandment Law (which they call the Law of God), and the rest of the Law (which they call the Law of Moses), they do not make the distinction which Christendom has

8. November, 1971; "How Did Christ Magnify the Law?"; p. 23
9. Ibid.

made down through the centuries between the *moral* and the *ceremonial* law. Evangelicals, of course, believe that the moral law is every bit as binding today as it has ever been. They teach that the ceremonial law, which was the *shadow* of Christ, has been fulfilled in His coming, the *substance.* But the Armstrongites, in their usual deceptive manner, attack the straw man they set up, pretending that evangelicals are now in favor of adultery, murder and other violations of God's moral law.

As a sample of this amazingly dishonest distortion, here is Mr. Armstrong's comment regarding Romans 7:7: "When God inspired that question, He knew that multiple thousands of professing clergy of today's deceived 'Christianity' would be saying that God's Law is EVIL—it is BAD—it is a yoke of BONDAGE—that it is bad for us—that Jesus 'nailed it to His cross'—that that 'terrible Law' is 'done away.' So God inspired the ANSWER: '*By no means*!'. . .

"Yes indeed—it is a SPIRITUAL Law—a Law of SPIRITUAL PRINCIPLES of living—the HOLY, GOOD, SPIRITUAL WAY OF LIFE! Yet God says the CARNAL mind hates it—is hostile to it, not subject to it (Rom. 8:7). According to THAT inspired Word of GOD, a vast segment of the clergy professing 'Christianity' is CARNAL minded! Tragic, but true!"[10]

Regarding the distinction between the Ten Commandments and the rest of God's Law, Armstrong says: "You will remember that *to the Ten Commandment law, God added no more* (Deut. 5:22). Any other law, or Covenant, coming later, is NO PART OF IT, but a separate law or Covenant. Paul makes this plain: 'Though it be but a man's covenant, yet if it be confirmed, no man disannulleth it, or addeth thereto' (Gal. 3:15)."[11]

---

10. *What Do You Mean. . . "The Unpardonable Sin"?* ©1967,1971,1972; p. 14
11. *Which Day Is The Christian Sabbath?* ©1962,1964,1968,1970,1971; p. 51

While we have already dealt with Armstrong's false distinction between the "Law of Moses" and the "Law of the Lord" in a previous chapter, we might point out here that Ezra 7:6 describes Ezra as "a ready scribe in *the law of Moses*," but just four verses later we read he "had prepared his heart to seek *the law of the Lord*, and to do it, and to teach in Israel statutes and judgments." There is nothing in the context to distinguish or intimate any difference. In fact, it is when it is described as "the law of the Lord" that the ceremonial features are mentioned. The same interchange of terms is found in the eighth chapter of Nehemiah where, in verse 1, it is called "the book of *the law of Moses*," and in verse 8 it says about that book, "they read in the book in *the law of God* distinctly."

Actually, Armstrong's insistence that all of the law is binding today becomes a little sticky, even for him. On one occasion he said: "This world is not taught to OBEY GOD! Its false 'Christianity' teaches that God's law is 'done away.' It actually puts human conscience, actuated by Satan's false teaching, in place of God's law! It does not teach, as did Christ, that we must actually *live by* every word of GOD—of the BIBLE!"[12]

But does Armstrong do this? *Of course he doesn't!* For example, he does not follow the Bible in Numbers 15:32-36 and stone to death anyone picking up sticks on the Sabbath day. Actually, for Armstrong to accept the law in its fulness, as he claims to do, he would need temple, altar, priesthood, animal sacrifices and all the rest.

Do the Armstrongs and the Worldwide Church of God members live by every word of God? Do they have a high priest, clothed in a robe and ephod, wearing a breastplate of Urim and Thummim and having a golden crown upon his head? Do they have a con-

12. Ibid.; p. 55

tinual burnt offering? Do they have peace offerings, sin offerings, meal offerings, trespass offerings? Do they have an ark of the covenant containing a mercy seat of pure gold? Do they go to Palestine to observe their feasts (Leviticus 23:10)? To ask these questions is to answer them. They have simply taken the portions they want to accept and rejected the portions they do not find feasible to follow in our day.

Strangely, however, the cult rigidly follows the ceremonial instructions about clean and unclean food given in the Levitical system. They do this in spite of Paul's clear teaching in I Timothy 4:1-5: "Now the Spirit speaketh expressly, that in the latter times some shall depart from the faith, giving heed to seducing spirits, and doctrines of devils; Speaking lies in hypocrisy; having their conscience seared with a hot iron; Forbidding to marry, and COMMANDING TO ABSTAIN FROM MEATS, which God hath created to be received with thanksgiving of them which believe and know the truth. For EVERY CREATURE of God is good, and NOTHING TO BE REFUSED, if it be received with thanksgiving."

Mr. Armstrong has a hard time seeing the whole picture. He delights in reminding his readers, "God's Law is not a horrible monster!"[13] He quotes an abundance of Scripture showing that God's law is perfect, just, holy, righteous, pure and spiritual. To all this we acquiesce, of course. However, Armstrong seems to be unable to locate the passages which speak of the law as a "ministration of death" (II Corinthians 3:7), "the ministration of condemnation" (II Corinthians 3:9), or "the enmity" (Ephesians 2:15). This, frankly, is because of his inability to understand *the purpose* of the law, previously pointed out in Romans 3 and I Timothy 1. Instead of being God's looking glass to show us His standards and point out our sin, Mr.

---

13. *Tomorrow's World,* August, 1971; p. 5

Armstrong wants us to make it a condition of eventual salvation. But Galatians 3:11,12 warn us: "That no man is justified by the law in the sight of God, it is evident: for, The just shall live by faith. And the law is not of faith: but, The man that doeth them shall live in them."

Armstrong and Sabbath Observance

The Sabbath is a big issue with Armstrong. In fact, it was right here that the starting point of his error was launched. His wife became entangled in this aspect of legalism first. In a "Personal" column, he describes it: "Then two successive major business depressions, and circumstances beyond my control, brought three successive total business failures. It was then that a Bible-believing woman, neighbor of my parents in Salem, Oregon, convinced my wife that the Bible enforced observance of the seventh-day Sabbath in this New Testament time of grace! The facts of my outraged reaction at this 'religious fanaticism' have been published many times.

"I was unable to talk, reason, argue, cajole, or threaten her out of her new-found conviction. I was literally angered into my first STUDY of the Bible—to *prove* to her that 'all these churches couldn't be wrong'—and that the Bible commanded and enforced the observance of Sunday, in this New Testament period."[14]

In another "Personal" column, he added: "I started my study in an effort to *refute* a Biblical truth the big denominations had lost. My determined motive was to prove these denominations were RIGHT. But in the BIBLE *itself*, and checking with all these 'helps' besides, many of which had even then deliberately distorted the facts on this subject, the TRUTH reluctantly emerged. I was faced with an uncomfortable

---

14. *Tomorrow's World,* June, 1971; p. 1

decision. I didn't want to accept it. To do so meant some DOING. It meant being a DOER of God's Law—not a 'hearer' only."[15]

The purpose of the Sabbath? Armstrong declares: "So here we find a GREAT PURPOSE in the Sabbath. It *identifies* GOD! The very day which GOD set aside for assembly and worship points as a memorial to WHOM we are to worship—the CREATOR-RULER of all that is!

"But *that is not all*!

"The Sabbath also was given as a SIGN which identifies WHO are the PEOPLE of God and who are NOT!"[16]

Eventual salvation, according to the Worldwide Church of God, hinges on keeping the seventh-day Sabbath. They are among those "who insist the seventh-day Sabbath is still binding. Failure to keep it, they claim, is SIN—and the punishment is DEATH for eternity!"[17]

Mr. Armstrong says: "Thus did God reveal *which day* is HIS SABBATH, and also that it DOES MAKE LIFE-AND-DEATH DIFFERENCE — for to break God's Holy Sabbath is SIN, and the penalty is eternal DEATH!. . .

"Yes, this is the TEST COMMAND—the one on which YOUR VERY SALVATION and ETERNITY DEPENDS!. . .

"You must make your own choice. Rebellion means eternal PUNISHMENT of everlasting DEATH. God will *save* no person He does not RULE."[18]

He says again: "TIME LOST? If so, then you and I are LOST, for it is SIN to profane God's Sabbath! That is the 4th point of the Law."[19]

---

15. *Tomorrow's World,* August, 1971; p. 2
16. *Which Day Is The Christian Sabbath?* p. 56
17. Ibid.; p. 9
18. Ibid.; pp. 35,58,93-94
19. *Has Time Been Lost?*©1952,1968,1970,1972; p. 22

In fact, he teaches that if one were really a Christian it would be impossible *not* to keep the seventh day. He says: "Now *IF* Jesus Christ is *IN YOU* (and you are not a truly converted Christian unless He is!) will He, *in you*, profane His Holy Day, and observe a pagan day?

"*IMPOSSIBLE!*"[20]

He even goes so far as to claim that Christ is not present in any assembly unless it is on the Sabbath. He says: "Now what joins the many branches of that vine to one another? When *people* meet on *their own human-appointed day*, trying to JOIN THEMSELVES together in a church group, Christ is *not* present with them in that fellowship. He never put HIS PRESENCE in that day! They are like a lot of grape branches, cut off from the vine, trying to join themselves together!"[21]

How foreign is such teaching as this to our Lord's words in Matthew 18:20, "For where two or three are gathered together in my name, there am I in the midst of them." Notice that Christ's presence hinges on the *purpose* of the meeting, not on the *day* or the *time.*

Mr. Armstrong denies that the Sabbath was a covenant between God and Israel. He says that, beginning right with Adam, all of God's people have always observed the seventh-day Sabbath. His argument that Abraham observed the Sabbath is typical. He writes: "But Abraham *kept* God's commandments 430 years before his descendants reached Sinai.

"READ IT IN YOUR OWN BIBLE! 'Abraham obeyed my voice, and kept my charge, *MY COMMANDMENTS, MY STATUTES, AND MY LAWS'* (Gen. 26:5). GOD is speaking. He is explaining *why* He made the great promises to Abraham.

"So ABRAHAM KEPT GOD'S SABBATH!"[22]

---

20. *Which Day Is The Christian Sabbath?* p. 90
21. Ibid.; pp. 84,85
22. Ibid.; p. 30

But his "proof text" proves too much! If it means what he is claiming it means, then he is proving, for example, that Abraham kept the feast of unleavened bread and other statutes which were not given until centuries later. That, obviously, is not what Genesis 26:5 is saying. The only thing that passage says is that Abraham did whatever God told him to do; he was fully obedient to God's orders. It certainly is not a proof of seventh-day Sabbath-keeping on Abraham's part.

Armstrong goes on with this thesis: "Adam was created and living when sunset came that sixth day of creation week—when God rested from His *work*. Adam knew which was the seventh day. Jesus called Abel 'righteous' (Matt. 23:35), so Abel *kept* the Sabbath. Enoch 'walked with God,' so Enoch kept the Sabbath—and he was 'translated' less than a hundred years before Noah.

"...and Noah kept it, because Noah was a preacher of RIGHTEOUSNESS (II Peter 2:5)—and 'all thy commandments are righteous' (Psalm 119:172)."[23]

This is typical of how Armstrong proves his points "from the Bible," as he likes to say. You can read, reread and meditate upon all of the above "proof texts" until you can mumble them in your sleep, but you will not find the slightest reference to Sabbath observance. One could just as easily and just as scripturally say that because Jesus called Abel "righteous," that means he was baptized! Baptism is a biblical command, is it not? But, one might argue in rebuttal, baptism was not given as a command for God's people until much later. *Exactly so*! And the command about Sabbath-keeping was not given to God's people as a command until long after the days of Adam, Abel, Enoch, Noah and Abraham.

---

23. Ibid.; pp. 30,31

In fact, if one wanted to throw Scripture around to suit his own purpose, those who worship on Sunday might argue their point from Adam thusly: Adam was created on the sixth day. Since the Scripture says that God worked six days and rested on the seventh and man is to do the same (Exodus 20:9,10), Adam was the first rebel! Because the seventh day came the day after his creation, this means he rested his *first* day and then *labored the following six*! So one might "prove" from this that it is right to rest the first day, then labor on the six following days! Naturally, we offer no such argument because we do not believe in twisting Scripture to fabricate favorable support.

But in reply to Armstrong's thesis that God's people, before the law was given to the children of Israel on Mt. Sinai, observed the seventh-day Sabbath, we merely refer to the testimony of Scripture found in Nehemiah 9:13,14: "Thou camest down also upon mount Sinai, and spakest with them from heaven, and gavest them right judgments, and true laws, good statutes and commandments: And madest known unto them thy holy sabbath, and commandedst them precepts, statutes, and laws, by the hand of Moses thy servant."

As Dr. C. I. Scofield points out, "This important passage fixes beyond all cavil the time when the sabbath, God's rest (Gen. 2.1-3), was given to man. Cf. Ex. 20.9-11. In Ex. 31.13-17 the sabbath is invested with the character of a sign between Jehovah and Israel."[24] None observed the seventh-day Sabbath before the days of Moses for the simple reason that God's people did not know about it. He had not revealed it to them, the Scripture says.

Armstrong's argument is that God worked Sunday through Friday, then rested on Saturday. Perhaps so,

---

24. From *The Scofield Reference Bible*, edited by C. I. Scofield. Copyright 1917,1944 by Oxford University Press, Inc., and reprinted by permission; p. 550

but that is *not* what the Scripture says. It merely says God worked six days and then rested the seventh. Whether those days corresponded with our Sunday through Saturday, we do not know. Perhaps they did, but the Bible does not say so.

The truth of the matter is that God "starts time" as He sees fit. For example, the reason why God's calendar of months and man's calendar of months are not in harmony is because God started His own calendar for the Jews when He brought them out of Egypt. At a time that corresponds to the April in man's calendar, we read: "And the Lord spake unto Moses and Aaron in the land of Egypt, saying, This month shall be unto you the beginning of months: it shall be the first month of the year to you" (Exodus 12:1,2). While we do not say it was, we do say *it could have been the same with the Sabbath*, which was also instituted at the time of Israel's coming out of Egypt. To say that the Sabbath had to be on our calendar Saturday is going beyond what God has written.

Armstrong, in a desperate effort to find seventh-day Sabbath-keeping in the New Testament points to Hebrews 4:9. In a major article, "Does It Matter Which Day You Keep?" William F. Dankenbring declares: "Therefore, God says to us in the book of Hebrews, in the New Testament, 'There remaineth therefore a *rest* [margin, KEEPING OF A SABBATH] to the people of God' (Heb. 4:9). 'Rest' is an improper translation in this verse. . . .The original Greek word is *sabbatismos* and refers to the Sabbath day!"[25]

Again the writer proves too much! In the first place, this promise is something pertaining to the future. It is something that "remaineth." For another thing, it is something to be entered into, not something to

25. *Tomorrow's World,* March, 1971; p. 36

be observed. Two verses later we are told: "Let us labour therefore TO ENTER INTO that rest, lest any man fall after the same example of unbelief" (Hebrews 4:11). So, if this is talking about Sabbath-day observance, it is talking about something for the future, not something for the present. Then, finally, we must point out that the writer in Hebrews is referring to Psalm 95. His application of the quotation is to the effect that the people in Psalm 95 did *not* enter into God's rest, so a future rest awaited them—*yet these were people then observing the seventh-day Sabbath*!

A favorite Armstrong argument for Sabbath observance is taken from the statement of Hebrews 13:8. For example, talking about how Jesus went to the synagogue on the Sabbath, he declares: "Jesus Christ is still the SAME, today, as He was yesterday, and will be *forever* (Heb. 13:8). *Do you believe that*? Is your Bible an AUTHORITY? Do you accept it as *AUTHORITY*? Unless Jesus Christ, in Spirit, is today living *in your flesh*—actually living your life for you—you are none of His—you are not a Christian (Rom. 8:9). And if He is, HE HAS NOT CHANGED—He is *still* putting His presence in His Sabbath!"[26]

He said again: "Does it make any difference? It certainly made a lot of difference to GOD! And He says He has not changed—He is the *same* yesterday, today, and forever! (Heb. 13:8)."[27]

This is begging the issue! Hebrews 13:8 is simply saying that His *Person* is the same; His *Being*, His *Character* change not. This cannot, by any stretch of the imagination, be construed to mean that His economy of doing things is necessarily the same. What Armstrongite understands this to mean that Jesus today has nowhere to lay His head? Would he under-

---

26. *Which Day Is The Christian Sabbath?* p. 28
27. Ibid.; p. 76

stand it to mean that Jesus is still needing donkeys to ride upon? Does this mean that God is still making donkeys talk like humans? *How absurd*! Because God does one thing in one dispensation does not necessarily mean He wants the same thing in some other dispensation. Even Armstrong has no temple in Jerusalem, does not send a scapegoat into the wilderness on the day of atonement, has no Levitical priesthood and, in fact, does not practice many things God ordered in ages past. The use of Hebrews 13:8 does not at all prove his point, it merely muddies the water.

Armstrong also argues that the Sabbath was a special covenant with Israel—in addition to the covenant of the Ten Commandments—and, "if one tries to argue that the Old Covenant is 'abolished' and that therefore the Ten Commandments are abolished,"[28] the Jew would still be bound to observe it. He says: "So, then, the Jew can be a converted CHRISTIAN! Indeed, the Church at the beginning was nearly altogether Jewish! So the JEW, even though a Christian, in God's CHURCH, is BOUND to keep God's Sabbath as a perpetual covenant, throughout his generations FOREVER!

"Now, does God have TWO KINDS of Christians? Is it SIN for a Jewish Christian to break the Sabbath, and sin for all others to KEEP it? Must Jewish Christians assemble on the Sabbath, and those of other nationalities on Sunday? Didn't Jesus say a house divided against itself would fall?

"Are there TWO KINDS of Christians? Read Galatians 3:28-29: 'There is neither Jew nor Greek, there is neither bond nor free, there is neither male nor female: for ye are ALL ONE IN CHRIST JESUS. And, if ye [ye Gentiles] be Christ's, then are *ye* Abraham's seed, and heirs according to the promise."[29]

---

28. Ibid.; p. 60
29. Ibid.

It is true, as Armstrong emphasizes with his capital letters, that all believers are one in Christ Jesus! But the very passage Armstrong is quoting condemns his philosophy. It says, "There is NEITHER JEW nor Greek. . ." God is not dealing with the Jew as a Jew in this dispensation. See Romans 9-11.

Armstrong, however, instead of recognizing this truth, seeks to tie his Sabbath-keeping in with his Anglo-Israelism theory. He says: "But there is *another answer* to this argument: The peoples of the United States, the British Commonwealth nations, and the nations of Northwestern Europe *are,* in fact, the peoples of the TEN TRIBES of the HOUSE OF ISRAEL. The Jewish people are the house of JUDAH."[30] We will be dealing with this false philosophy in Chapter VIII; we merely quote the claim here to show that, after making all the Anglo-Saxon people into Israelites, he uses their Israelitish "origin" to prove they ought to be keeping the seventh-day Sabbath. This is circular reasoning with a vengeance!

Since, from apostolic times, the expression "the Lord's Day" has been used to signify the first day of the week, Armstrong must get rid of it in some way. His explanation is most unique! He writes: "Right here, let's put an end to the rebellious ARGUMENTS about Sunday being the 'Lord's Day.' I will make to any reader this challenge: Produce any passage in the Bible identifying Sunday—or the first day of the week—as 'the Lord's Day,' and I will proclaim the truth of that passage to the millions of people who hear *The* WORLD TOMORROW program on the air in every inhabited continent on earth, and publish it prominently in *The* PLAIN TRUTH, which now has a reading audience of over four million people around the world. . . .

30. Ibid.; p. 61

"The BIBLE sets apart *only the Sabbath* as God's Holy Day for joint assembly and worship. I will pay anyone who can show any passage in the Bible which sets apart Sunday as a Sabbath, or as 'the Lord's Day' or as a HOLY Day, or which commands its observance, $1,000 for the information.

"For ANY BIBLE AUTHORITY WHATSOEVER which commands the regular observance of Sunday, I will pay $1,000. Why don't you try to find it? The Bible is the AUTHORITY OF GOD! WHAT AUTHORITY DO PEOPLE HAVE FOR SUNDAY?"[31]

How silly! That would be like my offering $1,000 to anyone who could prove that the Bible commanded Christians assembling for worship to lock the doors (as they do in the Worldwide Church of God services!), or that one ought to get on radio and television to preach, as the Armstrongs do.

If the first day of the week, the *resurrection day*, is not the Lord's Day, what day is? What does this expression, "the Lord's Day," mean? Armstrong has a ready answer, saying, with reference to Revelation 1:10: "In spirit, IN VISION, John was carried forward some 1900 years—projected, as it were, into THE LORD'S DAY, which is simply 'THE DAY OF THE LORD'—the time of God's judgments and plagues upon sin at the end—where John sees in symbols in this vision, these age-end events leading up to, and climaxing in, THE SECOND COMING OF CHRIST!"[32]

Just as simply as that—*presto-chango*—Armstrong transforms "the Lord's Day," a historical day, into "the Day of the Lord," a prophetical day. He does violence, however, to both reason and history. There is ample written evidence, dating all the way back to approximately 100 A.D., showing that this term, "the Lord's Day," was used for the first day of the week,

---

31. Ibid.; pp. 47,86
32. *The Key To The Book Of The Revelation,* Written Anonymously; ©1952; p. 4

the day on which Christians assembled for worship. There is absolutely no justification whatsoever for trying to make the expression deal with end-time judgment. It is, quite frankly, the dishonest ruse of a desperate false prophet seeking to destroy damaging evidence which repudiates his unscriptural tenet.

Armstrong does not like to have the Sabbath referred to as Jewish. He says: "*You cannot find* any such term as 'the Jewish Sabbath' anywhere in the Bible!"[33] However, he titles his book on the subject, "*Which Day is the* CHRISTIAN SABBATH?" We would like to remind Mr. Armstrong again: "*You cannot find* any such term as 'the *Christian Sabbath*' anywhere in the Bible!" This is just another example of the straw men he invents to knock down.

Where did Sunday worship come from? Well, for one thing, Armstrong says: "It came out of *paganism*!"[34]

Again, as we saw in Chapter II, he claims ". . .Jeroboam changed the Sabbath day from the seventh to the eighth—that is, to the day *following* the seventh day, which, actually of course, was the *first* day of the WEEK. Thus he set the day for worship to coincide with the pagan DAY OF THE SUN, now called Sunday!"[35]

In addition to the above, he parrots the silly claim of the Roman Catholic Church that it, by its own infallible authority, changed the day of worship from Saturday to Sunday, even offering a photostat copy from the page of the late Cardinal Gibbon's book, *Faith of Our Fathers*, as proof.[36] In all three of his charges—paganism, Jeroboamism, Catholicism—there is not a single shred of evidence other than that which has been fabricated in the minds of those who teach it.

---

33. *Which Day Is The Christian Sabbath?* p. 88
34. Ibid.; p. 35
35. Ibid.; p. 63
36. Ibid.; pp. 13,86-87

Observations About the Sabbath

Before we leave the Sabbath issue it might be helpful to express some thoughts on the subject. No one denies that the Sabbath was revealed to Israel and incorporated into Old Testament law. No one denies that Jesus, in His fulfilling of the law, honored the Sabbath. No one denies the Sabbath was a "holy" day.

However, we do object strenuously to the repeated references by Armstrong and other seventh-day observers arguing that Sunday is "the day of the Sun" and, therefore, anyone who worships on the first day of the week is worshiping the sun! It would be every bit as logical to offer the counter-argument that, since Saturday is named for Saturn and is "the day of Saturn," anyone who worships on the seventh day of the week is worshiping Saturn. *How silly*!

The fact that Sabbath observance was a *ceremonial* law, not a *moral* one, is evidenced by the fact that it could be modified. Moral laws (those pertaining to adultery, murder, stealing, idolatry, etc.) can never be modified. Yet, during His earthly ministry, Jesus modified the Sabbath observance on numerous occasions. In fact, His attendance at the synagogue on the Sabbath (which Armstrong and others like to point out as proof of their thesis) was a modification of the Sabbath observance, since the Sabbath was *never* a day of worship, it was merely a day of *rest*!

Christ modified the Sabbath when His disciples plucked corn on that day. When the Pharisees protested, our Lord did not claim their actions were perfectly lawful for the Sabbath, instead He pointed to a higher law, saying, "The sabbath was made for man, and not man for the sabbath: Therefore the Son of man is Lord also of the sabbath" (Mark 2:27,28). And to justify this modification of the Sabbath, He referred the Pharisees to what David did in violating another ceremonial law, eating the shewbread which was to be consumed by the priests alone. A moral law could not be modified; a ceremonial law could.

We might point out, in defense of our calling one of the Ten Commandments ceremonial and not the others, that the Fourth Commandment alone pictures Christ in His redemptive work. You may go down the list, commandment by commandment, and none except the Fourth is picturing a result of Christ's redemptive work? Does the command prohibiting idolatry picture His redemptive work? Does the command about adultery? Does the command about murder? Does the command about stealing? Does the command about coveting? No, nor does any other *except* the Sabbath commandment.

There is other evidence that the Sabbath command was ceremonial, not moral. It, alone, of the Ten Commandments served as a memorial. In fact, its commemorative value was twofold. For one thing, it was a memorial of creation (Exodus 20:11). For another thing, it was also a memorial of Israel's deliverance from the bitter bondage of Egypt (Deuteronomy 5:13-15).

Permit us to interject a humorous note. Armstrong argues, in trying to free himself from the impact of stoning people to death for picking up sticks on that day: "LET'S UNDERSTAND! The prohibition against 'picking up sticks,' or 'kindling a fire' on the Sabbath was part of the added CIVIL and RITUALISTIC or CEREMONIAL law of Moses—no part of the Ten Commandment SPIRITUAL law!"[37]

If stoning someone to death for picking up sticks on the Sabbath is ceremonial, we would like to know what it ceremonializes! (and it wasn't something "added," as Armstrong says; it was "an interpretation" by God Almighty Himself concerning what breaking the Sabbath law entailed.)

37. Ibid.; p. 91

Incidentally, to those who want to be Sabbath-keepers, we would like to point out that God not only forbade picking up sticks or building fires, He did not even allow them to carry a package in or out of their houses on that day: "Thus saith the Lord; Take heed to yourselves, and bear no burden on the sabbath day, nor bring it in by the gates of Jerusalem; Neither carry forth a burden out of your houses on the sabbath day, neither do ye any work, but hallow ye the sabbath day, as I commanded your fathers" (Jeremiah 17:21,22).

Armstrong and other seventh-day worshipers make much of the apostles going to synagogues on the Sabbath in the Book of Acts. But on not one single occasion did they go to the synagogue for worship, nor is there any record of them worshiping *anywhere* on the Sabbath as a day separated from the rest of the week. The apostles went to the synagogues to preach to the unconverted Jews who were assembled there at that time. In any and every New Testament reference to apostolic *worship*, it was on the first day of the week (John 20:19; John 20:26; Acts 20:7; I Corinthians 16:1,2).

The resurrection of Christ from the grave was on *the first day of the week.* Christ's first meeting with the disciples assembled for worship was on *the first day of the week.* His second meeting with His disciples assembled for worship was on *the first day of the week.* Pentecost and the mighty outpouring of the Holy Spirit took place on *the first day of the week.* This was the day God honored, blessed and hallowed on this side of the cross.

We conclude this section with three indisputable facts.

Fact Number One: The "Sabbaths" were part of the "handwriting of ordinances" nailed to the cross and taken out of the way. Paul told the saints at Colosse: "Blotting out the handwriting of ordinances that was against us, which was contrary to us, and took it out of the way, nailing it to his cross; And having spoiled principalities and powers, he made a shew of them openly, triumphing over them in it. Let no man therefore judge you in meat, or in drink, or in respect of an holyday, or of the new moon, OR OF THE SABBATH DAYS: Which are a shadow of things to come; but the body is of Christ" (Colossians 2:14-17). Sabbath observances—these days of physical rest—were ceremonial observances looking forward to the spiritual rest received in Christ. Now that Christ has come, the Sabbaths, along with the other ceremonial matters which looked forward to His coming, are done away. There is no *need* for them.

Fact Number Two: There is a measure of Christian liberty in this dispensation which God has carefully highlighted. Paul said to the church at Rome: "Him that is weak in the faith receive ye, but not to doubtful disputations. . . .Who art thou that judgest another man's servant? to his own master he standeth or falleth. Yea, he shall be holden up: for God is able to make him stand. One man esteemeth one day above another: another esteemeth every day alike. Let every man be fully persuaded in his own mind. He that regardeth the day, regardeth it unto the Lord; and he that regardeth not the day, to the Lord he doth not regard it" (Romans 14:1,4-6).

Fact Number Three: In the original Sabbath instructions, it was not "Saturday" that the Israelites were told to hallow, but "the Seventh Day." This may or may not have coincided with the Saturday of our calendar week.

CHAPTER VII

The Armstrong Teaching About Hell and Heaven

Garner Ted Armstrong is the only preacher we know about who is certain as to the *exact* location of Hell. He has been there. He has looked into it.

Where is Hell according to Armstrong? *It is a suburb of Jerusalem*!

In an article in *Tomorrow's World*, he says: "During Christ's time, the Valley of Hinnom, just outside of Jerusalem, was the place where refuse and the bodies of criminals were thrown—into fires that were kept burning. God uses this as a *type* of the coming *lake of fire*! My father, mother, brother and I *saw* this valley, called 'Gehenna' in the Bible—and thus were actually looking into HELL, believe it or not!

"During the millennial reign of Christ and His saints, this valley will once more be kept perpetually burning—and the incorrigibly wicked ones who WILL to continue in rebellion against God's laws will be THROWN INTO this 'lake of fire' as a stern witness to all the rest of the world! (Isa. 66:24.)"[1]

Aside from the fact that his "proof text" does not substantiate his charge, as with most of the cult's proof texts, notice that Mr. Armstrong makes no effort to explain how there will be "incorrigibly wicked ones" in the millennium with Satan chained in the bottomless pit during that time (Revelation 20:1-3).

Leaders in the Worldwide Church of God scoff at the traditional concept of Hell. In an article in *Tomorrow's World*, "What is this place called HELL?" the writer said: "The concept of 'hell' is part and parcel of the folklore and mythology of the whole world. Most of the world's religions have some sort of a belief in a

---

1. June, 1971; "What Is Satan's Fate?"; pp. 7,8

'hell' as a place of punishment and torture of the wicked."[2]

How do the Armstrongites get around clear biblical statements about "everlasting fire" and "unquenchable fire"? It is very simple, if one does not mind how he tampers with what the Bible really says—as apparently these religionists do not.

For example, in "What is this place called HELL?" the writer says: "In the book of Matthew, Jesus Christ twice uses the expression 'everlasting fire' (Matt. 18:8; 25:41). Notice 2541—'Then shall he say also to them on the left hand, Depart from me, ye cursed, into *everlasting fire*, prepared for the devil and his angels.'

"What did Jesus mean by 'everlasting'? The Bible does not contradict itself (John 10:35).

"He used a Greek word—*aionios*—which comes from the Greek *aion*, meaning an 'age.' The word *aion* is translated 'AGES' in Ephesians 2:7 and Colossians 1:26. The *aionios* fire Jesus spoke of refers to the age-ending fire which will occur at 'the end of this world,' and which will introduce the 'world to come'! It is an *epochal* event!

"This is why Jesus calls it *aionios* or age-ending fire! The translation 'everlasting' is misleading, since the fire itself will not burn forever."[3]

Once again, *too much* is proved! The same *aionios* is used twice just five verses further, where our Lord says: "And these shall go away into *everlasting* punishment: but the righteous into life *eternal*" (Matthew 25:46). If the punishment is only age-ending, then the life is only age-ending. Since the same identical word is used for both, simple sanity and common honesty demand both be understood alike. If one is temporary, so is the other; if one is permanent, the other must be, too. Incidentally, the same *aionios* is

2. July-August, 1970; William F. Dankenbring; p. 14
3. Ibid.; p. 18

used in John 3:16; John 3:36; John 5:24; John 6:47; Galatians 6:8; I Timothy 1:16; and Romans 6:22; where it is understood by all to mean forever, not merely age-lasting.

As for his trying to pass off *aionios* (an adjective) by *aion* (a noun), suffice it to say that such outstanding Greek scholars as Moulton and Milligan *(Vocabulary of the Greek Testament)*, Herman Cremer *(Biblico-Theological Lexicon of New Testament Greek),* Joseph Henry Thayer (*A Greek-English Lexicon of the New Testament*), and Liddell and Scott *(Greek-English Lexicon*) are unanimous in saying that while *aion* can refer to "an age" (just as it can—and often does—refer to "unending," the context determining its meaning), *aionios* is exclusively a term designating forever, unending.[4]

The writer's interpretation of Matthew 25:41, seeking to disprove its impact, is not an honest one. Nor is the same writer's effort to disprove, in the same article, the teaching of unquenchable fire. He writes: "Another much misunderstood scripture is Mark 9:43 where Jesus speaks of 'the fire that never shall be quenched.'

"Does this mean the fire burns forever?

"Not at all. Take a match, light it and set a piece of paper on fire. Let it burn. Don't put it out, or snuff it out. Just let the paper burn, until it burns up. Soon it will burn itself out.

"Now, what do you have? A burned-up piece of paper. But did you put it out? Did you 'quench' it? No, you left it unquenched. It was *not* quenched. Not at all!

"Even so, the final *Gehenna* fire will not be 'quenched,' or 'put out'. Nevertheless, in time it will burn itself

4. Quoted in *Treasures From The Greek New Testament,* Kenneth S. Wuest; Copyright, 1941; Wm. B. Eerdmans Publishing Company, Grand Rapids, Michigan; pp. 34-36

out, when the wicked and all their wicked works are burned up!"[5]

We leave it to our readers whether or not this does violence to intelligence. No one could honestly read the passage in Mark 9:41-49 and conclude our Lord was speaking of anything but a fire that never burns out.

But the argument is stronger than this. In that passage in Mark, where our English word "quenched" is found five times, the original actually has two different words. In verses 42, 46 and 48, the word is *sbennumi.* This word is used eight times in the New Testament, and seven times it is translated as here, but the other time (Matthew 25:8), it is translated "go out." (And the margin has it "be going out.") So it is honest to say that the fire Jesus spoke of is fire that *cannot be going out*! It is not just fire that can't be *put out*—it can't go out!

The other word for quenched, found in verses 43 and 45, makes the case even stronger. This is the Greek *asbestos.* It is found only four times in the New Testament and in both other cases it is translated "unquenchable." Those references are Matthew 3:12 and Luke 3:17. The fire of Hell is "unquenchable," not merely fire that isn't quenched.

The Worldwide Church of God, as with all the other cultists who are seeking to extinguish Hell's eternal flames, makes much of the fact that different words are used in the New Testament which are translated "hell." One of these New Testament words is "hades" ("sheol" in the Old Testament). This, we are told, never means Hell; it always speaks of "the grave."

Garner Ted Armstrong, referring to the use of the word with reference to Christ, wrote: "No, Jesus did not lie—neither did He go into a burning HELL—but into 'hades' which NEVER, by the wildest stretch of

---

5. "What is this place called *Hell?*" op. cit.; p. 18

the imagination, has anything whatsoever to *do* with infernal fires, but means, simply, 'the GRAVE.' Check ANY reliable concordance, commentary, or lexicon for proof of this."[6]

That statement simply is not true! Probably the most reputable concordance in existence, one referred to repeatedly by the Armstrongs, is *Young's Analytical Concordance to the Bible.* It gives as the meaning of *sheol*, "the unseen state," and the meaning for *hades*, "the unseen world." *And that is exactly the meaning*!

Sometimes, quite frankly, *sheol* and *hades* do refer simply to the grave, although always in the sense that it is part of the unseen state, the unseen world. But just as frankly and just as explicitly, sometimes it could not possibly, by any stretch of the imagination, refer merely to the grave. Actually, *sheol* is found 65 times in the Old Testament and it is translated *grave* 31 times, *hell* 31 times and *pit* 3 times. Regarding *hades*, it is found 11 times in the New Testament and translated *grave* once (with *hell* in the margin), and it is translated *hell* 10 times—with *grave* in the margin one of those ten times.

Another word translated "hell" in the New Testament is the Greek *gehenna*. This is found 12 times in the New Testament; 9 of those times it is translated *hell* and 3 times *hell* [*fire*]. This is what the cult tells us ". . .refers to the ancient dwelling place of the sons of Hinnom, a valley just outside the city of Jerusalem which came to be used as a garbage dump or rubbish pit. Filthy, dirty garbage, dead bodies, and corpses of criminals were thrown into this valley and burned up. Jesus used this figurative expression as a symbol of the final HELL FIRE which will consume the bodies of the incorrigibly wicked!"[7]

Regarding this, Herbert W. Armstrong wrote: "Jesus

---

6. *Tomorrow's World,* July-August, 1970; "Will *You* get to *Heaven!*"; p. 12
7. "What is this place called *Hell?*" op. cit.; p. 17

said the 'soul' can be DESTROYED in gehenna fire (Matt. 10:28)."[8] In other words, he makes this destruction to be an annihilation—*a ceasing to be*! But once again, trying to make "destroy" mean "annihilate," he finds himself proving too much. His son Garner Ted, in discussing the fate of Satan, refers to God's promise of destruction in Ezekiel 28:16, "I will destroy thee." Yet the Armstrongs teach that Satan will never be annihilated, so Garner Ted wrote: ". . .Satan and his demons shall be tormented day and night forever and ever!

"This expressly states Satan will be tormented for the AGES OF THE AGES! (See *International Critical Commentary*, an interlinear or other such Bible helps.) This expression in the Greek means for all eternity—for time everlasting!"[9]

Something must be done to explain away the discrepancy.

Here it is: "The word *destroy* is explained by the word FROM! God does NOT say Satan is to be DESTROYED! He DOES say Satan is to be DESTROYED FROM a certain place—the midst of the stones of fire, or the location of God's seat of authority."[10] We leave our readers to ponder over such a use of semantics.

Armstrong errs in trying to make "destroy" (Matthew 10:28) mean "cease to be." It is the Greek *apollumi* and the same word is translated "lost" concerning the house of Israel (Matthew 10:6). Would Armstrong be willing to admit Israel had ceased to be—and annihilate his Anglo-Saxon/Israel theory? We think not. The same word, incidentally, is used for the sheep and the coin (translated "lost") in Luke 15:6,9, and of bottles (translated "perish") in Matthew 9:17.

A third word translated Hell is *tartaroo* and it is

---

8. *What'll You Be Doing In The Next Life?* © 1967, 1969; p. 2
9. *Tomorrow's World*, June, 1971; p. 9
10. Ibid.

used only one time in the Bible, II Peter 2:4, "cast down to hell." This reference is disposed of in a hurry. David Jon Hill simply says: "It is used *only once* in the Bible. . . .The word here, very loosely translated hell, is not a place but a condition. It refers to the *condition of restraint* that God has imposed upon those angels which rebelled against Him and followed Satan the Devil. This term—*tartaroo* hell—is never used in reference to man.

"When Satan and his demons rebelled against God, He put them in a condition of restraint—much as modern governments put criminals in a condition of restraint—where they must remain until their time of judgment (Jude 6).

"Science has never observed this *tartaroo* hell! Churchmen are confounded by it! God's truth is very plain concerning it!"[11]

Suffice it to say, there is not one iota of support for his claim that *tartaroo* is a condition, not an actual place. Yet he has the audacity to say this truth "is very plain." And what the assertion "Science has never observed this *tartaroo* hell" has to do with the matter, we are at a loss to explain. Science has never "observed" Heaven, either.

Right here, incidentally, is one of the trademarks of religious error: *tampering with biblical teaching about Hell.* Almost every cult whose sun has ever risen has been guilty, probably because banking the fires appeals to the flesh of carnal, sensual mankind. The Worldwide Church of God joins Mormons, Unitarians, Jehovah's Witnesses, Spiritists, New Thoughtites, Seventh-Day Adventists, Universalists, and almost all other sects in seeking to explain away Hell's eternal fires. "The conscious punishment will not last forever," the false prophets are unanimous in declaring. Armstrong, like Ellen G. White and "Pastor" Russell, tells

---

11. *There Is A Real Hell Fire!* © 1962,1963,1971; p. 3

us that lost sinners will merely be cast into the fire and burned up—consumed, cease to exist, be annihilated! *But this is not what the Bible teaches.*

In the case of Armstrong and his followers, Hell is not too much to get excited about anyway since they do not think many are going there. With their belief in an opportunity to get saved after death, few will end up in Hell—only those who refuse to accept the Armstrong gospel.

What is the lake of fire to the followers of Armstrong? Believe it or not, it is the world being burned up at the end of the age! We are told: "What about this 'hell fire'? Where will it be? How hot? How big? How long will it last?

"Peter helps us understand. 'But the day of the Lord will come as a thief in the night; in the which the heavens shall pass away with a great noise, and the elements shall melt with fervent heat, the earth also and the *works* that are therein shall be *burned up*' (II Peter 3:10).

"Notice verse 7: 'But the heavens and the earth, which are now, by the same word are kept in store, reserved unto fire against the *day of judgment* and perdition of ungodly men'!

"How plain. This great fire is the same as the 'lake of fire,' mentioned in Revelation, when God judges the incorrigibly wicked. It will sweep around the entire earth! The elements themselves will be dissolved, the surface of the earth will be purged and consumed with tremendous heat. Every remnant of man's sin, every sign of iniquity, every last trace of evil will be devoured by the heat of this fire."[12]

We could not imagine a more unjustified mingling of unrelated Scriptures. It is like someone reading about astronauts in training at Houston having chocolate ice cream for supper, and later noting the same

12. "What is this place called *Hell?*" op. cit.; p. 17

astronauts had taken off for the moon, then putting the two news items together to prove astronauts eat chocolate ice cream in outer space! It does violence to every known rule of hermeneutics and exegesis. But it "proves" the Armstrong theory—and that is all, seemingly, that matters to the leaders of this strange cult.

One of the most popular "proof texts" that the wicked are just going to be burned up, quoted repeatedly by the Worldwide Church of God, is Malachi 4:1-3: "For, behold, the day cometh, that shall burn as an oven; and all the proud, yea, and all that do wickedly, shall be stubble: and the day that cometh shall burn them up, saith the Lord of hosts, that it shall leave them neither root nor branch. But unto you that fear my name shall the Sun of righteousness arise with healing in his wings; and ye shall go forth, and grow up as calves of the stall. And ye shall tread down the wicked; for they shall be ashes under the soles of your feet in the day that I shall do this, saith the Lord of hosts." The fact that this has nothing to do with Hell, referring rather to the Day of the Lord on earth, means nothing to this cult.

Garner Ted Armstrong writes about this passage: "Notice that the wicked (the *same* ones Christ referred to) are to be ASHES under the feet of the righteous! (Mal. 4:3.)"[13] According to him, these ashes are material, literal ashes, hence proof that the wicked will be "consumed" by fire with only ashes remaining. But if the ashes are literal, what about the *stubble*? What about the *root*? What about the *branches*? What about the *wings*? Are they literal? Now, if Armstrong is going to be honest, he is either going to have to accept symbolic, figurative *ashes*, or literal stubble, root, branches and wings! One cannot pick and choose,

13. "What Is Satan's Fate?" op. cit.; p. 7

making part literal and part figurative according to how it suits his fancy. This is a case of not being able to have cake and eat it, too.

In referring to the beast and false prophet being cast into the lake of fire (Revelation 19:20), Armstrong says: "These two are human beings—physical, breathing *men*, who are alive and drawing breath at this instant! The fire will CONSUME them. *This lake of fire is going to be burning all during the millennium*! (Isaiah 66:23-24.)"[14]

Aside from the fact that Armstrong dabbles in the field of date setting by saying that these men who will be such prominent figures during the Great Tribulation are alive right now (and were alive in 1958 when he first wrote those words), plus the fact that he is completely out of context in his proof text for the millennial fire, note that he says the fire will "consume" these men. Yet, in Revelation 20:10, we find the same pair still alive and still being tormented over a thousand years later. The Bible says: "And the devil that deceived them was cast into the lake of fire and brimstone, where the beast and the false prophet are, and shall be tormented day and night for ever and ever."

Armstrong brushes this off by saying, "Next, turn to Revelation 20:10. 'And the devil that deceived them was cast into *the* lake of fire and brimstone, where the beast and the false prophet [WERE CAST].' There is *no* verb 'are' in the original Greek, as the King James revisers have added in italics!"[15]

True, but who is guilty of the greater sin? The King James translators for adding *one* word, "are"; or Garner Ted Armstrong for adding *two* words (and putting them in all capital letters, at that!), "WERE CAST"? There is an added difference: what the King

14. Ibid.
15. Ibid.; p. 8

James translators did is consistent with the Greek text; what Mr. Armstrong did is not.

While the Armstrongs teach annihilation for incorrigible wicked sinners, they do not let Satan and his demons off as easily. Referring to Revelation 20:10, David Jon Hill tells us: "Simply by applying the rules of grammar you will see that the latter part of this sentence, 'and shall be tormented day and night for ever and ever,' refers to the *devil*, and to his demons, who are the subject of this entire sentence. Yes, God's Word plainly says Satan the devil and all his demons are going to be tormented day and night forever and ever. Since the devil faces this horrible sentencing, he has endeavored to make mankind think that the punishment of sin for *mankind* is going to be an eternal punish*ing*—in order to get sympathy for himself."[16]

Once again, too much is proved. The same expression regarding the duration of Satan's punishment—"for ever and ever"—is used of the torment for humans who worship the beast and his image in Revelation 14:9-11: "And the third angel followed them, saying with a loud voice, If any man worship the beast and his image, and receive his mark in his forehead, or in his hand, The same shall drink of the wine of the wrath of God, which is poured out without mixture into the cup of his indignation; and he shall be tormented with fire and brimstone in the presence of the holy angels, and in the presence of the Lamb: And the smoke of their torment ascendeth up FOR EVER AND EVER: and they have no rest day nor night, who worship the beast and his image, and whosoever receiveth the mark of his name."

This phrase "for ever and ever" is literally "to the ages of the ages." As the Cambridge Bible points out, it comprises "as strong an expression for absolute

16. *There Is A Real Hell Fire!* p. 5

endlessness as Biblical language affords." So if "for ever and ever" proves Satan and his demons are going to be tormented forever, not annihilated—*and it does*—then the same identical term proves human sinners will be punished for the same duration, never annihilated. The same expression is applied to both.

It is in the area of Satan's punishment that Armstrong comes up with a new twist, original and unique. On the one hand, he teaches that Satan's punishment is eternal. On the other hand, he has theorized that the lake of fire is only a temporary matter. How can a temporary fire provide an eternal punishment? Here is Garner Ted Armstrong's novel explanation: "The Bible plainly reveals Satan will be cast into the lake of fire, but the lake of fire will *end* when the new heavens and new earth are established, and Satan is to be tormented unto the *ages of the ages*! It also shows his torment *while* in that fire is going to be MENTAL, at seeing all he has strived toward, worked for, plotted for, *burned up*."[17]

Rational readers may inquire as to why Satan will be cast into a literal fire in the first place, if it doesn't do any harm! Why not just let him stand alongside and watch "all he has strived toward, worked for, plotted for, *burned up*"? But let it be noted that it is IN "the lake of fire" where Satan is going to be "tormented day and night for ever and ever." We suggest that those "rules of grammar" David Jon Hill referred to be applied in this area, just as in any other. And we would like to point out that Jesus said in Matthew 25:41, "Depart from me, ye cursed, into EVERLASTING fire, prepared for the devil and his angels." Even one of Armstrong's principal writers is forced to confess: "Jesus here plainly showed that the everlasting fire was prepared for Satan and his angels."[18]

17. "What Is Satan's Fate?" op. cit.; pp. 9, 10
18. *There Is A Real Hell Fire!* p. 5

One of the arguments used to prop up the annihilation theory is: "A *human body* doesn't burn *forever*. It finally turns to ashes in the fire."[19] But trees don't burn forever, either. Yet we remind our readers of Exodus 3 and the story of the burning bush. Just as God can violate natural law and cause a bush to burn as long as it suits His purpose, so He can easily overturn physical laws in the burning of human bodies. Leave God out of it and you have one story; put God into it and it is an entirely different matter. It is the same with lost souls in Hell! For a Bible believer the issue is never can God do what He says, but what has God said He will do?

One of the biggest stumbling blocks for every false prophet in banking the eternal fires of Hell is the story Jesus told about the rich man and Lazarus (Luke 16:19-31). Every false cult has tried to explain away the truth of this passage; in fact, it is absolutely essential to its theology that such be done. Hence it is not surprising that Herbert W. Armstrong and his Worldwide Church of God publish a special book to explain away the impact of this passage of Scripture. However, the interpretations set forth in that anonymously written book are rare indeed. Having read it carefully a number of times, we confess to admiration for the author's fertile imaginative powers, even though we are compelled to condemn his conclusions in the light of the Word of God.

Consider some samples of the Worldwide Church of God's exegesis of this Scripture.

"Abraham's bosom" simply refers to one becoming a recipient of the kingdom promises given to Abraham. We are told: "Lazarus here is pictured as a person, perhaps even a Gentile, who receives salvation. Do Gentiles, upon being converted and becoming Christ's, enter into any intimate relationship to Abraham? They

---

19. *Lazarus And The Rich Man*, Written Anonymously; © 1953,1971; p. 19

certainly do! To the Gentile-born Galatians, the Scriptures written by Paul say definitely: 'If ye be Christ's, then are ye Abraham's seed [children], and heirs according to the promise' (Gal. 3:29).

"Through Christ they become the children of Abraham. Through faith we all become 'the children of Abraham' (Gal. 3:7). That is an intimate relationship with Abraham. That is being taken into Abraham's bosom!"[20]

The fact that Jesus in Luke was talking about what happened to some individuals *after they had died* means little to this cult. Its leadership switches the setting to *before death* and acts as if nothing is amiss.

Lazarus being "carried by the angels into Abraham's bosom" is uniquely explained. Apparently a concordance was consulted and a verse or two located where the word "angels" was used, then applied to this passage. The way those verses are strung together is absolutely incredible. First of all, the reader is asked: "When do the angels come down from heaven? In Matthew 25:31, quoted above, we saw that it was at the second coming of Christ—*at the time of the* RESURRECTION."[21]

As if this were the only time angels came down from Heaven! But, continuing, the writer goes on: "Again, Scripture reveals: Christ shall 'send his *angels* with the great sound of a trumpet, and *they* shall gather together His elect from the four winds'—out of their graves in a RESURRECTION (Matt. 24:31). The TIME when the angels carry LAZARUS and the saints into sharing the INHERITANCE with Abraham—into Abraham's bosom—is a time of the RESURRECTION. Lazarus is to be resurrected, and carried by the angels through the air to meet Christ, at His return, *and to be with Abraham*, in the intimate relationship of father and son! Yes, HOW PLAIN! Lazarus will then enjoy

20. Ibid.; p. 7
21. Ibid.; p. 11

the fond embrace of his father through Christ, Abraham—both then resurrected and LIVING forevermore, in the promised LAND, then inherited!"[22]

The fact that the rich man's five brothers are still alive on earth in need of someone to warn them about Hell and plead with them to repent, is of little consequence to this cult. Facts are switched around and juggled in utter confusion to try to make them conform to its evasive philosophies.

There is a problem also in the fact that, in the words of Jesus, as soon as the rich man died he was in Hell and "lift up his eyes." So we are given an explanation about this lifting up of the eyes. We are told: "Now once again, Jesus did not say *when* this rich man, 'in hell,' lifted up his eyes. Jesus pictured him as one of the wicked, or lost. We must look to other Scriptures to tell us *when* the unjust will lift up their eyes in their graves."[23]

We are then treated to quotations of Daniel 12:2 and John 5:28, 29, complete with the "bracket" explanations so necessary to this cult's theology. For example, Daniel 12:2 is given: "And many of them that sleep [*their eyes closed*] in the dust of the earth [*their graves—buried—in hades*], shall awake [*lift up their eyes*] some to everlasting life, and some to shame and everlasting contempt."[24]

This, we are told to accept, is what Jesus meant when the rich man died, went to Hell, and "lift up his eyes." The trouble with this explanation, however, is that the order is reversed. The Armstrong cult would have us believe that the wicked will lift up their eyes *before* they are cast into Hell. Jesus said the rich man went to Hell and *then* lifted up his eyes. But, in light of such major perversions and twistings of Scripture

22. Ibid.
23. Ibid.; p. 14
24. Ibid.

as the Armstrongs habitually engage, this would be a minor matter to them. Armstrong has been known to even quote the last half of the verse first, changing the order without indicating anything amiss, in order to "prove" a point.

Jesus said the man in Hell was tormented by the flames and begging for a moist finger to touch the tip of his tongue. We learn from the Armstrongs, however, that the man was not in fire at all—it was merely his terror at the thought of being burned up by fire that made his mouth go dry! Believe it or not, that is what we are told to believe and accept! The writer says: "Now, opening his eyes in his grave, this rich man SEES Abraham, and Lazarus in his 'bosom'—his embrace!. . .he also sees this awful flame of fire—this LAKE OF FIRE which is about to destroy him forever! He is *terrified*!

"What happens when one is suddenly so horrified with fear? His mouth goes dry. His tongue sticks to his mouth and throat!. . .

"The flame, he said, was 'tormenting' him. This word 'tormented,' used in verses 24 and 25 is translated from the Greek word *odunomai*. This is defined in any Greek-English lexicon as 'to cause pain, to pain, distress; pain of body, but also, *pain of mind*, *grief*, *distress.*'

"Why, of course! This rich man opens his eyes in his grave in a resurrection. He is resurrected MORTAL, just as he was before he died—not immortal like Lazarus. He sees this lake of fire. Now he *knows* the frightful, the AWFUL doom he is to be thrust into—to be *burned up—destroyed*! He is suffering mental anguish such as he never experienced in his lifetime. HIS TONGUE IS DRY. He breaks out in cold sweat. He cries for a little water on the tip of Lazarus' finger TO COOL HIS TONGUE! He is in a condition of WEEPING and GNASHING OF TEETH!"[25]

25. Ibid.; pp. 16,17

Such an incredible explanation of what it means to be "tormented in this flame" does not deserve to be dignified by a reply. It does violence to the English; it does violence to the Greek; it does violence to the intelligence.

The reader is also treated to a unique explanation of "the gulf fixed." Believe it or not, we are told it is "mortality." The author says: "There is a great gulf fixed between this doomed sinner and all the glorified saints in God's Kingdom.

"What is that great GULF?

"The *gulf* mentioned by Abraham which prevents the wicked from escaping death by hell-fire, and which also keeps the righteous from being burned, is *immortality*. . . .

"Don't forget, this is a *literal fire* and the rich man is *human being* composed of flesh and blood. *Only* the saved possess immortality as the gift of God (Rom. 2:7), but the wicked reap anguish and wrath that shall devour the adversary — fiery indignation (Heb. 10:27)."[26]

We cannot help being amused at the insistence of the writer that the fire is literal, while, at the same time, making everything else figurative. This kind of reasoning is a far cry from honest interpretation or manifesting the reverence with which one should approach the Word of God.

What about the five brothers, still living on earth, for whom the rich man intercedes? As already indicated, this is a real problem for anyone trying to explain away the force of the story. The Armstrongs make a stab at it, but the result is very feeble. Readers are told: "The rich man at last realized he was DOOMED! He now comprehended the gulf that existed between him and those who had been made

26. Ibid.; pp. 18,19

immortal. Abraham had made clear the utter *impossibility* of the rich man crossing that gulf into immortality. He had had his chance during his lifetime. He had passed it up for this world's material riches and pleasures. There was no hope for him. He was now DOOMED to perish in this lake of fire.

"His last thought flashed finally to his five brothers. He gave one last cry to Abraham, begging him to send Lazarus to his father's house to plead with his brothers, lest they come to his terrible fate. Abraham replied they had the writings of Moses and the prophets. But the rich man realized they would not hear these Scriptures."[27]

However, if this is at the time of the great judgment morning, when the rich man is to be cast into the lake of fire, one wonders what his five brothers are still doing at home! For the rich man to have died before the time of Christ and the five brothers still be living at the close of the millennium—without having tasted death—is a little bit more than our imagination can fathom.

We are not blessed with the kind of credulity that can accept explanations like the ones above. We much prefer to accept the plain, clear-cut teaching of the Lord Jesus Christ in the Luke 16 passage, just exactly as He taught it. There is absolutely no scriptural basis for *anyone* trying to explain it away.

Armstrong's "Heaven!"

We have put the word *Heaven* above in quotes because members of the Worldwide Church of God really do not believe in a Heaven. As already noted, "Abraham's Bosom" (Luke 16:22) is just a term of "an intimate relationship with Abraham" to them. Oh, they believe in a Heaven in the sense that it is where

27. Ibid.; p. 20

God's throne is, but they do not believe in a Heaven where saved people will spend eternity. In fact, writer after writer ridicules any such thought in words dripping with sarcasm.

Garner Ted Armstrong refers to ". . .deluded men [preaching] the ancient, *pagan* doctrine of 'going to heaven.'"[28]

Note how he puts the expression "going to heaven" in quotes, indicating his contempt of the thought. And note how he calls it a "pagan" doctrine, accusing anyone who preaches it of being "deluded." His father, Herbert W. Armstrong, says boldly and bluntly: "There is absolutely NO SCRIPTURE in all the Holy Bible that promises HEAVEN as the reward the saved shall inherit."[29]

Technically, that statement is half true and half false. Of course there are no Scriptures offering Heaven as a "reward," because rewards have to do with works. Heaven has to do with grace. Heaven is not a reward given to people because of their works on this earth; it is an inheritance granted absolutely free to those who trust Jesus Christ. So there are, in truth and in fact, no Scriptures promising Heaven as a reward. On the other hand, there are a host of Scriptures saying "the saved shall inherit" Heaven.

The problem the Worldwide Church of God has in this area results not only from its utter confusion regarding works and grace, but its equally confused jumbling of Scripture pertaining to Christ's coming kingdom on earth (which the Scripture certainly teaches) with equally forceful Scripture regarding the inheritance of the redeemed in Heaven. Armstrong will quote Scriptures speaking of Christ's earthly kingdom (and there are many which speak of it!) as

28. "Will *You* get to *Heaven?*" op. cit.; p. 10
29. *Tomorrow's World,* November, 1971; "What Is The *Reward* Of The Saved. . . *Heaven?*"; p. 47

proof that there is no Heaven. All of which would be like my showing photographs of Chicago as "proof positive" that there is no Los Angeles!

Let us look at a few examples.

In an "Answers" column of *Tomorrow's World*, a reader had written to inquire: "What did Jesus mean when He told His disciples '. . .Be exceeding glad: for great is your reward *in heaven*'? (Matt. 5:12). Doesn't this prove the reward of the saved is heaven?" The reply began: "Only a few verses before Christ said, 'Blessed are the meek: for they shall inherit *the earth.*' Now do some of the saved—'the persecuted' (verses 11-12)—go to heaven to collect their reward, while others—'the meek'—inherit the earth? Did Jesus contradict Himself in His very next breath? Certainly NOT!"[30]

But why try to make a contradiction between Matthew 5:12 and Matthew 5:5? Why not accept the beautiful harmony that is there: one emphasizing Christ's coming earthly kingdom and the other recognizing the inheritance of Heaven? Why try to make an issue that does not exist; why try to force a contradiction that is not present?

Herbert W. Armstrong mixes rewards and inheritance, the Kingdom of Christ on earth with the inheritance of Heaven, then seeks to make the truth about the one annihilate the other. He says, in commenting about Galatians 3:16 and 29: "The Christian is *not* a possessor of his reward—he is an *heir*—and what he shall inherit, if saved, is the PROMISE made to Abraham. Whatever shall be the reward of the saved, wherever we shall spend eternity if saved, is a definite, specific promise of God. That promise was made to Abraham, who is called, in this same book of Galatians which was written for Gentile converts, the FATHER of the faithful. If one is converted, whether Jew or Gentile—

30. September, 1971; p. 48

regardless of race or color or sex—if one is Christ's, then he becomes one of Abraham's children, and an HEIR of the PROMISE made to Abraham. What he is to *inherit,* is whatever was promised to Abraham."[31]

From there Armstrong proceeds to show the promises about Abraham's earthly inheritance, offering them as proof that this is the "inheritance" today's Christians will eventually receive. Now while, admittedly, these promises to Abraham are *part* of what God has planned for His own, they certainly do not embrace all. In fact, they didn't even for Abraham and his successors. In Hebrews 11 we are told that Abraham "looked for a city which hath foundations, whose builder and maker is God" (vs. 10). Was this some earthly city of an earthly kingdom? Obviously not.

The Scripture continues: "These all died in faith, not having received the promises, but having seen them afar off, and were persuaded of them, and embraced them, and confessed that they were strangers and pilgrims on the earth. For they that say such things declare plainly that they seek a country. And truly, if they had been mindful of that country from whence they came out, they might have had opportunity to have returned. But now they desire a better country, that is, an heavenly: wherefore God is not ashamed to be called their God: for he hath prepared for them a city" (vss. 13-16).

Abraham was not merely interested in an earthly country, he was looking for a heavenly country as well, a "better country"! Mr. Armstrong simply is not honest with his readers when he tries to limit Abraham to an earthly inheritance.

One of the major problems in explaining away Heaven relates to John 14:1-6. In trying to blunt the force of this passage, Garner Ted Armstrong wrote: "But what about the time-honored songs, the hopes

31. "What Is The *Reward* Of The Saved. . .*Heaven?*" op. cit.; p. 3

of millions, the cherished 'Christian traditions' of the 'homes above' that so many have talked about, sung about, written about, all down through these years?

"*Turn* to this scripture. You read it in John, the 14th chapter. 'In my Father's house are many mansions [margin, 'abodes']: if it were not so, I would have told you. I go to prepare a *place* for you. IF I GO and prepare a PLACE for you, I WILL COME AGAIN, and receive you unto myself, that *where I am*, there YE MAY BE ALSO' (John 14:2-3).

"Notice it—NOWHERE DID JESUS SAY SAINTS GO TO HEAVEN! He said, rather, there are PLACES, HABITATIONS, ABODES, MANSIONS, RESIDENCES which HE IS PREPARING. These 'places' are NOW 'IN' HEAVEN. But Jesus went *on* to say, 'I will COME AGAIN.' Come where? To THIS EARTH, as Jesus repeated so many times. He said also, 'that where I AM, there ye may be also' (verse 3).

"Where will Jesus BE?

"If Jesus COMES AGAIN TO THIS EARTH—then He will *BE* ON THIS EARTH! The EARTH, and a definite, specific location ON the earth, will be where Jesus said He is going to BE. If *we* are to BE WITH HIM where He is to BE—then we, also, are going to BE ON THIS EARTH!"[32]

Such an understanding, of course, does tremendous violence to the plain statement Jesus made. Armstrong is trying to tell his readers Jesus was really saying, "If I go and prepare a place for you, I will come again, and let you receive me unto yourselves, that where you are, I may be also." But this is not what He said!

Furthermore, the context shows that the disciples did not understand Him to say any such thing. The very next verse goes on to record Jesus saying to them: "And whither I go ye know, and the way ye

32. "Will *You* get to *Heaven?*" op. cit.; p. 11

know." That certainly was a superfluous statement if He were talking about dwelling with them on earth. The disciples did not understand it thus, Thomas immediately questioning: "Lord, we know not whither thou goest; and how can we know the way?" He did not ask here about when Jesus was *coming*, but where He was *going*! Thomas was not wanting to know about an inheritance on earth, he asked plainly the way to that house of many mansions where Jesus was going.

Neither did Jesus tell the disciples they had misunderstood Him (the obvious time to do so if they had)—that He was not talking about being with them in Heaven, but, rather, about coming back to be with them on earth. Quite the contrary, He immediately and forcefully answered Thomas' question about getting to Heaven, saying: "I am the way, the truth, and the life; no man cometh unto the Father, but by me."

Any other understanding of John 14 does violence to the plain statements of the Word of God. So, in this matter, we would like to quote Garner Ted Armstrong's words back to him, namely: "Simply *scoffing* at the *real meaning* of these plain scriptures will NOT CHANGE them. Not *wanting* to believe the precious, glorious, PLAIN TRUTH of the Bible will not *do away* with it!"[33]

Further, we might ask why the Lord should trouble to catch His own up into the clouds—off this earth—when He returns, if He is only coming to be with them on earth anyway? In that classic passage in I Thessalonians 4, the 17th verse assures us: "Then we which are alive and remain shall be caught up together with them in the clouds, to meet the Lord in the air: and so shall we ever be with the Lord." He is coming to take us to be with Him; He is not coming to be with us.

Incidentally, Armstrong's teaching that Christ is now in Heaven preparing "places, habitations, abodes,

---

33. Ibid.

mansions, residences" to bring back with Him to this earth has lately begun to seem illogical even to him, apparently. On page 48 of the March, 1973, *Plain Truth*, in a footnote attempting to answer a reader's argument about Christians' going to Heaven, we find this new explanation of the mansions in John 14: "*Jesus was not talking about 'homes,' but rather, rooms or offices—positions of responsibility in the Kingdom of God. Christ is now preparing the offices, jobs and responsibilities which He will bestow upon true Christians when He returns.*"

This is the argument of a false prophet in the throes of desperation, grasping for a straw, since there is not even the slightest foundation in the original for such reasoning. The word "mansions" in the King James is the Greek *mone.* It is utterly impossible to translate or interpret it as "offices, jobs and responsibilities." James Strong, in his Greek Dictionary of the New Testament, gives it: "a *staying*, i.e. *residence* (the act or the place):—abode, mansion." W. E. Vine, in his *An Expository Dictionary of New Testament Words*, describes it: "primarily a staying, abiding (akin to *meno*, to abide), denotes an abode (Eng., manor, manse, etc.), translated 'mansions' in John 14:2; 'abode' in ver. 23." For Armstrong to interpret it as he has is one more flagrant example of his dishonest and deceitful handling of the Word of God.

Another major stumbling block to Armstrong's "no Heaven" philosophy relates to the Lord's promise to the dying thief in Luke 23:43: "And Jesus said unto him, Verily I say unto thee, To day shalt thou be with me in paradise." All cults teaching soul sleep (most of whom, however, acknowledge the truth of Heaven), have had to do something to explain away this passage. The majority of them have found it simplest to resort to grammatical tricks; the Armstrongs are no different.

Here is Garner Ted Armstrong's explanation: "Now

turn to Luke 23:43. Read it carefully. Jesus APPEARS to have said, by the placement of the *comma*, in the English version, 'TODAY SHALT THOU BE WITH ME IN PARADISE.' And yet Jesus KNEW He was not going to enter into Paradise ON THAT DAY—or for the next THREE OR FOUR DAYS!

"Now put the comma where it BELONGS, to preserve the *sense* of this scripture as *proved by all other scriptures* on the subject (remember, the Bible *interprets itself*). 'And Jesus said unto him, Verily I say unto you today, THOU SHALT BE WITH ME IN PARADISE!' Jesus said it THAT DAY, and promised the thief WOULD BE in paradise—but He most certainly DID NOT promise paradise to the thief *that very day.*"[34]

Mr. Armstrong makes several gross errors in these two paragraphs. First, he is wrong in charging that Jesus knew He was not going to enter Paradise that day—He did enter Paradise that day, just as He said He would. Second, he is wrong in saying that all other Scriptures on the subject prove that the comma is out of place. *They prove no such thing*! Third, he is wrong in his basic assumption; that is, that the comma is misplaced.

Dr. George Lawlor, professor of Greek and Bible at Cedarville College, dealt with this charge in our magazine, *The Biblical Evangelist*, some time ago. His article is too lengthy to reproduce in its entirety, but here is the heart of it:

". . .the text of Luke 23:43 is so assured by reliable evidence that *any* change based on textual grounds must be rejected. All is clear where *seimeron* ['today'] and the punctuation of the sentence are concerned. The KJV is right: the comma belongs where it is—after the pronoun 'thee' [the Greek order reverses the pronoun and the verb, but retains the same sense].

34. Ibid.; p. 12

Again, as previously in the Gospel records, we meet the seal of verity and sovereignty in '*Amen*' ['Verily' in the KJV] coupled with the declaration of authority: '*I say unto thee*' [the Greek text places the dative pronoun before the verb: 'To thee I say'], followed correctly by the comma. Any attempt to join the word 'today' with the clause 'to thee I say' violates common sense, ignores the textual evidence, and destroys the forces of the Lord's promise.

"It should not even be necessary to explain that the comma is not to be moved so that the word 'today' must be construed with 'I say to thee.' To be sure the Lord is saying these words TODAY—*this is self-evident*! When else would He be saying them? The thief heard the words and knew the Lord was talking to him AT THAT MOMENT—today—and believed what the Lord said. Never did Christ so redundantly and emphatically express Himself. Hence the [Armstrong] insinuation is groundless—yea, dangerous, for the Lord's great promise in this remarkable statement would lose all of its precision, meaning and blessedness if based upon the [Armstrong] interpretation that there is no passage of the soul into the presence of the Lord.

"Without doubt, the adverb 'today' is an essential part of the Lord's promise to the thief. In fact, its place forward in the last clause bears a degree of emphasis. While it is perfectly obvious that the Lord is making this remarkable statement TODAY and not YESTERDAY or TOMORROW, the stress is upon the fact that TODAY, *this very day, today already—the thief will be with Christ in paradise.* Frequently, in the normal course of things, it would take perhaps two or three days until a man would die hanging on a cross, so lingering was death by crucifixion. But our Lord Jesus Christ assures this thief that his sufferings will cease TODAY, *and that the thief will be with the Lord, where He is*—TODAY.

"The adverb 'today' [Greek, *seimeron*] stands first

and immediately with the prepositional phrase 'with Me' [*met' emou*], which is followed by the rest of the sentence in order: 'shall be in paradise' [*esei en to paradeiso*], so that the whole clause reads literally: 'Today with Me (pronoun emphatic) thou shalt be in the paradise.' The position of 'today' [*seimeron*] in immediate proximity with the words 'with me' [*met' emou*] argues for the fact that it belongs to the second clause. . . .

"Our Lord's reply to the thief's humble plea assured the thief of continued existence in the state of blessedness into which he would enter immediately after death—that state of conscious union and perfect fellowship with Christ. The thief would not have to wait until the Lord returned to be with Him—TODAY HE WOULD BE WITH HIM WHERE HE WAS. Such is the true meaning of the Lord's promise and it imparts consolation and comfort to every believing heart since it assures all true believers of the immediate translation of their spirits into the presence of the Lord at the instant of physical death. The scheme of transferring the comma and thus making the word '*today*' a part of the first '*I say to thee*' dishonors the Lord and belongs to a subtle, satanically-devised system of teaching that denies Heaven *ad interim* to the soul that dies in Christ. But let no true Christian be troubled or disturbed. The Scriptures leave no doubt for us on this point."[35]

(We will deal further with the subject of life beyond the grave in Chapter X.)

How thrilling and assuring are Paul's words to the saints at Philippi, placed by the Spirit of God in the divine canon for us as well: "For our conversation is in heaven; from whence also we look for the Saviour, the Lord Jesus Christ" (Philippians 3:20). The word unfortunately translated "conversation" here by the

35. November, 1970; "Did The Thief on the Cross Go Immediately to Paradise?"; p. 6

King James translators is the Greek *politeuma* and literally means citizenship, commonwealth, enfranchisement!

Thank God, the believer's citizenship is in Heaven!

CHAPTER VIII

The Armstrong Teaching About Israel

One important facet of the Worldwide Church of God doctrinal platform includes the imaginative speculation—held by many different cults over the years, especially during the nineteenth and twentieth centuries—that Anglo-Saxon people are the "lost Ten Tribes of Israel." Calling it the "Anglo-American Miracle,"[1] Britain is identified as Ephraim while America is announced as Manasseh. How "Ephraimites" leaving England for the New World landed in America as "Manassites" is not explained. (They must have experienced something much more potent than the usual seasickness on that voyage!)

Although, as one Jewish scholar expressed it, "not a scintilla of sacred or secular history can be found to support it,"[2] Armstrong calls this "the vital KEY, needed to unlock prophetic doors to understanding,"[3] saying that although it had long been lost, he rediscovered it. This claim is made even though the theory, with only slight variations, has long been held by the movement known as British-Israelism. In fact, it "owes its modern success to Richard Brothers (1757-1824), a half-pay officer of eccentric habits in the English navy." He authored 15 books, mostly endeavoring to prove Israelitish ancestry for the English, and insisted "Israel" was about to be restored to the Holy Land where he (Brothers) would be exalted as "Prince of the Hebrews and Ruler of the World." Brothers was eventually confined to an institution for the mentally unbalanced, but his "Correct Account of the Invasion of England by the Saxons, Showing the

---

1. *The Plain Truth*, October-November, 1970; p. 3
2. *The Shofar*, Second Quarter, 1963; Dr. James A. Voss; p. 2
3. *The United States And The British Commonwealth In Prophecy*, Copyright, 1954; p. 1

English Nation to be Descendants of the Lost Ten Tribes" spawned all the followers of the theory to this day.[4]

Herbert W. Armstrong says: "The United States, Great Britain, and the democracies of northwestern Europe are actually modern ISRAEL—descended from the so-called lost Ten Tribes." Again he declares: "The peoples of the United States and British Commonwealth (Britain, Australia, Canada, etc.) are the descendants of the ancient Israel of your Bible. So our peoples are mentioned in Bible prophecy."[5]

He says again: "The people of ten-tribed Israel also migrated northwest. Though the Assyrians had taken Israel into captivity, the Israelites did not remain as slaves of the Assyrians in Europe. They continued on a little further—into Western Europe, the Scandinavian peninsula, and the British Isles!. . .

"After several generations, the tribe of Joseph divided into the *two* tribes of Ephraim and Manasseh which today are the British and American people."[6]

This is, of course, *pure fiction*!

Regarding the other eight tribes, Armstrong declares: "Suffice it to say here, that there is ample evidence that these other eight tribes have descended into such northwestern European nations as Holland, Belgium, Denmark, Northern France, Luxembourg, Switzerland, Sweden, Norway, Finland, and at least portions of western Germany. The people of Iceland are also of Viking stock."[7] He does not offer his readers any of this "ample evidence"; apparently they are expected to take his word for it.

One of the Armstrong writers, in a *Tomorrow's World*

4. See *Hastings' Encyclopedia Of Religion And Ethics,* Section "Anglo-Israel"; Quoted in *The Delusion Of British-Israelism,* Anton Darms, n.d.; Loizeaux Brothers, Neptune, New Jersey; pp. 15-17
5. *Will Russia Attack America?* © 1956,1970,1971; p. 1
6. *Which Day Is The Christian Sabbath?* © 1962,1964,1968,1970,1971; pp.63, 64
7. *The United States And The British Commonwealth In Prophecy,* p. 22

science article, "The DEATH of the OCEANS," steals a passage pertaining to Israel and applies it to the Anglo-Saxons. He assumes: "SPEAKING TO the peoples of modern United States and the British Commonwealth of nations, God levels this stinging rebuke:

"'Hear the word of the Lord, oh people of Israel, the Lord has filed a lawsuit against you listing the following charges: There is no faithfulness, no kindness, no knowledge of God in your land. You swear and lie and kill and steal and commit adultery. There is violence everywhere, with one murder after another. That is *why* your land is not producing: it is filled with sadness and *all living things grow sick and die*: the animals, the birds and EVEN THE FISH BEGIN TO DISAPPEAR' (Hosea 4:1-3, *Living Prophecies* version).

"This is a vivid description of our MODERN 20TH-CENTURY WORLD! Who could deny the obvious connection between this prophecy and today's impending 'terracide'?"[8]

The author's reasoning is: *our oceans are being polluted, so that makes this a fulfillment of God's prophecy to Israel through Hosea!* In fact, he announces the Bible "scooped the news of this mind-boggling prospect." In typical Worldwide Church of God fashion, the writer merely lifts "fish" out of the text, offering no explanation of animals, birds or even "your land is not producing." We imagine the latter phrase was ignored for the obvious reason it certainly could not, even by an Armstrongite flight of imagination, apply to the most productive land in the world today: the United States of America. This is merely one illustration of the foolish conclusions resulting from trying to apply Israel's prophecies to Britain and America.

---

8. August, 1971; K. C. Lee; p. 24

Armstrong does not believe Anglo-Saxon people are Gentiles at all. He speaks of "...the dumfounding, astonishing TRUTH that the people of the United States, the British, the peoples of Northwestern Europe, are, in actual fact, those very 'Lost' Ten Tribes of the nation ISRAEL—and not by birth Gentiles at all!"[9]

How did these non-Gentiles get confused and forget they were Israelites? Armstrong tells his readers it was when they abandoned the seventh-day Sabbath. He writes: "When ISRAEL rejected this identifying SIGN, it most assuredly *did not* identify them—period! It did not distinguish them from Gentiles—they came to believe that *they* were Gentiles. The Gentile people of the world CALLED THEM GENTILES. The JEWS called them Gentiles!"[10]

According to a writer in *Tomorrow's World,* "The word 'Gentile' is a relative term. It means an outsider. In the Biblical usage it means a person who is not a physical Israelite, i.e., a descendant of Jacob. Inasmuch as most of the world is today unaware of the identity of *eleven* out of the twelve tribes of Israel, the word 'Gentile' is commonly used today to mean a non-Jew. There are many non-Jews, however, who are Israelites."[11]

We might point out that the Hebrew word is *goi* and is translated in the King James Version 373 times "nation," 142 times "heathen," 30 times "Gentile," 3 times "people," and once "another." The New Testament word is *ethnos* and is translated 93 times "Gentiles" (plural), 64 times "nation," 5 times "heathen," and 2 times "people."

Mr. Armstrong tells his readers that the coming Great Tribulation is the "greatest time of trouble of all history, the time of 'Jacob's trouble,' meaning

9. *Which Day Is The Christian Sabbath?* p. 65
10. Ibid.; p. 70
11. May, 1971; p. 45

U.S. and British nations. . ."[12] And the Day of the Lord "is the time when God will first intervene supernaturally in this world's affairs, to END the Great Tribulation, into which the world is now heading, and to punish the Gentile nations for having so frightfully punished Britain-U.S. and the Jewish people in World War III, and the imminent Tribulation."[13]

Here is a sample, from Obadiah 15, of how Armstrong and his "ever ready brackets" endeavor to prove the point. His version is: ". . .As thou hast done, it shall be done unto thee. . . .But upon Mount Zion [Jerusalem] shall be deliverance, and there shall be holiness [at Christ's coming]; and the house of Jacob [U.S.-British, *not* Jews] shall possess their possessions. And the house of Jacob shall be a fire, and the house of Joseph [U.S.-British] a flame, and the house of Esau [Turkey] for stubble, and they shall kindle in them, and devour them; and there shall not be any remaining of the house of Esau; for the Eternal hath spoken it."[14]

Another sample is his quotation of Genesis 35:9-12, which he gives as follows: "And God appeared unto Jacob. . .and God said unto him, Thy name is Jacob: thy name shall not be called any more Jacob, but ISRAEL shall be thy name. . . .I am God Almighty: be fruitful and multiply; a nation [today the United States] and a company of nations [today the British Commonwealth] shall be of thee, and kings shall come out of thy loins; and the LAND which I gave Abraham and Isaac, to thee I will give it, and to thy seed after thee will I give the land."[15]

In order to make this thesis work, it is necessary to limit "Jews" to Judah. He says: "The term 'Jew'

---

12. *Tomorrow's World,* November, 1971; "Personal"; p. 48
13. Ibid.
14. Ibid.
15. November, 1971; "What Is The *Reward* Of The Saved. . .*Heaven?*"; p. 5

is merely a nickname for 'Judah.' It applies to one nation, or House of Judah ONLY—never to the House of ISRAEL.

". . .It is wrong to call the Jews of today 'Israel.' They are not Israel,—they are JUDAH! And wherever ISRAEL is today, remember that ISRAEL *does not mean JEW!*"[16]

It is very simple to prove from the Scripture that this claim does not hold water. For example, Paul, in his letter to the Church at Rome, spoke of the Jews, saying: "What advantage then hath the Jew? or what profit is there of circumcision? Much every way: chiefly, because that unto them were committed the oracles of God" (Romans 3:1,2). Yet, in the same letter, he later says: "Who are Israelites; to whom pertaineth the adoption, and the glory, and the covenants, and the giving of the law, and the service of God, and the promises" (Romans 9:4). Here "Jew" and "Israelites" are used interchangeably for describing to whom the Old Testament was committed.

Again, in the same epistle, Paul repeatedly speaks of both Jew and Gentile. By way of example, he warns of judgment for the wicked to "the Jew first, and also of the Gentile" (Romans 2:9); he offers blessing for those who work good, "to the Jew first, and also to the Gentile" (Romans 2:10); he describes "both Jews and Gentiles" as being "under sin" (Romans 3:9); he speaks of God being "the God of the Jews" and "of the Gentiles also" (Romans 3:29); he insists God's calling is "not of the Jews only, but also of the Gentiles" (Romans 9:24); and he offers salvation to anyone who will call upon the name of the Lord, since "there is no difference between the Jew and the Greek" (Romans 10:12,13; see also Romans 1:16).

16. *The United States And The British Commonwealth In Prophecy,* p. 7

Are we to understand that judgment, blessing, sin, God, calling and salvation are all matters concerning Jews and Gentiles, but not Israelites? To ask the question is to answer it. Peter addressed the inhabitants in Palestine as "men of Israel" (Acts 3:12), exactly as Paul did the Jews out of Palestine (Acts 13:16,17).

As for Jew and Israelite being used interchangeably, we would like to point out that Paul said of himself, "I am verily a man which am a Jew" (Acts 22:3), yet he insisted every bit as strenuously, "Are they Israelites? so am I" (II Corinthians 11:22).

Again, in that classic passage where Paul divided saved and lost mankind into three classes—"Give none offence neither to the Jews, nor to the Gentiles, nor to the church of God" (I Corinthians 10:32)—did he err in not adding a fourth classification, "nor to the lost ten tribes"? Armstrong's philosophy would have us think so.

Are we to conclude that when Paul described the reaction of Jews and Greeks to the preaching of the cross in I Corinthians 1:18-25, he just "forgot" about Israel? Was he wrong in just discussing "Jews by nature" and Gentiles by nature in Galatians 2:11-15, ignoring Israel? Did he make another mistake in Galatians 3:28, saying, "There is neither Jew nor Greek. . .in Christ Jesus," when he should have said, "There is neither Jew, nor Israelite, nor Greek"?

One more word: When Paul called the Ephesian elders around him at Miletus and reminded them of his anointed ministry in their midst, he said: "I kept back nothing that was profitable unto you, but have shewed you, and have taught you publickly, and from house to house, Testifying both to the Jews, and also to the Greeks. . ." (Acts 20:20,21). Remember, this was Ephesus—not Judea. According to Armstrong, the "Jews" were in Palestine, not "northwest" of Palestine, across the Mediterranean in Asia. If Armstrong's theory is right, Paul should have said he had been "testifying both to the *Israelites*, and also to the Greeks." However, we think Armstrong made the mistake, not the Apostle Paul. Frankly, the claim that "Jew" always refers to Judah has more holes than a fisherman's seine.

While we cringe at the thought of using this much space, in order to be fair to his position, we will reproduce an entire section wherein Armstrong "locates" *lost* Israel. He writes: "Without further suspense, let us see where prophecy locates these Birthright holders, now possessing the throne of David and earth's richest national blessings.

"Remember they are distinguished from Judah—the Jews—by various names, 'Ephraim,' 'Joseph,' 'Jacob,' 'Rachel,' (the mother of Joseph), Samaria, (the former home) 'Israel.'

"According to Hosea 12:1, 'Ephraim followeth after the east wind.' An 'east wind' travels west. Ephraim must have gone *west* from Assyria.

"When the Eternal swore of David to perpetuate his throne, he said: 'I will *set* his hand (sceptre) *in the sea.*' (Psalm 89:25). The throne is to be 'set,' planted, 'in the sea.'

"Thru Jeremiah the Eternal said: 'Backsliding Israel hath justified herself more than treacherous Judah. Go and proclaim these words *toward the* NORTH and say, Return thou backsliding Israel, saith the Lord.' (Jer. 3:11-12). Israel is clearly distinguished from Judah. And in these last days messengers are to go 'toward the NORTH' (of Jerusalem) in order to locate lost Israel and proclaim this warning. So the location, we now find, is toward the north, also west, and in the sea.

"The 18th verse, same chapter, says: 'In those days the house of Judah shall walk with the house of Israel, (margin, *to* the House of Israel), and they shall come together *out of the land of the north* to the land that

I have given for an inheritance unto your fathers.' At the future Exodus, at Christ's coming, they are to return to Palestine out of the land of the NORTH!

"After saying, 'How shall I give thee up, Ephraim?' the Eternal, speaking thru Hosea, says: 'then the children shall tremble *from the WEST.*' (Hos. 11:8,10).

"Again: 'Behold, I will bring them *from the north country*, and gather them from *the coasts of the earth.*' (Jer. 31:8). This prophecy is for consideration in the 'latter days' (Jer. 30:24; 31:1), and is addressed to 'Israel,' (verses 2,4,9,) to 'Ephraim,' (verses 6,9,) and 'Samaria,' (verse 5). Here is added another hint—'the coasts of the earth'—evidently they are dominant at sea.

"Referring to the House of ISRAEL (not Judah) in Isaiah 49:3,6, God says: 'Behold these shall come from far: and lo, these *from the* NORTH *and from the* WEST; and these from the land of Sinim.' (Isa. 49:12). In the Hebrew, the language in which this was originally inspired, there is no word for 'NORTHWEST,' but this term is designated by the phrase, 'the north and the west.' It means, literally, the NORTHWEST! The Vulgate renders 'Sinim' as Australi, or 'Australia.' So we now have the location NORTHWEST of JERUSALEM!

"Hence, Israel of TODAY—Israel of the day of Jeremiah's 'planting' of David's throne—is located specifically as NORTHWEST of JERUSALEM, and IN THE SEA!

"Let us locate this land more specifically!

"The same 49th chapter of Isaiah begins with this: 'Listen, *O Isles,* unto me.' The people addressed, Israel, are called 'O Isles,' in the first verse and 'O Israel' in the third verse.

"The 31st chapter of Jeremiah, locating Israel in the 'north country,' says: 'I am a father to Israel, and Ephraim is my first born. . .Hear the word of the Lord, O ye nations'—(Ephraim, Manasseh)—'and declared *in the isles* afar off.' (Jer. 31:9-10).

"Again: 'Keep silence before me, O islands. . .thou, Israel, art my servant Jacob whom I have chosen.' (Isa. 41:5,8).

"In Jer. 31:7, the message to be declared 'in the isles afar off' (verse 10), is to be shouted in 'the CHIEF OF THE NATIONS.'

"So, finally, today, as in Jeremiah's day, the House of ISRAEL is IN THE ISLES, which are '*in the sea*,' the CHIEF of the nations, NORTHWEST of Jerusalem! A coast-dwelling, and therefore sea-dominant people.

"Certainly there can be no mistaking that identity!

"Take a map of Europe. Lay a line due NORTHWEST of Jerusalem across the continent of Europe, until you come to the sea, and then to the islands in the sea!

"This line takes you direct to the BRITISH ISLES!"[17]

It is fantastic that such an unrelated conglomeration of twisted texts should be put together to make Israel some "islands," "northwest of Jerusalem" and "chief of the nations"! How cleverly Armstrong took west and north and combined them into northwest! Yet by no stretch of the imagination (or ruler placed on a map) could Australia be northwest of Palestine. So he discovers a Vulgate rendering of *Sinim* as Australi, although Strong's Hebrew and Chaldee dictionary identifies it as "a distant *oriental* region," hardly a description of Australia!

We trust our readers will look up all the Scriptures Armstrong quotes in the above passage, read the entire verses with their context, and his theory will prove to be even more fantastic. He has Ephraim going west because it says in Hosea 12:1 that Ephraim "followeth after the east wind," and he says that "travels west." But the same verse says that Ephraim

---

17. Ibid.; pp. 16,17

"feedeth on wind," and he conveniently ignores trying to make a literal interpretation of this part of the verse.

The next verse referred to, Psalm 89:25, finds him quoting only the first half of the verse, "I will set his hand also in the sea," in order to identify *hand* as "sceptre," since he needed to get David's throne "in the sea." But the latter half of the verse, which he ignored, goes on to say, "and his right hand in the rivers." If "setting his hand" is planting the throne of David in the sea, what, pray tell, is "setting his right hand in the rivers," especially since "right hand" speaks of superior strength? Furthermore, the promise regarding "the sceptre" was not given to Joseph (or Ephraim or Manasseh), but to Judah. Genesis 49:10 says: "The sceptre shall not depart from Judah, nor a lawgiver from between his feet, until Shiloh come. . ." Yet Armstrong wants to take that non-departable throne from Judah and give it to Ephraim, he wants to remove it from Judah and put it on an island in the Atlantic Ocean!

Notice also, in the above quotation from Armstrong's pen, how he quotes the Scripture speaking of "the isles afar off," because he is trying to establish a point identifying those "isles" as the British Isles, yet surely one with even an elementary understanding of Scriptures is aware that the phrase "in the isles," as most marginal renderings give it, is "the coasts," or, more literally, "a habitable spot"—land, coast or island. Even considered "islands," it would make every bit as much sense to identify Jeremiah 31:10 with the Philippine Islands as the British Isles. As for the "isles" of these passages, they are identified as peoples from afar, in contrast to Israel—that is, Gentiles! So rather than proving Armstrong's theory, it disproves it. And what a stretch of the imagination it takes to call once mighty, now feeble Britain "the chief of the nations!"

Fantastic is the only way to describe some of Armstrong's fanciful flights in seeking to establish his thesis. He has Jeremiah traveling to Ireland with David's throne and a young Hebrew princess, the daughter of Zedekiah, there to marry a young prince eventually crowned King Herremon. To which he breathlessly adds: "The crown worn by King Herremon and the sovereigns of ancient Ireland had TWELVE POINTS!"[18] The inference being, of course, that the twelve points in the crown represented the twelve tribes of Israel. But perhaps the twelve points represented the twelve apostles! Or perhaps they signified the twelve gates in the New Jerusalem!

Armstrong's "twelve points" in the crown conflict with another of his amazing coincidences, however. Offering what he calls "overwhelming" proof that Manasseh is America, he announces: "The proof that we are Manasseh is overwhelming. Manasseh was to separate from Ephraim and become the greatest, wealthiest single nation of earth's history. We alone have fulfilled this prophecy. Manasseh was, in fact a *thirteenth* tribe. There were twelve original tribes. Joseph was one of these twelve. But when Joseph divided into TWO tribes and Manasseh separated into an independent nation, it became a *thirteenth* tribe. It started with *thirteen* colonies."[19]

Note how conveniently Armstrong's "tribe count" fluctuates back and forth to fit his imaginary evidence. If the crown has twelve points, then he points to twelve tribes. If the founding of America was launched with thirteen colonies, then he just as happily points to thirteen tribes. In the name of sanity, *he cannot have both*!

In trying to identify the throne of Queen Elizabeth II with David's throne, Armstrong—after first telling his

18. Ibid.; p. 19
19. Ibid.; p. 22

readers the "real ancient history of Ireland is rather vague, now colored with some legend,"[20] —in case anyone checks history and discovers it doesn't agree with what he says, he'll have an out—has the tribe of Dan landing in Ireland about 700 B.C., then Jeremiah arriving with Zedekiah's daughter about 580 B.C., bringing with them "the stone of destiny."[21] Armstrong says: "The stone rests, today, in Westminster Abbey in London, and the Coronation Chair is built over and around it. A sign beside it labels it 'Jacob's pillar-stone.' (Gen. 28:18.)"[22]

The thought of this stone being the stone used by Jacob for a pillow at Bethel is as fantastic as the Prophet Jeremiah's sojourn to Ireland. The sandstone of the Bethel region is *white*; the sandstone in the coronation chair is *red*. If it came from Bethel it is either the only piece of red sandstone ever to be found in that area, or it had a miraculous color transformation while crossing the sea. This "Stone of Scone," as it is also known, was brought from the Abbey of Scone by Edward I in 1296. Scientists say it is sandstone such as found in Western Scotland, not Palestine.

The illustrious Horatius Bonar, one of England's mightiest pulpiteers of yesteryear, writing about the supposed migration, points out: ". . .if the Anglo-Israelite Theory be true, the Ten Tribes poured in upon Great Britain and settled themselves there, drove back the Aborigines, but left their religion, their books, their priesthood, their language, their names, behind them like cast-off clothes, in order to prevent themselves from being identified, as if ashamed of their ancestry. . . .

"There is no evidence in the Bible, or in history, or tradition, for any such Israelitish emigration. Such a

20. Ibid.; p. 19
21. Ibid.
22. Ibid.

flood could not have passed over Europe, either north or south, without leaving some trace or being mentioned in history. If some two or three millions of Israelites did pour into this remote and barbarous island of ours, it must have been before the Romans came; and such a flood of Easterns must have made it a populous island, which certainly it was not. . . .

"Noah's prophecy stands out clear and sharp with its threefold ethnology; Shem, Ham and Japheth are the roots of the nations, and God has kept them distinct: let us beware of confounding them. History tells us that our pedigree is to be traced to Japheth. The modern discoveries in ethnology confirm this beyond a doubt; Eastern monuments, whether of Assyria or Egypt, tell the same story."[23]

Twisting Scripture to establish a point, as we have already seen, is an Armstrong trademark. So obsessed is he with his "lost ten tribes" theory—although nowhere does the Bible refer to any "lost" tribes; it does speak of *scattered* and *dispersed*, but never *lost*—that Mr. Armstrong thinks he sees "lost tribes" in many references. For example, referring to the parable of the pounds, Armstrong says: "Jesus had come 'to His own,' the Jews—the remnant of the Kingdom of JUDAH—and 'they received Him not' (John 1:11), so Jesus turned to 'the lost sheep of the House of Israel' (Matt. 15:24), and sent His twelve apostles to them (Matt. 10:6). That is, to the so-called 'Lost Ten Tribes' of Israel. They were then, most of them, in Northwestern Europe and the British Isles. . ."[24]

But, in the first place, the expression "lost sheep" is not compatible with "lost tribes." In the second place, if we were to admit they were compatible, would this mean that the apostles went to England? Did they go to the United States? Did they go to Ireland?

---

23. "Are We the Ten Tribes?"; quoted in *The Delusion Of British-Israelism*, pp. 138,139
24. *What'll You Be Doing In The Next Life?* © 1967,1969; p. 5

Did they go to Denmark? No, they went into the towns of that particular area. Luke 9:6 describes it: "And they departed, and went through the towns, preaching the gospel, and healing every where."

Another mistake Armstrong makes is in his claim that Israel never returned after the captivity to Palestine. He says: "They did NOT return to Palestine with the Jews in the days of Ezra and Nehemiah, as some erroneously believe. Those who returned to rebuild the temple and restore worship in Jerusalem at that time, 70 years after JUDAH's captivity, were *only* those of the House of Judah whom Nebuchadnezzar had carried to Babylon."[25]

That statement simply will not stand up under examination. For example, Ezra 2:70 says, "So the priests, and the Levites, and some of the people, and the singers, and the porters, and the Nethinims, dwelt in their cities, and all Israel in their cities." Note the expression, "all Israel," a term Armstrong says does not refer to the Jews.

In Ezra 6:16,17, at the time of the dedication of the temple, we are told: "And the children of Israel, the priests, and the Levites, and the rest of the children of the captivity, kept the dedication of this house of God with joy, And offered at the dedication of this house of God an hundred bullocks, two hundred rams, four hundred lambs; and for a sin-offering for all Israel, twelve he goats, according to the number of the tribes of Israel." Note that it was "the children of Israel" who were included in this time of dedication—and *twelve* he goats were offered representing all twelve tribes.

In Ezra 7:27,28, we read: "Blessed be the Lord God of our fathers, which hath put such a thing as this in the king's heart, to beautify the house of the Lord

25. *The United States And The British Commonwealth In Prophecy,* p. 9

which is in Jerusalem: And hath extended mercy unto me before the king, and his counsellors, and before all the king's mighty princes. And I was strengthened as the hand of the Lord my God was upon me, and I gathered together out of Israel chief men to go up with me." Notice where he gathered these chief men: "*out of Israel*"!

The Book of Nehemiah tells the same story. For example, in Nehemiah 7:6,7: "These are the children of the province, that went up out of the captivity, of those that had been carried away, whom Nebuchadnezzar the king of Babylon had carried away, and came again to Jerusalem and to Judah, every one unto his city; Who came with Zerubbabel, Jeshua, Nehemiah, Azariah, Raamiah, Nahamani, Mordecai, Bilshan, Mispereth, Bigvai, Nehum, Baanah. The number, I say, of the men of the people of Israel was this." Note that these returnees to the Promised Land after the captivity are called "the people of Israel." Incidentally, verse 61 of the same chapter speaks of some who could not prove their Israelitish background, saying of them, "they could not shew their father's house, nor their seed, whether they were of Israel."

Daniel's seventy sevens is further proof (Daniel 9:24-27). That prophecy was given to Daniel and referred to those going back to Palestine—in fact, the prophecy was to start with "the going forth of the commandment to restore and to build Jerusalem." Yet it was addressed to "thy people" (vs. 24), earlier identified in the chapter as "my people ISRAEL" (vs. 20). And Malachi, the last of the post-exilic prophets, addressed the people in the land as "Israel" (Malachi 1:1).

Regarding whether only Judah returned to Israel following the captivity, Anton Darms, who was mixed up in Anglo-Israelism for over thiry years himself, writes: "The prophets did not say that all of Judah or all of Israel, but that only A REMNANT OF JUDAH and A REMNANT OF ISRAEL, would return. Enough of the ten tribes of Israel returned with Judah to warrant Ezra and Nehemiah using the terms 'Israel' and 'Jew' interchangeably. 'Israel' appears in these two books *sixty-two* times, whereas 'Jew' appears but *nineteen* times. Even the larger and more inclusive term 'children of Israel' is used six times in Ezra and ten times in Nehemiah.

"If, as British-Israelism teaches, the Jews are persons belonging to the tribe or house of Judah only, and only Jews returned to Palestine, as they say, then of a certainty the term 'children of Israel' would not have been used in these historical records, and the term 'Jews' only, would appear."[26]

To this the noted Hebrew scholar, David Baron, adds: "As to those who remained behind in the one hundred and twenty-seven provinces of the Persian Empire, which included all the territories of ancient Assyria, Anglo-Israelites would say they were of the kingdom of 'Israel'; but in the Book of Esther, where we get a vivid glimpse of them at a period subsequent to the partial restoration under Zerubbabel and Joshua, they are called forty-five times by the name 'Jews,' and not once by the name 'Israel'!

"In the New Testament the same people who are called 'Jews' one hundred and seventy-four times are also called 'Israel' no fewer than seventy-five times."[27]

This is incontrovertible evidence of the falsity of the Armstrong position.

It is amazing that Armstrong and his Worldwide Church of God would put Queen Elizabeth on the throne of David, but that is exactly what they do. A writer in *The Plain Truth* boldly announces: "The world may scoff and sneer at the truth, the world may deny the *facts of history*, but Queen Elizabeth

---

26. *The Delusion Of British-Israelism*, p. 50
27. *For Bible Students Only*, n.d.; Dunham Publishing Company, Findlay, Ohio; p. 26

is ruling over part of Israel—the tribe of Ephraim. She sits upon the throne of David!—the very throne that Jesus Christ shall take when he returns to rule the world...

"Yes, on the throne of England reigns a daughter of David, a descendant of King Zedekiah's daughter whom Jeremiah the prophet took to Ireland together with the stone of destiny. From the marriage of that young princess has descended a dynasty that has ruled Ireland, Scotland and England for over 2500 years! And all of them have been crowned over the stone of destiny, Jacob's pillow stone."[28]

After a wild flight of imagination, in which Herbert W. Armstrong makes part of Jeremiah's ministry tearing down the throne of David in Palestine and planting it in Ireland through the daughter of Zedekiah, whom he identifies as Tea-Tephi (called by some others Tea-Zephia), then having that throne overturned and transplanted in Scotland, then overturned again and transplanted in England, he says: "In view of the linking together of Biblical history, prophecy, and Irish history, can anyone deny that this Hebrew princess was the daughter of King Zedekiah of Judah, and therefore heir to the throne of David?—That the aged patriarch was in fact Jeremiah, and his companion Jeremiah's scribe, or secretary, Baruch?—And that King Herremon was a descendant of Zara, here married to the daughter of Pharez, healing the ancient breach?—That when the throne of David was first overturned by Jeremiah, it was re-PLANTED in Ireland, later overturned a second time and replanted in Scotland, overturned a third time and planted in London, from where it cannot be overturned or moved again UNTIL THE COMING OF CHRIST, when it

28. July, 1959; p. 32

once again shall be overturned and transplanted back in Jerusalem?

"The Royal Family of the British Commonwealth possesses a chart showing its ancestry, *every generation,* back to Herremon and Tephi, to Zedekiah, on back to David, and thru the scriptural genealogy clear to Adam! The writer has a copy of this chart, and also his own genealogy for each generation back into the line of ancient British kings, and therefore has the complete record of his genealogy thru the House of David clear to Adam—believe it or not!"[29]

We are certainly glad that he gives us a choice of believing or not believing. If there were such a chart that would prove the genealogies for "each generation back into the line of ancient British Kings" clear to the House of David, you may be sure that Armstrong would publish such *amazing*, ASTOUNDING proof in his book. No such evidence is offered! If he refers to what we think he does, however, we have the same phoney chart in our possession. Perhaps it would be helpful here to remind Mr. Armstrong of Paul's admonition to Timothy: "Neither give heed to fables and endless genealogies, which minister questions, rather than godly edifying which is in faith: so do" (I Timothy 1:4).

Two of Armstrong's principal proof passages for his Anglo-Saxon theory are Ezekiel 17 and Ezekiel 21. In the latter, he emphasizes: "And thou, profane wicked prince of Israel, whose day is come, when iniquity shall have an end, Thus saith the Lord God; Remove the diadem, and take off the crown: this shall not be the same: exalt him that is low, and abase him that is high. I will overturn, overturn, overturn it: and it shall be no more, until he come whose right it is; and I will give it him" (vss. 25-27). He says: "Does

29. *The United States And The British Commonwealth In Prophecy,* pp. 19,20

this mean the throne—the crown—is to cease to exist? Not at all! How could it be OVERTURNED three times—that is, TRANSFERRED from one to another, if it ceased to exist?"[30]

We have already seen that Armstrong identifies these three turnovers as the throne of David being transplanted from Palestine to Ireland, then to Scotland, then to England. But in truth and in fact, God is merely stating through Ezekiel the removal of Judah's final three kings: Jehoiakim, Jehoiachin and Zedekiah. Nothing more; nothing less. Furthermore, the word for overturn is the Hebrew *avvah* and simply means overthrow. There is not the slightest thought of a "transplanting"—that is purely an Armstrong invention to fit a preconceived theory.

The other favorite, Ezekiel 17, finds Armstrong emphasizing verse 22: "Thus saith the Lord God; I will also take of the highest branch of the high cedar, and will set it; I will crop off from the top of his young twigs a tender one, and will plant it upon an high mountain and eminent." Armstrong exults: "Ah! 'A tender young twig!' The twigs of this highest branch represent the children of King Zedekiah! Certainly a tender young twig, then, represents a DAUGHTER!

"'. . .and will PLANT it.' Could symbolic language say plainer this young Jewish Princess is to become the royal seed for PLANTING again of David's throne? Where?

"'. . .upon a high mountain and eminent,' says the Eternal! A 'mountain' in symbol always represents a NATION. But WHICH nation?

"'In the mountain of the height of ISRAEL will I plant it,' answers the Eternal! David's throne now is to be planted in ISRAEL, after being thrown down from JUDAH! Could language be PLAINER?"[31]

---

30. Ibid.; p. 13
31. Ibid.; p. 14

Frankly, we think it could! As Anton Darms points out: "The promise that God 'will crop off from the top of his young twigs A TENDER ONE' (ver. 22) and will plant it 'in the mountain of the height of Israel' has no application whatever to Tea Tephi or to the bringing of David's crown to Great Britain. It refers directly to the coming of the Promised Messiah, who more than a century prior to Ezekiel's time was described by Isaiah as 'A ROD OUT OF THE STEM OF JESSE, AND A BRANCH growing out of his roots' (Isaiah 11:1). This tender twig was also known to Jeremiah as 'A RIGHTEOUS BRANCH' raised up unto David, 'A KING WHO SHALL REIGN AND PROSPER,' who will 'execute judgment and justice in the earth' (Jeremiah 23:5)."[32]

Is it possible that a descendant of David could actually be on the British throne? God's promise to David, in II Samuel 7, was limited to a seed proceeding "out of thy bowels," that is, of his own flesh, and it was to that fleshly seed that God promised to "establish the throne" forever. In fact, II Samuel 7:16 puts it: "And thine house and thy kingdom shall be established for ever before thee: thy throne shall be established for ever." This promise was to the "house" of David; that is, to his family. Now, as anyone can discover by checking the Scripture, David was of the tribe of Judah. Yet, according to Armstrong, Judah is the only tribe not lost, located now in the land of Palestine and called "Jews" by everyone. So Queen Elizabeth could not possibly be a descendant of David, and she could not possibly be entitled to sit on David's throne. Anyway, we find it a little absurd to think that God would have *a woman* on David's throne! Doesn't Armstrong know God said, "Suffer not a woman to. . . usurp authority over the man. . ." (I Timothy 2:12)?

---

32. *The Delusion Of British-Israelism*, p. 112

Jeremiah 33:17 says: "For thus saith the Lord; David shall never want **A MAN** to sit upon the throne of the house of Israel." The word "man" is the Hebrew *ish*, applying to a male; the Hebrew for woman is *ishshah*. Furthermore, four verses farther on, God identifies it as "A SON" to reign on David's throne (Jeremiah 33:21).

Armstrong places heavy emphasis on the fact that someone must be continuously reigning from David's throne, although that is not what the Scripture says. In fact, if the above passage in Jeremiah of the throne of David being occupied continuously, as he interprets it, hinges on whether "God's promise has failed," then things look bad for God. The same passage says: "Neither shall the priests the Levites want a man before me to offer burnt-offerings, and to kindle meat-offerings, and to do sacrifice continually" (vs. 18). The time God refers to here will see lack in *neither* throne *nor* priesthood, something hardly true in Britain or America today. When Armstrong deals with this passage he "jumps" from verse 17 to verse 19, omitting the portion which annihilates his position.

Armstrong continues: ". . .But HOW can Jesus Christ, when He returns again to earth, take over and sit upon a throne that long ago ceased to exist?

"IF the throne of David ceased with Zedekiah, then it does not exist today. And if it does not exist, *how shall Christ sit upon a non-existent throne*? See Luke 1:31-32. And, since it was to continue through *all* generations, how about those many generations between Zedekiah and the birth of Jesus?"[33]

But the prophet Hosea, who ministered to Israel up to and even into the Syrian captivity, warned: "For the children of Israel shall abide many days without a king, and without a prince, and without a sacrifice, and without an image, and without an ephod, and

---

33. *The United States And The British Commonwealth In Prophecy*, pp. 5,6

without teraphim: Afterward shall the children of Israel return, and seek the Lord their God, and David their king; and shall fear the Lord and his goodness in the latter days" (Hosea 3:4,5). In other words, Israel was to be without rulers for "many days," something that is certainly not true of the British Commonwealth or the United States of America. And note that this fate of being without rulers was to continue until they "returned, and seek the Lord their God, and David their king." Neither Britain nor the United States—in all their godlessness and iniquity—could qualify for this stipulation, yet both have rulers. In fact, because of our refusal to listen to Armstrong, here is how one of his writers describes us: "Today the conditions are similar to Noah's day and becoming so more all the time (Matt. 24:37). And as Noah's words fell on deaf ears, so the words of this Work bounce off the flinty foreheads of a rebellious and stiff-necked nation!"[34]

In one of Balaam's prophecies about Israel, pronounced with the Spirit of the Lord upon him, he said: "For from the top of the rocks I see him, and from the hills I behold him: lo, the people shall dwell alone, and shall not be reckoned among the nations" (Numbers 23:9). By no stretch of the imagination could this be considered true of either Great Britain or the United States. Neither the British Commonwealth nor America dwells alone, refusing to be numbered among the nations. The covenants and treaties of both countries with other nations are almost as numerous as the stones on the Mississippi River bottom!

Again, in Leviticus 26—the chapter to which Armstrong refers so repeatedly for his unexplained 2,520 years—Jehovah warned Israel, speaking of the third chastisement: "I will also send wild beasts among you, which shall rob you of your children, and destroy

34. *Tomorrow's World,* September, 1971; Brian Knowles, "What 'on Earth' Is God Doing?"; p. 13

your cattle, and make you few in number; and your highways shall be desolate" (vs. 22). To ask the question, "When have the inhabitants of Great Britain or the United States become few in number?" is to show how ridiculous it is to apply this passage to these nations. The last time we checked, for example, the United States was the fourth most populous nation in the world! This hardly fits the "few in number" tag.

We think it would be both fitting and helpful to quote a rebuttal of the Anglo-Saxon theory from the pen of J. Oswald Sanders: "In the realm of SCHOLARSHIP, it is discredited. The theory is chiefly concerned with history, ethnology, philology and anthropology, all of which can be tested by secular scholarship. Tested factually, British-Israelism makes a very poor showing.

"In the realm of *philology* there is no more affinity between English and Hebrew than there is between English and Chinese.

"As to *physiognomy*, there is strong contrast rather than striking similarity between the large-boned, fair-haired, blue-eyed Briton, and the thick-set, swarthy, brown-eyed Israelite.

"As to *graphology*, Israel has always written from right to left, while the Anglo-Saxons have always written from left to right. Such a radical change would be impossible except by direct compulsion, but evidence of such a change is totally lacking.

"*Racially*, the British, and Americans even more so, are extra-ordinarily mixed. Unlike the Hebrews, they have freely inter-mingled with other races, and to a large extent racial identity has been lost. Unlike the Hebrews, too, they are uncircumcised, and have therefore forfeited any claim to blessing under the covenant. Gen. 17:14; Gal. 6:15.

"*Historically*, it is unsubstantiated. The theory is thoroughly untenable on historical grounds. So far as we are aware, no competent and reputable historian has identified himself with the movement. Some of the 'missing links' in genealogical tables in support of British-Israelism, we have perused, would utterly discredit any historian who sponsored it."[35]

Incidentally, regarding the Anglo-Israel theory, none other than Garner Ted Armstrong, being interviewed by the Rev. Lester Kinsolving, a syndicated religious writer for the public press, when queried about it, smiled and replied: "It's a likelihood, but it can't be proved. It's an interesting aside. We certainly don't regard this as a required belief, if that's what you're getting at."[36] When Kinsolving pointed out that in 1963, during an investigation of Ambassador College by the Pasadena City Attorney, it was learned that the school's constitution and by-laws, adopted in 1951, restricted the student body "to the race of Israel, whom we believe now to be the white, English-speaking Anglo-Saxon and Celtic people, and the democratic peoples of Northwestern Europe, in addition to the Jews descended from the Kingdom of Judah," he said Armstrong appeared surprised and hurriedly said: "That must have been while I was in the Navy. It's been altered dramatically. We have no such restrictions now."

Yet this is the same Garner Ted Armstrong who, in the Worldwide Church of God release, "WHY PROPHECY?" declared dogmatically and assuredly: "If you have not yet seen the startling identity of the lost ten tribes of Israel PROVED, write immediately for our FREE book, *The United States and British Commonwealth in Prophecy*!"[37]

Which makes one wonder—if Armstrong were whole-

---

35. *The Reaper,* New Zealand; quoted in *Prophecy Monthly,* September, 1944; pp. 31,32
36. *Fort Wayne News-Sentinel,* March 11, 1972. Kinsolving, incidentally, described Garner Ted's private office as being worthy of the White House or the office of a General Motors president. This is how some of the "tithes and offerings" of the faithful are expended.
37. © 1960,1970; p. 3

heartedly sincere when he wrote that—how sincere he is when he makes his dogmatic, all-capital-letter, italicized, bold-faced declarations regarding his other doctrines!

In closing this chapter, we can sum it up best by quoting our Lord's words to the church at Smyrna in Revelation 2:9: ". . .I know the blasphemy of them which say they are Jews, and are not, but are of the synagogue of Satan."

The same would be true of those who say they are Israelites. . .*and are not*!

CHAPTER IX

The Armstrong Teaching About the Church

Herbert W. Armstrong's followers are very specific about when the True Church was organized and when the apostasy began to set in. Garner Ted Armstrong announces, "On the Day of Pentecost, when the Church was built. . ."[1] In another article he gets more specific: "Immediately after the day of Pentecost, Monday, June 18, 31 A.D., the Church of God began to grow by leaps and bounds."[2]

Yet his father contradicts this statement (as well as his own claims in other places), saying: "Most people think the CHURCH was first started after the resurrection of Christ—on the Day of Pentecost. That was merely the NEW Testament Church. But the Church started long before that—it started way back in the days of MOSES!"[3]

The Armstrongs are just as specific and just as obliging with dates for the apostasy. Although he starts by confusing what he said in the previous paragraph, in one of his "Personal" columns, Herbert W. Armstrong declared: "Jesus Christ started God's Church in 31 A.D. And in 33 A.D. the Great Conspiracy got under way to organize and build the GREAT FALSE CHURCH—Satan's Church! The Great Conspiracy sought to destroy the true Church of God, and to blot out the Word of God, by *counterfeit* doctrines. They appropriated the NAME of Christ, and called themselves 'Christian'—then presented a *false* Christ and a *false* 'Christianity.' "[4]

We are not quite sure how to take his reference to these conspirators calling themselves "Christian." The

---

1. *Do You Have An Immortal Soul?* © 1957,1969,1970,1971; p. 6
2. *Tomorrow's World,* May, 1971; "Should You *Join* A Church?"; p. 11
3. *Does God Heal Today?* Copyright, 1952; p. 3
4. *Tomorrow's World,* August, 1971; p. 1

Word of God tells us that when Paul and Barnabas ministered for a year among the saints at Antioch, teaching much people: ". . .the disciples were called Christians first in Antioch" (Acts 11:26). So the term "Christian" was not started by the great conspirators of Satan's church calling themselves by that term; it was applied to Christ's very own *disciples* in Antioch who were won to Christ by Paul and Barnabas.

In another article, Mr. Armstrong develops this *counterfeit* Christianity of the great conspiracy, saying about its source: "BUT—marvel of marvels—the actual SOURCE of what is commonly accepted as 'Christianity' today is altogether different from what professing Christians call the HEATHEN religions. Yet almost no one knows what it is.

"It is a NEW THING in the earth; and it originated, not from the philosophies of a human mind *apart from* the truth of God and of Christ, but in actually seizing upon the true religion of Christ and *counterfeiting* it in order to exalt and deify human man. . . .

"Differing totally from all previous pagan religions, the true Christianity was *counterfeited*, with a former pagan belief or practice substituted for almost everything vital in the *true* belief and practice which came from GOD, and yet seizing on the NAME of Christ, and the NAME of God, and labeling this religion 'Christianity.' Vehemently it *professed* to abolish idolatry, by substituting the NAMES of God and of Christ for pagan gods, while substituting pagan beliefs and practices for those of Jesus Christ!

"And all the world is DECEIVED!"[5]

Further in the same article, under the bold-faced heading, "'Christianity' Not Founded on the Bible," Mr. Armstrong declared: "*I found that there is absolutely NO organized religion on the face of the earth*

5. *Tomorrow's World,* May, 1971; "Why God Is Not Real to Most People"; p. 5

that has AS ITS SOURCE of faith and practice the HOLY BIBLE."[6]

The True Church

A *World Tomorrow* writer says: ". . .to be kept *in the Father's name* (John 17:11) means to be kept In His only True Church—*the Church which belongs to and is ruled by God.*

"And of all the denominations bearing the name 'Church of God,' only *ONE* could be the true Church of God—the one that obeys *all* the commandments of God and maintains the faith delivered once for all time."[7]

Does Armstrong know which church is that True Church, the one Jesus Christ organized in 31 A.D.? Absolutely! It is *his* church! As Garner Ted Armstrong humbly declares: "There is only ONE CHURCH on the face of this earth that has been consistently, through *many years* of labor, preaching the ONE true Gospel of the Kingdom of God, telling you exactly what these times MEAN!

"There is only ONE Church that has dared to tell you in definite, specific, point-by-point, detailed order the events that are yet to occur, what *will happen* in Europe, what WILL happen here in our country and all over the world, and what is sure to happen in the Middle East!. . .

"Where is that ONE Church Jesus built?

"It is where the WORK of that Church is being done!

"And THIS WORK that you are reading of *right now*—that you *hear* over The WORLD TOMORROW—this Work is the only genuine Work that is carrying out Jesus' very commission just as He said it would be doing!"[8]

---

6. Ibid.; p. 7
7. *Tomorrow's World,* February, 1971; David Albert, "In the *Name* of *Jesus*"; p. 19
8. "Should You *Join* A Church?" op. cit.; p. 11

What proof do the Armstrongs offer that their Worldwide Church of God is the one True Church of Christ on earth today?

Very frankly, *not much*! Verses like Luke 12:32; John 15:18,19; and Revelation 3:8 are strung together, then readers are told this conclusively *proves* the World Tomorrow group is God's True Church on earth! It is not surprising that nearly every other false cult—such as the Jehovah's Witnesses, the Mormons, etc.—offers the same proof that they are God's True Church on earth.

Before one runs out to join the Armstrong group as God's True Church, however, he should be warned that Armstrong has been wrong about the True Church before—*by his own admission*! In a rare (for him) confessional session, Herbert W. Armstrong acknowledges: "When I was first ordained, I accepted a very small salary from what I then believed to be God's True Church."[9] This reference is to the Seventh-day Adventist splinter group, "Church of God (Adventist)," with headquarters at Stanberry, Missouri—now in Denver, Colorado. But he had a falling out with the leadership, men he calls "envious and scheming ministers, influential near the top," and he departed from that "True Church" to start his own.

The Worldwide Church of God is not only confident about the date when the True Church was organized, and what or who it is today, the leaders are just as confident about its name. When a *Tomorrow's World* reader wrote to inquire, "What is the name of the True Church of God?" he was told: "Twelve times in the New Testament, the name of the *one* true Church is given as *the Church of God*. Churches are often named after men, after the system they have devised, or after a significant doctrine they emphasize. But wherever the *one* true Church is, it will *always*, with-

9. *Tomorrow's World*, August, 1971; p. 2

out exception, be named the CHURCH OF GOD."[10]

While this is not exactly true—our "Church of Christ" friends make much of Romans 16:16, "The churches of Christ salute you," and New Testament churches were also marked by other identifying features, such as location—we will merely point out that putting the name "Church of God" in front of a building or on a letterhead doesn't make it thus, any more than putting a sign in front of our Biblical Evangelism office, "INDIANA STATE HOUSE," would make it the State House, or putting The White House on our letterhead would make our headquarters the executive mansion. So even if "Church of God" (not *Worldwide* Church of God; or, horrors, "Radio" Church of God, as the Armstrong group was first called) were the correct name, we agree with the cult's leadership when it says: "One caution should be mentioned here. Even *some* who have the correct name are *not* proclaiming the KINGDOM OF GOD. . ."[11]

The Armstrongs have a "size" problem with their True Church, also. In our first expose of the movement, back in 1961, they were making much of the statement that Christ's church was "everywhere prophesied thru the New Testament as the 'little flock'—never as a great, large popular universal church."[12] At that time, the work was small and the prophecy fit them very nicely, they thought. Now, thanks to the tremendous advertising techniques which they have applied, the work is large and prosperous. Herbert W. Armstrong himself speaks of the time when "the work of God was small," but says now "The Work has grown worldwide and very large."[13] On another occasion he said, "God has blessed His Work, and caused it to

---

10. May, 1971; p. 45
11. Ibid.
12. *Easter Is Pagan,* Written Anonymously; Copyright, 1952; pp. 7,8
13. *Tomorrow's World,* July-August, 1970; "Just What Is the Church?"; p. 6

grow into a tremendous worldwide activity, with offices around the world."[14] Again he boasted: ". . .it is a BIG, WORLDWIDE WORK."[15] So we are not sure whether they want to be known as a "little flock" or as a "great worldwide organization." In all honesty, they cannot be both!

Armstrong is very clear in warning that one should not attend any church but his. In answer to a question from a reader of *The Plain Truth*, we find: "While we are instructed, in Heb. 10:23-25: 'Let us hold fast the profession of our faith without wavering; and let us consider one another to provoke unto love and to good works: *not forsaking the assembling of ourselves together*, as the manner of some is; but exhorting one another: and so much the more, as ye see the day approaching'—yet, notice carefully, we are not instructed to assemble with blinded, deceived people in the denominations. The instruction is not to forsake the assembling of *ourselves* together—that is, true Christians who have the TRUTH, who are filled with God's Holy Spirit, truly converted, and WALKING IN THE LIGHT, living by every Word of God. . . .

"All Protestant sects and denominations contain a certain mixture of false Roman doctrines which have been handed down from the ancient Babylonian idolatry. They constitute an ORGANIZED SYSTEM, even though divided into hundreds of sectarian organizations. Shall the true Christian JOIN, and thus become a *part of* this apostate system?. . .

"The truth is, GOD DID NOT PLANT THESE CHURCHES. And Jesus said, 'Every plant, which my heavenly Father hath not planted, shall be rooted up. *Let them alone*: they be blind leaders of the blind. And if the blind lead the blind, both shall fall into the ditch' (Mat. 15:13-14)."[16]

---

14. *The Seven Laws Of Success,* © 1961,1968; p. 61
15. *Just What Is The Church?* © 1970; p. 2
16. *The Plain Truth,* April, 1958; p. 19

Translated, this means: "Don't attend any church but ours!"

Garner Ted Armstrong wrote: "*Church attendance* is not the most important thing! Church attendance by itself does not mean Church membership in God's sight!

". . .it is, where *God has made it possible*, a MEANS to an end. God *does* instruct His true servants *not* to forsake the assembling of themselves together—and shows by His Word that *an assembly should NOT meet unless one of God's true MINISTERS is present to* FEED and GUIDE the flock! Only the genuine worship of God in His Church is acceptable to Him!"[17]

He goes on to identify those "true ministers," in case any one doubted, as representatives of the Worldwide Church of God. (No telling what a group of the faithful might come up with if representatives from Pasadena were not around to keep things in check!)

Armstrong also warns: "*Should you join a church*? NO! BECAUSE ANY CHURCH YOU CAN 'JOIN' IS NOT THE CHURCH OF GOD!"[18]

Technically, one cannot join the Worldwide Church of God, but, theoretically, "converts" just as truly "join" it as any other church. They are baptized, supposedly, into the "Body of Christ," but, since they identify the Body of Christ with their own organization on an exclusive basis, it is actually one and the same in their eyes. In fact, when describing one of its assemblies, an official brochure of the cult declares: "These people are MEMBERS of the Church of God, known in our day as the Worldwide Church of God. This church is unique in practicing Christianity as A WAY OF LIFE as well as a faith—even as it did originally in the days of the first-century apostles.

"Its MEMBERS are motivated with PURPOSE, in-

17. "Should You *Join* A Church?" op. cit.; p. 12
18. Ibid.

spired by knowing the transcendent human potential. They know the true values. They have found THE WAY that makes life truly meaningful, rewarding, abundant!"[19] [Bold-faced emphasis is the author's!]

This "membership," incidentally, is of the human, organizational kind capable of experiencing excommunication if the leadership is crossed!

The Ordinance of Baptism

The Worldwide Church of God teaches "baptismal regeneration." That is, they believe and teach that baptism is a necessary requirement for salvation and, unless one is baptized, he can never be saved. Dennis D. Luker, in a *Tomorrow's World* article, "BE BAPTIZED!" put it like this: "BAPTISM is a Biblical command. It is an *essential requirement* for salvation. You must be baptized to become a true Christian. . . .

"Then, and only then, can you begin to grow and eventually be born as a Son in God's eternal, ruling Family!"[20]

Another writer, George Geis, in the same issue of the same magazine, trying to explain baptismal regeneration, says: "What actually makes remission of sins possible at the time of baptism is that the blood of Jesus Christ is applied to you personally (Rom. 5:9). Your sins are transferred to the body of Jesus and Christ dies in your place. (Don't let this world's sickly sentimental usage of the phrase 'the blood of Jesus Christ' turn you off. What I'm talking about here is a real thing, divorced from any improper sentimentality.)

". . .you emerge from a few seconds under the waters of baptism completely justified and righteous in God's sight."[21]

---

19. *This Is The Worldwide Church Of God,* Written Anonymously; © 1970,1971,1972; p. 6
20. February, 1971; pp. 16,17
21. "For the Remission *Of Sins"*; p. 20

Note in the above quote the hostility of this cult to "the blood of Jesus Christ," a factor which appears repeatedly in its writings. For some reason, the idea of the blood of Christ—and the blood of Christ *alone*—completely blotting out forever an individual's sins, is a suggestion which incenses them. Note also that the writer talks about Christ's death in the present tense, not the past tense, when he says "Christ *dies* in your place" during baptism. This smacks of Roman Catholicism's "elevation of the host." Hebrews 10:10-14 tells us that Jesus Christ died *once for all*, back on the cross. He does not "die in the sinner's place" each time someone is baptized.

We also remind our readers not to be confused when the above-quoted writer speaks of emerging from the baptismal waters "completely justified and righteous in God's sight." By no stretch of the imagination does he mean that the individual is "saved"! Baptism is merely what "starts" an Armstrong convert "down the highway" toward what he hopes will be eventual salvation.

They teach, nonetheless, that baptism is a *very vital cog* in that regeneration. Herbert W. Armstrong says: "I have shown that it is the living Christ who puts members into His Church—and it is done BY the Holy Spirit. Notice, now, the conditions for receiving God's Spirit—Acts 2:38: 'Repent, and be baptized every one of you in the name of Jesus Christ for the remission of sins, and ye shall receive the gift of the Holy Spirit.' This is speaking of being baptized in water—after which they shall receive the Holy Spirit, which, in turn, baptizes—puts them into—the Church."[22]

This verse, incidentally, is a key one in the whole Armstrong theology and, obviously, it hinges on the interpretation given the word "for." The Greek word *eis* can mean either "in order to" or "with reference

---

22. *Just What Is The Church?* p. 2

to." It can be looking either forward or backward. The same is true of the English word used here. As we have commented elsewhere:

"Those who say baptism is necessary for the remission of sins make that to read: 'be baptized. . .*in order to receive* remission of sins.' *That is not what it says*!

"It says 'for' remission, not 'in order to receive' remission. *That is all the difference in the world*! The Greek word translated 'for' is the word *eis*. This same word is sometimes translated 'upon,' or 'because of,' or 'into,' or 'with reference to.' Peter was simply saying what every Bible believer tells new converts, 'be baptized. . .UPON remission of sins.'

"The English word 'for' means the same thing. A man is arrested *for* stealing. That doesn't mean he was arrested 'in order to' steal; it means he was arrested 'because of' stealing. A man is hung *for* murder. He is hung *because* he murdered, not *in order to* murder. There are innumerable illustrations we might give to show that the word 'for' does not necessarily mean 'in order to.' Be saved *first* and have your sins forgiven, *then* be baptized because they *are* forgiven."[23]

In the Worldwide Church of God, who makes the decision as to whether one should be baptized? That decision, the leadership is very dogmatic in saying, rests entirely in them. If fact, we are told that their decision is actually the very decision of Jesus Christ!

David Elbert says: "Christ holds His servants strictly accountable for everything that is done 'in His name,' so extreme care must be taken by the ministry—as well as by the individual—to see that no errors are committed.

"Many fail to understand that they are in fact *appealing* this first decision of their Christian life directly to

---

23. *Does The Bible Teach That Water Baptism Is A Necessary Requirement For Salvation?*; Copyright, 1970; Biblical Evangelism Press, Brownsburg, Indiana; p. 11

Jesus Christ, and that He makes that decision *through* His ministers!. . .

"The decision as to who will be baptized for the remission of sins, and who will later receive the *laying on of hands* for the receiving of God's Holy Spirit must be made by someone who has been given the authority to act 'in Jesus' name'—usually *an ordained minister of Jesus Christ*—or else someone directly and specifically commissioned to act in that capacity, such as Ananias in Acts, chapter nine, for Paul's baptism."[24] The ordained ministers from Ambassador College are identified as the ministers meant.

As to the actual baptism, we are told: "Therefore, *putting it all together*, at the time of baptism the repentant believer is asked if he has repented of his sins and accepted Jesus Christ as his personal Saviour. If he indicates that he has—and his works *prove* that he has—the person performing the baptism will say to the individual (giving his name), 'As a result of the repentance of your sins and acceptance of Jesus Christ as your personal Saviour, I do therefore baptize you *into* the name of the Father, and the Son, and the Holy Spirit, *in the name of*, that is, *by the authority of*, Jesus Christ for the remission of your sins. Amen.' (Notice carefully that *neither important part is omitted*!) He will then totally immerse the person in the water."[25] In other words, the baptism of the Worldwide Church of God is a baptism into the name of two Gods—one quantitatively inferior in deity to the other—and a power!

It is almost humorous, going through the organization's literature, to notice how the leaders repeatedly "invite" people to be baptized, then say, in effect, "This is not an invitation!" For example, Garner Ted Armstrong says: "Also as a part of the ADULT EDU-

24. "In the *Name* of *Jesus*" op. cit.; p. 18
25. Ibid.

CATIONAL PROGRAM, we now have TRAINED MEN—graduates of AMBASSADOR COLLEGE—available in all parts of the United States and in many parts of the world, ready to counsel with you PERSONALLY—to answer questions—to help you with any spiritual problems—even to baptize any who are ready for it, if any should, voluntarily, and with no solicitation from us, so desire. Please do not construe this announcement as an 'invitation' of any sort—but from time to time, people write to us, wanting to know if a *personal* visit is possible."[26]

In a single issue of *Tomorrow's World*,[27] I noted that, on page 13, Roderick C. Meredith was saying: "If you feel that this is a *very work of God*—preaching Christ's message as a *witness* to this dying world—perhaps you would like to write us about being counseled or baptized." Two pages further, on page 15, A. E. Carrozzo was telling the readers: "If you feel you *need* personal counsel from one of God's ministers, write and ask for one of our representatives to call on you. You must make a personal request." And just two pages beyond that, on page 17, Dennis G. Luker was appealing to the readership clientele: "If you have deeply repented and sincerely want to be baptized, or if you are desirous of just discussing these vital subjects in relation to your life with a qualified and dedicated servant of God, then *do* write and let us know.

"God's true ministers. . .are stationed throughout the world to counsel and baptize people like you."

Even that wasn't all! On page 23, Robert L. Kuhn was begging: "There is a concrete act that you must do. You cannot baptize yourself. You *must* have a true representative of Jesus Christ baptize you.

"How can you arrange this? As many of our readers already know, God has His ministers within easy reach

26. "Should You *Join* A Church?" op. cit.; p. 12
27. February, 1971

of all areas of the United States, British Commonwealth and Western Europe. . . .if you want to meet and counsel with one of these men, write. . ." Then mailing addresses were given, along with a further word of admonition: "This is all *you* have to do. Then it becomes *our responsibility* to arrange the most convenient time and place."

One writer, in a scary article, "*False* Conversion—A MORTAL DANGER!" after pointing out, subtly of course, that none is converted apart from the Armstrong system, wound up his warning: "Even as this article is being written, five nationwide baptizing tours from Ambassador College—directed by God's servants—are preparing to visit personally with hundreds of people from coast to coast. . .

"These people *know* that this is the work of God's true Church on earth today. They realize the *importance* of *personal contact* with the true ministers of Jesus Christ who are actually DOING His work of preaching the message of the Kingdom of God as a last witness to this earth.

"If you would *wire* or write *air mail*, it would still not be too late for most of you to be contacted by these tours. If you realize the vital necessity of this personal contact and guidance of the true servants of Jesus Christ, then tell us and send your name and address immediately. . ."[28]

The Ordinance of the Lord's Supper

Since Jesus and His disciples were observing the Passover Supper at the time He instituted His memorial service, the Armstrongs understand the Lord's Supper to be a continuation of the Passover—*officially the Passover Observance*! Herbert W. Armstrong writes: "Now notice Exodus 12:17,24. The Passover was insti-

---

28. *The Plain Truth,* July, 1959; Roderick C. Meredith; p. 16

tuted as *an ordinance* FOREVER. Just as circumcision was not done away, but was changed—today it is of the HEART (Romans 2:29). In both cases God meant FOREVER, and so, as we have seen, at the last Passover supper Jesus CHANGED the manner of observance of this ordinance. No longer do we kill a lamb and eat it, since the Lamb of God has been sacrificed once for all. Instead, we take the bread, symbolizing His broken body, and the wine, symbolizing His shed blood, as a memorial, looking back to His death."[29]

We trust our readers will, as Armstrong invites, notice Exodus 12. When God said, in that 24th verse, the Passover was to be "an ordinance to thee and to thy sons for ever," to whom and of what was He speaking? *He was talking to the Israelites who were brought out of the bondage of Egypt*! It was to them God said, "YE shall keep it a feast to the Lord throughout your generations; YE shall keep it a feast by an ordinance for ever" (vs. 14). *And it was a memorial of deliverance from Egypt!* Today's Christian is not an Israelite from the standpoint of "generation," and he certainly was not delivered from Pharaoh and Egyptian bondage! To try to make the Lord's Supper a continuation of the Passover results in utter confusion and total misunderstanding of the Word of God.

Because the Armstrongs equate the Passover with the Lord's Supper, naturally, they feel it should be observed only once a year, on the Passover date. As Armstrong says: "Jesus set us an example, and by following His example in observing this sacred ordinance at the same time He did—the same time the Passover always was observed, commanded to continue FOREVER—we do continue to *remember* His death, annually, on the very anniversary of His crucifixion. It is the most solemn and sacred occasion of the year—

29. *Tomorrow's World,* March, 1971; "How Often Should We Partake of the *Lord's Supper?*"; p. 4

especially when observed at this correct scriptural hour!"[30]

Incidentally, Armstrong understands the disciples' meeting together to break bread as simply eating a meal, not observing the Lord's Supper. He says: "This bread-breaking was not the 'Lord's supper,' but eating a *plain meal.*

". . .In fact, this term is NEVER used to designate the 'Lord's supper' in the New Testament."[31]

Armstrong, as is quite common in his case, takes issue with competent and reliable scholarship when he makes such a statement. As one authority, referring to the words "break bread," says: "The very same Greek words occur in the *Didache* or 'Teaching of the Twelve,' which dates from about A. D. 100, to denote the observance of the Lord's Supper. This parallel proves that Luke's words refer, not to a social meal (as some have contended) but to the Holy Communion."[32]

Laying on of Hands

An integral part of the Worldwide Church of God is the laying on of hands. In a special article dealing with the subject, Richard A. Wiedenheft declared: "THE MOST basic doctrines of Christianity are listed in Hebrews 6:1 and 2—repentance, baptism, faith, and the resurrection. Among them is the *laying on of hands.*

"Yet you have probably never heard of the *laying on of hands.* Most so-called Christian churches seem oblivious to this basic Biblical teaching—and those who do recognize it, misunderstand, misapply, or misuse it. . . .

"God has ordained that His Church employ *the laying on of hands* as a *physical symbol of the authority*

30. Ibid.; p. 5
31. Ibid.
32. *Another Look At Seventh-Day Adventism,* Norman F. Douty; Copyright, 1962; Baker Book House, Grand Rapids, Michigan; p. 83

that God placed in His Church and with His true ministers. . . .

"Christ gave the ministers of His Church the authority to baptize those who have truly repented of their sins. Along with the physical act of baptism is promised the Holy Spirit—through *the laying on of hands.*

"Millions have supposedly been baptized, but very few have ever had hands laid on them for the receipt of the Holy Spirit after baptism. And fewer still have had hands laid on them by a person who had authority from Jesus Christ to baptize."[33]

Armstrong teaches that no one today has the Holy Spirit—or can receive Him—apart from the laying on of hands by ministers of his organization.

Divine Healing

Number the Armstrongs and the Worldwide Church of God as among those believing healing to be in the atonement, applicable as such today, and that all Christians everywhere should be able to be healed when sick. Herbert W. Armstrong, who sends out anointed handkerchiefs to all who write in requesting prayer for healing,[34] [although, as Bob Ross points out, there is no more biblical justification for this than telling lepers to dip in the Jordan River], says: "This wonderful 53rd chapter of Isaiah tells us the Messiah was to come in human flesh, to grow up, to bear our afflictions and *our sicknesses.* Yes, HE was to be WOUNDED and to suffer for our physical as well as spiritual transgressions, so that by His stripes—His BODY broken for us—*we* are to be *healed* when sick! *Many of us* do not fully grasp *that* truth, even today!"[35]

He tells of an Ed Smith, emphasizing "the name is not fictitious," whose wife and son were in a State

---

33. *Tomorrow's World,* April, 1971; "The Laying on of Hands"; pp. 41,42
34. *Does God Heal Today?* p. 14
35. *Tomorrow's World,* December, 1971; "Should We Use the Old Testament?"; p. 5

Hospital suffering from tuberculosis. Smith came to Armstrong, "according to the command of James 5:14, and both his wife and son were completely healed and returned home."[36]

Mr. Armstrong confesses, however, that healing does not always work for everybody, even members of his own family. Referring to 1927, he says: "My wife was miraculously healed—even a dumfounded doctor was forced to admit that. Then I was blessed with my first son. Years later, God tried me to see whether I would be willing to give *him* up. Struggling in prayer, I told God I was willing—not for a moment believing He would require it of me. But, He did."[37] The wife was healed—*the son died*!

So insistent is Armstrong that doctors and medicines are wrong for healing that, under the subhead "Scripture Labels Other Modes of Healing IDOLATRY," he declares: "God says, 'I am the Eternal that heals you,' and He isn't going to let anyone else *heal* you. He says, 'Thou shalt have no other Gods before me,'—no other *healers*, in other words."[38] His next subhead announces "Medicine Condemned as Idolatry," and although he recounts the case of King Asa in II Chronicles 16 as his proof,[39] there is absolutely nothing in the passage to substantiate his point that God calls medicine idolatry.

His next subpoint is "The Pagan Origin of Medicine" and his readers are told: "Now there, my friends, is where medical 'Science' (falsely so called) came from. From the heathens."[40] Later he says, ". . .medical science came out of the ancient heathen practice of medicine-men supposed to be in the good graces of imaginary gods of medicine. . ."[41] And still later he

36. *Tomorrow's World,* November, 1971; "The Man Who Couldn't Afford to Tithe"; p. 29
37. *Tomorrow's World,* June, 1971; p. 2
38. *Does God Heal Today?* p. 4
39. Ibid.; p. 5
40. Ibid.
41. Ibid.; p. 11

laments: "WHY, then, do people place their faith and their trust in human men who have no power to help them—sometimes spend all their money on these men of a 'science, falsely so called,'—and be utterly unable to place any FAITH in GOD to heal them?"[42] In a special section, "God's Instruction to Those Sick TODAY," Armstrong quotes James 5:14,15, then observes: "He does not say, call the doctors and let them give medicines and drugs, and God will cause the medicines and drugs and dope to cure you. Yet that seems to be the way many professing Christians believe, because it's what they practice."[43]

One of the cult's chief writers, a senior editor on both the public magazines, Roderick C. Meredith, called the use of doctors and medicine "Substituting Human Devices for Obedience to Divine Law." Under that heading, he wrote: "In regard to the thousands of *hospitals* put up in the name of religion, did it ever occur to you that the Christ you read of in *your Bible* supernaturally HEALED people of sickness and disease? And that He did this *without* resorting to drugs, knives and the terribly expensive and painful procedures men now employ in this 'enlightened age' in which we live?

". . .Jesus will call the *false prophets* to account for not teaching their flocks real *faith* in GOD for the *true healing* which He has promised. And they will be rebuked for refusing to teach the people the *physical laws which would prevent* MOST *sickness and disease in the first place*!

"The terrible financial drain, the use of poisonous drugs and knives, the suffering and loss of work, and the cultivation of *faith in men* in overcrowded, gloomy, antiseptic-smelling modern hospitals is NOT God's way to health and healing! If anything, it is a mighty poor

42. Ibid.; p. 12
43. Ibid.; p. 15

second best to *obedience* to the physical laws of God to PREVENT SICKNESS in the first place, or Divine *healing* by Him if some unwitting infraction or carelessness does result in sickness or an accident."[44]

Armstrong does not completely rule out doctors. It would be a little embarrassing to do so in light of the fact that two books of the New Testament, Luke and Acts, were written by one designated by God Himself as the "beloved physician" (Colossians 4:14). So he acknowledges doctors might be needed for child-bearing, setting broken bones and a few other trivial matters—but nothing having anything to do with healing. His followers are left with the clear impression that use of doctors and medicines comprises mighty weak faith. In fact, they are taught that sickness is entirely the result of sin in the life—and when one gets forgiveness, he will be healed. Armstrong insists: "It isn't natural to be sick. It's unnatural, and wrong.

"So sickness is only the *penalty of physical transgression,* and whenever one is sick, he is paying that penalty! The penalty of transgressing these physical laws that regulate the human body is PAIN, suffering, sometimes the first or physical DEATH. It's a physical transgression, or sin—and there's a physical PENALTY for that sin.

"*Consequently, healing is nothing more or less than the* FORGIVENESS OF SIN—the consequent removal from us of the PENALTY we have incurred—and no human doctor, no medicine, no drug, has ever been given power to forgive sin—whether spiritual or physical."[45]

Armstrong understands the breaking of Christ's body to mean He took our infirmities upon Himself. Therefore, he reasons, when we partake of the broken bread in the Lord's Supper (the Passover, to him), if we do

44. *The Plain Truth,* November, 1959; "*Revival* in Our Time?"; p. 19
45. *Does God Heal Today?* p. 8

not understand that "Jesus' body was broken FOR OUR HEALING," we are taking this bread unworthily. Not only so, but he adds: "We take the broken bread UNWORTHILY if, and when, we take it at communion service and then PUT OUR TRUST IN DOCTORS AND MEDICINES, instead of in Christ—thus putting ANOTHER god before HIM! So, many are sick. Many die!"[46]

The idea of praying "if it be Thy will" with regard to healing is openly scoffed at and ridiculed. According to Armstrong, *it is* ALWAYS *God's will to heal*! He reasons like this: (1) Sickness is always a result of sin; (2) Forgiveness of sin results in healing; (3) It is always God's will to forgive sin; (4) Since it is always God's will to forgive sin, it also must always be His will to heal. He writes: "Now let's settle this question—'Is it God's WILL to heal me?' once and for all. . . .

"Jesus healed. It was *always* His will. . . .

"The Word of God says Jesus Christ is THE SAME, yesterday, today, and forever. Then it is still HIS WILL today!"[47]

This hardly proves his point. As we have noted previously, Hebrews 13:8 is merely stating that the *character* and *person* of Christ are unchanging, not necessarily His method of operation. That it is not always God's will to heal should be obvious to even a casual Bible reader. Paul left Trophimus at Miletum, sick (II Timothy 4:20). Rather than a stinging rebuke about sin or a challenge about faith, the same apostle offered medical suggestions to a young preacher who was troubled with "often infirmities" (I Timothy 5:23). In his own case, Paul was plagued with a physical problem he described as "a thorn IN THE FLESH," and concerning which he cried to God repeatedly for

46. Ibid.; pp. 10,11
47. Ibid.; pp. 12,13

deliverance. Each time he was refused healing and told, "My grace is sufficient for thee: for my strength is made perfect in weakness." This caused the mighty Apostle Paul, unlike Armstrong, to exclaim, "Most gladly therefore will I rather glory in my infirmities. . . Therefore I take pleasure in infirmities. . .for when I am weak, then am I strong" (See II Corinthians 12:7-11). Paul apparently had a speech defect (II Corinthians 10:10), and his eyesight was so faulty those who loved him would have gladly given him their own eyes, if it had been possible (Galatians 4:15). We note, incidentally, that Herbert W. Armstrong has worn eyeglasses for over a half-century to correct *his* faulty vision. Mr. Meredith, whose emphatic statements about healing are also quoted above, is troubled with the same infirmity of the flesh. Neither has experienced healing.

While Armstrong is insistent that God alone can heal, he is equally dogmatic that deity has delegated the job to leaders of the Worldwide Church of God. He writes: "GOD ALONE has power to HEAL. But Christ Jesus *delegated this power* to HIS MINISTERS whom He was sending out to preach! Show me where the Eternal GOD, who *alone* has the power to heal, ever delegated that power to the doctors, physicians, of medical science! HE NEVER DID! *They do not HAVE the power to heal*, but every true minister of Jesus Christ—if he is one whom God has called to the ministry—DOES HAVE THAT POWER! Well, what a shame that most ministers today do not KNOW that they have been given that power, and most people who are sick do not know it either!"[48]

We have quoted sufficient statements elsewhere, making repetition unnecessary here, proving Armstrong limits "true ministers of Jesus Christ" to his own leadership.

48. Ibid.; p. 13

As one might suspect with those who teach laying on of hands as a prerequisite for the gift of the Holy Spirit, the same is taught regarding healing. One of the cult's writers says: "The most ignored and misunderstood aspect of *the laying on of hands* is its application to the miraculous healing of sickness. . . .

"Christ said that His true ministers and servants would *lay hands on the sick*—and the sick would recover. . . .

"James 5:14 is a command from God to those who are sick. No minister's hands are special or holy. No olive oil has any mysterious power. It is God Himself who heals through His Holy Spirit; but He has prescribed a physical act to show our faith and trust in Him and to show that we know where He is working on the earth today—to show our acceptance of the authority He has placed with His servants."[49]

What about failure? Armstrong blames that failure on his followers, not himself, even after quoting James 5:14-15: "Is any sick among you? let him call for the elders of the church; and let them pray over him, anointing him with oil in the name of the Lord: And the prayer of faith shall save the sick, and the Lord shall raise him up; and if he have committed sins, they shall be forgiven him."

Armstrong says: "I have answered the call of thousands, who have come to me for prayer for healing. Many *have* been healed—miraculously—of even cancer and an advanced case, in a hospital, of leukemia. On the other hand, many *have not* been healed. Yet I have prayed with the same faith for the one as the other.

"WHY are many not healed? Jesus said it is ACCORDING TO YOUR FAITH. Perhaps they did not fully believe. Perhaps they were not obedient. Perhaps

49. "The Laying on of Hands" op. cit.; pp. 42,48

they should read James 4:3, where it says: 'Ye ask, and receive not, *because*. . . .' And you may read the answer yourself."[50]

The Apostle James and the Prophet Armstrong seem to be in disagreement here. Armstrong is saying that lack of faith and lack of obedience on the part of *the sick* cause the failure. But James said, "And THE PRAYER of faith shall save the sick. . ." That is, success hinges on the faith of *the one doing the praying*, not the one being prayed for!

The Church's Main Business

Starting with the founding of the New Testament church by Christ and His apostles, the main business of that church has always been considered the reaching of the lost for Christ. What is the Worldwide Church of God's position regarding this vital issue? While we have already dealt with it in another chapter, we will repeat it here: *they don't get very excited about it*! This is due, beyond question, to the cult's fatalistic approach as to whom God is calling in this age.

Herbert W. Armstrong sets the pace for his followers, boasting: "I never try to talk *anyone* into accepting Bible truth or being converted. . . .that's GOD'S WAY!!"[51] One of his writers, Richard A. Wiedenheft, in an article seeking to show that "trying to 'convert' others" is a mistake, declared, with reference to Matthew 24:14: ". . .the preaching part of that commission was given specifically to Christ's apostles, who had been ordained as ministers." Then he adds: "It is simply not the duty of the laymen to preach to their community. That responsibility rests on the shoulders of those called and chosen by God to do that Work."[52] By this is meant, of course, only the ones who are

50. *Tomorrow's World*, April, 1971; p. 48
51. *Should You Try To Convert Others?"* © 1966,1970,1972; p. 3
52. *Be Seen And Not Heard*, © 1971,1972; p. 4

authorized by the Pasadena headquarters of the Worldwide Church of God. In almost his closing paragraph, Wiedenheft warns: "As you learn new truth, don't TELL the whole world about it—that is the job of God's chosen servants."[53]

Garner Ted Armstrong even denies that Christ came to win men to Himself. Trying to describe the "real Christ" to his readers, he invites them: "Discover the Christ who was utterly unconcerned about saving the world then—who came to deliver a vital message, not to convert men's souls. . ."[54] What a strange comprehension regarding the ministry of the One who said: "For the Son of man is come to seek and to save that which was lost" (Luke 19:10). Paul added his testimony: "This is a faithful saying, and worthy of all acceptation, that Christ Jesus came into the world to save sinners; of whom I am chief" (I Timothy 1:15).

In order to prove this peculiar philosophy, Scripture is made to fight against Scripture, as is so often the case with this cult. For example, Herbert W. Armstrong writes: "But, some will ask, didn't Jesus tell us we are the light of the world—and that we must let our light SHINE?

"Oh yes! But do you notice HOW He said we must let our light shine? LISTEN: 'Ye are the light of the world. . .Let your light so shine before men, that they may SEE your GOOD WORKS. . .' (Matthew 5:14,16). NOTICE THAT CAREFULLY! He did NOT say 'that they may HEAR your good ARGUMENTS.' He said 'that they may SEE your GOOD WORKS!'"[55]

Mr. Wiedenheft agrees with his leader, declaring: "Christ said in Matthew 5:16, 'Let your light so shine before men, that they may *see your good works*, and glorify your Father which is in heaven.'

53. Ibid.; p. 6
54. *Tomorrow's World,* March, 1971; "The 'Jesus Trip'"; p. 5
55. *Should You Try To Convert Others?* p. 1

"Notice, He said, 'SEE *your good works*'! WORKS not *words*!

"Peter exhorted all Christians, 'Maintain good conduct among the Gentiles, so that in case they speak against you as wrongdoers, they may SEE *your good deeds* and glorify God on the day of visitation' (I Pet. 2:12, RSV).

"Others should SEE, *not hear*, all the benefits of living by God's Word."[56]

This is only a half truth! Of course we are to let our light shine and our good deeds are to be seen. But that does not nullify the plain commands God has given regarding verbal witness. Mark's version of the Great Commission says: "And he said unto them, Go ye into all the world, and preach the gospel to every creature" (Mark 16:15). Neither avenue—shining nor speaking—is to be used to the exclusion of the other. For Armstrong and his followers to use Matthew 5:14,16 and I Peter 2:12 to "prove" witnessing is wrong is as wicked as it would be for me to use Mark 16:15 to "prove" Christians shouldn't shine!

While antagonism to *personal* evangelism is under discussion here, perhaps it might be a good place to mention that the movement does not pass up any opportunity to sneer at *mass* evangelism by evangelicals. Just by way of example, in an article by Herman L. Hoeh discussing apostolic preaching, we read: "This was not some kind of uncontrolled pseudo-spiritual, humanly generated, emotional ecstasy often witnessed in evangelistic campaigns."[57]

The Saints

We close this chapter on the church by giving the cult's definition of a saint, admitting we find it slightly

---

56. Op. cit.; p. 5
57. *How You Can Be Imbued With The Power Of God!* © 1958,1967,1970,1971; p. 1

amusing that the Worldwide Church of God acknowledges "saints" today. Since it does not believe in "salvation" during this life, this makes the cult the only religion we know of with "unsaved saints"!

In a *Tomorrow's World* article, "What Is a Saint?" by James L. Chapman, we are told: "Paul makes it *very clear* that the saints were those people who were true followers of Christ, keeping God's Law in spite of severe criticism and persecution, and that they were people who were alive and active in God's Church. (See Eph. 2:19-22; Col. 1:2; Eph. 5:3; Phil. 1:1.)"[58]

We would point out to our readers that the writer, when he speaks of "keeping God's Law," means the interpretation of that law for today as this cult outlines it. However, their definition goes way beyond the bounds of the biblical understanding since, according to the Word of God, anyone who has put his faith and trust in Jesus Christ is a saint—even though he may not be living very saintly at the time!

The church at Corinth is certainly an example of this fact. Paul called them "saints," but they were having all kinds of internal divisions, they were going to law one against another before unbelievers, they were guilty of creating disorders at the Lord's table, they were confused about and were abusing "tongues," they were honoring human leadership above and beyond scriptural procedure and practice, and these Corinthian Christians were otherwise proving how unsaintly it is possible for a saint to be.

You will note, also, that Mr. Chapman did not include the Corinthians in his reference about saints in the passage quoted above.

To do so would have annihilated his position!

---

58. July, 1971; p. 16

CHAPTER X

The Armstrong Teaching About Life After Death

In order to understand what the Worldwide Church of God teaches in this area, it is necessary to know what it means by death, the soul and immortality.

Death, to the Armstrongs, is merely *ceasing to be.* The individual who dies does not exist again until the resurrection. If it happens to be the resurrection of life, then he will continue to exist forever. If it is the resurrection to death, then he will die the second time and cease to be forever. Garner Ted Armstrong writes: "Death is the *absence* of life, the cessation of life—not the continuation of life under different circumstances."[1]

Regarding the soul, it is not distinguished from the body—and it is this error which causes the cult much of its confusion. The Senior Armstrong, following the line that man is strictly a body, actually attempts to tie the evangelical teaching about the soul into a wrong attitude toward sex. He declares: "*It was from this 'immortal soul' doctrine that the concept of sex as evil in itself stemmed.*

"Notice how it developed!

"This 'immortal soul' doctrine teaches that man is DUAL. While it claims falsely that the 'immortal soul' is the real man, and the body is merely the prison in which he is held, yet it teaches inconsistently that man is DUAL—both soul and body."[2]

He dismisses man's spirit in almost the same breath, denying it is a part of man. Says Mr. Armstrong: "This spirit essence is NOT the man, but something IN the *wholly physical man.*"[3]

---

1. *Do You Have An Immortal Soul?* © 1957,1969,1970,1971; p. 2
2. *The Missing Dimension In Sex,* Herbert W. Armstrong, written in collaboration with 5 Ambassador College faculty members and 1 medical doctor; © 1964,1971; p. 51
3. Ibid.

In defining the soul, Garner Ted Armstrong quotes Genesis 2:7, then exclaims: "There is the answer! Man *became* a living SOUL; that is what man IS—a *soul.* Notice there is no mention that man has a soul, but that man *is* a soul!. . .

"You have already read—as quoted from YOUR BIBLE—the PROOF that a *soul* is an ANIMAL, a BODY, and CAN DIE!"[4]

He argues: "Since man IS a soul, and since man can die, and a soul can die, it is obvious that man and soul are one and the same thing!"[5] (By this reasoning, of course, we could prove that Garner Ted Armstrong is a baboon! A baboon can die. Garner Ted Armstrong can die. Therefore, because both a baboon and Armstrong can die, they are one and the same thing!)

You will note Armstrong says "a *soul* is. . .a BODY." Not that a soul *has* a body, but it *is* one. We can disprove this very simply by both the Bible and Garner Ted Armstrong himself. Looking at the Word of God, I Thessalonians 5:23 says: "And the very God of peace sanctify you wholly; and I pray God your whole spirit and soul and body be preserved blameless unto the coming of our Lord Jesus Christ." Note that man is made up of three separate things: spirit, soul and body. The spirit is not the soul; the spirit is not the body. The soul is not the spirit; the soul is not the body. The body is not the spirit; the body is not the soul. There are three different, separate things. God said so!

When it comes right down to it, Armstrong himself doesn't believe the soul and body to be one and the same. Or, if he does, he hasn't convinced one of his key writers. Robert L. Kuhn, an Associate Editor of *Tomorrow's World*, in an article, "Science Vs. Theology? Life After Death?" says: "Jesus Christ plainly stated that *both* the *body and* the *soul* can be *destroyed* in

---

4. Op. cit.; p. 2,3
5. Ibid.; p. 2

gehenna fire (Matt. 10:28)."[6] Without entering into a discussion here as to what Christ meant by "destroy" in this verse, we simply note that the body and soul are separate—two things, not one!

The same writer says again: "When a human being dies, he is *dead*—which means that his body, mind *and soul* are *all dead.* He simply *stops 'being.'*"[7] Here Kuhn not only distinguishes body from soul, but throws in "mind" as well.

Armstrong errs grievously in seeking to make body and soul one and the same.

The Worldwide Church of God does acknowledge man to have a spirit, but insists it is not the man. Herman L. Hoeh says: "Your Bible reveals there is a spirit *in* man. It is not the man—it is something in the man. Connected with physical brain, it forms human *mind.* It imparts the power of intellect and personality that no animal can have. This spirit in man is not conscious *of itself.* It cannot know apart from the brain. It is spirit *essence.*"[8]

The understanding of *death* and the understanding of *soul* held by this cult have dictated its understanding of immortality. Some of the movement's strongest guns are used in scoffing at the thought of "an immortal soul." For example, Robert L. Kuhn, in the previously mentioned article, says: "An 'immortal soul' is *not* the Biblical understanding of a life after death. As a matter of fact, the phrase 'immortal soul' is not even mentioned in the Bible. Ezekiel twice emphasized that 'the soul that sinneth, it shall *die*' (Ezek. 18:4, 20)."[9]

We quickly respond to this straw man by saying, "Neither is the phrase 'mortal soul' even mentioned in the Bible!" The only way the Armstrong confusion

---

6. February, 1971; p. 40
7. Ibid.; p. 41
8. *How You Can Be Imbued With The Power Of God!* © 1958,1968,1970,1971; p. 3
9. Op. cit.

in this area can be brought about is by making, as we have already seen, the soul and body one and the same.

Is death ceasing to be? Is the soul "mortal"? Garner Ted Armstrong writes: "Satan began his deception by introducing the doctrine of the 'immortality of the soul' to Eve in the Garden of Eden. He told her, 'Ye shall not surely die' (Gen. 3:4). Since that time, the devil has succeeded in palming off *his own aspirations* and *his ultimate destination* on gullible human beings as their chief religious doctrines—which are NOT found in the Bible!"[10]

Once again, the passage to which Armstrong points for proof, proves too much. Just what had God told Adam and Eve? He had declared: "But of the tree of the knowledge of good and evil, thou shalt not eat of it: for in the day that thou eatest thereof thou shalt surely die" (Genesis 2:17). If physical death is referred to here—and if death is ceasing to be—then the Bible is in error. Death was not only to be the result of sin, it was to be the *immediate* result the *very day* man sinned. We know that Adam and Eve did not die *physically* the day they partook of the forbidden fruit; they certainly did not *cease to be* in any sense of the word. Adam lived hundreds of years after the incident and Eve probably lived nearly as long (the average woman today lives longer than the average man).

Contrary to what Armstrong would have his followers believe (he calls it "manufacturing a new definition"),[11] death in the Bible is simply separation. *Physical death* is the separation of the soul and the spirit from the body. *Spiritual death* is the separation of the individual from God because of his sin. And the *second death* is simply a final, complete, absolute separation from God and everything that comes from God. With regard to

10. *Tomorrow's World,* June, 1971; "What Is Satan's Fate?"; p. 6
11. *Just What Is The Church?* © 1970; p. 6

none of the three is death ceasing to be.

Paul said of the Ephesians, "And you hath he quickened, who were dead in trespasses and sin" (Ephesians 2:1). Did he mean that they had ceased to be and had now been brought back into existence? Of course not. Paul warned Timothy, "But she that liveth in pleasure is dead while she liveth" (I Timothy 5:6). How could people "cease to be" at the very time they were "living in pleasure"? The thought is absurd! But it is certainly possible for sinners to be "separated from God" at the time they are so living!

First John 3:14 is a good illustration of the absurdity of Armstrong's definition. It says: "We know that we have passed from death unto life, because we love the brethren. He that loveth not his brother abideth in death." How could it be understood that one loving his brother had passed from a state of ceasing to be to a state of being? How could one who hates his brother be living in a state of ceasing to be? Armstrong's version of the latter part of that verse would have to be: "he that loveth not his brother is existing in non-existence!" Scores of kindred illustrations could be given regarding the use of *dead* and *death*.

What the Worldwide Church of God teaches regarding death, the soul and immortality relate to one of the key doctrines of the movement—a philosophy held by just about every false cult since apostolic days, namely,

Soul Sleep[12]

This expression means that when anyone dies—believer or non-believer—he is simply put into the earth to sleep until a future resurrection morning. In Kuhn's article purporting to answer whether or not there is life

12. In Armstrong's case, he does not like the expression "soul sleep," saying, ". . .the soul doesn't sleep—it *dies!*" [*The Plain Truth*, August, 1972; "Animal Brain Vs. Human Mind"; p. 38] However, we are using the term here because it describes what the theological world has always meant by it.

after death, following page after page of suspenseful build-up in typical Armstrong style, near the end he finally tells his readers: "But this brings us to the ultimate answer: *There indeed IS a life after death — eventually!*"[13] Not immediately upon death, only "eventually!" conforming to the cult's doctrine of soul sleep.

What about Abraham? According to the Armstrongites, he has been sleeping in the ground about 4,000 years. Robert L. Kuhn says: "So we can be sure that Abraham will be resurrected."[14] Keep in mind that, according to Worldwide Church of God theology, this does not mean Abraham's body will be resurrected, as evangelicals have always believed, but that the "whole" Abraham is now sleeping and will eventually be resurrected.

What about the answer our Lord gave to the Sadducees of His day — who not only believed in *temporary* soul sleeping, but the *permanent* kind: "Ye do err, not knowing the scriptures, nor the power of God. . . .have ye not read that which was spoken unto you by God, saying, I am the God of Abraham, and the God of Isaac, and the God of Jacob? God is not the God of the dead, but of the living" (Matthew 22:29,31,32)? While, admittedly, the main thrust of this argument has to do with future resurrection, note that our Lord did not say, as would have been necessary if the Armstrong philosophy were true, "I am the God of Abraham. . .God is now the God of the dead, but He will eventually be the God of the living."

To get away from the devastating impact of this declaration by Jesus Christ, Herbert W. Armstrong descends to the level of quoting the devil's crowd for an answer. He says: ". . .the Scriptures tell us that Abraham IS DEAD. When the New Testament was written, many hundreds of years after his death, Abra-

13. Op. cit.; p. 41
14. *Tomorrow's World,* June, 1971; "Your Destiny — *The God Family*"; p. 36

ham was STILL DEAD, as recorded in John 8:52-53. There you read the plain words: 'Abraham is DEAD. . . .' "[15] But, as anyone can quickly see by checking the context of the reference, the statement "Abraham is dead" came from the lips of the very ones of whom Jesus said, "Ye are of your father the devil" (John 8:44).

One can either believe, as Armstrong says he does, the words of the devil's crowd that Abraham is dead, or he can believe what Jesus Christ said, that God is the God of the living—and because He is called the God of Abraham, Abraham is now living somewhere. As for us, we prefer to believe God.

The heresy of soul sleep comes, as already indicated, from Armstrong's inability to distinquish between *soul* and *body*. In every instance in the Word of God where death is spoken of as a "sleep," the reference is to the body, not the soul or the spirit. For example, we read in Matthew 27:52: "And the graves were opened; and many BODIES of the saints which slept arose."

Yet C. Paul Meredith argues: "Notice this: if people are in heaven, purgatory or hell where most preachers today say they are, then they are still alive; therefore they could not be resurrected—for the very word 'resurrection' itself implies that those resurrected are dead!

"Therefore a resurrection is necessary if a person who once died is brought to life again! How sadly and without reason have the Bible teachings been distorted!"[16]

That simply is not true! The soul and the spirit are already in Heaven or Hell, depending upon what the individual did with Jesus Christ. There must be a

---

15. *Tomorrow's World*, November, 1971; "What Is the *Reward* of the Saved. . .*Heaven?"*; p. 6
16. *If You Die. . . Will You Live Again?* © 1958,1971; p. 6

resurrection *only for the body*, which now sleeps in the bosom of the earth.

Herbert W. Armstrong says: "We are now flesh—vile corruptible flesh subject to rotting and decay. But at Christ's coming, when we shall be born of God, this vile body shall be changed, and made exactly like Jesus in His glorified body!

"Yes, I know this is probably too wonderful for you to grasp!. . .

"The Bible, which is God's message and instruction to mankind, nowhere teaches any such thing as a pagan doctrine of an 'immortal soul' going to heaven at death."[17]

He is wrong when he says "we are now flesh." We are not flesh. We *have* flesh, but the soul and the spirit are entirely different from the flesh. Paul wrote in II Corinthians 5:1,2: "For we know that if our earthly house of this tabernacle were dissolved, we have a building of God, an house not made with hands, eternal in the heavens. For in this we groan, earnestly desiring to be clothed upon with our house which is from heaven."

He said we have an earthly house, a tabernacle. What is this house, this tabernacle? Paul answers in verse 6: "Therefore we are always confident, knowing that, whilst we are at home in the body, we are absent from the Lord." Note: "at home in the body"! In other words, while we are tabernacling, dwelling in this body, we are not present with the Lord. However, as soon as we do leave the body, speaking as a Christian, of course, we are immediately present with Him. Paul said in verse 8: "We are confident, I say, and willing rather to be absent from the body, and to be present with the Lord." We would like to ask the Armstrongs—and all other soul sleepers—just when they expect to

---

17. *Tomorrow's World,* October, 1971; "Just What Do You Mean. . .*Born Again?*"; p. 47

be absent from the body and present with the Lord. All this confusion results from failure to distinguish between body, soul and spirit.

Garner Ted Armstrong argues that Paul is sleeping in the ground right now because he has not yet received his crown. After quoting the apostle's farewell words in II Timothy 4:6-8, Armstrong declares: "The Apostle Paul isn't in 'heaven.' He said he won't get his reward until that day—the day Christ returns!

"Christ said, in Revelation 22:12, '*MY REWARD IS WITH ME*'!

"But Christ isn't here yet. The Apostle Paul is *still* dead and buried."[18]

No one is claiming that Paul has already received his reward. Of course he doesn't have it yet! That reward will not be given until the Judgment Seat of Christ. What does that have to do with where Paul dwells now while he is waiting for his crown?

Absolutely nothing!

As to where Paul is right now, it would be well to let him answer for himself. When he was writing to the church at Philippi, talking about the burning twofold desire he had—staying on earth and serving the Lord, versus the "gain" of departing and being with Christ—he said: "For to me to live is Christ, and to die is gain. But if I live in the flesh, this is the fruit of my labour: yet what I shall choose I wot not. For I am in a strait betwixt two, having a desire to depart, and to be with Christ; which is far better: Nevertheless to abide in the flesh is more needful for you" (Philippians 1:21-24).

Note the following incontrovertible facts in this passage: (1) Paul equates "to die" with "to depart." (2) This dying, this departing, this going somewhere, he says, is "to be with Christ." (3) If Paul expected to sleep in the bosom of the earth for 2,000 years after dying, there would have been no hurry about it

18. *What Is Death?* © 1966,1967,1969,1970,1971; p. 3

and the whole passage instantly has lost the force of its impact. Paul obviously expected to go immediately to be with Christ the moment he died. There is no other intelligent explanation of the passage.

Because of this soul sleep doctrine, the Worldwide Church of God position is: "The Bible shows us plainly that no one is in heaven except God, Jesus Christ and the angels."[19]

Someone might ask, "What about Elijah?" He never did die; the Scripture says, ". . .there appeared a chariot of fire, and horses of fire, and parted them both asunder; and Elijah went up by a whirlwind into heaven" (II Kings 2:11). What about Enoch? He never did die; the Scripture says, ". . .Enoch walked with God: and he was not; for God took him" (Genesis 5:24).

In one of the cult's *"Answers"* columns, Elijah gets this treatment: "Elijah *was* taken 'up by a *whirlwind* into heaven,' but as Jesus clearly said, 'No man hath ascended up to heaven, but he that came down from heaven, even the Son of man'! (John 3:13.) Clearly, the 'heaven' where Elijah was taken was *not* the same place to which Jesus referred.

"There are, in fact, *three* 'heavens' mentioned in the Bible—not just one.

"The *third* heaven is God's throne, where Jesus is today. Jesus, as God's High Priest, is the only one who has the right to be in that heaven with the Father. The *second* heaven is the vast space in which we see the stars, the sun and the moon, the comets and planets (Ps. 8:3). And the *first* heaven, the one into which Elijah was taken by a wind, is the very one in which birds and airplanes fly, the *atmosphere* around our planet (Gen. 1:20). It would be physically impossible for a *whirlwind* to travel beyond the heaven that is this earth's atmosphere."[20]

---

19. *Tomorrow's World,* July, 1971; James L. Chapman, "What Is a Saint?"; p. 16
20. January, 1972; p. 33

This reduces one of the Bible's greatest miracles into a pre-20th century airplane ride in the realm where sparrows habitually fly! And to say that this phenomenon was "physically impossible" is an insult to God's veracity and exactly what the world's infidels have always said about God's other claims of the miraculous. Hasn't Mr. Armstrong ever entered the realm of Jeremiah's conviction: "Ah Lord God! behold, thou hast made the heaven and the earth by thy great power and stretched out arm, **AND THERE IS NOTHING TOO HARD FOR THEE"** (Jeremiah 32:17)? We suggest the writer of the above "explanation" meditate long and hard on Gabriel's words to Mary: "For with God nothing shall be impossible" (Luke 1:37).

Regarding Enoch, the same column of the same magazine declared: "At this moment Enoch is dead and in his grave. We know this because it is clearly stated in Hebrews that Enoch *died* in faith, not having received the promises (Heb. 11:5,13). And Genesis 5:23 plainly says that ALL THE DAYS of Enoch were 365 years. On the other hand, God *did* deal with Enoch in a highly unique manner. . . .

"We are not informed of the conditions that made it necessary for God to 'translate' (transfer, transport) Enoch from where he had been, but it is clear that God did this to save his life (Heb. 11:5). Enoch was *not* taken to the heaven of God's Throne—he was removed by God to a safer location on the earth. Conditions were so bad that Enoch would have perished at the hands of men—had not God intervened."[21]

In another *"Answers"* column in another issue of *Tomorrow's World,* explaining the longevity of the world's inhabitants before Noah, the writer says: "The deaths by natural causes were based on figures for death because of *old age*. Noah, for example, lived for 950 years. Most of those listed in Genesis 5 lived be-

21. Ibid.

tween 900 and 1000 years. Even all of these did not die of *natural* causes—Enoch, for example, who lived only 365 years."[22]

What a dishonest perversion of Scripture is this! The Word of God says, in Hebrews 11:5: "By faith Enoch was translated that he SHOULD NOT SEE DEATH; and was not found, BECAUSE GOD HAD TRANSLATED HIM: for before his translation he had this testimony, that he pleased God." God said plainly that **Enoch did not see death;** the Worldwide Church of God says **he died,** but not of natural causes. The Bible says God "**translated him**"; the Worldwide Church of God says he was **simply switched to another place on the earth.**

As for the writer's dishonest attempt to prove his point through tying Hebrews 11:13 with Enoch (vs. 5), saying, "it is clearly stated in Hebrews that Enoch *died* in faith, not having received the promises," it is necessary only to turn to the passage and read the context. Rather than speaking of Enoch (or Abel, or Noah), this statement pertains only to those who "sprang" from Sarah's seed "as the stars of the sky in multitude, and as the sand which is by the sea shore innumerable" (vs. 12). Shame on the Armstrongites for trying to pretend that Enoch was a descendant of Abraham and Sarah! This is just another phase of the utter confusion wrapped up in Worldwide Church of God theology.

Garner Ted Armstrong, in attempting to answer the question, "Do You Have An Immortal Soul?" discusses some whose hearts have stopped beating, then revived, saying: "And if the *conscious* 'you' *leaves* the body immediately at death, *why is it* that NOT ONE of the persons can remember ONE SINGLE THING during the time they were 'dead'?"[23]

---

22. *Tomorrow's World,* November, 1971; p. 45
23. Op. cit.; p. 2

That argument rules out God, of course. But the explanation is really a very simple one. With non-biblical cases of apparent death and return to life, we doubt seriously that the individual stepped either into Heaven or Hell. An omniscient God knew, of course, that the individual's heart would be beating again in a matter of moments and we presume he was merely unconscious, although giving every outward indication of actual death.

In the biblical cases, we have one very definite explanation; it was given by Paul in II Corinthians 12:2-4: "I knew a man in Christ above fourteen years ago, (whether in the body, I cannot tell; or whether out of the body, I cannot tell: God knoweth;) such an one caught up to the third heaven. And I knew such a man, (whether in the body, or out of the body, I cannot tell: God knoweth;) How that he was caught up into paradise, and heard unspeakable words, which it is not lawful for a man to utter." Note carefully the words: "not lawful for a man to utter." God simply forbade the telling! It is as simple as that.

Already discussed in a previous chapter is the fact that Christ, while purchasing redemption on the cross, promised the dying thief he would go to be with Him in Paradise that very day. There was to be no soul sleep for that new convert!

What About the Resurrection?

We have already dealt pretty well with this subject, but permit just a few additional comments. The Worldwide Church of God does not believe in a resurrection of the body. As Herman L. Hoeh writes: "In Hebrews 12:9, the Almighty is called 'the Father of Spirits.' We are ultimately, at the resurrection, to be composed of spirit—members of the Divine Family (John 3:6).

"In the resurrection the mortal bodies we now have

will be changed to '*spiritual* bodies' (I Cor. 15:44) imbued with the power of God."[24]

On the contrary, the word for resurrection is *anastasis* and it carries the thought of bringing back what has been. These very same bodies of the flesh are going to be "brought back" in the resurrection. They will be changed and made like Christ's body—yes—but they will still remain *physical* bodies, just as did His.

You will recall that we quoted C. Paul Meredith as saying: "Christ's body did disappear though! Christ was resurrected as a divine spirit being!"[25] To conform to their "spirit bodies" doctrine, even our Lord is denied a physical resurrection body—attributing a disappearing act to it that would make Houdini green with envy. Since it conflicts with their theories—although there is not even one single shred of scriptural support, they merely announce to the gullible: "It disappeared!"

Job expected to have a physical body in the resurrection. He testified, in the midst of the dark waters of his soul's tribulations: "For I know that my redeemer liveth, and that he shall stand at the latter day upon the earth: And though after my skin worms destroy this body, yet IN MY FLESH shall I see God" (Job 19:25,26).

In the Worldwide Church of God's system of theology there are three resurrections. Garner Ted Armstrong explains it thusly: "Believe it or not, the Bible shows there must be a THIRD and FINAL resurrection! This time, a resurrection to all DEATH—by *fire*—for those who have deliberately and willfully sinned.

"Remember, there are THREE CLASSES OF PEOPLE with whom God is dealing. Those who *have* repented, and, whether living or dead, will rise to meet Christ

24. *How You Can Be Imbued With The Power Of God!* p. 4
25. *If You Die. . .Will You Live Again?* p. 6

in the air (I Thes. 4:15-18), coming down ON THAT DAY with Him to the mount of Olives (Zech. 14:4) to RULE with Him for 1,000 years (Rev. 2:26; 3:21; 5:10; 20: 4). Then there are the millions of those who *have never* understood—the 'REST' of the dead (Rev. 20:5).

"And then there are those who WILL not choose to repent—who are finally to *lose out* on salvation."[26]

We suppose we are numbered by Armstrong in the latter classification since we have not chosen to accept his message after going over carefully everything his cult has to teach. Actually, what he is saying amounts to universal salvation—apart from a handful who reject the teaching of Armstrong and his Worldwide Church of God after being fully enlightened by it.

The thought is as *fantastic* as it is *unscriptural!*

26. *What Is Death?* p. 6

CHAPTER XI

The Armstrong Teaching About Prophecy

As previously noted, utter lack of humility is a besetting sin with Herbert W. Armstrong and other Worldwide Church of God leaders. Over and over, readers of their literature and listeners to their broadcasts are deluged with inference upon inference—and, not infrequently, outright claims—regarding "inside information" available nowhere else. This is especially apparent in the area of eschatology.

Although disclaiming to be prophets in the biblical sense, the claims they make regarding *interpretations* for existing prophecies in the Word of God are tantamount to revelations which could not be more original or revealing if delivered by a heavenly archangel over the combined NBC, CBS and ABC networks! For example, Herbert W. Armstrong says: "Did you ever notice that *The* WORLD TOMORROW program makes plain the REAL MEANING of today's world news, and that it REPORTS *tomorrow's* world news *before it happens?*"[1]

Sometimes readers are treated to outright crystal ball gazing—much to the later embarrassment of the Pasadena seer. For example, twenty-five or twenty-six months after the now-famous Six-Day "Holy Land" War (June, 1967), readers were assured: "Many prophecies show that the 'times of the Gentiles' have not ended. The greatest proof that the 'times of the Gentiles' have not yet ended is the simple fact that the Gentile Arabs are still in possession of the old city of Jerusalem. THEY WILL REMAIN IN CONTROL OF THIS CITY UNTIL THE SECOND COMING OF CHRIST, AT WHICH TIME HE WILL DELIVER

---

1. *Should You Try To "Convert" Others?* © 1966,1970,1972; p.1

JERUSALEM, THE JEWS AND ALL ISRAEL FROM GENTILE DOMINATION."[2]

Barely two years later Mr. Armstrong was red-facedly eating crow.

In this chapter about the second coming, we will show first how the cult seeks to interpret the *time* of Christ's coming in a way that is, for all practical purposes, the date setting forbidden by our Lord. Then we will point out some of their absurd and extreme views concerning our Lord's return and His coming kingdom.

Predictions About the "Time" of Christ's Coming

In a *Tomorrow's World* article collaborated on by David Jon Hill and J. Orlin Grabbe, "Noah's Day—Today!" the writers try to prove Christ will return in our time. They say: "Christ's forecast, 'As things were in Noah's days, so will they be when the Son of Man comes. In the days before the flood they ate and drank and married, until the day that Noah went into the ark, and they knew nothing until the flood came and swept them all away. That is how it will be when the Son of Man comes' (Matt. 24:37-39, *New English Bible*).

"Now if Christ were *really* going to return, and come back at a time when the whole earth *is* the way it *was* in Noah's day, and if our newspapers were to say that's the way the world was *now*—we'd be concerned!

"So we are. Because He is. Because society is living Noah's day all over again."[3]

The writers then go on to point out that, just as in Noah's day, we are having a population explosion, there is violence for the sake of violence, and population pressures are bringing stresses upon all mankind. Because of this, they argue, Christ *must* return shortly.

---

2. *The Plain Truth*, May, 1965; p. 21; quoted in *The Plain Truth About The Armstrong Cult*, Robert G. Grant; n.d.; Published by the Author, Glendale, California; p. 22
3. May, 1971; p. 26

We invite, however, our readers to examine the passage in Matthew 24:37-39 more closely, either in the version given by the writers or in the Authorized Version, the King James. Where does it say one word about population explosions, violence or stresses being the identifying feature announcing Christ's return? This is neither what the passage is saying nor the meaning it intends to convey. Actually, it teaches the very opposite. Instead of saying that certain characteristics will help us to identify Christ's coming, it is teaching that His coming will be without warning—in absolute suddenness. It is simply saying that, just as without warning the flood struck in Noah's day (they "knew not until the flood came, and swept them all away"), so "shall also the coming of the Son of man be."

A favorite *proving ground* for writers of the Armstrong cult in developing this particular thesis pertains to the "signs" our Lord gave in Matthew 24. They like to argue that the wars and rumors of wars, the earthquakes, the pestilences and these other things are evidence that this generation is the one which will be alive when Christ returns. Without going into detail here, we will simply point out that we have two books in our library written in the 19th century, both of which *proved* Christ would have to come in that generation, using the same identical arguments. One of the books even gives the actual dates, listing Jerome Napoleon, head of the Bonaparte dynasty, as the antichrist and predicting Christ would descend to Mount Olivet at "about 3 p.m., the hour of the Jewish Evening Sacrifice," on "the last day of Passover Week, Thursday, April 11, 1901," with the "Commencement of the Millennium" immediately taking place.[4]

Brian Knowles, writing about "the end of the world" in *Tomorrow's World*, insists, "*This Work has never*

4. *Forty Coming Wonders,* M. Baxter; Sixth Edition, 1887; Christian Herald, London and New York; pp. iii, 430

set an exact date for the return of Christ! After all, who are we to dictate to Christ when He must arrive on this earth?"[5] Yet the same writer, in the same article, says, "*You are living in that one generation* during which almost 90% of prophecy will be fulfilled! Read Matthew 24:34."[6]

Does Matthew 24:34 say that almost 90 per cent of prophecy is going to be fulfilled in our day? We answer by simply quoting the verse: "Verily I say unto you, This generation shall not pass, till all these things be fulfilled." Does it say what Mr. Knowles claims it does? *It most certainly does not*! In fact, it would be helpful to quote a footnote in the original Scofield Reference Bible regarding this word "generation." Dr. Scofield says: "Gr. *genea*, the primary definition of which is, 'race, kind, family, stock, breed.' (So all lexicons.) That the word is used in this sense here is sure because none of 'these things,' i.e. the world-wide preaching of the kingdom, the great tribulation, the return of the Lord in visible glory, and the regathering of the elect, occurred at the destruction of Jerusalem by Titus, A.D. 70. The promise is, therefore, that the generation—nation, or family of Israel—will be preserved unto these things'; a promise wonderfully fulfilled to this day."[7]

Knowles further argues, "God dogmatically states whenever He does a major act, *He will inform His servants beforehand* (Amos 3:7)."[8] Again, the proffered proof text says no such thing. The passage in Amos merely stated that God was going to reveal His plan to His servants regarding a particular instance in that day and time, not that He is going to give advance information about everything He ever does.

---

5. August, 1971; "What Do You Mean—'*The End* of the *World'?*"; p. 13
6. Ibid.
7. From *The Scofield Reference Bible,* edited by C. I. Scofield. Copyright, 1917,1944 by Oxford University Press, Inc., and reprinted by permission; p. 1034
8. Op. cit.; p. 13

Are we to conclude, for example, that God tells Mr. Armstrong when He is going to lash the coast along the Gulf of Mexico with a hurricane, or when He is going to cause a tornado to sweep through St. Louis? We think not. Nor has God made any such guarantee with regard to informing His servants about the return of Christ.

Mr. Knowles goes on to argue, "Though we cannot know at this time the precise day of the return of the Messiah, *we can know the approximate time in history*. We can watch the news of the world fulfill the specific and meticulous end-time prophecies of God's Word. When we see these prophecies being fulfilled (which they are!), we can also recognize the imminency of Christ's arrival. As John the Baptist prepared the way for the first coming of Jesus, *this Work is preparing the way for His second arrival*! (Mal. 4:5-6)."[9]

Ignoring the "modest" reference to the Worldwide Church of God—and even ignoring the "source" of the cult's inside information (*the newspapers*!)—consider the claim that "the approximate time" of Christ's coming can be ascertained. The disciples of our Lord, following the crucifixion and resurrection, asked the Savior, "Lord, wilt thou at this time restore again the kingdom to Israel?" (Acts 1:6). In other words, "When are you coming? When will your Kingdom be established on earth?"

The very next verse tells us: "And he said unto them, IT IS NOT FOR YOU TO KNOW THE TIMES OR THE SEASONS, which the Father hath put in his own power." In other words, not only are we unable to know "the precise day," we cannot even know "the seasons." Our Lord was warning, if words mean anything at all, not to attempt estimating even the approximate time of His coming.

---

9. Ibid.

Incidentally, another writer in the same issue of the magazine, trying to answer the objection that "*there have ALWAYS BEEN false prophets, wars and rumors of wars, famines, pestilences and earthquakes,*" says: "Matthew 24:22 gives the answer: The time of Christ's second coming and the end of the present age would occur at a time when mankind would be on the brink of the ultimate abyss of complete destruction. All human life on earth would not only have to be in danger, but in fact, literally about to be obliterated.

"This is precisely the situation *today*.

"It has *never* been this way before.

"*This is the end time*!"[10]

Note that Mr. Kuhn does not say, "This might be the end time!"; he dogmatically states that it *is* the end time!

Garner Ted Armstrong says the beast Christ will destroy at His coming is alive today. In an article on Satan he declared: "When Jesus returns to this earth as KING, His first act will be to destroy, NOT *ALL* the wicked, but that 'wicked ONE' who is going to be working miracles and deceiving the world! (II Thes. 2:8.) Together with this great False Prophet, Christ will lay hold of the Beast who is yet to arise, and throw them *both* into a *lake of fire*, burning with brimstone! (Rev. 19:20.)

"These two are human beings—physical, breathing *men*, who are alive and drawing breath at this instant! The fire will CONSUME them. *This lake of fire is going to be burning all during the millennium*! (Isaiah 66:23-24)"[11]

Notice the bold assumption—offered as a plain statement of fact—that this "beast" is alive right now! The article was first published in 1958—*15 years before the publication of this book*!

---

10. Robert L. Kuhn, "Is This The Time of *The End?*"; p. 16
11. *Tomorrow's World,* June, 1971; "What Is Satan's Fate?"; p. 7

Part of the problem in interpreting prophecy on the part of the Armstrongs and their co-workers pertains to the fact of their obsession with their own importance. Mr. Armstrong, as we have already seen, teaches that when he launched his ministry on January 7, 1934, this triggered the fulfillment of ninety per cent of all biblical prophecy. He divides this fulfillment into two 19-year time-cycles, the second commencing on January 7, 1953,[12] and being completed on January 7, 1972 (we would think completion would have been January 6, but this is the date Armstrong gives). Writers of the cult's literature, along with Mr. Armstrong himself, obviously felt something of tremendous significance would take place on or about that date. It is an honest inference to say they expected the return of Christ and the launching of the millennium at that time.

Although it probably is not very gracious of us to admit it, one of the most humorous articles we have ever read was Armstrong's "Personal" column in the first issue of *Tomorrow's World* after January 7, 1972, came and went without event. No Roman Catholic confessional booth ever revealed a greater baring of soul or acknowledgement of human frailties. He reminded his readers that his commission (which he

---

12. He bases his argument for 19-year cycles on a claim that "God has set time running in cycles of 19 years. Just once in every 19 years the *days,* divided by the sun; the *months,* marked by the new *moon;* and the *years,* divided by the revolution of the earth around the *sun,* all come into conjunction." Armstrong sets Pentecost, 31 A.D., as "the day" the "early Church. . .*started* on its mission." Exactly 19 years later to the very day, he has "reason to believe," the door was opened for the Apostle Paul "to get the Message into EUROPE." Nineteen years later, in 69 A.D., the apostles fled, with the destruction of Jerusalem taking place the following year. He offers no authority for this supposed fleeing, nor any *why* they fled or *to where*— just "they fled"! (He also attempts to concoct two 19-year cycles for getting Jeremiah to Ireland with the Throne of David!) Armstrong thinks his second cycle began, like that of the early Church, with the launching of his European ministry. The only significance he was able to attach to January 7, 1972, was "the purchase of advertising space" in the *Reader's Digest* and receiving from his bankers "the signed, sealed and delivered financing for 80%" of a new auditorium at Ambassador College—neither of which could be considered of any earth-shaking importance! [All references and quotes in this footnote are from Armstrong's "Personal" column, *Tomorrow's World,* February, 1972; pp. 1-4, 30-33]

spells with a capital "C"!) was "*not* to become an infallible expert on, or to preach, chronology." He admitted feeling "at present" [note the loophole for a future pinpointing of dates] "the whole question of chronology is in confusion" [thanks to Armstrong!], "and no one can be positively SURE of dates." He added, "As of the present" [again note the loophole] "I, and a majority of our historians in Ambassador College, and researchers in the School of Theology" [are you duly impressed with this scholarly array of background, as Armstrong intends for you to be?], feel that it is utterly unsafe to try to SET DATES in regard to future prophesied events, especially the return of the living Christ in supreme Power and Glory to rule all nations of the earth." We will go farther than Armstrong and say it is not only utterly unsafe "as of the present," but at any time!

But back to Armstrong's confessional booth. He says, ". . .we are only human, and it is natural that we should have been curious to know, as far as possible, how much time we had to GET THE JOB DONE." Lest readers think he is *too* human, however, he says: "But when God chooses His human instruments, He is more concerned about the sincere and honest of HEART. He calls imperfect (*all* men are, anyway) but sincere and dedicated human instruments. THEY ALL MAKE MISTAKES! This fact needs NO APOLOGY!" However, we are not blaming Armstrong for being wrong with the dates he set (anyone who sets dates will be!), *we are blaming him for trying to set those dates in the first place*—clearly contradicting plain biblical prohibitions.

Armstrong proceeded to explain how imperfectly his understanding of "true Biblical teaching" had been over the years and how, repeatedly, he has had to change, correct and amend what he had previously understood and taught. Lest anyone get the wrong idea, however, he throws in a comparison of himself with the Apostle Paul, saying both were not taught by men, but by God Himself. Also, he reminded the faithful: "Even though it is God's Work, directed, empowered and blessed by Him, He carries it on through frail, weak HUMANS, and we humans are *ALL* of us subject to mistakes!" For good measure, he reminded his followers that "Peter made mistakes."

Armstrong then quoted from some of his past writings where he admits it "appeared" he was setting dates. One was after he discovered there would be a second 19-year cycle (he originally taught there would only be one), and his explanation is: "I admit we were somewhat excited by this realization of FACT. We are HUMAN! Our hearts are IN God's Work to which He has called us. This was, to some extent, an emotional revelation. Would YOU have the same normal human reaction, had you been in our place? I think all but dour, prejudiced, hostile critics, who would like to see God's Work destroyed, would have reacted as we did!" As we write these lines, the poor man is intimating there will be a *third* 19-year cycle and, we predict, his successors will be announcing new cycles every 19 years from now until Christ returns!

How important are the repeated Armstrong errors regarding dates? He says: "Our human interest, and enthusiasm about facts and indications pointing to the probable amount of time we had left is of MOST MINOR consequence compared to the BIG point of the Commission—WHICH WE HAVE BEEN GETTING DONE!" It may be "of MOST MINOR consequence" to Armstrong, but it is proof positive to the rest of the world that he is a false prophet, as phony in his claims as a $17 bill! After all, one of the signs of a false prophet is his failure in prediction: "When a prophet speaketh in the name of the Lord, if the thing follow not, nor come to pass, that is the thing which the Lord hath not spoken, but the prophet hath spoken it presumptuously: thou shalt not be afraid of him" (Deuteronomy 18:22).

Armstrong acknowledges that Herman L. Hoeh, in the cult's publication, *A True History of the True Church*, claimed God had given His Church "*just two* nineteen-year cycles in which to carry the Gospel to the world!" Armstrong's only comment about this prediction: they did get it into all the world before the second cycle was completed! (Although earlier in the article he admitted there might "be a very few little countries virtually unheard of into which we have not penetrated"!)

Armstrong made much of explaining away his zeal in the booklet *1975 in Prophecy* (which an ex-member of the cult says co-workers have been told to destroy), listing the author, Gordon Ratray Taylor, along with scientists such as Sir Philip Noel Baker, John Platt, Dr. Binay Sen and the "Federation of American Scientists" in 1960, as, about the same time his booklet appeared, predicting the end of the world by 1975. What this proves escapes our understanding, however, since they were only giving personal observations, not thundering forth supposedly divine and infallible predictions from the Word of God, as Armstrong was implying to his followers. Fortunately for Armstrong, he had the foresight to throw in a number of "possiblies," "probablies" and "it appears"—to point out after January 7, 1972, came and went without incident.

The confession goes on: ". . .we were SO overwhelmingly impressed—perhaps more than we should have been—by the FACT of what happened after 19 years, we did, a few times, go further than we should with it [*that is the understatement of the year*!—R. L. S.]—though basically, we continued, time and again, to say 'we do not set dates.' But some statements gave the IMPRESSION that we did set the date, January 7, 1972. It is difficult to control sincere, dedicated enthusiastic ZEAL; and we were human!"

Before he finished, he compared himself with Moses, Abraham, David, Elijah, Peter and "ALL MEN God has ever called and used" (they made mistakes, too). Then he wound up the confession by declaring, in effect, "So we were wrong in our predictions! You've still got to stay with us because we are the only ones who have the Truth!" Here are his exact closing words: "You know, I'm reminded of the time Jesus was criticized, persecuted, misrepresented by His enemies. He asked His disciples, 'Will ye also go away?'

"'Then Simon Peter answered him, Lord, to whom shall we go? THOU hast the words of Eternal Life!'

"And we in His work, today, have those SAME WORDS OF ETERNAL LIFE!

"Yes, *all systems are 'Go!'*

"With renewed energy, greater than ever before, WE PLUNGE ON TO FINISH THE WORK WE HAVE BEEN GIVEN TO DO!"

Actually, in a move unprecedented in the long history of false prophets, Mr. Armstrong actually tried to use his abominable failures in this entire area of wrong date setting to his advantage, a lesson he learned early in his "pre-conversion" advertising days from John R. Patterson, president of the National Cash Register Company.[13] He argues that his failures, now

---

13. This incident is described in his autobiography and had to do with a meeting Armstrong attended of the NCR sales staff, conducted by Mr. Patterson. The latter told his staff: "Men, you are wondering why I called all of you here. Now I will tell you. Every one of you loses sales because your prospects put up objections you are unable to overcome. An idea flashed into my mind the other day that will enable you to turn *every* objection into your strongest selling point. It's so simple you'll all wonder why you never thought of it. *Whatever* the objection, you are to answer immediately, with a smile of complete assurance: 'Why, *certainly!*—and *that's* the *very reason* you need this National cash register!'" Armstrong confessed: "I have found this principle of salesmanship effective, perhaps hundreds of times, even in 'selling' men the *Free* salvation to which they so often put up every objection against receiving." [*The Plain Truth,* May, 1958; p. 15] We dare say Mr. Armstrong never found "this principle of salesmanship" any more effective than when he used it to try and make his amazing, astounding blunders and mistakes in the field of date setting proof the boners were *added evidence* his work is "the True Work of God on earth today!"

that he has confessed them (but, like the kid caught with his hands in the cookie jar, *what else could he do*?), prove his work and message are the true work and message of God on earth today!

Listen to this: "Let me ask you this question. Do you know of any large, established, well-recognized professing Christian denomination which has PUBLICLY confessed it had been WRONG in what it had been teaching, and which then CORRECTED the error, and turned to the TRUTH?

"No, the big established churches and denominations feel they cannot afford to admit having had any error—having ever mis-taught the people. . . .

"If I were looking for God's one true Church, I would assuredly *look for one that had confessed and corrected its errors! For all have had them*—even the early churches (Rev. 2:4,14,20).

"Any criterion that assumes God's TRUE Work through humans is absolutely perfect, unable to be wrong or make mistakes or hold to any error, is a false measuring stick and will mislead you.

"You may ask, do I, then, feel that we in this Work are full of errors, misleading the people? MOST EMPHATICALLY *NO*! We have not had to correct error many times. But each time we have corrected an error, we have had one fewer error left. If we KNEW of any error still remaining, now, we would CHANGE it! If and when we find one in the future, we shall correct it!

The one who follows that principle is THE *MOST* FREE FROM ERROR!

"So, confessing such an error is one of the SUREST proofs to identify the people through whom the living Christ IS WORKING—and whom HE IS USING!"

We trust our readers will study carefully the *astounding* claim in that last paragraph!

Another major problem the Worldwide Church of God has in interpreting prophecy pertains to the fact that absolutely no distinction is made between the rapture, which is called "this vile doctrine,"[14] and the revelation. Just as Israelites before Christ's first coming confused and failed to distinguish prophecies relating to the Messiah's *passion* and His *power*, His coming to *suffer* and His coming to *reign*, so the Armstrongs fail to recognize Bible teaching regarding our Lord's coming *for* His saints, over against the teaching of His coming *with* His saints. Both sets of prophecies are jumbled into one, resulting in utter chaos and confusion.

An example of this failure to distinguish can be seen in the following paragraph from the pen of Herbert W. Armstrong, mingling statements about rapture and revelation together: "JOHN 14:1-3: This text is also used as a proof text for going to Heaven. Jesus said, 'If I go. . .I WILL COME AGAIN, and receive you unto myself.' He receives us unto Himself WHEN HE WILL HAVE COME AGAIN—right here on the earth. We are to meet Him IN THE CLOUDS, and airplanes fly higher than that every day. That same day we come on down WITH HIM upon the Mount of Olives (Zech. 14:4,5). 'That where I am, THERE ye may be also.' After Jesus receives us unto Himself, He will remain here on this earth. We shall ever BE with Him. We shall sit with Him IN HIS THRONE—which is the throne of David ON THIS EARTH."[15] The passage in John, about Christ returning *for* His saints to take them to the Father's house of many mansions, is welded into a prophecy in Zechariah about Messiah's return to set up His earthly kingdom—an entirely different event.

Armstrong and his followers have no plans for experiencing the woes of the tribulation, however. Herman

---

14. *The Plain Truth,* July, 1959; Herman L. Hoeh, "The *'Secret Rapture'* fact. . .or fiction?"; p. 20
15. *Tomorrow's World,* September, 1971; "Where Will The *Millennium* Be Spent?"; p. 6

L. Hoeh explains: "But how and where are the Christians who watch and pray going to escape? Turn to the 12th chapter of Revelation. Here we find the answer!

"Here we find the true Church—the Church of God—pictured. A woman, remember, is the symbol of a Church (II Cor. 11:2). This chapter pictures the true Church, whereas the 17th chapter of Revelation pictures the false churches—a mother church and her daughter churches. Notice verse 6 of chapter 12. In the tribulation during the Middle Ages 'the woman [the true Church] fled into the wilderness, where she hath there a place prepared of God.' That tribulation is merely a type of the coming great tribulation—a time of trouble of such magnitude as has never occurred on earth before. Now turn to verse 13:

"'And when the dragon [Satan] saw that he was cast down to the earth, he persecuted the woman'—this is the persecution that is yet in the future, a persecution that is being secretly planned at this very moment! How does the Church escape? 'And the two wings of the great eagle were given to the woman that she should fly TO THE WILDERNESS to her place' for 3½ years.

"The Church is NOT taken to heaven, but to the *wilderness*—to a desert region *here on earth*. 'And the *earth* helped the woman' (Rev. 12:13-16).

"Could anything be plainer?"[16]

This fleeing to the wilderness by the "watching" and "worthy" ones of the cult is to be to Petra, "an ancient city in northern Arabia, the stronghold and treasury city of the Nabataeans. . .situated in the desert of Edom, near the points of intersection of great caravan routes from Palmyra, Gaza, Egypt, and

16. Op. cit.; pp. 17,18

the Persian Gulf."[17] The same authority describes it: "An impregnable fortress. . .approached by a chasm or ravine, which in some places is only 12 ft. wide and has rocky walls of red sandstone towering to a height of more than 100 ft."[18] This sanctuary, the Armstrongs feel, will keep them safe from "the wrath of Satan" during the Great Tribulation.

Not all the Church will escape, however. Hoeh continues: "But what happens to those not accounted worthy to escape? 'And the dragon. . .went away to make war with the rest of her seed'—the remainder of the Church that did not escape. The people whom Satan hates—and against whom he stirs up the nations—the people who 'keep the commandments of God and hold the testimony of Jesus' (verse 17)."[19]

By the way, those who believe in the biblical teaching of the rapture are not given much comfort by Hoeh. He warns: "It is time you opened your eyes to this HERESY that has stemmed from 'BABYLON THE GREAT, the Mother of Harlots and Abominations of the Earth' (Rev. 17:5). Unless you recognize this vile doctrine for what it is, YOU AND MILLIONS WITH YOU ARE PLUNGING STRAIGHT FOR THE MOST FIENDISH, DIABOLICAL TIME OF TORTURE EVER INSTITUTED BY MAN! IT IS NOW BEING PLANNED IN EUROPE! There is only one way of escape—'Watch world events and pray constantly.'"[20]

As for the evidence of the cult's date setting, note these paragraphs from the pen of A. E. Carrozzo: "It is through this 'sure word of prophecy' that we can understand the truth about the return of Jesus Christ. And the Bible reveals that Jesus Christ will return to set up His world-ruling kingdom *in your lifetime and*

---

17. *The New Funk & Wagnalls Encyclopedia,* Copyright, 1950,1951; Unicorn Publishers, Inc., N.Y., N.Y.; Vol. 26, p. 9503
18. Ibid.
19. Op. cit.; p. 18
20. Ibid.; p. 20

mine! (That is, barring any unforeseen termination of your life or mine!) *Christ's return will occur in this generation*!

"Did you notice we did not say 'maybe,' 'perhaps,' or 'it might occur'? [*We noticed*!—R. L. S.] It *will* happen in your generation! It is entirely possible that YOU, as an individual, will live to witness this greatest event in contemporary history!

". . .No thinking person today doubts we are in the end of the age. . . .There is no question about it—Jesus Christ was talking about THIS GENERATION. . . .

"When will Jesus Christ return? Not tonight! On the other hand, He will come in THIS GENERATION—your lifetime and mine! Will you be ready?"[21]

Part of the cult's dogmatism regarding the time of Christ's second coming relates to its teaching that God only planned to deal with man for 6,000 years. Herbert W. Armstrong expressed it: "And this very SAME Bible inspired by the LIVING GOD *fore*tells precisely what God is going to DO about it all—yes, and in OUR TIME!

"It reveals that God made man a free moral agent—that God DECREED from the beginning that MAN MUST *CHOOSE* whether to believe and obey God, or to reject God and set up on earth his *own* systems of religion, government, and society; and that God set apart a duration of 6,000 years for man to *cut himself off* from the very real GOD, and to learn his lesson by writing it in cruel *human experience*."[22]

He says again: "God had set a definite PLAN with a definite time-program, for working out His PURPOSE here below! It is a 7,000-year plan of seven millennial 'days' of which the first seven literal days of re-creation were a type. The first six of these millenniums were allotted for man, of his own free volition (though

---

21. *Tomorrow's World,* August, 1971; "This Generation *Shall NOT Pass*. . ."; p. 9
22. *Tomorrow's World,* May, 1971; "Why God Is Not *Real* To Most People"; p. 7

swayed by Satan) to go his own way. Also, in effect, they were allotted as the six millennial 'days' for Satan's 'labor' of deception over humanity, to be followed by the millennial 'Sabbath,' in which Satan will observe *enforced* rest from his work of deceiving the nations, and God will teach humanity His TRUTH!"[23]

David Jon Hill follows the same line when he writes: "God's plan of salvation is a 7000-year plan. For 6000 years of this time God has allowed mankind to go his way, under the influence of his own mind and directed also by the mind of Satan the Devil."[24]

Now, God *may* or *may not* be operating on a 7,000-year plan for mankind on this earth. One thing, however, is absolutely positive: *if He is, the Bible nowhere declares it*![25] Such a conclusion is merely a hypothesis set up in order to "prove" that Jesus Christ is coming in this generation. And, we hasten to point out, it must rest upon such ancient chronological charts as that by James Ussher (1581-1656)—long since disproved by the findings of modern scholarship—in order to make it realistic. As one who believes thoroughly in the imminent return of Jesus Christ, it grieves us to see this blessed truth prostituted in such a dishonest, scheming manner before an unbelieving, cynical and skeptical world.

But the Worldwide Church of God narrows the time of Christ's coming down to a finer point than merely "this generation." Herbert W. Armstrong writes: "What

---

23. *Tomorrow's World*, October, 1971; "Just What Do You Mean. . .*Born Again?*"; pp. 4,5
24. *There Is A Real Hell Fire!* © 1962,1963,1971; p. 6
25. Edmond C. Gruss, in his work on a kindred cult, *The Jehovah's Witnesses And Prophetic Speculation* (Presbyterian and Reformed Publishing Company, Nutley, N. J.; Copyright, 1972; pp. 59,60), points out that there is nothing new (it goes back centuries, even B.C.), nor Christian (Jews, Islams and even pagans among the Egyptians, Chaldeans and others have taught it), in this philosophy. The highly speculative aspect of the theory is seen when E. B. Elliott (*Horae Apocalypticae*) is quoted regarding the dates some of antiquity's scholars held would complete the first six thousand years and usher in the seventh: Sibylline Oracles, c. A.D. 196 (the earliest); Cyprian, c. 243; Hippolytus, 500; Lactantius, c. 500; Constantius, c. 500; Hilarion, 500; Sulpitius Severus 581; and Augustine, 650. While acknowledging that some evangelicals today teach this theory, we dogmatically insist it rests entirely on *speculation*, not *revelation*.

WONDERFUL, almost INCOMPREHENSIBLE, *GLORIOUS GOOD NEWS*!

"And the BEST NEWS is, that the COMING OF CHRIST is now drawing VERY NEAR! Just a very few more years! And then—the PEACEFUL, HAPPY, GLORIOUS *WORLD TOMORROW*!"[26]

So it is not merely "this generation," it is just "a few more years!"

Armstrong sets the date even closer than this! The first edition of the book you are holding in your hands came from the presses in 1973. Armstrong has made astounding predictions for this very year! In his book, "The *Proof* of the BIBLE," he says: "Here is a book—The Holy Bible—that dares to write out the future history of this world in advance—that dares to prophesy what is actually going to *happen* within 15 or 20 years to specific nations, including Russia, the British Commonwealth, China, the United States, Italy, Turkey, Ethiopia, and many others—most of the major nations of this world."[27]

Armstrong's statement was made in 1958, fifteen years ago, making the fulfillment "within 1973 to 1978." Later in the book he says: "Notice! This same God is telling what is going to happen to our modern nations today, yes, Russia, Germany, Great Britain, the United States, Australia, Italy, China, all of the great nations, and many of the *minor* nations of the world, pronouncing sentence on *us*—warning of things that are to happen to us in the next 20 years. *Can He do it*? Was He able to do what He said about ancient *Tyre*?"[28]

Then, still later, he says: "Always, everything that has been previously prophesied in your Bible for the past centuries has been fulfilled. But there are many,

26. "Just What Do You Mean. . .*Born Again?*" op. cit.; p. 49
27. © 1958; p. 3
28. Page 11

many more prophecies that are to be fulfilled *from this moment on*! We are just coming now to the grand smash climax of this whole age when there are far more prophecies — far more world-shaking events — to happen in the next 15 or 20 years *than ever happened before in the history of the world*!"[29]

However, when he winds up the book, no doubt feeling the need for a little more safety in his prediction, he subtracts 5 and adds 5 from his time schedule. In the final three paragraphs of the book, he says: "But now finally what is the true significance of all this? Simply this: One third, approximately, of the Bible is PROPHECY. Only about *one-tenth* of the prophecies pertain to these cities and nations of old — prophecies *already fulfilled*! *NINE-TENTHS* OF PROPHECY IS DEVOTED TO WORLD EVENTS *NOW* TO HAPPEN *IN OUR TIME*!

"Think of it! Almost one-third of YOUR BIBLE is devoted to revealing to us, today, in advance, *what WE are going to live through during the next ten to twenty-five years*!

"*WE* LIVE IN THE EXCITING *TIME OF THE END*! The 'END OF THE WORLD'—of *this age*—is upon us."[30]

An article in *The Plain Truth* in 1963 said: "The world you live in won't be here 15 years from now!"[31] An ex-member of the cult points out that Armstrong first predicted final destruction for 1938, then switched the date, of necessity, several times. The *pro tem* time is now the late 1970's, apparently. As that time draws near it will be moved again, no doubt. This date-setting dilemma has necessitated, according to the same former member, Armstrong getting out word to the faithful to destroy copies of previous releases, including

29. Page 37
30. Pp. 40,41
31. December, p. 7; quoted by Robert G. Grant, op. cit.; p. 18

1975 in Prophecy, because the dates were too specific and too faulty![32]

Thus Herbert W. Armstrong falls into the same foolish trap and heads toward the same tragic fate of such previous founders of false cults as "Pastor" Charles Russell, William Miller, Ellen G. White and others who vainly imagined they had discovered inside information about dates relating to the end times.

Regarding the time of His coming, our Lord said, "Behold, I come as a thief. Blessed is he that watcheth, and keepeth his garments, lest he walk naked, and they see his shame" (Revelation 16:15). Thieves do not send advance telegrams or herald their approach with blasting trumpets! They come suddenly, swiftly, without warning. This is how our Lord is going to come. In fact, He said elsewhere: "But of that day and that hour knoweth no man, no, not the angels which are in heaven, neither the Son, but the Father. Take ye heed, watch and pray: for ye know not when the time is" (Mark 13:32,33).

We are absolutely sure that if our Lord, during His earthly ministry, did not know the time of His second appearing, no one in the Worldwide Church of God today knows!

Confusing Prophetic Errors

In the remaining section of this chapter on prophecy, we would like to point out some of the erroneous statements regarding Christ's coming and His Kingdom made by Mr. Armstrong and other Worldwide Church of God leaders. Let us just list a few of them.

(1) Armstrong teaches that the second coming of Christ is the "climax" of events of "the Day of the Lord." We are told: "And so the THEME of *The Revelation* is the events of the 'DAY OF THE LORD,'

32. *The Marson Report*, Richard A. Marson; © 1970; The Ashley-Calvin Press, Seattle, Washington; pp. 1,8

climaxing in the second coming of Christ."[33] We would not object to this except Armstrong means by it the *first* and *only* coming of Christ. As already noted, he does not believe in the rapture of the saints.

Because of this, the cult puts nearly as much emphasis on reading the newspaper as reading the Bible. In the summary of R. A. Wiedenheft's article based on Luke 21:36, "Are You Watching?" he wrote: "You don't need to be saying 'peace and safety' when sudden destruction comes!

"You don't need to be in darkness that that day should overtake you as a thief.

"Read and know God's Word. Know what God said would happen in our day.

"Then watch what's going on around you. Listen to people. Read the newspapers and magazines, listen to radio and TV newscasts. Continue to read TOMORROW'S WORLD and watch prophecy being fulfilled!

"Watch! And pray!—that *you* may be accounted worthy to escape!"[34]

(2) Along this line, the Worldwide Church of God makes the "last trump" synonomous with the "trump of God" in Christ's coming for His own, saying that the saints alive at the coming of Christ will go directly to Jerusalem and begin ruling. One of the cult's leaders, C. Paul Meredith, describes it: "The first resurrection of man to immortality that has ever occurred in this world (except Christ), will occur when Christ comes at the last trump. I Thessalonians 4:16-17 describes this: 'For the Lord himself shall descend from heaven with a [great] shout, with the voice of the archangel, and with the trump [last trump] of God: and the dead in Christ shall rise first.

"Then we which are alive and remain shall be caught up together with them in the clouds to meet the Lord

33. *The Key To The Book Of Revelation,* Written Anonymously; © 1952; p. 4
34. *Tomorrow's World,* September, 1971; p. 40

in the air: and so shall we ever be with the Lord.' But they will go *immediately* to Jerusalem to start their 1000-year rule. Read Zechariah 14.

"This is the resurrection just ahead now! I Corinthians 15:51 through 56 describes this same resurrection and Revelation 11:15 describes the blowing (sounding) of the 'last trump' which ushers this period in. Read these verses!"[35]

This confusion causes Herman L. Hoeh to say: "There is no secret rapture before the tribulation *or at any other time*! The resurrection is at the mighty sound of the seventh trump IN the Day of God's wrath which *follows* the tribulation. The tribulation is *not* the Day of the Lord."[36]

What a hopeless confusion of Scriptures-out-of-context!

(3) Armstrong, while not a postmillennialist, has the "clean up the world" philosophy of those who are. William F. Dankenbring, talking about the millennium, says: "Make no mistake. When Christ returns, He is NOT going to 'do it all Himself.' The saints—true *Christians*—are going to help Him clean up this world!"[37]

This cleaning up is not going to be any little job, either. In fact, we are told it will take several generations to accomplish! A writer in *Tomorrow's World* informs us: ". . .we're not saying that God's new educational system will spread over the entire earth instantaneously, even at the return of Jesus Christ. Time will be required to train parents and teachers. In some areas of the world, it may take two or three generations just to reach 100% literacy. But pilot projects will rapidly begin in many places. Even whole countries will first be developed as show cases to other nations, demonstrating to them the fabulous benefits

---

35. *If You Die. . .Will You Live Again?* © 1958,1971; p. 6
36. *"The 'Secret Rapture'* fact. . .or fiction?"; op. cit.; p. 19
37. *Tomorrow's World,* December, 1971; "What Should You Do Until *Christ Returns?"*; p. 33

of the new system. And no nation, once it sees the benefits, will want to have part in other educational systems."[38]

What a far cry this is from the biblical picture of righteousness covering the earth like waters cover the sea, the moment Christ sets up His kingdom. And with Satan bound in the bottomless pit during that period (Revelation 20:1-3), one wonders why it will take so long to clean up the world.

(4) According to Armstrong, it is going to take 1,100 years for the judgment of the nations. Garner Ted Armstrong writes: "Jesus said He is going to cast unrepentant, carnal-minded HUMANS into 'everlasting fire, *prepared for the devil and his angels*' (Matt. 24:41). This parable of the sheep and the goats is another example of a parable of Christ's that makes no special reference to the *time element*, but is showing a spiritual lesson and principle to be learned! The *separation* in verse 32 takes place over a period of 1,100 years!—to the end of the 100-year period after the millennium."[39]

By what authority Armstrong makes this judgment last the entire millennium and 100 years beyond—and how he comes up with that 100-year figure—is not revealed. It is simply stated as a fact which the faithful are to unquestionably accept as gospel truth.

(5) Probably most Christians have the idea that Christ Himself is going to rule the world during the millennium. Not so, the Worldwide Church of God tells us, the ruler will be Abraham. A *Tomorrow's World* article reveals: "After a lifetime of testing, teaching and training, Abraham became qualified to ultimately rule *the entire earth* under Jesus Christ in Tomorrow's World! (Romans 4:13.) He was called the 'father of

---

38. September, 1971; George Geis, "Education in Tomorrow's World"; p. 39
39. *Tomorrow's World*, June, 1971; "What Is Satan's Fate?"; p. 7

the faithful.' "[40] Nowhere is a single line of Scripture found to support this statement. It is merely a fabrication of the writer's imagination—and not a very good one at that.

(6) Many evangelicals, although not all by any means, believe that the old Roman Empire is to be revived and headed up by the anti-christ. One revival for the Roman Empire is small potatoes to Armstrong. He teaches it already has been revived *nine times* and is good for one more! According to Herbert W. Armstrong: "This same GOD inspired the writing, 2,500 years ago, that *this* great Empire, which was the Roman Empire, was to be overthrown, but to be resurrected *ten times*! NINE of those resurrections have already come and gone, and that same GOD wrote in those same *prophecies*, 2,500 years ago [some of them 1,900 years ago], that yet IN *OUR* TIME, there would be *another* resurrection of that EMPIRE."[41]

He offers no proof of these ten resurrections; he merely states them as fact.

(7) Armstrong has a "throne" conflict. In an article about the millennium, Herbert W. Armstrong says: ". . .WHERE WILL JESUS' THRONE BE, when HE LEAVES His Father's throne—when the time of restitution of all things comes—and when He sits on HIS OWN throne? He does not say that the saints shall sit with Him on the Father's throne *in heaven*. He says they shall sit with Him IN HIS THRONE. Will His throne, too, be in heaven? Will there be TWO thrones in heaven? Will Jesus have a throne there, competing with the Father?

"A Kingdom with TWO thrones is a kingdom divided, and Jesus said a kingdom divided against itself cannot stand. Jesus is not now, at this time, sitting on HIS own throne, but on HIS FATHER'S throne, reigning

---

40. September, 1971; Brian Knowles, "What 'on Earth' is God Doing?"; p. 10
41. "Why God Is Not *Real* To Most People"; op. cit.; p. 6

WITH His Father in exactly the same manner as the saints shall sit with Him, on HIS THRONE, reigning with Him. . . .

"Now notice carefully. GOD'S throne is in heaven. DAVID'S throne is existing today on EARTH. At THIS time now, Jesus is on HIS FATHER'S throne, *in heaven*—but when the saints reign for a thousand years, they shall be sitting with Him, on HIS throne, the throne of DAVID, which throne is located ON THE EARTH!"[42]

Notice several things about this. For one thing, he tries to make Jesus' throne and the Father's throne in Heaven one and the same. Yet Jesus is not sitting on the Father's throne in Heaven, the Father is seated on it. The Scripture plainly tells us that Jesus is seated *at the right hand* of the Father on His own throne (See Hebrews 8:1; Hebrews 12:2, Colossians 3:1). Second, he would, to prove his point, intimate that two thrones in Heaven would make a kingdom divided against itself. Yet the Book of Revelation speaks of numerous thrones in Heaven, not once intimating in any way division or competition. Third, note the statement that David's throne is existing today on earth. This is a reference to the cult's teaching that the throne of David and the throne of Queen Elizabeth in England are one and the same!

(8) Herbert W. Armstrong, in the same article on the millennium, sets up another straw man to attack. He opens the article: "WHERE are the saints of God going to REIGN for the coming thousand years in Tomorrow's World?

"Some say: 'On the earth!'

"Others say, 'Up in Heaven! All unsaved people shall be destroyed by the brightness of Christ's coming. The earth will be desolate during this thousand years.'"[43]

42. "Where Will The *Millennium* Be Spent?"; op. cit.; p. 4
43. Page 3

Later, talking about some of the millennial events, he says: "That cannot be PRIOR to the millennium. The earth could not be full of the knowledge of the Lord if it were then desolate, and without an inhabitant! This proves the place of the thousand years is ON THE EARTH!—*not* in heaven as some teach."[44]

This straw man is entirely a figment of Armstrong's imagination. We know of no responsible evangelical who denies that the millennium will be on the earth. This is just a subtle way, in typical Armstrong fashion, of trying to deny the reality of Heaven. He has bungled the effort badly.

(9) While discussing the millennium, Armstrong, seeking to prove that God has not cast Israel away (so he can identify the Anglo-Saxon people as Israelites!), declares: "Back in the 26th chapter of Leviticus we read how God warned His chosen race that IF they would not obey Him, He would PUNISH THEM—for a duration of 2520 years! Not with eternal loss of salvation—but a duration of 2520 long years—the prophetic 'seven times' mentioned in verse 28. The children of Israel became divided into TWO NATIONS—one called the House of Israel, the TEN tribes—the other the House of JUDAH, consisting of Judah and Benjamin, called the Jews."[45]

Notice how suavely he put in a "duration of 2520 years!" The fact that Leviticus 26 does not mention any 2,520 years (it simply says, God "will chasten you seven times for your sins"), means nothing to Armstrong. A figure of 2,520 suits his purpose, so he puts it in without any explanation of where he got it. A "seven times" which would result in 2,520 years would have to be 360 to start! If we are allowed to hazard a guess as to how Armstrong came up with such a figure, we would presume that he took a pro-

44. Ibid.; p. 5
45. Ibid.

phetic year of 360 days and multiplied by seven, getting the 2,520 days, then arbitrarily and without justification changed the 2,520 days into 2,520 years. This is hermeneutical skulduggery at its very lowest level. We would have every bit as much right, in regard to the four *days* Lazarus was dead and buried (John 11:17,39), to say Christ raised him from the dead after he had "lain in the grave" four *years*. Not only so, but since this "seven times" is repeated four times in Leviticus 26, honesty would make it, if days are to be turned to years, a total of 10,080 years—not just 2,520.

(10) Coming up with long years of duration is nothing new for Armstrongites. Dealing with their understanding of the True Church, an anonymous writer says: "The prophecies bring this Church into concrete focus in the 12th chapter of Revelation. There she is shown spiritually, in the glory and splendor of the Spirit of God, but visibly in the world as a persecuted, Commandment-keeping Church *driven into the wilderness*, for 1260 years, thru the middle ages!"[46]

He says again: "Finally, in order to keep the true Way of God, a large portion of the true Christians (composing the true Church) 'fled into the wilderness,' as foretold in Rev. 12:6, where they were fed on the pure Word of God 1260 long years!"[47]

As we previously pointed out: "In neither instance does he attempt to offer an excuse or even admit that he has changed the days into years; he simply makes the statement as if it were fact. Yet THE PLAIN TRUTH is that the language of Revelation shows those 1,260 days to be *literal days* and *the same days* are in other places called 'forty and two months' and, again, 'a time, and times, and half a time,' or, three-

---

46. *Easter Is Pagan,* Written Anonymously; Copyright, 1952; p. 9
47. Ibid.; p. 12

and-a-half years (Rev. 11:2,3; Rev. 12:14)."[48]

Some of Armstrong's defenders have berated me for questioning this changing of days into years, saying, "God says one day is as a thousand years, and vice versa, II Peter 3:8." But, as I always pointed out in my reply, that would make it 1,260,000 years, not 1,260. Would it be right to say it rained forty years while Noah was in the ark, instead of forty days? Would it be proper to say that Jesus was in the grave 3 years, instead of 3 days? This is every bit as sensible and honest as Armstrong changing "a thousand two hundred and threescore days" (Revelation 12:6) into 1,260 years.

Prophecy, to Herbert W. Armstrong and his Worldwide Church of God, is merely a hodge-podge of Scriptures out of context, statements presented as biblical fact without one iota of corroborating proof, and various Scriptures mixed and jumbled to suit the mood of the moment. It has absolutely no resemblance whatsoever to the prophecy of the Word of God, or to the reputable interpretations of these prophecies given by evangelical scholars down through the centuries.

---

48. *Herbert W. Armstrong—A False Prophet,* Copyright, 1961; Sword of the Lord Foundation, Murfreesboro, Tennessee; p. 8

CHAPTER XII

The Armstrong Teaching About Liquor

Herbert W. Armstrong and his Worldwide Church of God do not get very excited about what the evangelical world calls "a separated life." In fact, readers can detect more than a slight sneer with regard to this in Armstrong's words: "WHY DO religious people often seem to feel that their religious life must be one of giving up all the fun and the enjoyment of living?—that in order to please God, they must endure a life of morbid gloom?

"Sin to many of these people consists of things that many other people consider to be most desirable. To them, sin is going contrary to a number of 'don'ts.' 'Don't smoke.' 'Don't dance.' 'Don't play cards.' 'Don't go to the theater.' 'Don't ever touch a drop of alcoholic beverage.' 'Don't do this!' 'Don't do that!'. . .

"Others feel that if they become, as they call it, 'saved,' that they must forever after live a gloomy life of giving up everything that they formerly enjoyed, and that their solemn, unhappy lives will somehow please their Creator. Of course, *that kind of religion is more or less a superstition*!"[1]

One of his writers sums it up: "Old-fashioned gospel preachers of a bygone puritanical Protestant era invented the idea that drinking, dancing, card-playing and theater-going were worldly."[2]

Prohibitions by the evangelical world against alcoholic beverages are especially singled out for attack by this cult. In fact, Jesus Christ is repeatedly set up as an example for using intoxicating beverages. For example, in the same issue of *Tomorrow's World* as the above

---

1. *Tomorrow's World,* December, 1971; p. 1
2. Quoted by R. E. Glasgow, *The Biblical Evangelist,* April, 1970; "'The Plain Truth': A False Magazine"; p. 6

Armstrong quote appeared, a reply to a query about the Essenes in the "Answers" section said, in part: "The Essenes were an ascetic sect that kept to themselves. They lived in the wilderness. They practiced celibacy, never drank wine, nor did they attend Temple services.

"Jesus clearly did not practice their tenets. Scripture shows Christ drank wine (Matt. 11:19; 26:29). . . ."[3]

Garner Ted Armstrong, in an article about the "Jesus People," wrote: "And shocking as it may be to many who believe in *total abstinence* from all alcoholic beverages, Jesus drank WINE from time to time (Matt. 11:19), and His *first miracle* involved creating fine WINE, MORE THAN A HUNDRED GALLONS OF IT, from water."[4]

In another issue of *Tomorrow's World*, replying to a Kentucky reader's letter berating the cult for its position on alcoholic beverages, Jesus Christ was again appealed to in the editorial defense, saying: "*Jesus Christ turned water into wine at a wedding feast (John 2:1-10). He came eating and drinking* [*alcoholic beverages*]—*His enemies accused Him of being a winebibber* [*an alcoholic—See Matt. 11:19*]. *Actually Jesus drank wine in true moderation. And also at the Passover (Matt. 26:27-29).*"[5]

Amazing as it may seem, however, the Worldwide Church, while putting its approbation upon intoxicating beverages, comes out strongly against the use of tobacco. Brian Knowles, one of the cult's writers, viciously attacks this habit, saying: "Smoking has been conclusively proven harmful to the body. Yet many persist in practicing a foul, dirty, disease-causing habit! Smoking befouls the breath, stains the teeth and fingers, costs a great deal of money and jeopardizes

---

3. *Tomorrow's World,* December, 1971; p. 36
4. *Tomorrow's World,* June, 1971; "The 'Jesus Trip' One-Way Ticket To Nowhere?"; p. 24
5. September, 1971; p. 49

the person's health and well-being. It is a factor in producing short-windedness, heart ailments, circulatory problems, lung cancer, emphysema and a host of other ailments. . . .

"Today's youthful cigarette smokers are in many cases tomorrow's cancer and heart patients!

"But *why* should anyone adopt such a habit?"[6]

While we do not want to be identified as one approving tobacco—and we are *strongly* against it—we cannot find the logic of being anti-tobacco and, at the same time, pro-alcohol. Of the two, alcohol is the more damaging and injurious by far. Have you read lately of any tobacco-caused highway fatality, for example? Over half the fatal accidents on our highways are connected with alcohol. But, then, consistency has never been one of the jewels found in the Worldwide Church of God coffers.

Followers of Armstrong are given this advice about booze: "Parents should be *educated* to have a balanced view of alcohol themselves, so they can set their children the RIGHT EXAMPLE of proper use. Parental *mis*use is a real factor in causing young people to imitate them and become alcoholics. On the other hand, if parents are teetotalers, and condemn the use of alcohol, then they run the danger of causing their children to REBEL, and become fanatical drinkers with a totally distorted view of alcohol.

"Clearly BALANCE and *moderation* should be primary goals of an EDUCATIONAL PROGRAM for both children and adults."[7]

How utterly asinine! There is only one proven method of averting alcoholism: **total abstinence**. As for prohibition causing children to rebel and become fanatical drinkers, why should this be true here any more than

6. *Tomorrow's World*, June, 1971; "Young People—Fill the Character Gap"; p. 34
7. *The Plain Truth*, October, 1971; William F. Dankenbring, "The Neglected Tragedy of *Alcoholism"*; p. 28

with any other prohibition? Why should telling children not to drink "run the danger of causing" them "to rebel" any more than telling them not to smoke? Mr. Dankenbring did not think through his argument very clearly, we fear.

The cult's position on liquor is described in detail in a Worldwide Church of God release written by one of its key leaders, Roderick C. Meredith, "Is Drinking a SIN?" The leaflet could easily have been published with pride in *The Brewer's Journal.* In fact, it is of the type and caliber that a local bootleggers' union might want to mimeograph and circulate with unconcealed and devilish delight. It would, without question, do justice as a feature article in any winery periodical anywhere in the world.

It is that bad!

We first saw the article when a Louisiana subscriber to our magazine, *The Biblical Evangelist*, sent us a copy. The remainder of this chapter consists of the rebuttal we prepared and published in our May, 1968, issue.

The Armstrong Position on Liquor

In a word: *prohibition is for the birds*! Followers of the Armstrongs and members of the Worldwide Church of God are openly invited to take a snort from the bottle any time they get thirsty. (*Only in* "moderation," *of course*!) Readers of Meredith's article are told to "rid" themselves of "blinding PREJUDICE" and to accept "*God's* will" about drinking with "open-mindedness and *honesty*!"

Statements in the Meredith Article

Let me quote a few of the word-for-word exhortations and misstatements of truth from the pen of Mr. Meredith. Seven—the scriptural number of perfection—should suffice to establish honestly his position.

(1) "The *principle* is this: Jesus Christ set us an

example that we should follow in His steps (I Peter 2:21). 'Jesus Christ is the *same* yesterday, and today, and for ever!' (Heb. 13:8). Jesus has *not changed*! He would still be living the *same* kind of life if He were to come in the flesh today as He did live 1900 years ago.

"Now notice His *example* in John 2:1-11. Here is the account of how Jesus turned water into *wine*. If you will look up the meaning of the word 'firkin' (verse 6), you will see that this amounted to many gallons of wine. . . .

"So He turned the water into *wine*—and it was real, *fermented wine*. . . ."[8]

Note that the author is seeking to establish that our blessed example, the Lord Jesus Christ, was a partner in the *fermented* wine-making-and-drinking business—and that we are commanded to follow His example and steps in doing the same! Such a defense of boozing is stooping pretty low and we will answer his argument in just a moment.

(2) "If properly used, wine is an aid to relaxation and affability at a special occasion."[9] And again, "It can help one *relax* at a meal or *rejoice* at a social occasion. . . ."[10]

Anyone who has ever been around a corner bar or a side street saloon can certainly testify to the *affability* and *rejoicing* power of alcohol. My, how they whoop it up! And as for the *relaxing* quality of the bottle, immediately comes to mind the scene seen frequently as a teen-ager in a small town. Every Sunday morning as we left for church, we would see anywhere from three to eight of the local tavern's "best" customers "sleeping it off" on the sidewalk, in the gutter, and on the bench in front of the place.

---

8. © 1961; p. 1
9. Ibid.
10. Ibid., p. 2

It *really* relaxed *them*!

(3) "There are many, many examples in the Old Testament where God's servants use *wine* in a proper way and with God's blessing."[11]

Well, Noah got rip-snorting drunk, but that was hardly in "a proper way" or "with God's blessing." And David got Uriah "drunk" when he wanted him to go down to his house and lie with his wife, Bath-sheba. But, once again, that could not exactly be called "a proper way" or "with God's blessing." Lot got drunk on wine in the mountain cave near Zoar and committed incest with both his surviving daughters, but that was not "a proper way" or "with God's blessing." Nor would such terms describe the party King Ahasuerus was throwing when he wanted Queen Vashti to show off her beauty before his drinking buddies. Nor would they fit the description of the drinkathon old Belshazzar was hosting when the mysterious fingers of a man's hand wrote MENE, MENE, TEKEL, UPHARSIN on the palace wall! One wonders just which Old Testament "servants" Mr. Meredith had in mind!

(4) "Some die-hards still cling to certain texts which *appear* (to them at least) to condemn wine, but in reality condemn only the wrong USE of alcohol."[12]

At least the author here acknowledges that there are some strong passages in the Word of God which have the APPEARANCE—on the surface, at any rate—of teaching total abstinence. But he shrugs these off as texts of "die-hards" who haven't the intelligence to read correctly what God is saying.

(5) ". . .*no condemnation* WHATEVER against the moderate, sensible use of wine, following Jesus' example."[13]

---

11. Ibid.
12. Ibid.
13. Ibid.

Meredith is seeking to make the point here that scriptural passages which condemn *intemperate* use of alcohol (a fact he is willing to acknowledge) are not proof of God's condemnation or prohibition of alcohol's *temperate* use. This would be true in principle, of course, UNLESS the passages quoted were actually forbidding *any* use of alcohol, not just the wrong use.

(6) ". . .wine has been given as a *blessing* from God. . . .It is a thing which *glorifies* God when it is used *sensibly* and *moderately*."[14]

Those statements are, you must admit, quite a mouthful! No doubt the boys at the neighborhood bar are totally ignorant of how they are "glorifying God" through their elbow-bending exercises!

(7) ". . .God gave us wine and alcoholic beverages to learn to use *properly*—and to develop CHARACTER by the proper exercise of *wisdom* and *self-control. Prohibition* is NOT God's way—and it does *not* develop character."[15]

We will come back to this startling revelation later, but suffice it now to note the astounding philosophy he is promoting: *character is not developed by restrictions!* Do you suppose Meredith thinks God was confused when He made eight of the Ten Commandments prohibitions, introducing each one with the words, "Thou shalt not"?

As fairly and honestly as humanly possible, I think the Meredith-Armstrong-Worldwide Church of God position can be summed up as follows: (1) Wine and other alcoholic beverages are gifts of God. (2) Wine and other alcoholic beverages are a blessing and aid in developing good character. (3) Only when used in excess do wine and other alcoholic beverages become sin and a violation of God's laws. (4) Jesus set us the example for using alcoholic beverages. (5) Any Scrip-

---

14. Ibid.
15. Ibid.

ture that seems to condemn wine and other alcoholic beverages is misunderstood.

Where This Position Leads

It should be apparent to anyone and everyone where such a "wet" road would lead its travelers. As our Lord observed about the teaching of false prophets: "Ye shall know them by their fruits. . . .Wherefore by their fruits ye shall know them" (Matthew 7:15-20). The "harvest" reaped by the Armstrongites from this false "tree" of moderation is sad indeed.

Let me take time and space to quote from just one or two letters.

A man in Amarillo, Texas, after running across my booklet, HERBERT W. ARMSTRONG: A FALSE PROPHET, wrote me: "With reference to your booklet about Herbert W. Armstrong, you don't know the half. You should be as I was for 10 years, overcome by his deception, to really know him. He got me for $2,500. I was really deceived until I found him doing right the opposite to his teaching. He and all his ministers drinking liquor, wine and beer, playing cards, going to dances, making trips abroad around the world with money the members intended to spread the gospel. . . .Somebody should get busy and stop such a way of robbing poor, ignorant people. . . ."[16]

The gentleman who wrote the above asked if I had a "representative" in his area with whom he could talk, so I asked a ministerial friend of mine to visit him at his home. My friend wrote me after the interview: "He is quite willing to give names and incidents if his testimony would be acceptable. For instance, in their meeting that they are compelled to attend each year, they drink wine and beer. It is served at their feasts. He cited an occasion when the head deacon

16. Personal letter to the author, January 20, 1964

and one of the ministers got drunk. He gave their names. . . ."[17] Without going into other matters here, suffice it to note that the position of the Armstrong movement is one which *can* and sometimes *does* lead to drunkenness—even on the part of its leadership.

Another letter is one I received from a woman who operates a motel near one of their churches. She wrote in part: "I am also glad for the booklets, HERBERT W. ARMSTRONG: A FALSE PROPHET. We have had our motel full of these Radio Church of God people, both last Fall and this Spring, when they came to observe these 'feasts' at the big tabernacle just six miles or so outside of G__________. I am glad to have more of an understanding of what they preach and teach.

"These people are told not to talk about the church and not to 'cram' it down people's throats, but I was able to learn much from the wife of one of the members. She is not a member and is heartsick to see how her husband and son have been drawn into it. The 22-year-old son is a minister and is now ready to go throughout the country baptizing converts.

"One of the terrible things to me is that they all drink. . .the sale of alcoholic beverages was up 300% in this county the eight days they were holding these meetings in April. . . ."[18]

For some reason, the liquor issue is one that makes *moderation* impossible. The proponents of temperance are invariably the ones who become intemperate—just as in the cases cited above. This is one reason why the Scripture warns: "Look not thou upon the wine when it is red, when it giveth his colour in the cup, when it moveth itself aright. AT THE LAST IT BITETH LIKE A SERPENT, AND STINGETH LIKE AN ADDER" (Proverbs 23:31,32).

---

17. Personal letter to the author, February 20, 1964
18. Personal letter to the author, May 14, 1963

But let us hurriedly take a brief look at some of the errors in this position.

Make no mistake about it, Meredith's article is literally loaded with untruths, misinterpretations and misunderstandings of Scripture; nonscientific and nonmedical conclusions; as well as almost total ignorance about the correct meanings of Hebrew and Greek words. It is a typical, fancy-worded Worldwide Church of God article using impressive and emphatic language calculated to fool the ignorant and the gullible, but never the enlightened or the scholar.

Let me point out a few of those glaring errors and misconceptions.

Wrong About the Wine in John 2

Meredith wrote: "So He turned the water into *wine*—and it was real, *fermented wine.* They would NEVER have said to the bridegroom, 'Thou hast kept the *good wine* until now'—if Jesus had provided only *grape juice* which they would have regarded as an inferior beverage for this occasion.

"Also, the original Greek word used here is 'oinos,' and it *always* means the *fermented* juice of the grape—nothing else."[19]

We will deal with the meaning of the Greek word *oinos* in a moment, but first it is important that we note three facts from John's inspired record: (1) The water was turned to wine after the "men had well drunk." If the wine is understood to be intoxicating wine, our Lord is automatically placed in the embarrassing position of providing more wine for men who had already *well drunk*! This even violates the position of the Armstrongites, since Meredith states: "Overindulgence in drink is NOT to be tampered with! *Alcoholism* is a growing CURSE in our land today!"[20]

19. Op. cit., p. 1
20. Ibid., p. 2

Ernest Gordon, in his *Christ, the Apostles, and Wine*, points out: "The six water pots of verse 6 each contained from two to three *metretas* apiece. This unit was almost nine gallons, according to Thayer's Lexicon. The total amount of wine then was between 108 and 162 gallons, certainly an invitation to drunkenness if the wine had been alcoholic."[21] Meredith has placed our Lord in the unsavory position of providing a flood of intoxicants for men already "well drunk."

(2) The second fact of note is seen in the descriptive term "good," used twice in verse 10 to describe the wine our Lord made. This is the Greek word *kalos* and is defined in Vine's *Expository Dictionary of New Testament Words*: "denotes that which is intrinsically good. . . ."[22] The same word is used three times in John 10:11,14 by our Lord in describing Himself as the Good Shepherd. The pure, sweet juice of the grape could rightly be denoted as "intrinsically good," but hardly the rotted, fermented, decayed, spoiled, intoxicating wine.

One automatically thinks of the term *"good"* to describe whatever our Lord makes. In summing up creation, Moses said: "And God saw everything that he had made, and, behold, it was *very good*" (Genesis 1:31). How unthinkable it is that He would have made corrupted wine at Cana! In His other acts of creativity during His earthly ministry—when He fed the 5,000 and, again, the 4,000—the bread He made was "good" bread and the fish was "good" fish. It would be as thinkable to suppose He served *moldy* bread and *spoiled* fish on those other occasions as to charge Him with providing fermented wine at the wedding. Remember, fermentation is a process of decomposition, just as are putrefaction and decay.

Pliny, (whom Meredith does not want quoted, as we

---

21. Copyright, 1944; The Sunday School Times Company, Philadelphia, Pennsylvania; p. 4
22. Fleming H. Revell Company, Westwood, N. J.; Vol. II, p. 164

shall shortly discover), expressly says that "good wine" was a term used to denote the juice destitute of spirit (Lib. iv. c. 13). Albert Barnes, after quoting this comment of Pliny, goes on to say: "The wine referred to here was doubtless such as was commonly drunk in Palestine. That was the pure juice of the grape. It was not brandied wine; nor drugged wine; nor wine compounded of various substances, such as we drink in this land. The common wine drunk in Palestine was that which was the simple juice of the grape. *We* use the word *wine* now to denote the kind of liquid which passes under that name in this country—always fermented, and always containing a considerable portion of alcohol—not only the alcohol produced by fermentation, but *added* to keep it or make it stronger. But we have no right to take *that* sense of the word, and go with it to the interpretation of the Scriptures. We should endeavor to get into the exact circumstances of those times; ascertain precisely what idea the word would convey to those who used it then; and apply *that* sense to the word in the interpretation of the Bible. And there is not the slightest evidence that the word so used would have conveyed any idea but that of the pure juice of the grape; nor the slightest circumstance mentioned in this account that would not be fully met by such a supposition."[23]

How strange it would be to suppose that the very first miracle Christ performed after being "filled with the Holy Ghost" was an act of creating intoxicating wine for a crowd of celebrants who were already "well drunk." *It is truly unthinkable*!

(3) Still another fact from the record in John 2 is that those men who had already "well drunk" praised the bridegroom for having kept "the good wine" until the last. In seeking to make the wine fermented wine,

23. *Barnes' Notes On The New Testament,* Albert Barnes; One Volume Edition, Kregel Publications, Grand Rapids, Michigan; p. 272

Meredith shows his nonscientific, nonmedical misunderstanding. It is a simple fact, not in the least profound, that alcohol, drunk to any excess, will deaden the tastebuds of the drinker. If the guests at the wedding party in Cana of Galilee had "well drunk" of *fermented* wine and then been given some different wine, *they would not have been able to tell the difference*! Only if they had been drinking the form of the vine's fruit that we know as grape juice—and then had been provided some new, fresh, sweet grape juice—would the governor of the feast been able to make the observation he did.

It is as simple as that!

Wrong About Prohibition!

Note again what Meredith said about prohibition: ". . .God gave us wine and alcoholic beverages to learn to use *properly*—and to develop CHARACTER by the proper exercise of *wisdom* and *self-control. Prohibition* is NOT God's way—and it does *not* develop character."[24]

Probably no more ASTOUNDING (a favorite Armstrong adjective) revelation was ever made by the Worldwide Church of God than *this* ASTOUNDING one: "*Prohibition* is NOT God's way—and it does *not* develop character."

Prohibition—*not moderation*—is God's way regarding murder. Prohibition—*not moderation*—is God's way regarding adultery. Prohibition—*not moderation*—is God's way regarding stealing. Prohibition—*not moderation*—is God's way regarding evil speaking. Prohibition—*not moderation*—is God's way regarding blasphemy. Prohibition—*not moderation*—is God's way

24. Op. cit., p. 2

regarding lying. Prohibition—*not moderation*—is God's way regarding covetousness. Prohibition—*not moderation*—is God's way regarding witchcraft. Prohibition—*not moderation*—is God's way regarding lasciviousness. Prohibition—*not moderation*—is God's way regarding sodomy. Prohibition—*not moderation*—is God's way in a thousand-and-one different matters.

And prohibition—not moderation—*is God's way regarding alcoholic beverages!*

It might be well also to repeat: Restrictions (*prohibitions*, if you please!) DO develop character. Any parent or pedagogist could tell Mr. Meredith that a child being raised without prohibitions (*restrictions*) will develop into an adult without character. This "prohibition" statement simply shows how hard pressed the author was to bolster an untenable position.

Wrong in Thinking "Oinos" Always Means Fermented Wine

Note again the writer's assertion: "Also, the original Greek word used here is 'oinos,' and it *always* means the *fermented* juice of the grape—nothing else."[25] He said further: "Again, the Greek word is 'oinos'—*fermented wine*, not grape juice!"[26]

Consider carefully his flat, authoritative statement that the Greek word *oinos* "always" means *fermented* wine and "nothing else." It is a simple matter to show that Mr. Meredith is not much of an authority on Greek! [*Incidentally, he bases most of his entire argument in favor of drinking on this point, so to prove him wrong here would be the equivalent of watching his whole thesis collapse like a house of cards in a Texas tornado.*]

What does *oinos* mean? Dr. Ferrar Fenton, a biblical

25. Ibid., p. 1
26. Ibid., p. 2

translater (*The Holy Bible in Modern English*), in his book, *The Bible and Wine*, lists six *different* meanings of this generic word: (1) Grapes, as fresh fruit; (2) Raisins; (3) A thick grape syrup; (4) A thick jam; (5) *Fresh* grape juice; and, (6) *Fermented* grape juice.[27] Dr. Lyman Abbott, in his *Dictionary of Religious Knowledge,* says of *oinos*: "It is tolerably clear that the word wine does not necessarily imply fermented liquor. It signifies only a production of the vine."[28] Abbott, by the way, called *fermented* wine the "least common" of all forms in biblical times and says that even then "the percentage of alcohol was small."[29]

Men who were fluently conversant with both Hebrew and Greek—the scholars who translated the Old Testament Scriptures from Hebrew into Greek (the Septuagint Version) two or three centuries before our Lord's birth—did not believe for a moment that *oinos* always meant fermented wine. As a matter of fact, on at least thirty-three separate occasions they used *oinos* as a Greek translation equivalent of the Hebrew *tiyrowsh.* And *tiyrowsh*—used two score times in the Old Testament—*never* meant anything other than the fresh, pure, unfermented juice of the grape. Not one single time was it ever used or associated with an evil such as drunkenness or debauchery!

Meredith, when developing his theme, wrote: "There are thirteen original Hebrew and Greek words for 'wine' in our English Bible. How can we know which one means fermented wine? To find the answer, do not go to Aristotle or Pliny, but go to the *Bible itself.* By comparing its usage, the Scriptural meaning of *wine* can be defined."[30]

Ignoring for a moment Meredith's blunder about the

---

27. Quoted in *The Bible And Its Wines,* Charles Wesley Ewing; Copyright, 1949; Published by the author; p. 12
28. Quoted in *Christ, The Apostles, And Wine,* p. 9
29. Ibid., p. 21
30. Op. cit., p. 2

number of Hebrew and Greek words translated *wine* in our English Bible (there are *thirteen* Hebrew and *eight* Greek, a total of *twenty-one*!), let us do as he suggested and turn to "the Bible itself" and sample its usage of *oinos*. One example would be our Lord's observation in Matthew 9:17: "Neither do men put new wine [*oinos*] into old bottles: else the bottles break, and the wine [*oinos*] runneth out, and the bottles perish: but they put new wine [*oinos*] into new bottles, and both are preserved."

Here, unquestionably, *oinos* is fresh, sweet, unfermented juice of the grape. If old wineskins were used for grape juice, the leftover yeast germs would begin immediately to ferment the juice and in short time the skins would be burst by the fermentating wine. If the wine was *already* fermented when placed in the old wineskins, there would be no expanding problem and no danger. If this *oinos* is to be considered *fermented* wine, the whole parable has lost the force of its meaning and message.

This should suffice to show that *oinos* does NOT *always* refer to fermented wine! Like our New England word "cider," which is used of both *sweet* and *hard,* so *oinos,* with the Greeks, described both *fermented* and *unfermented.*

Wrong in Thinking "Yayin" Always Means Fermented Wine

Just as Meredith is in error with his Greek, so he has blundered with his Hebrew. He wrote: "One of the original Hebrew words for wine is 'yayin'. . . .

"God Himself here gave *wine* to Abraham—*the father of the faithful.* And again, the original Hebrew word used *proves* that it was *fermented wine*—NOT grape juice. The original word is 'yayin'—and *always* means *fermented* wine."[31]

31. Ibid.

Not so, says all enlightened Hebrew scholarship! Meredith's procedure seems to be that he decides what he wants a word to mean. . .*and then defines it according to his desires*! Such a procedure fools the simple, perhaps, but it is given no credence by the informed or the scholarly.

Just what *does* the Hebrew word *yayin* mean?

Found 141 times in the Old Testament, it is used interchangeably, depending upon the context. Sometimes it *does* refer to fermented wine and other times to various forms of *unfermented* fruit of the vine. Fenton says it was used more frequently to describe a thick syrup or jam made from boiling grape juice than it was to describe fermented, intoxicating wine. Young's Analytical Concordance says it was used to describe "what is pressed out, grape juice."

Let us look at a passage or two as a sampling of *yayin's* usage other than fermented, intoxicating beverage. One such case is where Nehemiah described the returned Jews' violation of the Sabbath through harvesting on that divinely decreed day of rest. He lamented: "In those days saw I in Judah some treading wine presses on the sabbath, and bringing in sheaves, and lading asses; as also wine [*yayin*], grapes, and figs, and all manner of burdens, which they brought into Jerusalem on the sabbath day: and I testified against them in the day wherein they sold victuals" (Nehemiah 13:15). The fresh fruits harvested from the fields (and from the wine presses), then brought into Jerusalem on the Sabbath to be sold, included *yayin*. There was no possibility that fermentation could have this suddenly taken place; here is *yayin* as the fresh juice coming directly from the vineyard and the wine press.

The same thought is found in Zephaniah's warning to God's people of the impending captivity by Nebuchadnezzar and his hords of Babylonian warriors. He wrote: "Therefore their goods shall become a booty, and their houses a desolation: they shall also build houses, but not inhabit them; and they shall plant vineyards, but not drink the wine [*yayin*] thereof" (Zephaniah 1:13). Here is a message of judgment coming so suddenly that the victims would not even be able to drink the sweet, fresh juice of the grapes which were even then ripening in the vineyards. There is no thought whatsoever of fermentation in this usage of *yayin*.

Still another example is found in Isaiah 16:10, where the lamentation is: "And gladness is taken away, and joy out of the plentiful field; and in the vineyards there shall be no singing, neither shall there be shouting: the treaders shall tread out no wine [*yayin*] in their presses; I have made their vintage shouting to cease." Note carefully the phrase: "the treaders shall tread out no wine [*yayin*] in their presses"! Surely even the most dedicated winebibber must acknowledge that "fermented" wine does not come from the presses! Only sweet grape juice is "tread out" and long "fermenting" must take place before the wine becomes alcoholic!

Mr. Meredith's assertion that *yayin "always* means *fermented* wine" is simply NOT true or in accord with the known facts. The wish is the father of such a definition.

Wrong in His Explanation of "Contradictory" Texts

As sort of a "grand finale" for his article, Meredith "examined" some texts he said the "die-hards" use to prove alcohol wrong and contradict his position, but which, he insists, do not mean what the critics think.

He refers to only two such passages!

Let me quote that entire section:

"Some die-hards still cling to certain texts which *appear* (to them at least) to condemn wine, but in reality condemn only the wrong USE of alcohol.

"One of these is Proverbs 20:1: 'Wine is a *mocker,* strong drink is *raging:* and whosoever is *deceived* thereby is not wise.'

"The simple explanation is that wine certainly does *mock* and *deceive* many individuals who have not learned the proper, temperate USE of such beverages. Yes, God's way is *moderation* and *temperance*—NOT prohibition! And there is a *great difference* between these, which so-called 'temperance' people seem unable to recognize.

"Another text which is often twisted and misapplied is Proverbs 23:29-32. Here is a warning to those who 'tarry long' at wine. Of course! One who '*tarries long*' at wine is a 'winebibber,' or in modern terminology a 'barfly' or an 'alcoholic.'

"Such *excessive use* of wine is bound to bring harm on the person involved and on others. Therefore, it is breaking the spirit of God's law and is SIN. But this is *no condemnation* WHATEVER against the moderate, sensible use of wine, following Jesus' example.

"The latter part of this passage warns us not to 'look' upon the wine when it is 'red,' when it 'moveth itself aright.'

"In the *first* place, it is not a sin to LOOK on *anything* except in *lust. Secondly,* the terms 'red' and 'moveth itself' refer to wine when it is in the *process of fermentation.* This is BEFORE it is fully fermented. And if at this time you 'look' on it so as to finally *drink* it, you will become violently ill and possibly DIE!"[32]

The trouble with this "simple explanation" of the text in Proverbs 20:1 is that it is *too* simple! If Mr. Meredith will check this verse again, he will note that it does NOT—as he has implied—say: "Wine is SOMETIMES a mocker, strong drink is SOMETIMES

32. Ibid.

raging. . . ." It simply but forcibly says that wine IS "a mocker" and strong drink IS "raging". . .*and that anyone thinking otherwise has been* DECEIVED *by Satan!*

Could the "mocker" tag be indiscriminately applied to intoxicating wine if intemperance and "excesses" were the only causes of its mockery? *We think not!* Let's use honey to illustrate. In one biblical passage God calls honey "good" (Proverbs 24:13), but in another He warns of eating too much (Proverbs 25:16, 26). Honey is a food of blessing and benefit to mankind, yet one of the "sickest" experiences of my life was caused by eating an excess of this sweet, sticky substance. Would it be right to say, without qualification, "Honey is a mocker. . .and whosoever is deceived thereby is not wise"? *Of course not!* Delicious roast beef is harmful when eaten in excess. Would it be right to say, "Roast beef is a mocker. . . and whosoever is deceived thereby is not wise"? *To ask the question is to answer it!* Proverbs 20:1 is the language of something inherently evil, not a description of something good in itself which becomes *dangerous* only when partaken of in excess. *Alcoholic wine is* always *a deceiving mocker with stinging poison in its bite!*

Perhaps the best refutation of Meredith's explanation of the second passage, Proverbs 23:29-32, is for the reader to get out his Bible and read what God actually said. Meredith, you will note, did not quote it. That divinely inspired portion says: *"Who hath woe? who hath sorrow? who hath contentions? who hath babbling? who hath wounds without cause? who hath redness of eyes? They that tarry long at the wine; they that go to seek mixed wine. Look not thou upon the wine when it is red, when it giveth his colour in the cup, when it moveth itself aright. At the last it biteth like a serpent, and stingeth like an adder."*

God warns against *seeking* and *looking,* not only tarrying!

Regarding the "looking," one wonders if even Mr. Meredith could fail to note the contradictory definitions of "look" which he gave side-by-side above! First, he made "look" to mean "seeing," and said: ". . .it is not a sin to LOOK on *anything* except in *lust.*" Then he *immediately* turned around and made "look" to mean "drinking," saying: ". . .if at this time you 'LOOK' on it as to finally *drink* it. . . ." Undoubtedly, the gentleman is tragically confused as to just *what* he does mean!

The idea of "look" in Proverbs 23:31 is to "behold with favor or approval." Solomon was simply restating a divine principle that man should never look with favor or approval upon any fermented fruit of the vine. It has the curse, not the blessing, of God upon it.

To answer the question Meredith and the Worldwide Church of God raised, "YES, drinking *is* a SIN!"

CHAPTER XIII

The Armstrong Teaching About Money

"Remember, it's FREE, as Christ's Gospel is free, of course."[1] So says Herbert W. Armstrong in one of his "Personal" columns, while offering one of his booklets. This is a typical pitch in harmony with the "Everything's Free!" image the Worldwide Church of God seeks to present of itself before the general public.

A typical summation was made by Garner Ted Armstrong in an article aimed at convincing readers the religion of the Worldwide Church of God is the ideal religion for them. After announcing with customary modesty that their work is "the actual *Work of Almighty God* on this earth," he says under a subhead, "What Are Our Motives?": "You need to ask yourself—just what are we of *The* WORLD TOMORROW radio program, and TOMORROW'S WORLD magazine, 'after'?

"Listen to a few of the facts!

"First, you hear a straight-talk half-hour program which NEVER makes any emotional appeal, solicits funds, asks for contributions, or urges you to 'join' any kind of an organization!

"Secondly, you are receiving what we feel is the most finely printed, top-quality, beautiful magazine—chock-full of straight-from-the-shoulder articles trying to *serve*, and to *help you*—and all absolutely FREE of charge!

"At your request, you can join the multiple thousands who are receiving, *without tuition cost*, our Ambassador College Correspondence Course. This FREE course takes you in a step-by-step method through the *entire* Bible in a gripping, scintillating and absorbing manner.

"At your request, you may receive any one of the

---

1. *Tomorrow's World*, June, 1971; p. 2

many dozens of booklets and articles we send out, all absolutely FREE of charge. There is NEVER, in any of these booklets, any solicitation to 'join' an organization—or any request for money. . . .

"Again, *what are our motives?* Have we ever ASKED you for something? Or, on the other hand, don't you see us trying diligently to GIVE you something of *great* value—truly the 'pearl of great price,' the precious TRUTH of our Creator God, which comes to you FREE as the breath of air you breathe?

"Anything evil, anything sinister in that?"[2]

However noble and generous this may sound, it is not exactly quite that way! The reader of Worldwide Church of God literature—magazines and books—is constantly bombarded with the "soft sell" form of appeal, which insists it is not really an appeal at all. He is reminded over and over again how, while it may not be costing him anything, someone is going to have to foot the bill, of course.

Typical is a huge ad, nearly two-thirds of a page in size, in *The Plain Truth* magazine, purporting to explain how the reader's subscription has been paid. Getting down to the nitty-gritty, the third paragraph from the end informs the freeloading subscriber: "Although you cannot pay for your own subscription, we do gratefully accept contributions, voluntarily given, though we never solicit the public for financial support."[3] That very sentence is, of course, *a solicitation* for "financial support." It is the kind of double-talk, so common with this cult, which impresses individuals with low IQ's.

The masthead of the January, 1973, issue of *The Plain Truth*—as has every issue for some time—tells the reader his "already-paid subscription is made possible by the contributions of those who, voluntarily,

---

2. *Tomorrow's World,* December, 1971; "Which Is the Religion *Best For You?*"; p. 8
3. October-November, 1970; p. 38

have become co-workers in support of this worldwide work." Then he is told, along with a denial that it is solicitation, "contributions are gratefully welcomed." The *Tomorrow's World* masthead says the same.

Much is made of the fact that the "founder," Herbert W. Armstrong, has had this "no solicitation" policy from the very beginning. But, alas and alack, from the very beginning of his ministry he has made his famous "soft sell" appeals. Going all the way back to 1939, we find him sending out a letter to the clientele on his mailing list, dated February 4, saying in part: "I will have to tell you that we are very seriously in need of a new mimeograph machine. The present one is about worn out, and we are producing this issue of *The* PLAIN TRUTH under difficulties. I can get a very good used mimeograph, almost new, one capable of turning out the large amount of work that is necessary in this office, and that will last for several years, for $65. There is not one cent available for the mimeograph, unless some of our friends can send in a special and additional offering just for this purpose."[4]

Exactly two months and one day later found another letter going out over Mr. Armstrong's signature to his supporters, saying: "At last, after many unavoidable delays, we are sending you the *The* PLAIN TRUTH. This issue goes to about one thousand *new readers*. It is still mimeographed, because we have not enough funds to print it, as we did two issues last year. It is a tremendous task, and nearly all the work is done by Mrs. Armstrong, our daughter Beverly, who is office secretary, and myself."[5]

These appeals to the faithful continue every bit as strong in the present. Earlier in the book we pointed out how important Armstrong considers observance of the Old Testament holy days. Dr. Noel Smith, in his

---

4. *Tomorrow's World,* July, 1971; "The Gospel Must Be Published!"; p. 24
5. Ibid.

excellent expose of the cult, quotes from a letter sent to the membership urging attendance at the cult's Passover and Days of Unleavened Bread "Spring Festival." Armstrong pointed out that ". . .it is an absolutely *urgent requirement* which God lays upon us to attend these annual Feast days, ACTING OUT the very plan of Almighty God! To *miss* being with God's people during these joyous Feast days, absorbing the really *deep spiritual meaning,* and really LIVING a very part of the wonderful plan of God, is to miss one of the most vitally important parts of our Christian lives! Further, to miss taking part in these Feast days through negligence, carelessness, or simple 'forgetfulness' as some few have done in the past, is a tremendous SIN!"[6]

However, before the good gentleman finished his epistle, we find him warning the same faithful: "Brethren—please pay *special* attention to this vitally important point: Mr. Albert Portune, our new Business Manager and ordained Evangelist in God's Church, has asked me to call on EVERY SINGLE ONE OF YOU—URGENTLY—that you *do not* forget God's worldwide WORK during this Festival season! *Every year* when God's people travel to observe either the Spring or the Autumn Festival—it seems our business office finds itself in a REALLY SERIOUS BIND! Many brethren simply DO NOT SAVE all their second tithe—so they take travel money from their *own income*—CUTTING DOWN what they WOULD have sent in as offerings for God's Work—taking it for their travel expense! Brethren in Christ—FAR BETTER YOU HAD TO SUFFER BY MISSING MEETING WITH OTHERS DURING THIS SEASON THAN TO CRIPPLE GOD'S GREAT WORK! Yes, FAR better we LEARN THESE LESSONS than to hamper God's work so SERIOUSLY

---

6. *Herbert W. Armstrong And His World Tomorrow,* Copyright, 1964; Baptist Bible Tribune, Springfield, Missouri; p. 15

that these GRAVELY *HEAVY* BILLS CANNOT BE MET! THIS GREAT WORK OF GOD COSTS PRODIGIOUS SUMS OF MONEY! *Let's not forget God's work* during these Days of Unleavened Bread. Try to make sure you send in *MORE than usual*—instead of slacking off!"[7]

In other words, far better for the faithful to be guilty of what he himself called "a tremendous SIN!" than not to keep the shekels flowing into the Pasadena offices. What hypocrisy!

The solicitation for funds, always via the *soft sell* technique, of course, includes appeals for the cult to be remembered in the reader's will. By way of example, in the "Answers" column of *Tomorrow's World,* the same word-for-word question with the same word-for-word answer frequently appears. [We might point out here that one gets the impression in reading this particular column that the majority of the questions and answers are "staged"—that is, written by someone in the editorial department and then answered by the same writer—since they so frequently tie in with a particular article appearing elsewhere in that very issue.] Just now, however, the question and answer we speak of has to do with instructions for making out wills, along with an offer of free counsel from the cult's Legal Department. The question is: "I know your organization accepts tithes and general offerings as long as they are not intended to be direct payment for your magazines or other booklets. Then how do I go about naming your organization in my will?" While the answer contains the usual comment that "this should not be taken as a request for donations, but only as a notice that such information is available for those who are desirous of receiving it," we find it both strange and amusing that readers keep sending in the same word-for-word request for infor-

7. Ibid.; p. 16

mation and get the same word-for-word reply.[8] Perhaps this is not dishonest in the eyes of the Worldwide Church of God, but we find it *both* dishonest and misleading! "Beguiling unstable souls" (II Peter 2:14) describes it aptly.

Apparently this type of pitch works rather well. When we were in Southern California sometime ago, we noted an item in the *Los Angeles Herald-Examiner* to the effect that a gentleman had left the bulk of his $100,000 estate to Armstrong. A brother and two sisters were contesting it, saying the deceased was of "unsound mind" and "unduly influenced."[9]

In addition to frequent appeals for "unsolicited contributions," the cult—all the while pointing out that no one is ever visited apart from a personal request—appeals repeatedly for such a request to be made. A typical "invitation for an invitation" in *Tomorrow's World* says: *"The Ambassador College Graduate School of Theology has sent dedicated men (most are fully ordained ministers) into the vast majority of communities in the United States and British Commonwealth and into many cities of the world. These sincere individuals have no religious 'axe to grind,' no 'quota' to meet, no pressure to exert. Their main purpose in life is to help you gain eternal life. Of course, none will call on you unless you request it, but if you do have questions which you want answered, or you desire counsel concerning baptism, write to us and request this special, private appointment. Give us the pleasure of serving you."*[10]

Naturally, they have no "quota" to meet! We have previously seen (Chapter V) that the cult teaches if someone does not see "the light" now, it is only because God hasn't selected him to see it. He will

8. Examples: *Tomorrow's World,* April, 1971, p. 27; *Tomorrow's World,* December, 1971, p. 37
9. January 21, 1966
10. July, 1971; p. 49

have a chance in the next world, its leaders teach.

The closing two paragraphs of Herbert W. Armstrong's booklet, "What Do You Mean . . .'*The Unpardonable Sin*'?" tell the reader: "If you are one who really wants to repent and obey God—then here is GOOD NEWS! The Worldwide Church of God has dedicated, consecrated, converted, fully instructed and trained, ORDAINED MINISTERS in all parts of the United States and many other parts of the world—available to call on you, visit in your home, answer your questions, and explain the Bible to you. Of course, none of them will ever call on you, *unless* you of your own free will request it.

"But, if you of your own volition want to know more about the Bible, repentance, and the Christian life—why not request a personal visit (see addresses—page 41). We will have one of God's own ministers call on you."[11]

When the reader turns to page 41, he not only finds the mailing addresses, but there is a gentle reminder: "The publishers have nothing to sell, and although contributions are gratefully welcome, no solicitation is ever made to the public for financial support."[12] This is what might be called "solicitation through non-solicitation!"

In the September, 1971, issue of *Tomorrow's World* is a major article entitled, "What 'on Earth' is God Doing?" Written by Brian Knowles, it is, basically, an all-out pitch for readers to support the work of the Worldwide Church of God. The writer both laments and warns when he says: "Today over 150 million people are being exposed to the Gospel of the Kingdom of God via radio, television and the printing press. But only a *handful* are making it possible by their financial support and their fervent prayers. But those God has

11. © 1967,1971,1972; p. 39
12. Ibid.; p. 41

called to this Work are *dedicated and loyal* to the commission God has given them. They *love* this world as God did (John 3:16), but they do not love its *sins*.

"If YOU wish to have a more active part in this Work of God, He will not deny you! But it must be 'willingly and from the heart.' It behooves you to *prove to yourself* whether this is indeed where God is working today!

"Those who deny themselves in this end time and prayerfully support and do the Work of God will receive *God's* reward!

"'For God is not unrighteous to forget your work and labor of love. . .' (Heb. 6:10). Those who do the Work will be *rewarded according to their works!* (Prov. 24:12; Ps. 62:12; Matt. 16:27; Job 34:11.) (This does not refer to *salvation,* but rather to the *reward* they will receive after God has given them the free *gift* of salvation.)

"Remember the ringing words of the great Prophet Elijah:

"'HOW LONG WILL YOU SIT ON THE FENCE? If the Lord is God, *follow him;* but if Baal, then follow him. . . .And the people answered him. . .'?"[13]

The message is obvious!

"Keep Those Tithes and Offerings Coming In!"

Herbert W. Armstrong is a firm believer in the biblical injunctions which relate to tithes and offerings—*but only if they are sent to his headquarters!*

In fact, whether or not God wants to save you is tied into sending tithes and offerings to the Worldwide Church of God. In a major *Tomorrow's World* article, "Is God Calling You?" Alfred E. Carrozzo tells his readers: "If God is calling you, you will begin to wholeheartedly have a part in *doing His Work.* You

13. Page 13

will realize this tremendous knowledge of God's way is desperately needed by all the world. You will come to fully understand and know God's own physical people are actually being destroyed for a lack of this knowledge (Hosea 4:6). You will see the urgent need to *have a part in the very Work* that is disseminating this vital knowledge—this Gospel message of God's way to all the world. You will zealously *take part in the Work* that is teaching all nations the way of peace, happiness and joy brimful and running over.

"You will have the desire to GIVE, to share with and to help this wretched world. *You will put your whole heart into God's Work. . . .*

"If you have a part in God's Work, you will take great satisfaction in the knowledge that you are helping teach the world how to have happy homes, happy children, happy marriages and everything good and a full and abundant, happy life. You will even be willing to sacrifice to have a part in helping this world understand God's way.

"If God is calling you, *please understand* it is a fantastic, almost overwhelming calling to *help save humanity* by sacrificing to give this world what it needs most—*God's way, that leads to life.*"[14]

A major article in *The Plain Truth* by Associate Editor Roderick C. Meredith, *"Did JESUS Teach Tithing?"*—with a reminder that the tithe belongs in the coffers of the Armstrong cult—ties tithing into a hope of eternal life. In fact, the article closes with the warning: "Frankly, if you hope to enter God's Kingdom and inherit eternal life, *you had better learn to do what Jesus Christ says!* Speaking of *tithing,* He definitely states you had better NOT leave it undone!"[15]

What happens if a member does leave it undone? They are told to ante up immediately, *post haste,*

---

14. May, 1971; p. 33
15. September, 1958; p. 11

or they will have to pay double in addition to public confession of their sin! So says a former member who witnessed the threat carried out more than once.[16]

Herman L. Hoeh, writing a major article about how readers can "prosper" (pointing out that it comes through tithes and offerings sent to the Worldwide Church of God), laments: "*We are subsidized by no one!* Our work is made possible only through tithes and offerings received from those who, as Co-Workers, are interested in furthering the Work God has commanded to be done at this time—through the ones He has chosen to do it! We do not ask the public for contributions. Jesus didn't. But we are commanded by God to tell the people His laws just as Jesus did. It is up to the people to obey God!"[17]

In other words, they are not asking anybody for money, but if you ever expect to have the blessing of God, or if you ever hope to enter His Kingdom, you had better obediently mail in your check to them *post haste!* This kind of an appeal has all the subtilty of a vintage Mack truck!

In the February, 1971, issue of *Tomorrow's World,* Herbert W. Armstrong devotes his entire "Personal" column to making a pitch for the tithes and offerings of the readers. He gives a personal testimony telling how he discovered the requirement of tithing, saying: "We had frequently gone hungry before I was converted. Now we went hungry even more frequently. Then one day, it dawned on my mind that we, ourselves, were actually breaking God's financial law by not tithing! All of a sudden God made me see His financial law is something *personal*—not merely a doctrine to accept impersonally. It meant ME! That

16. *The Marson Report,* Richard A. Marson; © 1970; The Ashley-Calvin Press, Seattle, Washington; p. 15
17. *Tomorrow's World,* June, 1971; "Two Trillion Dollars In Debt—But You Can Prosper"; p. 16

very day I took 10% of what we had—and it was not enough to buy food—added an offering, and mailed it to the Church treasury.

"That very afternoon food came for a completely adequate meal. I don't remember how, but I do remember that *the very day* I REPENTED for not having accepted tithing as a *personal obligation,* instead of a mere doctrinal *argument,* THAT VERY DAY FOOD CAME!

"God did not bring us immediate financial prosperity. For some years more, for our own good, we were forced to live in very poor economic circumstances. But *that very day* our financial condition started upward."[18]

Armstrong, incidentally, does not explain here how putting a tithe into this "apostate" "church treasury" (this is the church he once "thought" was the True Church, then later discovered he had been deceived) resulted in God's blessing. That detail is left to the reader's imagination. However, before his column in this particular issue of *Tomorrow's World* is finished, Armstrong is making sure his readers make no such mistake. He says: "HOW do you pay your tithes to GOD? By putting them into GOD'S WORK—where God Himself is working—where HIS Gospel is being preached, not merely MAN'S Gospel *about* Christ, but the very message Christ preached. . . .

"WHAT does God *do* with His tithe? He uses it for HIS MINISTRY, to preach *HIS* message of REPENTANCE, FAITH IN CHRIST, AND BEING BAPTIZED BY HIS SPIRIT INTO HIS FAMILY—His message of the KINGDOM OF GOD—the WORLD TOMORROW! It is the message of GOD'S WAY. It is the message of true salvation. It is the message of a changed and a fuller, happier LIFE—the message

18. Page 2

of ETERNAL life, God's gift through grace!"[19]

He winds up his appeal, saying: "Even though the NATION is under a curse, *you,* as an individual, may come under GOD'S BLESSING! It's your BEST assurance of getting and holding a job—of *continuous* and *increasing* INCOME!"[20] Frankly, if that type of an appeal wouldn't get the shekels flowing into the Armstrong coffers, *no appeal on earth could!* After all, everybody wants to get and hold a job—with a "*continuous* and *increasing* INCOME!"

In a *Tomorrow's World* article simply titled, "ABOUT TITHING," A. E. Carrozzo goes all-out to make sure no one misunderstands. He enthuses: "So they then ask: '*Where* do I send my tithes?'

"The answer is simple—give God what is rightfully His. Give *God's* tithes to the ones *God* has chosen to fulfill His commission. Put God's resources into *God's Work.* It's as simple as that."[21]

And, lest anyone misunderstand his attempt at simpleness, he identifies further: "There is only one Work proclaiming the Good News of *Tomorrow's World!*

"That work is *this* Work.

"But you must prove it for yourself. Don't believe us—*believe your Bible.* Read Matthew 24:14 and Mark 13:10. Find out where God is working today. Find out where God's tithe will be used for *God's* Work."[22]

We trust readers will check the references cited. They have about as much to do with the Worldwide Church of God cult as they do with the Dallas Cowboys or the Metropolitan Opera! But the writer has made his point: *send your tithes and offerings to us!* And, remember, this is the organization which boasts of *never* soliciting funds!

---

19. Ibid.; p. 37
20. Ibid.
21. July-August, 1970; p. 33
22. Ibid.

In keeping with the cult's manner of soft-sell solicitation, frequent "testimonials" are printed in the "Letters to the Editor" section, telling how God blessed after the reader started sending money to the work. For example, a reader in Ohio wrote to say: "Nice timing on your *Ending Your Financial Worries* booklet, since a job and money happened to start coming my way in between the time I ordered it and the time I received it. It posed an interesting question, too. 'If I give to God the 10% that is rightfully His, will He make sure that the remaining 90% will cover 100% of my expenses?' Well, there is one way to find out: Here's another check for you. . . ."[23]

From down under in New Zealand, a reader wrote to testify: "Over the past six years I have been reading about tithing in *The Plain Truth.* I am a dairy farmer and over this period I have had many problems such as mineral deficiency, electric shocks in the cow shed, leptospiroses, contagious abortion, low fertility, and adverse weather conditions. After reading 'Tithing Pays' in the February edition of *Tomorrow's World* I have decided to take the bull by the horns and challenge God as in Malachi 3:10. Please find enclosed a cheque for my first tithe."[24]

R. E. Glasgow reports: "The very first edition of *Tomorrow's World* had a letter to the editor, '. . .the very next pay day after I began paying my tithe I received a 35 cent an hour raise.' Another letter in the same first edition, 'I have been wanting to send my tithes for a long while but just did not know how to go about it.'"[25]

Those who have both secretly and openly admired Armstrong for his "everything free" and "no solicitation" policies will not only be *shocked* to read this

23. *Tomorrow's World,* September, 1971; p. 49
24. *Tomorrow's World,* July-August, 1970; p. 49
25. *The Biblical Evangelist,* April 1970; "'The Plain Truth': A False Magazine"; p. 6

is not really, after all, true—they will be ASTOUNDED to find "soft sell" appeals not only being made to the faithful, but that unconverted readers are also told they should send in their tithes and offerings as well!

In fact, two major articles in one issue of *Tomorrow's World* emphasized this very thing. One was written by Herbert W. Armstrong himself and began with the account of a man named Ed Smith who argued that he not only couldn't afford to tithe, but he wasn't a Christian anyway and only Christians should tithe. Armstrong then said: "There are thousands who, like Ed Smith, reason in their own minds that they can't afford to tithe, even though, like Ed Smith, they realize the Bible commands it.

"I heard about the above conversation, and preached a sermon on the question of whether the *un*converted should obey the Ten Commandments and pay tithes, or whether, as Ed reasoned, these things are only for Christians. I pointed out that God's law was put in motion for *man's good*—it *is* THE WAY of life that brings peace, happiness, prosperity; the full, abundant, interesting life; success, joy *here and now,* as well as eternal life through Christ for the saved.

"I showed that it PAYS, and is the only sensible way of life, entirely apart from the matter of salvation—and that, even if one is finally lost, he who sins little shall be punished with *few* stripes, but he who sins much with *many* stripes (Luke 12:47-48). I pointed out God's promise to *prosper* the tithe-payer, and that this is a definite LAW God has set in motion, which operates inexorably and automatically on the just and unjust alike."[26]

Note that Armstrong not only teaches unconverted people should tithe, but offers them the solace that if they eventually do experience eternal damnation, it won't be quite as bad because they tithed! Naturally,

---

26. November, 1971; "The Man Who Couldn't Afford to Tithe"; p. 29

in order to do them any good, the tithes and offerings would have to be sent to him.

The other major article in the issue, "Should a Non-Christian Tithe?" was by Senior Editor Herman L. Hoeh. The subtitle asked: *"Is tithing only for Christians? Would God prosper non-Christians who tithe?"* In the article the reader is told: "A non-Christian who pays God his tithes automatically receives financial blessings because he is obeying a law set in motion to bring financial prosperity—to keep one out of needless debt.

"It is that simple!. . .

"Notice Malachi 3:9-12, a prophecy for today: 'Ye are cursed with the curse, Yet ye rob Me, even this whole nation' (Jewish Publication Society translation). That means professing Christian and non-Christian alike!. . .

"That is God's promise—and God cannot lie. God is no respecter of persons—it is not a matter of spiritual conversion. It is a financial matter."[27]

What does the Word of God say about financial contributions from the unconverted? For example, Proverbs 15:8 tells us: "The sacrifice of the wicked is AN ABOMINATION to the Lord. . ." Proverbs 21:27 adds, "The sacrifice of the wicked is ABOMINATION: how much more, when he bringeth it with a wicked mind?"

God is not hard up. He owns the cattle on a thousand hills and He does not need or want one penny from a single unconverted man, woman, or young person. Permit us to make our point even stronger: *we can assure our readers that Almighty God does not want one penny sent to such an apostate, heretical organization as that of Herbert W. Armstrong and his Worldwide Church of God!*

---

27. November, 1971; pp. 30,31

The Plain Truth About Armstrong and Finances!

As we have already seen, Armstrong's reputation for not soliciting funds is not altogether honest. As a matter of fact, he most definitely *does* boldly solicit funds if an individual has sent him a contribution more than once in any six-month period. In a letter I received from him, dated November 20,1959, he acknowledged: "*IF,* however, an interested listener and PLAIN TRUTH reader sends in, voluntarily, tithes or freewill offerings for this work TWICE within six months, then, because Jesus said that where our treasure is our HEARTS are also, we send them a nice letter telling them we believe they desire to be a co-worker with us in this wonderful work. I send a special CO-WORKER letter out to all such co-workers EVERY MONTH, keeping them informed of all the plans and progress of the work, and often *I DO* ask them for money. WHY? Because it is the BIBLE WAY! Moses did ask the Congregation of Israel for offerings! The Apostle Paul *did* ask God's own people for contributions!"

In fact, once Armstrong gets his hooks into an individual, there is apparently no limit to the financial assistance he expects. In addition to the minimum 20 or 30 per cent "tithes," members are expected to give "liberal" offerings from time to time, "special offerings" seven times a year, offerings for building funds, poor funds, emergency funds and on *ad infinitum.*

Let me list some case histories. A Christian lady in New South Wales, Australia, wrote me a lengthy letter in which she lamented, "I am in the unfortunate position of having a husband who is absolutely obsessed with the books and broadcasts of this False Prophet and is sending money to him which we can ill afford to send." That lady, mother of two lovely teen-aged daughters, said her home, after experiencing 24 years of a wonderful marriage, had become "a very unhappy one," thanks to the Armstrong cult.

A gentleman in Chicago, who had been delivered from the Worldwide Church of God after reading my previous expose, lamented that Armstrong had gotten him for $400 and wanted to know if he could demand his money back, possibly taking him to court for his deception, charging him with fraud.

A gentleman in Amarillo, Texas—who asked to be put in contact with one of our representatives and who was interviewed at length by a personal friend of mine, at my request—wrote me to say, in part: "With reference to your booklet about Herbert W. Armstrong, you don't know the half. You should be as I was for 10 years, overcome by his deception, to really know him. He got me for $2,500. I was really deceived until I found him doing right the opposite of his teaching." [Incidentally, this gentleman and his wife were both *baptized members* of the Worldwide Church of God, but were excommunicated when they began complaining about some of the cult's heretical teachings and practices. I have a copy of their letter of excommunication and one paragraph is especially pertinent to this discussion. The pastor, David L. Antion, said, "However, I have since found out that almost everyone in Amarillo knows about your objections—not only on the wine but pledges, childrearing, how the church handles its finances, 2nd and 3rd tithes. In fact, some say it is almost invariably brought up—that is, the subject on wine—when ever they visit you." Since tithe means tenth, a third tithe would obviously amount to 30 per cent!]

A mother of five children (aged 11 through 20), a superintendent of the Youth Department in her Sunday school in the Florida city where she lived, wrote to say, "Since my husband has been baptized into this corrupt mess, my family has been in constant jeopardy." Although she and the children had been forbidden by her husband to attend church, she said they would sometimes sneak the car keys and drive off hurriedly, before he could stop them. He finally jacked up the car and chained the wheels together to keep her from using it for church attendance. At the time of her letter, the husband had left for a 10 or 11-day trip to Alabama to observe the Passover Feast, planning to make another trip 50 days later for Pentecost. Saying he would also be spending a couple of weeks later in Texas during the cult's holy day celebrations there, she lamented: "He certainly wasn't financially able to go for we've even been short on groceries lately because he gives so much to Armstrong."

Writing early in 1963, she said that the previous year, when her husband's earnings totaled $5,466.42, plus some money he received from the sale of some cows, he paid $1,717.15 in tithe and $133.08 in offerings to Pasadena, plus a contribution of $62.30 for a convention in Alabama and $130.15 for a convention in Texas—a total of $2,042.68 in tithes and offerings to the movement in one year. This, of course, figures out to nearly 40 per cent of his income.

A lady in Georgia wrote a kindred heartbreaking story. She told how her husband's pastor instructed him to whip his wife when she did not do as he said (a report we have received from other wives, as well), and said, "I put my husband under a Peace Bond for slapping me, crushing me on my arms, legs, leaving blue, bloodshot places on my body for two and three weeks." Finally the leaders told him he could not return home until his wife agreed to their conditions, part of which she said was: "Thirty per cent of all his earnings each pay day in addition to free offerings such as a Poor Fund, Pledge and many others."

She said, "My husband's church requires a full 10 per cent of all his earnings for the widows in his church, but can't give wives any money or support under circumstances I just described." She said her husband's minister, a man she identified as Pastor Craig, had influenced him to borrow around $3,000 on their house, without her knowledge, and give the money to his church group. Then the church advised him to stop payments, putting his wife out of the house. The wife, who had ceased working six years previously because of poor health, had to buy the house back at a public auction, pay all the back taxes, then go to work to make payments on the house in order to keep it.

Another lady in Georgia said her husband lied to her and took their small daughter to one of the cult's meetings. She claimed the child became ill after being without food or water for over 24 hours, the father telling the daughter it was God's Holy Day and she could neither eat nor drink. Eventually her husband left her and the court ordered him to pay $45 a week support for the couple's two children. He did not do it. Quite the contrary, one day he waylaid the seven-year-old on the way home from school and disappeared with her. The distraught mother heard nothing from that time in April until October. Figuring he might be at the cult's Feast of Tabernacles celebration at Jekyll Island, Georgia, she and her lawyer waited outside the gate until the services were over. Sure enough, her husband and daughter came out—*and her husband was with another woman!* At the time I received the information, the husband was in an Atlanta jail charged with forgery, embezzlement and other charges, in addition to child desertion.

We have the letters referred to, along with full names and addresses, of course, in our files.

Tragic, indeed, are the homes broken on the divorce court rocks through the vicious influence of this cult. A brother in California wrote the author a heartrending letter about how his "mother-in-law with Herbert's 'Elders'" had convinced his wife that while they were married in the eyes of the law, since it was a second marriage they were "not married in God's eyes." They informed her that in order to be saved, she must repent, leave her husband, be baptized and then receive the Holy Spirit. He told how his wife truly loved him, did not want to leave him, "cried her heart out," lost thirty pounds in two months, "but to give me a chance to be saved too—she had to leave."

Well publicized was a kindred case in Akron, Ohio, where a Worldwide Church of God minister, David L. Antion (now a Vice-President in the cult), told Mrs. Isabel Bradesku she was living in adultery because of her husband's previous marriage—even though, at the time, she had been married to him for fifteen years and had borne him five children. In this incident, husband Melvin Bradesku filed a $150,000 alienation of affection suit against Antion, Armstrong, Sr., and Ambassador College, charging they had "wrongfully, willfully and maliciously designed and intended to estrange" Mrs. Bradesku's affections from her husband. The Summit County jury, composed of seven women and five men, found the defendents guilty and granted Bradesku $30.000 damages. Of this amount, blame was assessed: $5,000 against Antion; $8,000 each against Armstrong and Ambassador College, and $9,000 against the church. Mr. Bradesku was awarded legal custody of the five children—ranging in ages from 5 to 14—by the court.[28]

We think the court was wrong in this case and perhaps a higher court will reverse the decision. The Armstrongs and all others, under our constitution, have a right to believe anything they wish—no matter how false or how foolish. It is wrong, in our judgment, for a court to penalize others in any amount or in any manner for sincere religious convictions. But we list the account here because it highlights one of the tragic

---

28. *Akron Beacon Journal,* March 7, 1968; March 8, 1968; March 9, 1968; David Hess, Reporter

aspects of the Armstrong's false beliefs: *broken homes!*

While this, admittedly, may not refer to finances, we add it here for want of a better place. A mideastern pastor wrote us of a tragic case where a lovely young lady became ensnared in the Armstrong movement. After saying she had accepted Christ at an early age and gave every evidence of being truly saved, he related: "Two of her brothers invited her to listen to the broadcast of Herbert W. Armstrong one night. The messages they heard on prophecy and the world to come caused them to start listening on a regular basis. Eventually the brothers saw the errors of Armstrongism and urged their sister to stop listening to him also. She refused.

"Shortly after this she married a fine young man who was born again and sincerely loved the Lord. He joined the brothers in urging his young wife to cease listening to the Armstrong ministry. However, instead of taking their good advice, she joined the nearest group of Armstrongites and was baptized into that faith. When the couple's children were born, she did all she could to raise them according to the teachings of this false prophet, forbidding them to eat pork and insisting they observe many of the cult's other strange and unscriptural practices.

"This young wife's mother became very concerned and burdened for her daughter, eventually going to her home for an extended visit to see if she could help her see what she was doing to her home and marriage. Shortly after arriving she heard her daughter praying in her bedroom. About thirty minutes later there was a loud explosion. The mother ran into the bedroom to find her daughter sprawled out on the floor with a gaping shotgun wound in her stomach. She was crying and praying for the Lord to forgive her. . .*and died within minutes.* She was a tragic product of the demonic power of Herbert W. Armstrong and his devilish doctrines."

It is a sad, sad story. Yet how graphically it illustrates what our Lord said in the Sermon on the Mount: "Beware of false prophets, which come to you in sheep's clothing, but inwardly they are ravening wolves. Ye shall know them by their fruits. Do men gather grapes of thorns, or figs of thistles? Even so every good tree bringeth forth good fruit; but a corrupt tree bringeth forth evil fruit. A good tree cannot bring forth evil fruit, neither can a corrupt tree bring forth good fruit. Every tree that bringeth not forth good fruit is hewn down, and cast into the fire. Wherefore by their fruits ye shall know them" (Matthew 7:15-20).

CHAPTER XIV

The Armstrong Teaching About "This and That"

In what will be our final chapter, apart from a brief summary, we want to mention several Armstrong teachings, just in passing, which we did not feel merited more thorough coverage. On the other hand, to get the full picture of the entire organization, we are convinced they deserve at least a mention.

Biblical Inspiration

Armstrong and his followers believe in an infallible Bible, one written by the inspiration of the Holy Spirit of God. Not uncommon are statements such as, "The Bible stands PROVED to be the inspired book of Almighty God—His written revelation to man," "You... can rely on the Bible. You can TRUST it. You. . .can put your FAITH in *what it plainly says,*" "the inspired Word of God," "the sacred Word of God."[1] However, it is strange "inspiration" that comes from an impersonal force. We remind our readers that the Worldwide Church of God does not for a moment believe in the personality of the Holy Spirit, teaching that "it" is merely a power. How a "power" is able to inspire verbally—down to the least jot and tittle—is never made clear.

One is also compelled to wonder what the cult really means by inspiration when the same term, "the inspiration of God's Spirit," is given to Garner Ted Armstrong in his "World Tomorrow" radio broadcast! As a *Tomorrow's World* article described it: "When you add all this to what Mr. Armstrong already has in his mind, plus the inspiration of God's Spirit, then

1. All quotes, *Tomorrow's World,* July-August, 1970; Garner Ted Armstrong, "Will *You* Get to *Heaven?*"; pp. 9-13

perhaps you will realize how the facts come flowing so fluently out of the loudspeaker of your radio."[2]

Again, one has his curiosity aroused over the kind of "Word of God" which would flow from the pen of an unregenerate writer. In a *Tomorrow's World* article on adultery, written by Bill McDonald, the salvation of Solomon (whose pungent pen produced Proverbs, Ecclesiastes, Song of Solomon and some of the Psalms) is questioned and readers are told: "Solomon *may* even have missed his chance for eternal life. . ."[3] Apparently the cult believes we could have had a "Gospel of Judas" as easily as the Gospel of John. How strange to think that God would choose and inspire unregenerate men to write His Sacred Scripture.

We are a little perplexed also about Armstrong's claim that the selection of books to be included in the Divine Library, along with their preservation, was placed in the hands of the Church. This smacks strongly of Romanism. Seeking to answer the question of whether or not we have a complete Bible today, and whether or not the Apocrypha should be part of the Sacred Canon, Hermon L. Hoeh wrote: "God inspired His prophets to bear His message to the Old Testament Church. God placed His government in that Church. That Church became responsible—divinely appointed—to preserve His Word—*for all time!*

". . .God instituted His government in His Church—the Old Testament Church—through Moses. In Jesus' day *the Scribes and Pharisees* were sitting in Moses' seat, possessing his authority. . . .

"We now have the right Church—the Old Testament Church; the right tribe—Judah, the Jews; the right place—Jerusalem; the right leaders—the Scribes and Pharisees. Here is where we must look for the authority which determines what books belong to the

---

2. February, 1971; "The Ambassador College Radio Studio. . .An Inside Look"; p. 25
3. December, 1971; "Thou Shalt Not Commit Adultery!"; p. 27

'Old Testament.' Here was the only place on earth where God governed the preservation of His Word—the Old Testament."[4]

That type of reasoning is fraught with problems. Especially since Armstrong and his followers claim to be the successors of that church—hence the keepers of the authority.

While we do not consider it of vital importance, we note in passing that the cult habitually—although not consistently—substitutes "Eternal" in passages where "LORD" (English form of Jehovah) appears, without any indication whatsoever of any tampering with the translation. Sometimes *both forms* are used in the same quotation. As an example, here is a quote by Herbert W. Armstrong of Isaiah 58:13,14: "If thou *turn away thy foot from* the sabbath, from doing thy pleasure on my *HOLY* DAY; and call the sabbath a delight [not a yoke of bondage], the *HOLY* OF THE ETERNAL, *honourable;* and shalt *honour HIM,* not doing thine own ways, nor finding thine own pleasure, nor speaking thine own words: Then shalt thou *delight thyself in the LORD;* and I will cause thee to ride upon the high places of the earth, and feed thee with the heritage of Jacob thy father: for the mouth of the Eternal hath spoken it."[5]

The above is from the King James Version, which uses "LORD" three times. Armstrong arbitrarily changes it to "Eternal" in two of the places, leaving it "LORD" in the third—and all without any indication he is making any changes. He even bypasses his beloved brackets for this.

Creation

The Worldwide Church of God teaches the "Gap" theory (between Genesis 1:1 and Genesis 1:2), thus

4. *Do We Have A Complete Bible?* © 1959,1971; pp. 2,3
5. *Which Day Is The Christian Sabbath?* © 1962,1964,1968,1970,1971; p. 29

seeking to harmonize the age of the earth with some of the claims of science. Kenneth C. Herrmann discusses it: "'In the beginning God created the heaven and the earth'—this tells about the original creation. The second verse of Genesis 1 refers to a destruction which came upon the earth following the sin and rebellion of Satan and the angels who followed him. . . .

"Darkness was upon the face of the ocean. The renewing of our earth to a state of order followed in six days."[6] Incidentally, they believe these days to be literal solar days, comparable to our 24-hour day, as do we.

Robert E. Gentet adds: "The Hebrew words for 'without form and void' in Genesis 1:2 are *tohu* and *bohu.* They have the English meaning of 'waste, empty, confusion, and chaos.' The Hebrew word translated 'in vain' in Isaiah 45:18 is also *tohu,* the very same word used in Genesis 1:2.

"So we see that God did not create the earth in a state of *tohu,* but rather it had become that way. In the beginning the earth was not created in chaos. Something happened, however, that made it a chaos. Genesis 1, verse 2 reveals what most creationists do not understand. The earth was no longer in a state of order. It was (or had become) in a state of utter confusion and waste."[7]

What caused God's original creation to be wrecked? They teach that this world was originally the habitation of Lucifer and his angels; their rebellion wrecked it and God recreated it. Brian Knowles describes it: "It is not known how long ago God originally created the whole material universe. It could easily have been millions of years ago. It might have been more recently. In any case it was a beautiful creation. The angels of God (created earlier) rejoiced with singing

---

6. *How Long Were The "Days" Of Creation?* © 1958,1971; p. 1
7. *Dinosaurs Before Adam?* c 1963,1972; p. 6

at the harmony and beauty God had produced (Job 38:4-7). Certain angels under the leadership of a great cherub named Lucifer were placed in charge of this planet. After a time, however, mutinous feelings began to well up in Lucifer. *He was not willing to 'settle for earth'!* He persuaded one third of the angels to rebel with him, and then he attempted to overthrow the throne of God! Jude states that the angels '. . . kept not their first estate [this earth], but *left their own habitation. . . .*' Naturally their attempt at a 'coup' was unsuccessful. They were cast back down to the earth where they presently reside. They became known as 'demons' (Jude 6; Isa. 14:12-14; Ezek. 28:11-19; Luke 10:18).

"In their anger, these fallen spirit beings wreaked great destruction upon the material universe. Evidence of this can be seen in the cataclysmic condition of the solar system. Even the moon bears the scars of Satanic wrath."[8]

Note in the above: (1) how handily the writer uses the Armstrongian brackets to make Scripture mean what he wants it to mean, flaunting the context; (2) he endeavors to make "fallen angels" and "demons" one and the same; (3) he makes these fallen angels residing on earth today, instead of in Hell, chained and reserved unto judgment, as the Scripture says in II Peter 2:4; (4) he describes these fallen angels as wreaking destruction upon the entire material universe, including the solar system and even describing the moon as bearing "scars of Satanic wrath."

That is finding a lot, one must confess, in the blank space between those two opening verses of the Bible!

Sin

To Herbert W. Armstrong and his Worldwide Church

8. *Tomorrow's World*, September, 1971; "What 'on Earth' is God Doing?"; pp. 9,10

of God, sin is breaking the Ten Commandments. Whenever sin is defined, the reference is always to I John 3:4, "Whosoever committeth sin transgresseth also the law: for sin is the transgression of the law." And by transgressing the law, the Ten Commandments are invariably understood. For example, Garner Ted Armstrong writes: "*Sin* is the breaking of God's Ten Commandments—the transgression of His LAW (I John 3:4)."[9]

Strangely, the many other definitions of sin, scattered throughout the Word of God, are rarely, if ever, referred to. Definitions such as, "Whatsoever is not of faith is sin" (Romans 14:23); "All unrighteousness is sin" (I John 5:17); "To him that knoweth to do good, and doeth it not, to him it is sin" (James 4:17); and coming "short of the glory of God" (Romans 3:23), are habitually ignored. Apparently this obsession with just one aspect of sin stems from the strong legalistic foundation of the cult.

Speaking of strange things, we frankly do not know what to make of one of Herbert W. Armstrong's statements about cleansing from sin. He wrote: "If WE, who are already Christians, confess and REPENT of any sin we might, unhappily, commit (though we certainly SHOULD NOT SIN!!), the living Christ not only will forgive, but will CLEANSE US from doing it any more!"[10] Just what a cleansing "from doing it any more" means, we are not told.

However, the strangest of all Armstrong's strange teachings about sin is that God deliberately made man a sinner! He purposefully planned it that way, we are informed. One of the cult's prominent leaders, C. Paul Meredith, endeavoring to prove the cult's heretical doctrine of a day of salvation after death, says: "God has made it natural for man to reject truth and to do

9. *Tomorrow's World,* January, 1972; "Why Accidents?"; p. 7
10. *What Do You Mean. . ."The Unpardonable Sin"?* © 1967,1971,1972; p. 28

what is right in his own eyes, to want to sin—to want to break God's Laws."[11] He says again, about "the vast blinded majority who never had an opportunity" to be saved in this life: "Are they damned because God created them with a carnal mind which blinded them to the ways of salvation?"[12] And still again, in another article the same writer deals with the same subject: "These millions are not lost forever! They never were called to be saved!. . .

"Also, what about the great number since Christ's day who have shown very little interest in religion and have died? Are they lost forever? No, because they have never had a chance of salvation. They are blinded. God is not trying to save many now. He has blinded them!"[13]

Note carefully that the writer is saying God deliberately created man to sin, to reject truth; He deliberately blinded them because He did not want to save them in this life! This fits the pattern of Mr. Armstrong's teaching that God planned in advance to wreck His creation by sin, as we pointed out in our original brief expose. At that time we wrote: "Strange and unbelievable as it may seem, Mr. Armstrong makes God directly responsible for the sin and failure of mankind. For example, he says in one of his books: 'Now if Satan did *not* succeed in thwarting God's will, wrecking God's perfected and completed Creation, then the only alternative is to say that it all happened *according* to God's will—exactly as God himself originally planned!' (Page 8, *Why Were You Born?*)

"Again he states: 'Satan *did not* break into the Garden of Eden in spite of God—did *not* do one single thing contrary to God's great PURPOSE! All that has

11. *Is This The Only Day Of Salvation?* © 1958,1971; p. 2
12. Ibid.; p. 3
13. *If You Die. . .Will You Live Again?* © 1958,1971; p. 7

happened had been planned before of GOD—and all is progressing *exactly* as GOD WILLS.

"'Oh, what a WONDERFUL TRUTH!' (Page 9, *Why Were You Born?*)

"Mr. Armstrong's conception of what a 'wonderful truth' consists of contrasts sharply with this writer's opinion!. . .

"It would be absolutely and utterly impossible to harmonize his statements in the above quotations with the teaching of the Word of God in such places as James 1:13-16, where we read: 'Let no man say when he is tempted, I am tempted of God: for God cannot be tempted with evil, *neither tempteth he any man*: But every man is tempted, when he is drawn away of his own lust, and enticed. Then when lust hath conceived, it bringeth forth sin: and sin when it is finished, bringeth forth death. Do not err, my beloved brethren.'

"There is a world of difference between saying God *permitted* a thing, and that He *planned* a thing!"[14]

Satan and Demons

Do you know why Satan is currently the god of this world? According to Herbert W. Armstrong, it is because there is no bona fide successor to take his place! He says: "God governs by His spiritual Law—a Law based on the principle of LOVE. Love, first, to God with submission and obedience, and secondly to His creatures—the way of outgoing concern for the good and welfare of others. But Lucifer's heart was lifted up in vanity, because of his beauty and vast knowledge. He rebelled against God, mutinied, set out to organize his angels into an invading army and to conquer GOD—in order to rule the entire vast UNIVERSE. This disqualified him as earth's ruler.

---

14. *Herbert W. Armstrong—A False Prophet*, Copyright, 1961; Sword of the Lord Foundation, Murfreesboro, Tennessee; pp. 14,15

However, the very principle of God's Government requires that the ruler retain office *until* a successor qualifies and is inducted into office."[15]

Regarding demons, as previously pointed out, Mr. Armstrong thinks they are the same as fallen angels. Garner Ted Armstrong, in an article about Satan, declares: "God shows that fully one third of all the multiplied millions of the angels *followed* Lucifer in his rebellion, and were cast down to the earth with him! (Compare Rev. 12:4 with Rev. 1:20.) These fallen angels, remember, are SPIRITS, not human beings! To accomplish his *work* of deception, with the ultimate goal of *destroying* human beings, Satan utilizes these millions of disobedient spirits! He is called the PRINCE of demons (Matt. 12:24)."[16]

We previously quoted Brian Knowles as saying about the fallen angels, "They were cast back down to earth where they presently reside. They are become known as 'demons'. . ."

One *Tomorrow's World* writer explains that it was a "demon who impersonated Samuel" in the incident of Saul's visit to the witch of En-dor.[17]

The Unpardonable Sin

Herbert W. Armstrong's booklet, "What Do You Mean. . .'The Unpardonable Sin'?" is a good illustration of how he uses an abundance of words to muddy the waters, making it extremely difficult to tell what he really does believe. Our first impression was that he was saying it involved someone "on the road" [translated from Armstrongese, this means an individual who has hooked up with Armstrong's organization], then turning around and leaving the cult. Yet even

---

15. *Tomorrow's World,* October, 1971; "Just What Do You Mean. . .*Born Again?";* p. 4
16. *Tomorrow's World,* June, 1971; "What Is Satan's Fate?"; p. 7
17. October, 1971; William Stenger, "Do Liars Always Lie?"; p. 40

this seems to be "pardonable" according to Armstrong, if that wayward one returns to his fold.

As previously noted, Armstrong multiplies words without really getting down to the nitty-gritty. Even though the booklet is only 39 pages, the reader finds himself on page 25 before Armstrong announces, "Now we approach our final answer."[18] Then he must wade through another four pages before Armstrong says again, "Now we are ready to MAKE PLAIN what *IS* the 'unpardonable sin'—that sin that can never be forgiven, in this world or the next!"[19] Even then the reader is not told!

Here is what Armstrong eventually (on page 34!) seems to be saying is the unpardonable sin for a Christian: "To be 'saved'—to inherit eternal life in God's Kingdom—you must still be traveling THAT WAY at the end of your life! Stumbling—falling down—*on* that road, repented of, DOES NOT PUT YOU OFF THAT ROAD! But to deliberately *change roads,* to willfully go back on the world's road, or to let the false glamor and glitter of the world's road begin to dominate your life, may bring you to a place where you are unable to REPENT and get back on GOD'S WAY."[20]

In other words, one does not commit the unpardonable sin when he is guilty of "falling into sin," *as long as he is still going along with Armstrong and his movement.* But if he ever quits his organization, that is getting off the road. Even then, however, such a terrible act is not unpardonable: "Yet I am persuaded that anyone who does seriously REPENT, and earnestly SEEK Jesus Christ, may find Him, and forgiveness, and get back on the right road."[21] So even that is not

18. Op. cit.
19. Ibid.; p. 29
20. Ibid.; p. 34
21. Ibid.

unpardonable—if the prodigal returns to the Pasadena fold!

Perhaps Armstrong means that the "unpardonable" part of the act is waiting too long to "get back" with his organization—what he calls "back on the *right* road." He goes on to mention Esau finding no place of repentance and Judas Iscariot "repenting" but then hanging himself, pointing out it was "*too late*" for both of them. Then he says: "So far, we have treated only with the case of converted Christians, who have actually received the precious GIFT of God's Holy Spirit."[22] But to call Judas Iscariot, for example, a "converted Christian" who had "received the precious GIFT of God's Holy Spirit" is a tremendous contradiction of what the Bible teaches. Judas Iscariot was never a believer, was never converted, was an agent of Satan from the beginning—and Scripture makes it very plain (See John 6:64-71; John 13:10-11; John 17:12).

Armstrong then launched a discussion as to whether a non-Christian could commit the unpardonable sin. Here he appeared to make the unpardonable sin something entirely different, writing: "No ordinary sin, even by a Christian, is unforgivable. Jesus said plainly that ALL sins, and blasphemies—even against GOD—even against Jesus Christ—will be forgiven on repentance. It is ONLY premeditated, thought-out, planned, deliberate, intentional, willful indignity, insult, false accusation against God's HOLY SPIRIT that is unforgivable."[23]

We would assume this to mean someone like the author of this book who, after very carefully and minutely examining the doctrines of the Worldwide Church of God, rejected totally the teaching and called its leadership "false prophets," striking out strongly

22. Ibid.; p. 35
23. Ibid.; p. 37

in an attack upon the movement. We will be numbered among the very few, according to the Armstrong teaching, who will not even be given a chance in the next world to repent!

Yet when Armstrong gets to the next-to-the-last page of his book, he rules out the unpardonable sin for unconverted people. He says: "Remember, God *grants* repentance (Acts 11:18; 5:31). Yet of course God never *forces* repentance on one. When one has come to the place where he WON'T—can't—has totally, completely, lost all desire to repent—is UNABLE to repent—he has 'fallen away.'

"And of course this is NOT speaking of UNCONVERTED people—those who never had been converted—but only those who had been.

"The TEST is this: IF and WHEN one really does DESIRE to repent—*does* feel completely disgusted and abhorrent of himself—does DESIRE to repent and get back into God's grace—*HE CAN!*"[24]

Universalism

We do *not* say that the Worldwide Church of God teaches a doctrine of universalism; that is, that all mankind will eventually be saved. The cult *does* believe that a relatively few people will be cast into the lake of fire and annihilated. But, apparently, the number of individuals who will eventually be lost are so few that the leadership is able to talk like universalists.

Garner Ted Armstrong, writing about the "Jesus People," declared: "In the earlier 'Jesus Trip' article, I mentioned Jesus did not come to save the world THEN, and received many angry letters informing me of various scriptures in the Bible concerned with Jesus' death for our sins and transgressions, and statements concerning His position as Saviour of the world!

---

24. Ibid.; p. 38

"But I deeply and devotedly RECOGNIZE Jesus Christ as my own personal Saviour, and the eventual Saviour of *all the world!* But I also deeply recognize the plain, clear, written Word of God that Jesus Christ deliberately *concealed* His meaning during that time to the general populaces, and explained to His disciples that the general public COULD NOT understand."[25]

This, of course, is contrary to our Lord's declaration that a minority would be saved, not a majority. In the Sermon on the Mount, He revealed: "Enter ye in at the strait gate: for wide is the gate, and broad is the way, that leadeth to destruction, and many there be which go in thereat: Because strait is the gate, and narrow is the way, which leadeth unto life, and few there be that find it" (Matthew 7:13,14).

Easter and Christmas

The Armstrongs and their Worldwide Church of God have a vendetta against most holidays. Herbert W. Armstrong published a book, "*The* PLAIN TRUTH about CHRISTMAS," calling it paganism and seeking to trace its origin all the way back to old Nimrod himself![26] A writer in the *Plain Truth,* calling its observance heathenism, titled his article in the form of a question, "Where Does God Command *You* to Observe CHRISTMAS?" His subtitle announced: "Did you know that Christmas was observed by pagans 2000 years before the birth of Jesus Christ?—that neither the apostles nor the inspired New Testament Church observed it? Here are the astounding FACTS!"[27]

In typical Armstrong fashion, a straw man has been set up to gleefully knock down. We know of no one who ever said God commanded Christians to observe Christmas, nor that the apostles or New Testament

25. *Tomorrow's World,* June, 1971; "The 'Jesus Trip' One-Way Ticket To Nowhere?"; p. 27
26. ©1952,1970; pp. 10-15
27. December, 1958; Herman L. Hoeh; p. 5

church observed it. One might just as well ask the Worldwide Church of God: "Where Does God Command You to Publish *Tomorrow's World* or *The Plain Truth* Magazines?" Or, ask, "Where Does God Command You to Establish Ambassador College?" Or, "Where Does God Command You to Have a Tomorrow's World Radio or Television Program?" That is silly reasoning, intended only to impress the uneducated and underprivileged.

Yet the Worldwide Church of God makes eternal salvation hinge on observance or non-observance of Christmas. Herman L. Hoeh, in the above-mentioned article, declares: "It is time you looked to see WHAT IS RECORDED IN YOUR VERY OWN BIBLE!

"How, then, did Christmas—now revealed as an ancient pagan holiday celebrated 2000 years before the birth of Christ—creep into the Christianity of this Western World?

"And *DOES IT MAKE ANY DIFFERENCE* if you observe it?

"Consider! *Your eternal destiny* depends upon the answer!"[28]

That is slicing the baloney pretty thick, in our judgment!

Do not misunderstand. We are against all the wicked commercialism, the drunkenness, the wicked lies about reindeer flying through the sky, the myths of a big-bellied Santa Claus coming down the chimney, and all the rest of the crassness and crudeness of the world. Nonetheless, we are still grateful that all mankind—even though currently lying in the lap of the wicked one—is compelled once a year to acknowledge that Jesus Christ came into this world, born of a virgin, to provide a redemption for sinners. Frankly, we enjoy the sweet fellowship of friends and loved ones

---

28. Ibid.

at that season, with some of whom we are denied contact throughout all the rest of the year. We like the singing of the blessed songs about the birth of Christ. We thrill to the special emphasis put upon examining the Scriptures regarding His birth and the divine motivation behind it. And we think it both silly and wicked for someone to object about an emphasis which forces the world to acknowledge this Bible truth.

We were amused to note that Armstrong, while condemning the observance of Christmas, did not overlook the possibility of getting a nice contribution for his work at that season. He wrote: "Surely, for those who observe Christmas, the GIFT ought to go to Christ, most generously! But few think of that!"[29]

Easter is just as viciously attacked. In fact, one of the cult's booklets is "EASTER *Is Pagan!*"[30] Once again we emphasize that we do not defend falsehoods and myths. We are opposed to telling little children that rabbits lay eggs. We regret the "Easter bonnet" emphasis, having made it a practice never to purchase any of our new clothes at that time of the year, even when they were needed, lest someone think this to be our understanding of Easter. On the other hand, we have always been grateful that we could get people into our churches to hear the Word of God proclaimed on that day who would never attend the House of God otherwise. And we are excitedly grateful that once a year the world has been compelled to recognize that after three days and three nights in the belly of the earth, Jesus Christ tore the bars of death away and rose in resurrection power, making available an eternal salvation to all who desire it.

The Worldwide Church of God has published several articles condemning Halloween. Now, it just so happens, we don't care much for Halloween, either. It is a night

29. Letter received by the author from Mr. Armstrong, dated November 20, 1959
30. Copyright, 1952; Written Anonymously

dedicated to honoring demons and demonism, and we deplore teaching little children to go around the neighborhood begging for handouts—with a threat of retribution if the handout is not forthcoming!

On the other hand, we think anyone's objection ought to be an *honest* objection. Herman L. Hoeh, in the opening paragraph of his article, HALLOWE'EN *Where Did It Come From?"* says: "HALLOWE'EN is not a Christian holiday! Yet the 'Christian' world observes it. Why? Where does the Bible mention Hallowe'en?"[31]

In a later article, Hoeh, joined with co-author Gerhard Marx, tells us: "Since this holiday is called 'Christian' one assumes that the authority cited [for its observance] would be the Superior Authority of the *Christian* faith—Jesus Christ. The shocking point, however, is that NOWHERE can you find He commands, sanctions or alludes to this holiday in the Bible."[32]

It is an outright, boldfaced, blatant lie for Hoeh and Marx to say that the Christian world "observes" Halloween. If they are telling the truth, what services of the church are Halloween services? We dare say Mr. Hoeh and Mr. Marx cannot cite a single instance in the history of mankind where the Christian church has held a Halloween service for its worshipers. Some Sunday school class may have gotten together for a party on that date, bob for apples, play games, etc.—just as it might have a party on the 4th of July and shoot off fireworks—but that is hardly making it a "Christian holiday" or an "observance" of the Christian world. We think the leaders of this cult have stooped pretty low to try to make an issue like this. This is the argument of those in the throes of desperation.

Believe it or not, the Worldwide Church of God is

---

31. *The Plain Truth,* November, 1959; p. 21
32. *The Plain Truth,* October-November, 1970; p. 46

even against birthday celebrations! On the other hand, national holidays, such as Independence Day and Thanksgiving Day, are perfectly all right to observe. In answer to a question from a reader in *Tomorrow's World* about "Hanukkah" and "Christmas," the editor says: "Hanukkah is a Hebrew word meaning 'dedication.' The holiday commemorates the rededication of the Temple in Jerusalem by Judah Maccabee following the expulsion of the Seleucid Syrians under Antiochus Epiphanes in 165 B.C. The full account of the story can be found in Josephus' *Antiquities of the Jews,* Book XII, chapters 5-11.

"Hanukkah is a Jewish national feast of rejoicing. We read that Jesus was present at the festival of Dedication (since he was a physical Jew) in John 10:22. We learn from Christ's example that acknowledging national holidays not eminating from paganism (such as the American Thanksgiving Day) is not wrong and does not violate God's higher Law."[33]

Pacifism

While we were not able to discover much about this in wading through the voluminous writings of the cult, the following statement from the pen of Herbert W. Armstrong seems to indicate a position of pacifism, which harmonizes with their refusal to vote or otherwise take responsibilities with any form of "this world's" citizenship: "Christ said: 'LOVE your enemies,' so professing Christians—pretending to follow Him, HATE their enemies and go to war to kill them."[34]

On another occasion, Garner Ted Armstrong, who at one time served in the Navy, wrote: "A believer in Jesus shooting a machine gun is as purely hypocritical as a policy of peace through war, success through

---

33. May, 1971; p. 46
34. *Which Day Is The Christian Sabbath?* p. 46

cheating, or happy marriages through adultery."[35]

This conveniently ignores the repeated instances in the Word of God where Jehovah ordered His people to fight. It also bypasses the many clear statements in Scripture such as, "The Lord is a man of war: the Lord is his name" (Exodus 15:3); and, "Blessed be the Lord my strength, which teacheth my hands to war, and my fingers to fight" (Psalm 144:1).

There are times when war is *right,* when not to go to war is sin!

35. *Tomorrow's World,* March, 1971; "The 'Jesus Trip'"; p. 3

CHAPTER XV

Summary

We have loaded this volume with incontrovertible proof relative to the heretical teaching of Herbert W. Armstrong, Garner Ted Armstrong, and their Worldwide Church of God. We have shown that the success of the entire organization is founded upon deception, misrepresentation and the twisted perversion of scriptural truth.

We have pointed out that the blessed truth of the Trinity is denied, that the God the Father of Armstrongism is not the God the Father of the Bible, that the Person and Work of Christ are falsely presented by the movement—even to the extent of making Him inferior to the Father in *"quantitative"* deity. And we have noted that the cult denies the personality of the Holy Spirit, representing this blessed Comforter as merely a power, an impersonal force.

We have examined the strange and blasphemous "God Family" teaching of the Worldwide Church of God, whereby all its followers expect eventually to become gods and creators. In fact, we learned they teach that they will become *qualitatively* every bit as much deity as God the Father and God the Son.

We have examined carefully and in great detail what the movement teaches about salvation. We have seen that, contrary to repeated insistence that they believe in salvation by grace, the eventual salvation offered is gained primarily by works. We have seen that being born again is denied as something for this life; the new birth being nothing more than a pregnancy. We have discovered the cult has a strange and absurd idea of election, teaching that God does not even want to save many people in this life. We have noted that there is no security for anyone in the movement, not even the founder himself. But, perhaps worst of all, we have examined the cult's teaching of a "second chance" for salvation in the next world and learned its conclusions are not far from the universalism heresy.

We have seen that heavy and complex legalism is taught by the cult. We discovered that the entire Old Testament law is taught as binding for our day, including all of the various Levitical feasts and ceremonial observances. And we found an especially strong emphasis is placed on Saturday Sabbath observance, making eventual eternal life hinge on faithfulness to it.

We have looked at what the Worldwide Church of God teaches about Heaven and Hell, finding a denial that a single saved person will ever go to Heaven and a teaching that Hell is a suburb of Jerusalem, where a minority will eventually be annihilated.

We have examined the amazing Anglo-Saxon Israelism of the cult with its fantastic interpretation that Britain is Ephraim, America is Manasseh and Elizabeth's throne in England is really the Throne of David! We were astounded to find the cult actually believes the Prophet Jeremiah himself took that throne to Ireland during the days of Israel's captivity.

We have examined Armstrong's teaching about the church. We have seen his conflicting descriptions and identification of the True Church, what he teaches about baptism and baptismal regeneration, the Lord's Supper, the laying on of hands, healing for this age, his downgrading of soul winning, and his definition of a saint.

We have looked at the confusing Armstrong teaching about life on the other side of the grave, his understanding of what death is, what the soul is, and immortality. We have examined his teaching of soul sleep and found also that he denies the resurrection of the body.

We have looked at the Armstrong teaching about

prophecy, about the second coming of Christ, and about His earthly kingdom.

We have seen that the Worldwide Church of God is anti-temperance, arguing for and advocating the use of intoxicating liquors.

We have placed the cult's position about money under a microscope and examined the "everything free" boast. We have seen what it teaches about tithing—even for unconverted people—and we have noted some of the tragic consequences of this emphasis in the homes of Worldwide Church of God members.

We have even briefly noted what the cult teaches about such things as sin, Satan, demons, observance of holidays, and other matters.

Now after all this, we find ourselves in a position to repeat with even more dogmatic emphasis what we said, basically, at the close of our brief 24-page expose, HERBERT W. ARMSTRONG—A FALSE PROPHET, written a dozen years previously.[1]

First, beyond any question of doubt, Herbert W. Armstrong is a false prophet who proclaims a gospel contrary to that taught in the Word of God. His doctrine is wrong regarding the Person and Work of Jesus Christ, hence it is not Christian doctrine.

Second, because his work is not a Christian work, it does not merit the prayer, support or interest of Christian people. It would be as wicked to send money to Armstrong as it would be to give money to Satan himself. Money sent to Armstrong actually finances the devilish program of warfare against God's Word and God's dear Son.

Third, II John 9-11 says: "*Whosoever transgresseth, and abideth not in the doctrine of Christ, hath not*

1. Copyright, 1961, Sword of the Lord Foundation, Murfreesboro, Tennessee; p. 24. If readers would like this handy 24-page booklet for quantity distribution, it is available for only 10¢ per copy, either from the Sword of the Lord Foundation or the publisher of this volume.

God. He that abideth in the doctrine of Christ, he hath both the Father and the Son. If there come any unto you, and bring not this doctrine, receive him not into your house, neither bid him God speed: For he that biddeth him God speed is partaker of his evil deeds."

Note that anyone who helps Armstrong spread his wicked slander against the Person and Work of Jesus Christ becomes "a partaker of his evil deeds." But it is even more dogmatic than that! Simply welcoming him into the house makes one a co-laborer with him in his deviltry. It is not stretching truth at all to say that Armstrong is "received into your house" when you listen to his radio or television broadcasts. Good Christians who are desirous of pleasing their Savior will not listen to them or receive into their house such literature as *The Plain Truth* and *Tomorrow's World* magazines, or books and booklets written by leaders of the cult, or enroll in the Ambassador College Correspondence Course.

We will warn our readers of the *teachings* of Herbert W. Armstrong and the Worldwide Church of God, just as Paul warned the Ephesians of the *actions* of wicked men in their day: *"Let no man deceive you with vain words: for because of these things cometh the wrath of God upon the children of disobedience. Be not ye therefore partakers with them. For ye were sometimes darkness, but now are ye light in the Lord: walk as children of light: (For the fruit of the Spirit is in all goodness and righteousness and truth;) Proving what is acceptable unto the Lord. And have no fellowship with the unfruitful works of darkness, but rather reprove them. For it is a shame even to speak of those things which are done of them in secret. But all things that are reproved are made manifest by the light: for whatsoever doth make manifest is light"* (Ephesians 5:6-13).

Never were Paul's words to the Corinthians more applicable than with reference to the attitude twentieth-century Christians should maintain toward the Worldwide Church of God: ". . .they sacrifice to devils, and not to God: and I would not that ye should have fellowship with devils. Ye cannot drink the cup of the Lord, and the cup of devils: ye cannot be partakers of the Lord's table, and of the table of devils" (I Corinthians 10:20,21).

A Final Word

Before we close this book which, frankly, we found very distasteful but very necessary to write, just a warm word to one who has been following Armstrong and has learned, to his or her chagrin, he has been deceived by "doctrines of devils" (I Timothy 4:1). What should you do, apart from severing all ties with the group?

There might be a tendency, in the throes of bitter disappointment, to say, *"What's the use? Religion is a racket, preachers are deceivers, there is nothing to it!"* Such a conclusion and attitude would be as great a mistake as when you first started listening to the Armstrongs. The presence of error does not eliminate the possibility of truth.

Our blessed Lord said, "And ye shall know the truth, and the truth shall make you free" (John 8:32), adding a moment later, "If the Son therefore shall make you free, ye shall be free indeed" (John 8:36). The One who *is* Truth (John 14:6) can certainly *reveal* Truth.

His revelation regarding salvation's truth is: "For God so loved the world, that he gave his only begotten Son, that whosoever believeth in him should not perish, but have everlasting life. For God sent not his Son into the world to condemn the world; but that the world through him might be saved. He that believeth on him is not condemned: but he that believeth not is condemned already, because he hath not believed in the name of the only begotten Son of God" (John

3:16-18). He said again: "Verily, verily, I say unto you, He that heareth my word, and believeth on him that sent me, hath everlasting life, and shall not come into condemnation; but is passed from death unto life" (John 5:24).

Note that one receives everlasting life the very moment he puts his trust in Christ for salvation. The present tense is used to assure the believer he has passed from the death of sin to the life of God through that act of faith. The divine guarantee is his that he can never be brought into condemnation.

Will you make that personal and eternal surrender to Jesus Christ right now? If we can be of any further assistance in helping you settle this great transaction, feel free to write the author:

Dr. Robert L. Sumner, Director
BIBLICAL EVANGELISM
P. O. Box 157
Brownsburg, Indiana 46112

Epilogue

This book was completed and the type already set on all 15 chapters when the author had an opportunity to go to a major southern city and interview a couple who, as ex-members of the Worldwide Church of God and ex-employees of Ambassador College, were in a position to shed valuable light on the cult which could never be obtained from examining the literature of its leaders. The husband had been a member of the church for over ten years, the wife for nearly four. Both were paid employees of Ambassador College at the time of their withdrawal from the movement. He was a deacon in the church, with fourteen widows under his jurisdiction. They are personally acquainted with many of the leaders in the movement.

I stress their background so my readers will know they were "insiders," not mere novices. What they have to say is authoritative, factual, firsthand—not mere hearsay. And it might be helpful to also note that both attended college, are well educated and cultured. He was a successful businessman, an owner of a firm which had prospered sufficiently for him to retire before becoming connected with the cult. She had been an executive secretary.

One of my first impressions upon contacting this couple, first by telephone and then in person at their home, was the apparent fear—to an *unreasonable* degree, it seemed to me—they had of the Worldwide Church of God. While they did not fear *personal* retaliation so much, they desperately feared what might happen to relatives and friends if they talked too freely. For this reason the couple will not be identified here and the interview with the author, recorded and partly reproduced here, will simply identify him as "Husband," her as "Wife," with the author's remarks and questions identified as his, of course.

Perhaps I should also make clear that both withdrew from the Worldwide Church of God for doctrinal reasons, not personal. It was a result of diligent study in the Word of God which brought a clear conviction of salvation only by grace through faith, along with an understanding that the "new" covenant of liberty had replaced the "old" with its observances of Sabbaths, holy days and legalistic bondage. Galatians, Colossians and Hebrews were especially pertinent in bringing them to this biblical conviction.

Portions of our interview were as follows:

AUTHOR: Could you tell me a little bit about the Worldwide Church of God's position regarding marriage and divorce, applying it to your own particular case?

HUSBAND: My first wife and I were divorced years ago. Later I married a widow. When I first became interested in the Worldwide Church of God, one of its top ministers advised me that I was "probably living in adultery." He said the church would investigate and issue a disposition. In the meantime, he suggested we "separate," my wife staying in one part of the house and I in another. At that time, in the early 1960s, it was the church's policy to permit such couples to live together as brother and sister. This was later changed. In my case, we lived in that manner for three years, during which time the ministers deliberately introduced her to a potential husband. Since she had been a widow and not a divorcee, she was permitted by the leadership to remarry, and she eventually did. Our marriage was terminated without ever having established if my first wife were still living, and our property sold with the proceeds divided. The Worldwide Church, of course, was given its cut out of it, which was considerable.

AUTHOR: Are the leaders consistent in their dispositions determining whose marriage is valid and whose is not? For example, suppose Mr. and Mrs. A and Mr. and Mrs. B have similar situations. When the church finished its investigation, would there be cases where the A couple would be told, "You are living in adultery and ought to separate," while the B couple would be instructed, "Your marriage is all right"?

HUSBAND: There were many cases of that nature. The ministers are not at all consistent in their decrees about matrimonial status.

AUTHOR: You are saying that dispensation in every single case of a previous marriage not terminated by death is handled by the church authorities. They have the complete and final say-so. Is that correct?

HUSBAND: They have complete authority, just as with everything else in your life. I even know of a case where the ministers told a couple not to have any more children because they already had a rather large family.

AUTHOR: Then the Worldwide Church is like the Roman Catholic Church, where the pope in the Vatican tells the faithful, "You may remarry because your former marriage was not binding in the eyes of the church, and you may not remarry because yours was." Is that the idea?

HUSBAND: That is exactly the idea! In the Roman Church, if a politician carries enough weight, or a movie star has a big enough following, he or she is allowed to remarry. Some loophole is "discovered." It is the same in the Worldwide Church of God. Some are allowed to do things others are forbidden to do. I suspect that one of their pilots had special consideration given him when, after years of single life, he was suddenly permitted to remarry.

AUTHOR: Does the Worldwide Church of God recognize adultery as a ground for divorce?

HUSBAND: In all the years I was associated with the movement, I never knew of a single case of divorce on this ground.

WIFE: Their explanation of divorce on the grounds of fornication is where a man marries a woman he believes to be a virgin, then discovers she is not. That would be considered as fornication in her pre-marriage background, and he would be free. They make a distinction between adultery and fornication. They do not use the terms synonomously.

AUTHOR: How does the breaking up of these marriages with divorce in the background affect the lives of members involved?

HUSBAND: It wreaks havoc. I can think, at this moment, of several suicides which can be traced to this doctrine breaking up the home. It not only results in some suicides, but very much hardship, grief, drunkenness and, in general, it is a deplorable situation.

AUTHOR: What about a couple whom the leadership determines is "living in adultery," yet by that union four or five children have been conceived. Do they still advocate breaking up that home?

HUSBAND: Yes, they do! Even though it may create financial problems, and in spite of the hardships and heartbreak the children will go through, they order it, nonetheless.

AUTHOR: You mentioned the heartbreak the children go through. What about that? How does it affect the children? Can you give some personal observations?

HUSBAND: I recall one man who worked for the college and was helping build a feast site. Although he and his wife had twin boys about twelve years of age, they had separated on the authority of the church. I have never in my life seen any children so heartbroken as those two boys were. In fact, it almost brings tears to my eyes to think about it even now.

WIFE: Dr. Sumner, in my own particular case, my boy was four-and-a-half years old when I was divorced from his father as a result of the doctrine of the church. He then had five hard years, until I came out of the organization, living without his father and living within the legalistic doctrines of the church—no birthday celebrations, no Christmases, no Easters, none of the things kids normally enjoy. One teacher even told me she believed he had an inferiority complex over this. He also grew up during those years not knowing the truth about grace, because I didn't know it and couldn't give it to him. Fortunately, he now understands and has accepted Christ as his personal Savior, but I feel that one of the greatest harms of the organization lies in the fact these children are suffering innocent consequences of their parents' decisions. The adults make up their own minds, but the children have nothing to say. I think it is one of the most damaging things the cult is doing.

AUTHOR: Can you think of other cases where young people have been affected?

HUSBAND: I think of a couple who would probably be in their late seventies now. I got acquainted with them at a feast site about nine years ago. They were recent converts to the church and, although they had been married for forty-two years and were parents of grown children, the leadership of the church told them their marriage was not valid and made them break up their home. The man, especially, was beside himself with grief. Today he is nearly a mental case. The church refused to reverse the decision under any circumstances.

AUTHOR: Do you mean to tell me that after a man and woman had lived together for forty-two years, legally married in the eyes of the law, the Worldwide Church of God broke up the union?

HUSBAND: They did. And the couple is separated to this very day.

WIFE: I know of another very sad case. At a dance sponsored by the church, the so-called widows—not really widows, but women who had been caused to be divorced because of this doctrine and called widows by the church—had been invited. One was about thirty, the mother of three young children. During the course of the evening, this woman became very unhappy and finally she broke down and went to the ladies' restroom. She was totally inconsolable. Thinking it might be harmful to send her home in that condition, they asked me to go in and try to get her to return to the dance and "enjoy" herself. However, her only response to me was, "*I want my husband. I want my husband. I am miserable and very unhappy and this whole thing has brought back to mind how much I love my husband and want him. I need him.*" This is just one illustration of the untold agony these people go through over marriages broken by the church's doctrine. She had been married about seven years and had three pre-school children.

I remember another case where the wife was a very devout member and the husband was very much against it. The wife, naturally, was trying to raise their son according to the church's teachings and the husband, just as naturally, was very much opposed. The woman actually became ill from the nervous tension. She had stomach hemorrhages and very severe headaches.

HUSBAND: Dr. Sumner, I know of a case where the church recommended a separation of a man and his wife with the final decree pending. They had three children. He was about thirty-five and she about twenty-nine. They had been separated five or six years. I knew him well and talked to him many times. He told me it was almost unbearable, with his natural sex drives, to live such an unnatural life. It caused him many problems.

There was another man who had been divorced from his wife, but the church decreed he was free to marry. After some fourteen years of single life, he decided the wife of the first man was the woman he wanted to marry, so they went to the church leaders and were granted permission. But the lady's former husband went to the church officials and reminded them they had never ruled about his case. He and his wife had separated on advice of the ministers, who had promised to "investigate" their case and rule on it. They never had. So, when he protested, they took the case under advisement and finally ruled that he and his wife had been "legally" married all along. The plans for the other marriage were canceled and the protesting man was allowed to start living with his wife again.

AUTHOR: Do you mean to tell me that the leaders of the Worldwide Church of God broke up a marriage, promising to investigate, but at a later date, without ever having made an investigation, turned around and granted permission for this woman to marry some other man?

HUSBAND: That is exactly right. And she would have married him, too, if her husband hadn't asked for an investigation.

AUTHOR: That is absolutely incredible!

HUSBAND: I recall a similar case involving a lady who worked for me. Her husband worked for the college at Pasadena, California—headquarters of the church. They were separated eleven years. He was eligible for remarriage according to the church's decree. Although the officials had supposedly investigated the matter on several occasions, the wife begged for one more investigation since she heard he was about to marry again. This time they decided the couple had been married all along, so they allowed them to go back together—*after forcing them to live apart for eleven years!*

WIFE: A friend of mine, a young divorced mother who very nearly joined the church and, if so, would have had to remain single at the age of 21, said the only thing this doctrine did was make people wish their former mates would die!

AUTHOR: Apparently this cult believes that marriages are made in Pasadena, not in Heaven. But let's discuss a little about the finances of the Armstrong movement. As former members, you are very familiar with the "everything's free" pitch. As a bona fide member of the Worldwide Church of God for more than ten years, how much do you estimate you contributed to the cause? I realize they didn't take it by force; you gave on a voluntary basis.

HUSBAND: Well, I am going to express it in slightly different terms. I am going to say it cost me over a quarter of a million dollars. Exactly how much I gave in cash, I don't know. I kept a record of it for a good many years, but it was thousands and thousands of dollars. As for it being "voluntary," you either paid tithes or you were disfellowshiped.

AUTHOR: I understand, of course, that in the Armstrong group, as in any other, some followers are nominal and others are completely sold on the movement. But for an individual with an average income, what percentage of his income would you estimate goes into the work?

HUSBAND: My estimation, from past experience, is that a member completely sold on the movement will probably give between forty and sixty per cent of his income. He would only keep back what he needed to maintain his family. I've even known of cases where they gave what was needed for their families, having them go without food, clothing and heat.

AUTHOR: In other words, such a member would act on the basis, "How economically can I live? I will live as conservatively as I can and pour the rest into the church." Is this correct?

WIFE: Definitely! I remember one time a widow with a teen-age daughter received an unexpected bonus in her paycheck. I was so pleased because I thought now she could buy the clothes they needed. Instead she said, "I'm going to see just how fast I can get this off to headquarters!" Her daughter had to go without the badly needed clothes.

AUTHOR: Would you say that Herbert W. Armstrong and Garner Ted Armstrong live in a frugal and economical manner?

HUSBAND: No, I would not. I would say that they live as luxuriously as anyone anywhere in the world.

AUTHOR: What we call, down South, living "high on the hog"?

HUSBAND: They are as high on the hog as you can get.

AUTHOR: *Time* magazine reported, about a year ago, that Herbert Armstrong sports a watch worth $1,000 and that he squandered $2,000 on a cuff links/tie tack set for a Jerusalem junket. The same source said both Armstrongs have "elegant homes" in California, Texas and England.

WIFE: The first time I visited Big Sandy and took the bus tour of the college property they provide, which includes the dwellings of the ministers, I was absolutely amazed at the beautiful homes. One of my first impressions had to do with how well they lived. I am not trying to say it is wrong for ministers to live well, but when you have seen some of the abject poverty of some of the members, strictly because of the church's doctrinal teaching about money, then you do wonder why the ministry should live so luxuriously. Evidently the ministers sense how the members feel regarding this inequity because it was mentioned from the pulpit from time to time that we were not to look upon the ministry as living in luxury, because the ministers had very long hours, a difficult life and were entitled to the very best.

HUSBAND: I might add that it was generally felt among the lay members, because of this emphasis, that if you were not as prosperous as you thought you should be, you must be doing something wrong. Perhaps you were holding back on some of your tithes, or your offerings weren't as large as they should have been. Or perhaps you weren't keeping the Sabbath up to the last minute.

WIFE: I have actually heard the ministers say from the pulpit that spiritual growth was in direct contrast to how much "your heart" was in the work. Using Matthew 6:21, "For where your treasure is, there will your heart be also," they implied spiritual growth came about by giving to them.

AUTHOR: Tithing is stressed repeatedly in the movement. The cult has what it calls a first tithe, a second tithe, a third tithe and a tithe of the tithe. A tithe means tenth—10 per cent of the income—does it not?

WIFE: Yes. And this is 10 per cent of the *gross* income, not the net.

AUTHOR: Where does the first tithe go?

HUSBAND: The first tithe goes to the so-called "work of God" and is sent directly to headquarters in Pasadena. It is supposedly for the preaching of the gospel to the world. Sometimes, in special cases where Mr. Armstrong deems it necessary, it is used for other things. For example, he had plans to build a great "House for God," something like Solomon's temple, and he told the people that he was going to build it even if the money had to be taken out of the first tithe. However, it is supposed to be for the spread of the gospel.

AUTHOR: But this first tithe goes to Pasadena "to be spread," is that right?

HUSBAND: That is right. However, none of the members actually knows what is really done with it or how it is used, even though they do read a financial statement every year at the Feast of Tabernacles.

AUTHOR: What about the second tithe? What is it and where does it go?

HUSBAND: The second tithe is for the member to spend in keeping the Feast of Tabernacles, or, to put it somewhat more broadly, the holy days. It could be used at Pentecost, the Day of Atonement, or any other holy day.

WIFE: The first tithe is sent directly to headquarters each month, or each week, whenever you get paid. The second tithe is kept by the member in a bank account under his own name. No matter what financial straits he comes to, he is not permitted to touch it. If he borrows any of it for any emergency, the ministry calls it "stealing from God" and the guilty one is required to repay it with interest.

AUTHOR: Then the second tithe is used to pay motel bills, restaurant tabs, plane tickets, and things of that nature?

WIFE: That is right. And if there is an excess of second tithe—few people can spend 10 per cent of their annual income during an eight or ten-day period—you are asked to give the balance as a freewill offering on the last day of the feast. You are not permitted to keep that money under any circumstances. You must either give it then as a freewill offering, or send it to Pasadena as excess second tithe.

AUTHOR: What about the third tithe?

HUSBAND: It is taken every third and seventh year and is for the fatherless, the widows, the orphans, the strangers, as well as the Levites. The ministers of the Worldwide Church are considered the Levites. They administer the distribution of the third tithe and support, to some extent, some widows. But it has also been used by the ministry for personal items such as clothes, among other things.

WIFE: Whenever members approached a year with the third tithe, they tried to manipulate their finances so they wouldn't be in a tight bind. They did not dare complain, but they would talk about how "difficult" it was to manage. Thirty per cent of their income would be going for tithes, probably another twenty per cent for taxes, with only fifty per cent of their *gross* income to live on. And this does not count the freewill offerings or the holy day offerings one is expected to give. A tithe of the tithe is also required.

AUTHOR: What is this "tithe of the tithe"?

WIFE: It is 10 per cent of your second tithe which

you are saving for feast days. As the time approaches the big feast, which is the Feast of Tabernacles, you must send 10 per cent of whatever you have saved up in your second tithe to Pasadena. This, in turn, is supposed to go for preparing the feast sites and getting everything ready for the celebration.

HUSBAND: However, this is another area where the monies are not always used for their designated purpose.

AUTHOR: What about the offerings given in addition to all these tithes? Are they regular offerings, or are they just special occasions?

HUSBAND: The first offering is sent in with the first tithe. This can be an additional 2 per cent over your tithe, or whatever you can possibly spare. Each holy day you are required to bring another offering, and some of the people give offerings on new moons, too. I used to help count the money at the feasts and I remember one man from Denver who gave a $5,000 special offering. This was above all his tithes.

AUTHOR: No wonder *Time* estimates the cult's annual income at $55 million! However, when one discovers that the Armstrongs have been using this "tithes and offering" money—given by many poverty-stricken people at great personal sacrifice—for such items as a Grumman Gulfstream jet that "gobbles up at least $1.5 million a year," and a garbage digester "experiment" at Big Sandy costing at least a quarter-million dollars, one feels an angry sense of righteous indignation burning within his breast. But you spoke of counting the money. Could you give me any kind of idea as to how much money comes in on those feast days?

HUSBAND: At the last feast I attended, before leaving the movement, the first offering was $173,000 and the offering on the last day was nearly $200,000.

WIFE: Remember, they have 7 feast areas in the United States alone, and they made each area feel competitive with the other areas. They would break it down on a per capita basis, then let you know what other areas were giving so you could try to exceed them. They made you feel it was *very* important, *very* essential to reach way down to the lowest part of your pocketbook to get the last penny to give them. There was even an offering which was given to redeem your firstborn child!

HUSBAND: They would go as far as to ask, "How much do you think you can get home on? Could you do without one of those thick steaks?"

AUTHOR: We were discussing the third tithe a moment ago, supposedly for helping the widows and orphans. Perhaps you could give me some further word on how that money is used.

WIFE: Let me speak from my own particular case, first. I was considered a "widow" of the church, although divorced, because I didn't have a husband. I was fortunate to have a small income. When I first went with the movement I could just barely get by. However, in a very short time, due to the rising cost of living and my pre-school child, I found I could no longer make it. I was actually having to sell things of value from my home to live. I sold good china, furniture not absolutely necessary, and other things. This way I did not have to ask the ministry for help. The day finally came when I no longer had anything to sell and I was forced to request aid. I dreaded to do it, because of what other widows told me they had had to go through, but after figuring out the absolute minimum I would have to request to get by, I applied for $50 a month. Of course, I was putting more than $50 a month into the work. When the ministers came in and looked over my budget and my situation was explained, they took the information back and reviewed it among themselves. They finally consented to give me $47 a month. If they had been true ministers of God, they might have provided $60 a month. Instead, they cut my request $3 so the Armstrongs would have an additional $3 out of the widow, who really needed the money. They also said I would now be expected to work some for the church because I was on third tithe. I don't see where that was done in the Bible. And this was not only my case, but many, many other women experienced things like this. I knew of one "widow," mother of three small children, living alone with these babies, whom they refused permission to have a telephone. They called it a luxury. Another "widow" had to sell her car before they would help her with third tithe.

HUSBAND: As a deacon for the church, I was assigned to monitor 14 widow members who were financially supported by third tithe money from the church. I was to contact these widows twice monthly to check on their needs. Most of them lived in abject poverty such as 2 to 3 room shacks, leaking roofs, shortage of food, shabby clothing and no means of transportation. Whenever there was a need, I was to contact the ministers of the church to get additional third tithe money to take care of the case. However, during 3 years, I never at any time received any additional money whatsoever for these widows, although it was desperately needed and said to be available in the third tithe fund.

One widow's total income was less than $80 per month and yet when her utilities were cut off for non-payment, she was told by a minister in charge of the third tithe fund that she had to "learn to live within" her income. In contrast, this same minister needed a $3,000 down payment on a home for himself and it was financed out of the third tithe fund collected from the church members for the express purpose of helping the widows and the needy. I would estimate this minister's annual income, from his visible standard of living, to be somewhere between $15,000 and $20,000. By no stretch of the imagination could he have been considered "needy."

Money plays a big part in the Worldwide Church and the whole organization is geared to handle your finances. There are many sermons instructing lay members on how to make money, as well as to handle it and increase it. Of course, the more money the members make, the more money they will be able to send to headquarters.

AUTHOR: Can you enlighten me at all as to why the cult puts such an emphasis on getting tithes to Pasadena to get out the gospel when Herbert W. Armstrong says God has no intention of saving many in this age, anyway?

HUSBAND: Because Mr. Armstrong believes he has been commissioned to do the job of Elijah—to cry out and show the people their sins. I would add this, however: probably many of these non-profit, tax-free organizations need a thorough investigation of their status by the government.

AUTHOR: Let's change the subject. Mr. Armstrong, as you well know, has some theories about 19-year cycles, starting with January 7, 1934. What did they tell you about those 19-year cycles when you were in the organization?

HUSBAND: We were anticipating a flight to safety in early 1972—January to be exact. However, as early as the first part of 1971 the ministers began to tone this down, preparing the members for a shock with such statements as, "Do you realize Mr. Armstrong has never *said* we will be going to a place of safety?" But this idea had so permeated sermons and literature for years—geared to this 19-year cycle and flight to a place of safety—that 99 per cent of the people in the movement thoroughly believed it would happen.

AUTHOR: Then you would say that 99 per cent of the people, just listening to what the ministry had been saying, would normally and naturally get the impression, "This is it: January 7, 1972. We had better have our bags packed, our plane ticket in hand, all ready to flee to Petra—the place of safety." Is that right?

HUSBAND: That is right. And the ones who were in the top echelon, especially when the United States currency became fiat and they realized it might not be possible to get out of this country with ordinary money, began to store up silver and make other plans for getting their wealth out of the country.

WIFE: I would like to say, having gone through all I did with the movement and finally coming to understand what God really had in mind when He designed the plan of salvation through Jesus Christ, the ideal way to avoid falling into spiritual traps such as the Worldwide Church of God is by being taught by your parents what grace is. But if you are not that fortunate, as I was not, then the way is to have someone explain the difference between the Old and New Testaments, the old and new covenants. Many people become trapped in organizations like the Worldwide Church because they do not really understand the difference between works and grace. All that they teach about legalism can be proven from the Old Testament, and that is why keeping the Sabbath and the holy days seems to be logical in the eyes of those who do not know their Bibles. I didn't have enough sense to understand that this was only a shadow leading to Christ. People do not know how to rightly divide the Word of God.

HUSBAND: I believe it was Hosea who said, "My people are destroyed for lack of knowledge." You don't realize how true that is until you have spent ten or eleven years of your life as a semi-monk, and things like that. My advice to anyone seeking knowledge is as another ex-member said, "Cry out to Jesus Christ!" It is an individual thing. I wish there were some way I could reach every man—who feels, as I felt in times past, that he is a little smart—and tell him what he really needs to do is study the Bible.

AUTHOR: My impression is that the people who have come out of the Worldwide Church of God did so as a result of reading the Word of God for themselves, starting to study what the Word of God actually said. Would you consider that a proper evaluation?

HUSBAND: That is exactly what happened to me. After ten years of their teaching, I decided I needed to study the Bible on my own, without outside interference. Anyone who will do this, asking the Holy Spirit for guidance, will discover the truth.

AUTHOR: What is the position of the Worldwide Church of God regarding the Bible? Do the leaders encourage people to read and study it, or do they want the people to merely study the church's literature?

HUSBAND: In my case, when I began to study the Bible for myself and ask some questions of my own, they told me, "You act like you know more than the apostle, Mr. Armstrong." I replied, "No, but your own minister held up a Bible and said, 'Get back to the horse's mouth.' That's what I'm doing." They said, "True. But you are not to study *doctrine.* You read the pamphlets and we'll take care of the doctrine part of it ourselves."

WIFE: They always put a tremendous emphasis on studying their correspondence course. This is the way we were to study, with the outline of their correspondence course. We were not to deviate and get off on our own study. We were not to seek the Holy Spirit's leadership in trying to decipher doctrine for ourselves. We had to follow the lessons they put out, which were distinct outlines on their own doctrines. It is like the Roman Catholic Church, with the pope deciding the doctrines and the laity accepting them without digging into the Bible personally.

AUTHOR: I was interested, a moment ago, in your reference to Herbert W. Armstrong as "the apostle."

Is that what he is called within the movement?

HUSBAND: Yes.

AUTHOR: Do the members feel, then, that Mr. Armstrong is an apostle on a par with Paul, Peter, John and the New Testament apostles?

HUSBAND: That is their understanding. He is the only one in the world today who has the truth and the way of salvation.

WIFE: Regarding the belief that theirs is the true church, you will probably be amazed to know that Mr. Stanley Rader, one of Herbert W. Armstrong's closest friends and a "righthand man" who has traveled around the world with him repeatedly and who is described by Garner Ted Armstrong as "our general counsel and financial advisor," is not even a member of the church. Or at least he wasn't when we left the movement in 1971. He has never been convinced, apparently, that it is the true church.

AUTHOR: Are there other apostles in the cult, or is the founder the only one?

HUSBAND: Mr. Armstrong is the only apostle. Period.

AUTHOR: Does the church have prophets?

HUSBAND: I can only say that I remember at one feast, Garner Ted Armstrong said in one sermon, "I am a prophet of God." They evidently have one, a self-confessed prophet.

AUTHOR: What are your impressions regarding the break between Garner Ted and his father? You came out just before it happened, but you have some opinions, no doubt.

WIFE: My personal opinion is that Garner Ted Armstrong became aware of the fact that the holy days are no longer to be kept in this church age. Our own experience ties into this conclusion. We began studying the Bible on our own and came to see that the Sabbath and the holy days, which go together, are not for this age. A number of others were with us in this discovery. Some were kicked out of the movement; some of us resigned. Before we left, however, we asked for one final hearing on the subject. One particular minister, whom we felt was trying to be neutral and fair, was called and asked to come out and talk with us. He consented and came alone, something very rare as they usually go in twos. We explained to him what we had discovered in our studies and showed him many, many Scriptures. He asked a number of questions and appeared almost as if he were trying to find out if we knew something they didn't.

The very next night this minister was seen in a restaurant with Garner Ted Armstrong and Mr. Leslie L. McCullough, a vice-chancellor of the college. Another member of the cult was in the restaurant at the same time and overheard part of the conversation. They were discussing doctrine and the holy days, some of the things we had talked to the minister about the night before.

HUSBAND: Garner Ted Armstrong said, "They may be right. They could be right." Or words to that effect.

WIFE: It was shortly after this that the holy day observance came. Then, of course, Mr. Ted Armstrong traveled to all the different feast sites to speak to all the assemblies. It was during that time, it has been reported to us, he suddenly stopped in one of his sermons, at one of the feast sites, and said he couldn't go on. There was much comment, from many different channels, that he suspected the holy days were not to be kept. We definitely believe this was one of the causes of his difficulty with his father. The letters his father wrote sounded to us like a big cover-up. He tried to make it sound like something very personal and only related to Garner Ted, but we know how touchy the father is about anyone questioning the holy days. After Garner Ted returned to the movement, it was reported that the holy days would be phased out very gradually, perhaps dropping one holy day each year.

* * * * * * * *

As a postscript to the interview, let me offer the following documentation as a foundation for the above theory.

(1) It was late August or early September of 1971 when these people had the discussion with the minister, followed by the restaurant incident involving Garner Ted.

(2) The holy day observance, with Garner Ted's purported quitting in the middle of his message, took place a month or so later, in October.

(3) As late as September 26, 1971, in a letter to the membership, Herbert W. Armstrong spoke glowingly of his son, saying, "My son, Garner Ted, has been doing the jobs of five or six high-executive-caliber men. . . .lately he has been taking about 95% of my executive duties as President of the colleges and the Church." There was certainly no indication of a division at that time.

(4) In Herbert W. Armstrong's letter to the faithful, under date of October 14, 1971, he reported that Garner Ted had quit in the middle of his circuit of the festival sites. He wrote: ". . .after Squaw Valley, his fourth site, tensions had built up until his nerves were at razor-edge, and he could not continue.

"He is now on the leave of absence. It may take some weeks for full recovery. Therefore I have this morning called board meetings of both the Church and the College, at which we made official the relieving of all responsibilities from my son Garner Ted until recovery and return. The Boards have acted on my appointment of Mr. Albert J. Portune as *acting* Executive Vice President of both Church and College, and as Vice-Chancellor of Ambassador College."

(5) A brief letter to the members, dated October 27, 1971, carried this information: "My son, Garner Ted,

recovering from a near breakdown from overwork and too heavy pressures, seems to be making good progress."

(6) The letter to the "inner family," dated April 25, 1972, contained this information: "Last autumn I was dismayed to learn that my son had been so overcome with personal, emotional problems, that it led to conduct inconsistent with the high standard of the Work of the Church of God and the scriptural qualifications for a minister of Jesus Christ, and rendered him incapable of carrying on the duties of a minister. . ." In other words, Mr. Herbert W. Armstrong was not telling the *complete* truth, if *any* of it, in his previous letters of explanation on October 14 and 27. It was not Garner Ted's "nerves" which incapacitated him, it was his "conduct inconsistent with. . .the scriptural qualifications for a minister of Jesus Christ. . ."

Herbert W. Armstrong went on, in his lengthy letter of April 25, to quote exchanges of correspondence between the two, expressing undying love and devotion to one another. The letter from the son was a confession letter, part of which is quoted elsewhere in this book, and the father said: "The Boards and I did, as a result of this letter, receive him back. But subsequent events, attitude and conduct, to our great dismay, demonstrated to the Board members, ministers, and myself that the process of repentance was not yet complete."

(7) Under date of May 25, Mr. Armstrong sent another letter to the "family of co-workers," consisting mostly of a comparison of his persecution by the press with the persecution and crucifixion of Christ, along with glowing quotes from letters he had received, praising him and his work.

(8) On May 31, 1972, the Senior Armstrong sent out a letter announcing Garner Ted's full restoration to the church. Accompanying it, on his father's stationery, was a letter from Garner Ted, also dated May 31,

expressing "the combined feelings of vast relief, thanksgiving, humility, and joy over the events of these past few months."